75 SPIRITED YEARS:
WILL EISNER & THE SPIRIT

75 Spirited Years: Will Eisner & The Spirit
September 26, 2015 – March 7, 2016

Will Eisner's legacy in the world of comics is one of challenging the medium for all it was worth as he pushed the limits of form and function to get the greatest storytelling results possible.

In addition to championing the graphic novel, turning out "how to" instructions for the military, and inspiring multiple generations of creators, 75 years ago this master of the comic art form created The Spirit!

Join us for a retrospective on 75 years of The Spirit and a sampling of Will Eisner's other great works, **75 Spirited Years: Will Eisner & The Spirit** at Geppi's Entertainment Museum. Curated by Eisner's longtime friend, colleague and publisher Denis Kitchen, this exhibit showcases more than 50 pieces of original art and more!

www.geppismuseum.com
301 W. Camden Street • Second Floor • Baltimore, MD 21201 • (410) 625-7060

OVERSTREET'S COMIC BOOK MARKETPLACE Y·E·A·R·B·O·O·K

2015 - 2016

GRANT ADEY, DAVID ALLEN, STEPHEN BARRINGTON, MIKE BOLLINGER, SCOTT BRADEN, JON CHAMBERS, JOHN CHRUSCINSKI, ART CLOOS, BROCK DICKINSON, KEN DYBER, DOUG GILLOCK, STEVEN HOUSTON, BEN LABONOG, TIM LASIUTA, DOUG MABRY, JON McCLURE, JOSH NATHANSON, JAMIE NEWBOLD, CHARLES S. NOVINSKIE, TERRY O'NEILL, ROBERT M. OVERSTREET, MICHAEL PAVLIC, MATT SCHIFFMAN, FRANK SIMMONS, MAGGIE THOMPSON, J.C. VAUGHN, JASON VERSAGGI, CATHERINE SAUNDERS-WATSON, ALEX WINTER, AND CARRIE WOOD

CONTRIBUTING WRITERS

MARK L. HAYNES
WITH MARK HUESMAN
DESIGN & LAYOUT

MICHAEL SOLOF AND J. KEVIN TOPHAM
PHOTOGRAPHY

MIKE WILBUR
EDITING ASSISTS

MARK HUESMAN
J.C. VAUGHN
CARRIE WOOD
EDITORS

TOM GAREY, KATHY WEAVER, BRETT CANBY, AND ANGELA PHILLIPS-MILLS
ACCOUNTING SERVICES

GARY M. CARTER
FOUNDING EDITOR

BUTCH GUICE
ARTIST – X-O MANOWAR & BLOODSHOT cover
ISBN: 978-1-60360-180-1

HUGO PRATT
ARTIST – CORTO MALTESE cover
ISBN: 978-1-60360-181-8

MARK WHEATLEY
WILL EISNER
ARTISTS – THE SPIRIT cover
ISBN: 978-1-60360-182-5

GEMSTONE PUBLISHING • TIMONIUM, MARYLAND
WWW.GEMSTONEPUB.COM

Overstreet at 45: A Milestone for the Guide!

This year, Gemstone Publishing is celebrating the 45th anniversary of *The Overstreet Comic Book Price Guide*. As amazing as it seems to the rest of us, think for a moment how incredible it must seem to the man who started it all, Robert M. Overstreet.

When he started talking about doing a price guide, many folks volunteered to help. When it came time to actually get it done, there were, let's say, fewer folks who really showed up.

That's not to say there were none. In fact, we had such early Overstreet Advisors as Michelle Nolan and Larry Bigman along with *Comic Book Marketplace*'s founding editor, Gary M. Carter, at our "Overstreet at 45" panel at Comic-Con International: San Diego this year.

The panel itself was pretty amazing, too. Not only were we joined by Scoop columnist and former CBG editor Maggie Thompson, longtime *CBM* contributor and CCS President Matt Nelson, and Hero Initiative board member and CBCS President Steve Borock, but also by veteran comic book scribe Mark Waid, who's also become a comic book retailer in recent times.

The audience was packed with all sorts of Overstreet Advisors too, many of whom you'll see pictured in our Market Reports section. We thank everyone who participated, to the Comic-Con staff, and to our own Kevin Brennan and Mike Wilbur for helping us pull it off.

To keep the celebration going, we once again have a jam-packed edition of *Comic Book Marketplace Yearbook* for you in the form of character anniversaries, feature interviews (some great work by Jason Versaggi), market analysis and more.

The interview subjects include Rick Burchett, Sal Buscema, Chuck Dixon, Steve Epting, Tom Mason, Paul Ryan, Beau Smith, John K. Snyder III, Mark Wheatley and a Hall of Fame interview with the late, great Jerry Robinson, which we hope you'll agree is a pretty diverse selection. It's all built around a special retrospective on Dean Mullaney's Eclipse Comics and comes with a special look at his current efforts with The Library of American Comics and EuroComics as well.

And of course there's much more, but we trust you know we're required to say that at this point.

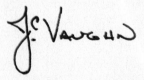

J.C. Vaughn
Vice-President of Publishing

Photo by Michael Solof

GEMSTONE PUBLISHING

STEPHEN A. GEPPI
PRESIDENT AND
CHIEF EXECUTIVE OFFICER

ROBERT M. OVERSTREET
PUBLISHER

J.C. VAUGHN
VICE-PRESIDENT
OF PUBLISHING

MARK HUESMAN
CREATIVE DIRECTOR

AMANDA SHERIFF
ASSOCIATE EDITOR

CARRIE WOOD
ASSISTANT EDITOR

BRAELYNN BOWERSOX
STAFF WRITER

WWW.GEMSTONEPUB.COM

GEPPI'S ENTERTAINMENT MUSEUM

STEPHEN A. GEPPI
FOUNDER AND
CHIEF EXECUTIVE OFFICER

MELISSA BOWERSOX
PRESIDENT

WWW.GEPPISMUSEUM.COM

Table of Contents

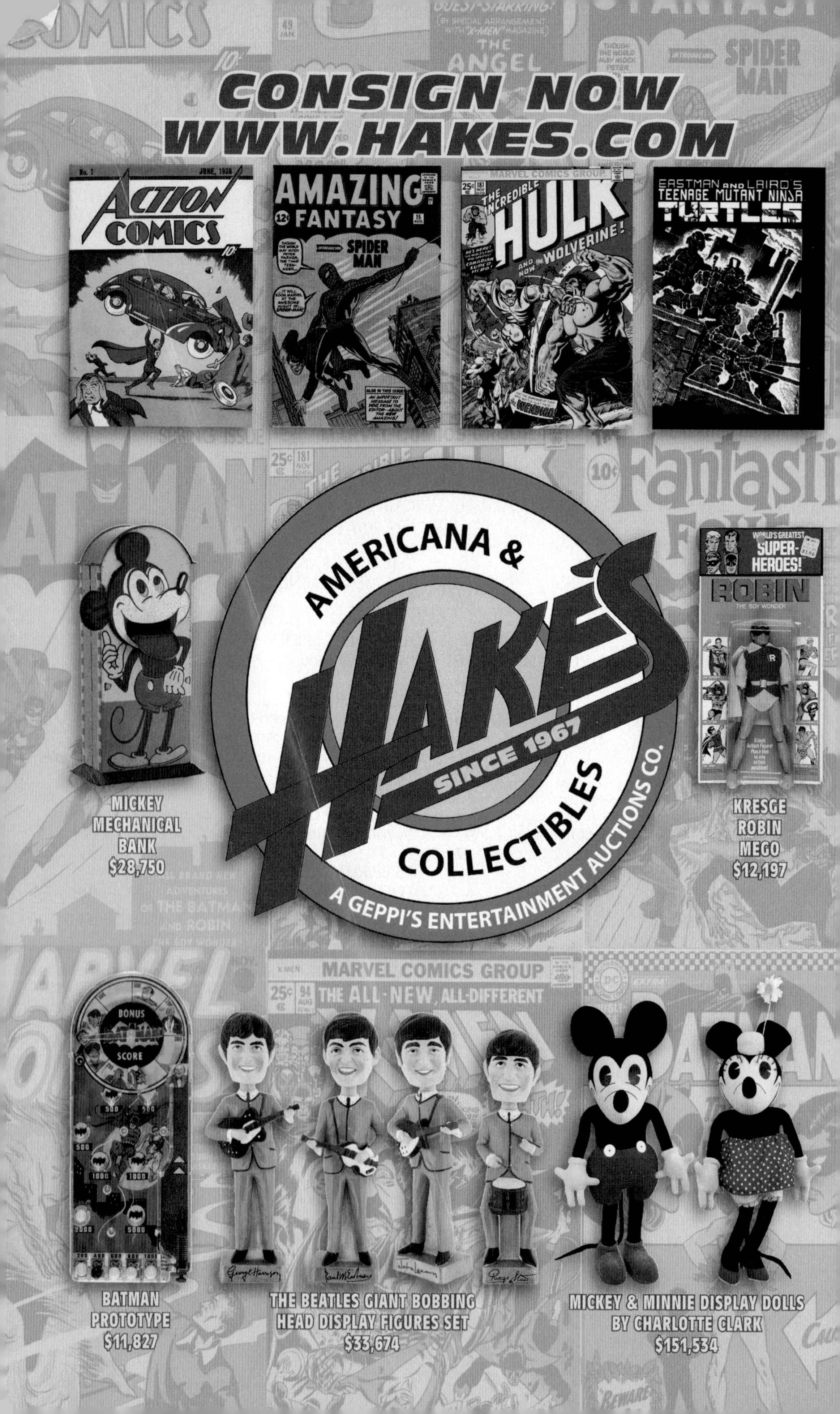
CONSIGN NOW
WWW.HAKES.COM
AMERICANA & HAKE'S COLLECTIBLES
SINCE 1967
A GEPPI'S ENTERTAINMENT AUCTIONS CO.
MICKEY MECHANICAL BANK $28,750
KRESGE ROBIN MEGO $12,197
BATMAN PROTOTYPE $11,827
THE BEATLES GIANT BOBBING HEAD DISPLAY FIGURES SET $33,674
MICKEY & MINNIE DISPLAY DOLLS BY CHARLOTTE CLARK $151,534

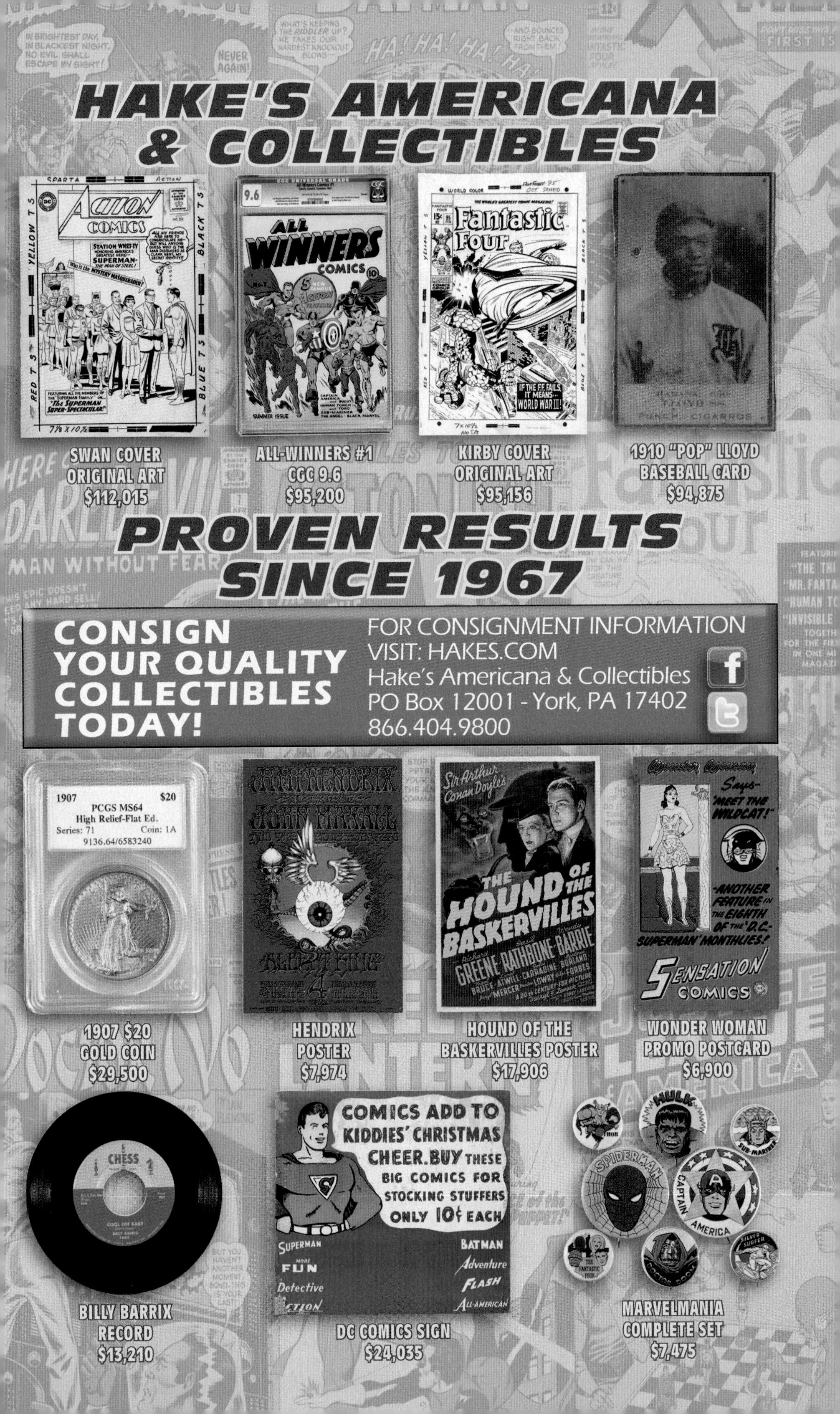
HAKE'S AMERICANA & COLLECTIBLES
SWAN COVER ORIGINAL ART $112,015
ALL-WINNERS #1 CGC 9.6 $95,200
KIRBY COVER ORIGINAL ART $95,156
1910 "POP" LLOYD BASEBALL CARD $94,875
PROVEN RESULTS SINCE 1967
CONSIGN YOUR QUALITY COLLECTIBLES TODAY!
FOR CONSIGNMENT INFORMATION
VISIT: HAKES.COM
Hake's Americana & Collectibles
PO Box 12001 - York, PA 17402
866.404.9800
1907 $20 GOLD COIN $29,500
HENDRIX POSTER $7,974
HOUND OF THE BASKERVILLES POSTER $17,906
WONDER WOMAN PROMO POSTCARD $6,900
BILLY BARRIX RECORD $13,210
DC COMICS SIGN $24,035
MARVELMANIA COMPLETE SET $7,475

Ten to Watch

BY **STEVEN HOUSTON**

Much like The Watcher, Torpedo Comics' Steven Houston keeps an eye on the back issue market, only he does so from many a convention floor, not the moon. We asked him what issues he's keeping an eye on at the moment, and here are the results...

MARVEL COMICS GROUP
25¢ 178 FEB
STRANGE TALES FEATURING:
WARLOCK
THE MAN WHO STALKED THE STARS!

MARVEL COMICS GROUP
25¢ 131 MAR
DAREDEVIL
THE MAN WITHOUT FEAR!
BULLSEYE NEVER MISSES!

DC
NO 474 DEC 35¢
BATMAN'S
DETECTIVE
COMICS
DEADSHOT'S REVENGE

DC TV COMIC
THE SATURDAY MORNING SUPER-STAR! WITH ONE MAGIC WORD...
30¢
SHAZAM!
THE WORLD'S MIGHTIEST MORTAL
BLACK ADAM?!? THIS IS IMPOSSIBLE! YOU'RE DEAD!
I'VE COME BACK TO DESTROY YOU AND THE OLD WIZARD!
THEN-- I'LL RULE THE WORLD!

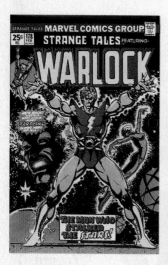

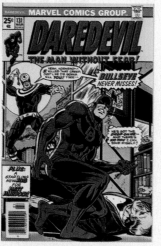

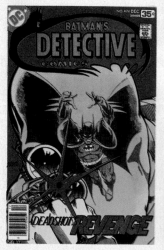

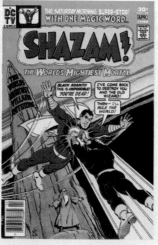

STRANGE TALES #178
(First Magus)
The news is still fresh that the Magus will be the featured in the *Avengers: Infinity War* movies, but prices have yet to explode – just wait until we see that first trailer with the Magus, we could see Thanos-like price increases.

DAREDEVIL #131
(First Bullseye)
Wait a minute! What's so new about this book Steve? I know this book has been 'hot' for years, but over the last three years this issue has been rather stable in price, something that could drastically change when Bullseye appears in the Netflix *Daredevil* series.

DETECTIVE COMICS #474
(Re-introduction of Deadshot)
Most contemporary collectors are not going to hunt down Deadshot's first appearance in *Batman* #59 (1950), however his re-intro featuring the classic costume readers know today could be where fans decide to swoop.

SHAZAM! #28
(Re-introduction of Black Adam)
Black Adam's first appearance in *Marvel Family* #1 (1945) is already out of the reach of most 'mortal' modern collectors, however *Shazam!* #28 from 1977 has been gathering dust for years. Say hello to Dwayne "The Rock" Johnson as Black Adam – just watch this book explode in demand.

MARVEL COMICS SUPER SPECIAL #16
(First comic book app. of Boba Fett)
Most Boba Fett fans are hunting down copies of *Star Wars* #42 for the first appearance, but issues #39-44 are technically reprints, the super-special came out months before issue #42 – better start looking in the magazine sections folks!

A MARVEL SUPER SPECIAL MAGAZINE
STAR WARS
THE EMPIRE STRIKES BACK
THE STAR WARS SAGA CONTINUES
THE OFFICIAL COMICS ADAPTATION OF THE MOST EAGERLY AWAITED SPACE FANTASY FILM OF ALL! THE COMPLETE STORY IN DAZZLING FULL COLOR!

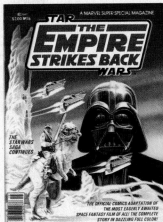

A-NEXT #7
(First Hope Pym)
Okay, most of you reading this may be saying ‘A-What?’ but back in this forgotten series from 1999, this book featuring an alternate future universe introduced the first comic book appearance of Henry Pym’s daughter. Depending on future cinematic appearances by the new Wasp (Hope), this book just may be a sleeper.

THE NEXT GENERATION OF AVENGERS!
A NEXT
AT LAST! WE REVEAL THE SECRET OF...
...MAINFRAME!

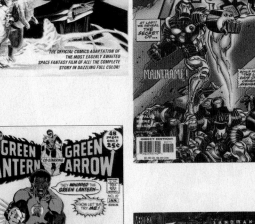

GREEN LANTERN #87
(First John Stewart)
Now this may be a shot in the proverbial dark, but with the next Green Lantern movie featuring the full ‘Corps’, many are making the leap that John will be featured heavily in the new movie. Right now this book is still reasonably priced, but who knows what will happen if this rumor has merit.

GREEN LANTERN CO-STARRING GREEN ARROW
48 PAGES ONLY 25¢
THEY WHIPPED THE GREEN LANTERN--
--NOW LET 'EM TRY ME!
INTRODUCING AN UNFORGETTABLE NEW CHARACTER WHO REALLY MEANS IT WHEN HE WARNS...
"BEWARE MY POWER!"
PLUS A NEW LIFE FOR GREEN ARROW "WHAT CAN ONE MAN DO?"
A CLASSIC EXTRA-- "EARTH'S FIRST GREEN LANTERN!"

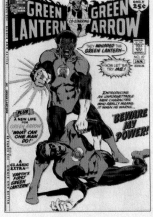

LUCIFER #1
Although some fans of the DC Comics Vertigo series have found the premise for the Fox television show distasteful, this show could just get a following and if so, this book will blow up – the reason: low print run, low print run, low print run…get the idea.

SANDMAN
Lucifer

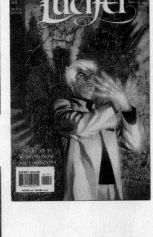

SHOWCASE #20
(First app. and origin of Rip Hunter)
Okay so this book has been around since 1959, so why is this book one to watch? Yes, you guessed it – the *Legends of Tomorrow* television show featuring good ‘ol Rip. Compared to the other major *Showcase* keys, this books is still reasonably priced – but not for long I think.

SHOWCASE presents
10¢
Rip Hunter... TIME MASTER
THERE'S ONLY ONE WAY TO SAVE BONNIE AND CORKY FROM THIS DINOSAUR!
"PRISONERS OF 100 MILLION B.C.!"

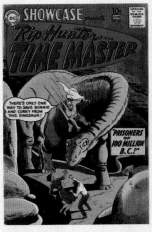

ETERNAL WARRIOR #4
(First Bloodshot in last panel cameo)
Are you kidding me, Steve? No, no, it’s true, a Bloodshot movie has been announced for 2017 and if this movie does see the light of day, then this book will be asked for not just by comic book insiders, but a whole new audience – umm, it’s that supply and demand thing again.

VALIANT
ETERNAL WARRIOR

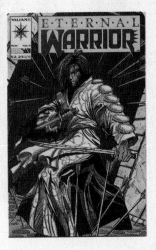

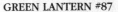

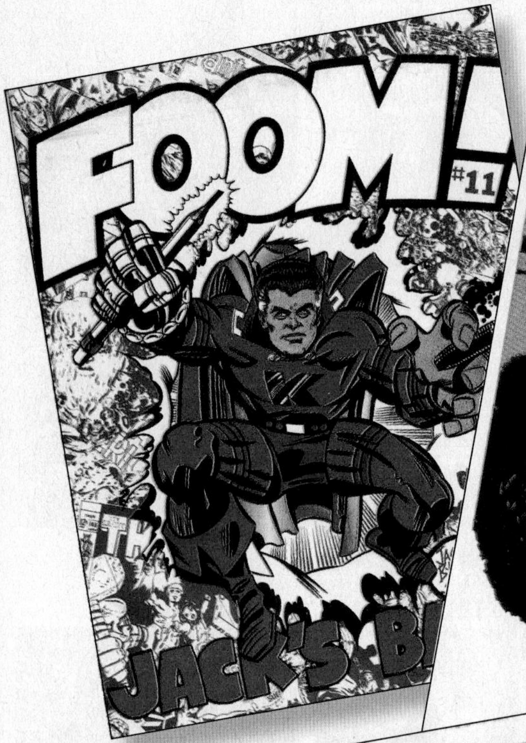
FOOM!
#11
JACK'S

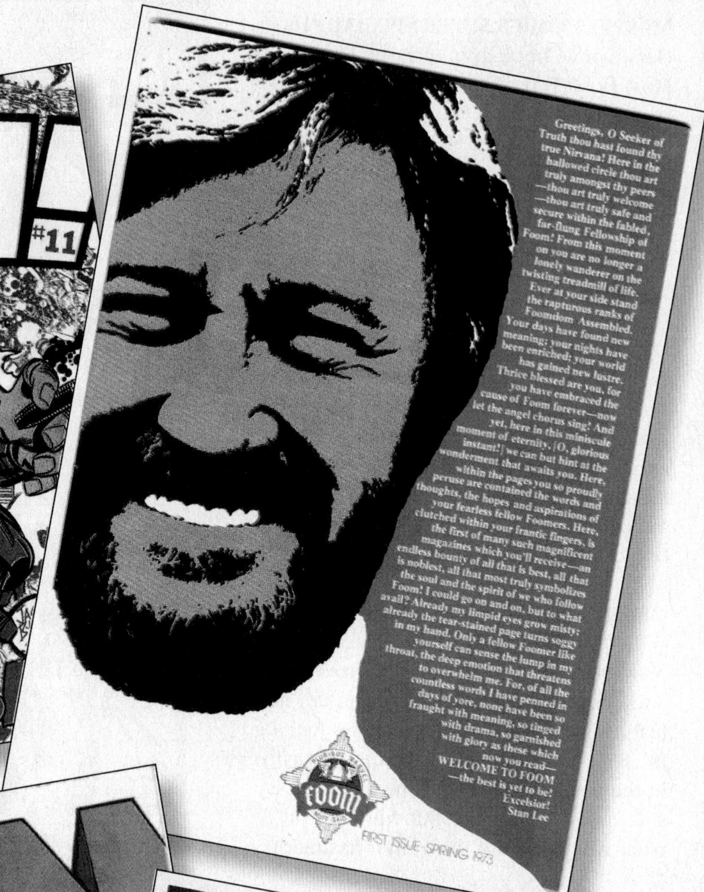
Greetings, O Seeker of Truth thou hast found thy true Nirvana! Here in the hallowed circle thou art truly amongst thy peers —thou art truly welcome —thou art truly safe and secure within the fabled, far-flung Fellowship of Foom! From this moment on you are no longer a lonely wanderer on the twisting treadmill of life. Ever at your side stand the rapturous ranks of Foomdom Assembled. Your days have found new meaning; your nights have been enriched; your world has gained new lustre. Thrice blessed are you, for you have embraced the cause of Foom forever—now let the angel chorus sing! And yet, here in this miniscule moment of eternity, [O, glorious instant!] we can but hint at the wonderment that awaits you. Here, within the pages you so proudly peruse are contained the words and thoughts, the hopes and aspirations of your fearless fellow Foomers. Here, clutched within your frantic fingers, is the first of many such magnificent magazines which you'll receive—an endless bounty of all that is best, all that is noblest, all that most truly symbolizes the soul and the spirit of we who follow Foom! I could go on and on, but to what avail? Already my limpid eyes grow misty; already the tear-stained page turns soggy in my hand. Only a fellow Foomer like yourself can sense the lump in my throat, the deep emotion that threatens to overwhelm me. For, of all the countless words I have penned in days of yore, none have been so fraught with meaning, so tinged with drama, so garnished with glory as these which now you read—
WELCOME TO FOOM
—the best is yet to be!
Excelsior!
Stan Lee
FOOM
FIRST ISSUE-SPRING 1973

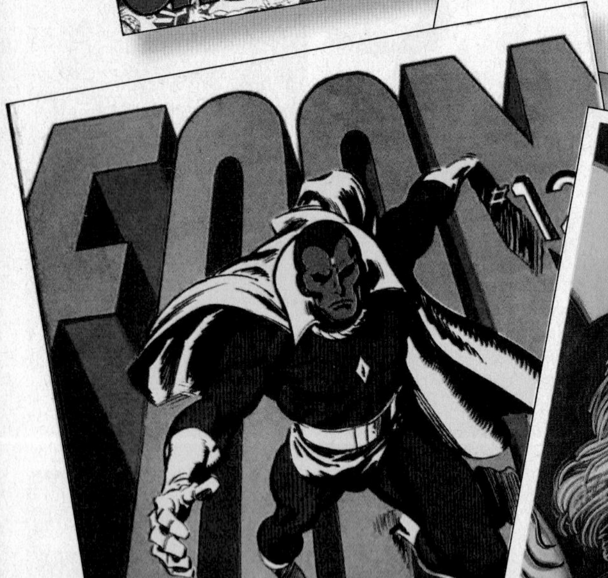
BUSCEMA RUSSELL

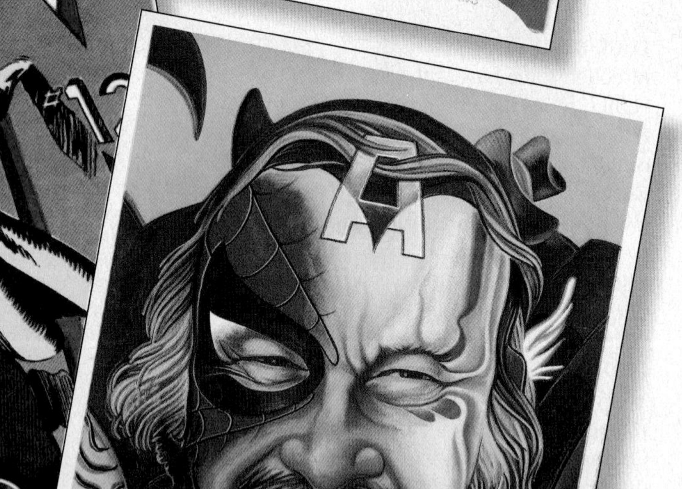
STAN THE MAN
MARVEL COMICS GROUP
25¢
10 OCT

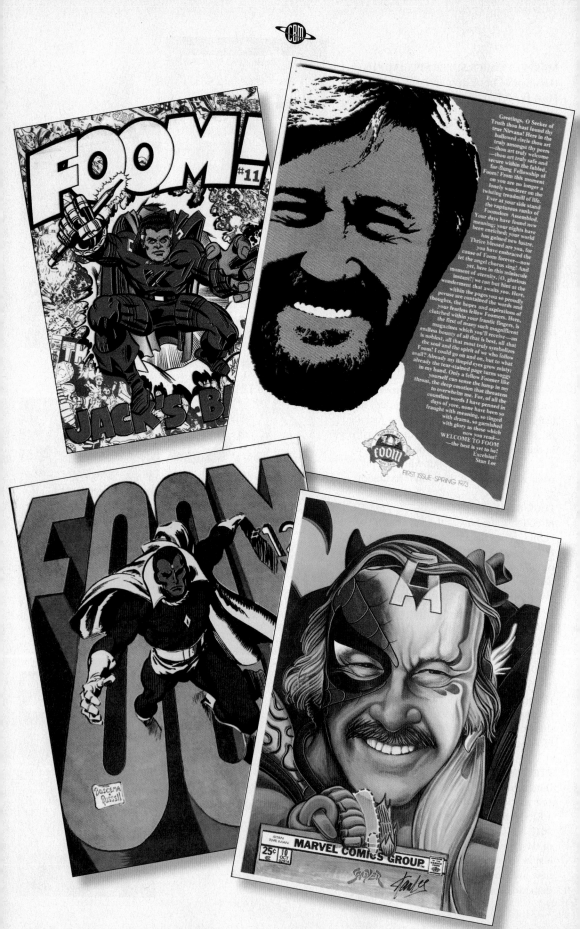

FOOM:
Friends of Ol' Marvel

BY **CHARLES S. NOVINSKIE**

Following the demise of Marvel's long-running fan club, Marvelmania, the House of Ideas introduced *FOOM—Friends of Ol' Marvel*, a magazine format publication, in the winter of 1973.

Under the auspices of Stan Lee, the book had a pedigree roster of contributors starting with Jim Steranko, who volunteered his services to spearhead Friends of Ol' Marvel. The initial staff was rounded out by the likes of Ken Bruzenak as Associate Editor with contributors Joel Thingvall and Gary Brown. Editor-in-Chief Roy Thomas was listed as Consulting Editor and said that in general he left running *FOOM* to others.

The first issue was packed full of bois and interviews with the likes of Stan Lee, Roy Thomas, John Buscema, Joe Sinnott, and Gerry Conway. The contents were very fan-centric with a crossword puzzle, and an "Infoomation" section offering tidbits on upcoming projects. A one-page humor strip, *Fantastic Fear*, had some great art rendered by Gil Kane and Wally Wood from a story written by Roy Thomas and Len Brown (*Mars Attacks*). The back cover featured Spider-Man by Steranko (*FOOM #2* has a Steranko-illustrated Hulk on the back cover).

Published quarterly, the fanzine ran 22 issues. A one-year, four-issue subscription was an incredible $3, or an extra buck if you wanted the full membership kit. The full $4 kit included not only the issues of *FOOM*, but a membership card, a poster, and six decals.

It didn't take *FOOM* too long to fall into a bit of a formula when it came to its contents, but the publication did feature the efforts of quite a few talented writers, editors, and artists, many of whom went on to become noted in the industry.

With issue #5 Steranko stepped aside, handing the reins to Tony Isabella. Ed Hannigan was responsible for its production, along with Contributing Editors Mark Evanier, Jim Salicrup, and Duffy Vohland. Eventually, Chris Claremont,

David Anthony Kraft (*Comics Interview*), and Ralph Macchio also contributed to its pages.

Issue #5 featured a drawing of Frankenstein on its Fan Art Gallery page and turned out to be one of the earliest pieces of Marvel art by John Byrne. The Fall 1974 issue (#7) featured one of Mike Ploog's earliest drawings of the Ghost Rider, and that same issue also announced the return of Jack Kirby to the House of Ideas after his stint at DC.

While *FOOM* may not have garnered a lot of respect during its short existence, the publication definitely has its following in the marketplace. Most issues are relatively hard to find and command high prices when offered for sale or auction.

As a fledgling Marvel Comics fan and high school student at the time, I cherished the first issue of *FOOM* as much as receiving my driver's permit. Both served to take me to places that I never would have been able to travel to without them. Growing up in the small coal mining town of Shamokin, PA, was akin to living in the next town over from Mayberry. Not much happened there, which is why any form of escape was greatly appreciated.

I often wondered what the mail man thought of those classic, white manila envelopes with the giant green Hulk on the front of it. I still chuckle over the address label fitting in the Hulk's open mouth! Coming home and finding that envelope on the coffee table was akin to waking up to a snow day from school!

A life-long fan of Marvel Comics, Charles S. Novinskie lives in Lake Havasu City AZ., with his wife, Kristine, and two dogs, Tayla and Odo. He currently serves as a Board Member of The Hero Initiative and is an Overstreet Advisor. He is the writer and Managing Editor of Lake Havasu LIVING Magazine and contributes to a number of comic and trading card publications.

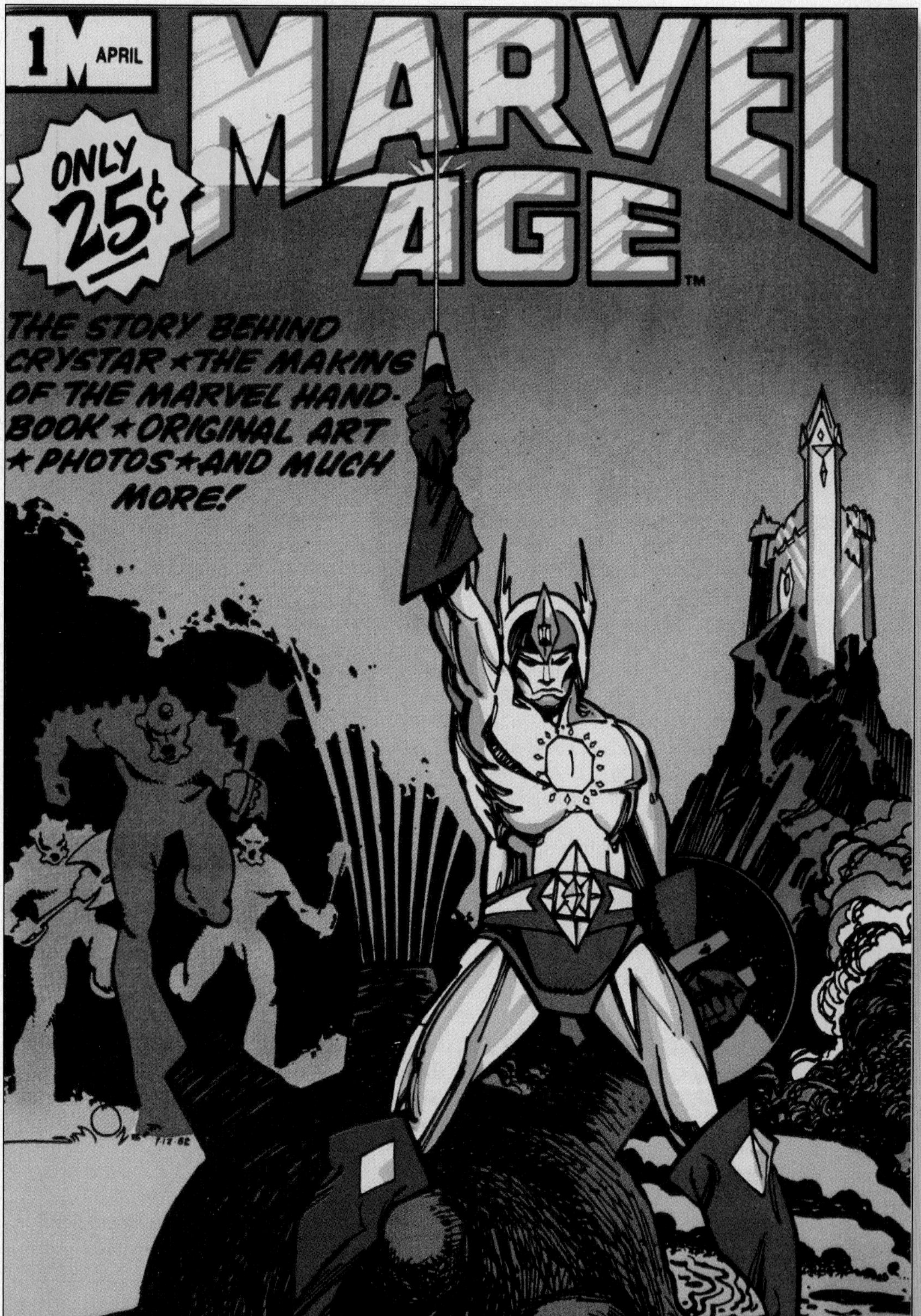
1 M APRIL
MARVEL AGE
ONLY 25¢
THE STORY BEHIND CRYSTAR ★ THE MAKING OF THE MARVEL HAND-BOOK ★ ORIGINAL ART ★ PHOTOS ★ AND MUCH MORE!

Marvel Age 1: *Marvel Age Magazine debuted in April of 1983. Helmed by Carol Kalish, the publication was seen as part sales tool, part fanzine.*

Remembering the Marvel Age

BY **CHARLES S. NOVINSKIE**

What became known in Stan Lee-speak as "The Marvel Age" began in the 1960s with the introduction of the Fantastic Four—superheroes with problems—introduced by Lee and Jack Kirby. But did you know that there was a second Marvel Age?

April 1983 saw the release of *Marvel Age* magazine, a fanzine for Marvel fans, written by fans that later became bona fide professionals. But you won't find the book listed in *The Overstreet Comic Book Price Guide*. In fact, you won't find it listed on anyone's Top 100 Must Read Comics list.

The reality is that the title ran 140 issues—from April 1983 to 1994, longer than most comic book titles. For anyone that grew up during that time period you will surely have fond memories of a wonderfully produced fanzine that wasn't afraid to entertain, laugh at itself, and provide behind-the-scenes info that made Marvel a cool place to want to work. A precursor to today's *Marvel Previews*, without the slick paper and full-page ads teasing things to come, this magazine was full of wacky, zany stuff, pre-production artwork, and editors' notes.

Printed on the familiar pulp paper of the day, the first issue ran 16 pages, not counting covers, and was a real bargain for 25 cents. The first issue sported a flashy cover of Marvel's newest book, *Crystar*, complete with a Walt Simonson original conceptual cover (the final cover of *Crystar* #1 was done by talented Bob Larkin). The feature article on *Crystar* had character sketches by John Romita Jr., as well as interior pencils and ink samples by Bret Blevins and Vinnie Colletta.

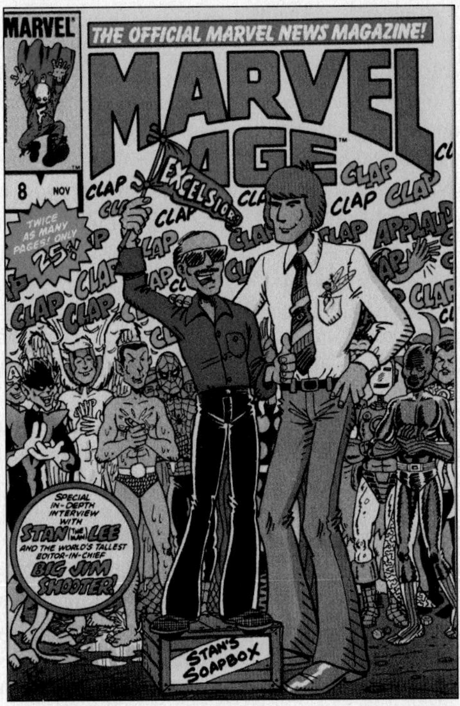
MARVEL
THE OFFICIAL MARVEL NEWS MAGAZINE!
MARVEL AGE
8 NOV
TWICE AS MANY PAGES! ONLY 25¢
EXCELSIOR!
CLAP CLAP CLAP
APPLAUD
SPECIAL IN-DEPTH INTERVIEW WITH STAN THE MAN LEE AND THE WORLD'S TALLEST EDITOR-IN-CHIEF BIG JIM SHOOTER!
STAN'S SOAPBOX

Marvel Age 8: *Now expanded to 32 pages, issue #8 featured an 11-page, in-depth interview with Stan Lee and then Editor-in-Chief Jim Shooter.*

The contents had a variety of features, including a Newswatch section featuring tidbits on upcoming projects and smatterings of behind the scenes doings of Marvel's staff and creators. Ample editorial notes from staff filled in "Marvel Zombies" (a term applied to anyone who purchased all Marvel Comics, regardless of content) wanting to know what was next on their buying list (like Peter Sanderson promoting Marvel's newest project—*The Official Handbook of the Marvel Universe*).

Subsequent issues featured an array of original covers by top drawer artists, many of whom were interviewed ahead of an upcoming special project. Rarely-interviewed John Byrne was interviewed in issue #2, promoting his Canadian-based superhero team Alpha Flight. Issue #4 kicked off another staple of *Marvel Age Magazine*, the letters page with submissions from around the world.

Changes began to appear with issue #7 when Jim Salicrup took over as Editor and Design Director. The page count doubled to

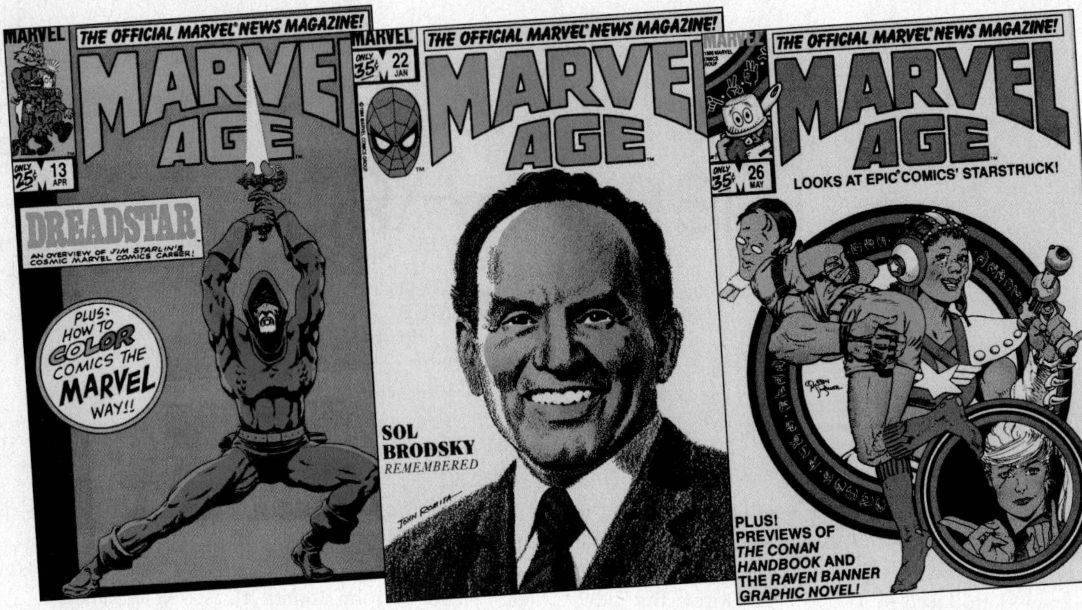
MARVEL
THE OFFICIAL MARVEL NEWS MAGAZINE!
MARVEL AGE
ONLY 25¢ 13 APR
DREADSTAR
AN OVERVIEW OF JIM STARLIN'S COSMIC MARVEL COMICS CAREER!
PLUS: HOW TO COLOR COMICS THE MARVEL WAY!!
MARVEL
THE OFFICIAL MARVEL NEWS MAGAZINE!
ONLY 35¢ 22 JAN
MARVEL AGE
SOL BRODSKY REMEMBERED
THE OFFICIAL MARVEL NEWS MAGAZINE!
MARVEL AGE
ONLY 35¢ 26 MAY
LOOKS AT EPIC COMICS' STARSTRUCK!
PLUS! PREVIEWS OF THE CONAN HANDBOOK AND THE RAVEN BANNER GRAPHIC NOVEL!

***Marvel Age 13* (left):** *How To Color Comics the Marvel Way was another one of those behind the scenes look at what went into coloring comics. Antiquated by today's computer coloring techniques, this feature shed light on how to color not only Marvel comics, but all comics during that era.* ***Marvel Age 22* (center):** *This issue featured a touching and sincere tribute to Sol Brodsky, one of Marvel's top executives and driving forces behind Marvel's early success.* ***Marvel Age 26* (right):** *One of the staples of Marvel Age—and a fan favorite—was the wacky Marvel Age Calendar that featured industry birthdays, sight gags, and fun facts and trivia.*

32 pages, all still priced at two bits. In his editorial, Salicrup explained how he ended up as an intern at Marvel at age 14 while announcing a new Talent Department that would feature art from new faces in upcoming issues. Issue #8 featured an 11-page double interview with Stan Lee and Jim Shooter (Editor in Chief at the time), conducted by then Assistant Direct Sales Manager, Peter David (long before anyone knew he could write).

After a year of publication, *Marvel Age* appeared to be picking up steam. A book that on the surface appeared to be nothing more than a publication prompting readers to pay money for Marvel hype, the book became the fans' mouthpiece for expressing their thoughts; letter's pages ran three pages an issue and fans, pros, and wannabe-pros were sending in letters. Marvel had successfully proven that the big guys could pull off something akin to a fanzine—a fan based publication. Issue #13 had an incredible feature--totally unexpected--and in-depth (seven pages) on "How to Color Comics the Marvel Way." The article, outdated by today's computer-rendered coloring techniques, provided a look at the work that went into the early days of coloring comics. The article even profiled the seven colorists on staff at Marvel. This issue also featured the start of a semi-regular feature, "Marvel Age," a look back at the history of Marvel starting with the year 1961.

Paper price increases saw *Marvel Age* #15 increase in price by 10 cents. The increase stuck for 26 issues with the dreaded "Only 50 cents" banner showing up on issue #41. Issue #22 featured a touching tribute to Sol Brodsky, one of Marvel's early pioneers who was a true unsung hero that worked mostly in production and eventually as VP of Operations. Sol was also a talented artist and writer before joining Marvel. A 17-page tribute and cover portrait drawn by John Romita Sr. made this a very touching and special issue.

Issue #26 saw the introduction of the back cover calendar—an illustrated, colorful look at industry birthdays, shameless plugs, and wacky sight gags. The calendar became a popular, regular feature along with the humorous comic strips of Fred Hembeck, future writer/artist on *Fred Hembeck Destroys the Marvel Universe*. In typical fanzine fashion, issue #35 featured "A Day in the Life of Marvel Comics!," a 20-page opus complete with an illustrated cover featuring office staff and an in-depth timeline of a typical day at Marvel. Photos of rarely-seen staff made this issue a treat for fans wanting to learn more about the faces behind their favorite comics.

"Stan's Soapbox" returned in *Marvel Age* #41 after quite a hiatus—complete with that infamous yellow box warning us of some big, exciting news. The piece was followed up by *The Stan Lee Story*, a

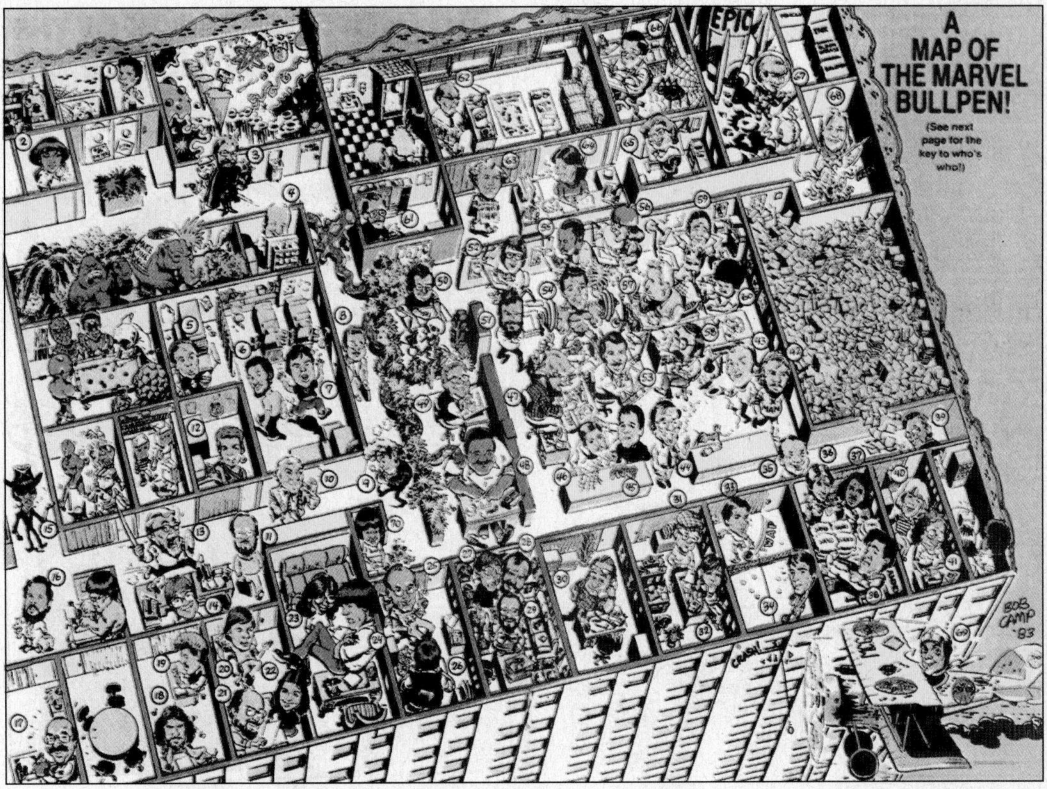
A MAP OF THE MARVEL BULLPEN!
(See next page for the key to who's who!)
EPIC
BOB CAMP '83

Marvel Age 7: Part of the fun was seeing that peek behind the curtain at what is was like to work at Marvel. Issue #7 saw this wonderful center-spread of the Marvel Bullpen!

four page look back written by none other than talented comic scribe, Kurt Busiek. Issue #50 arrived with the exclusive story of the wedding of Peter Parker and Mary Jane Watson and we all hit the jackpot with a cut-out Mary Jane paper doll featuring several outfits, including the wedding dress designed by real-life fashion designer, Will Smith.

After its meager beginning back in 1983, *Marvel Age Magazine* had blossomed into a full-fledged success that had crossed the boundary between slick Marvel book and fanzine. The editorial of issue #61 featured a letter from George Doro of Denver, Colorado, debating the term "Marvel Zombie" with Jim in his *Salicrup's Section* editorial. Salicrup continued his pattern of engaging fans in his editorials, making them part of the experience. Some of those fans went on to work professionally in the business—even getting the chance to work with Jim. (I know, I was one of them.) The issue also focused on graphic novels which were an up and coming commodity back then. The letters pages, still running three full pages, sometimes longer, also involved fans by using a different, fan-submitted title each and every issue. One of my favorites, "Attack of the Killer Fan Mail," complete with fan art, ran in issue #74. Issue #75 (June 1989), saw the addition of "Mark's Remarks," a popular, thought-provoking column written by one of Marvel's more outgoing and fan-oriented editors and writer, Mark Gruenwald. Mark always had a way of connecting with the fans and often featured their well thought out letters that he received. The column was carried over from the feature which ran in letters pages of books that he edited.

Issue #80 ushered in the biggest price increase yet—a 25 cent increase—to 75 cents, even though Salicrup had announced an increase to $1.00 several issues later. Of course the temporary increase only lasted six issues and went to the aforementioned $1.00 starting with issue #86. Every Marvel fan out there worth his weight in adamantium knows about the coveted "No-Prize," but Salicrup went into great detail to explain how it was awarded and that it was an envelope sent out, announcing that the recipient had received a no-prize; which meant exactly that--there was no-prize (or anything else) in the envelope. Mystery solved!

It was late 1989 when the *CBG (Comics Buyer's Guide)* Fan Awards selected *Marvel Age Magazine* as the Winner as Favorite Publication About Comics. It was January of 1990 when *Marvel Age Magazine* went from Direct Sales Only to also

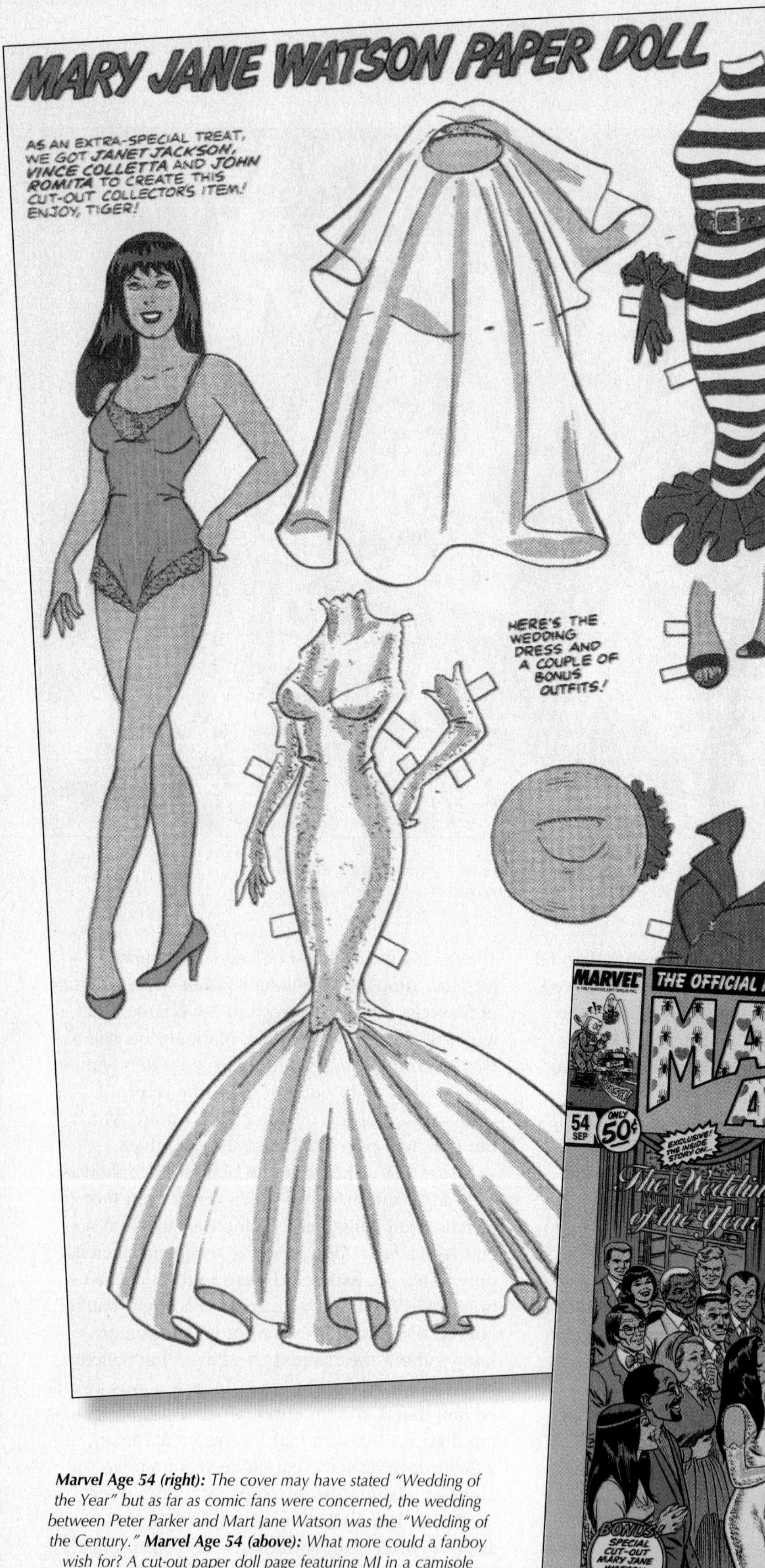
MARY JANE WATSON PAPER DOLL
AS AN EXTRA-SPECIAL TREAT, WE GOT JANET JACKSON, VINCE COLLETTA AND JOHN ROMITA TO CREATE THIS CUT-OUT COLLECTOR'S ITEM! ENJOY, TIGER!
HERE'S THE WEDDING DRESS AND A COUPLE OF BONUS OUTFITS!

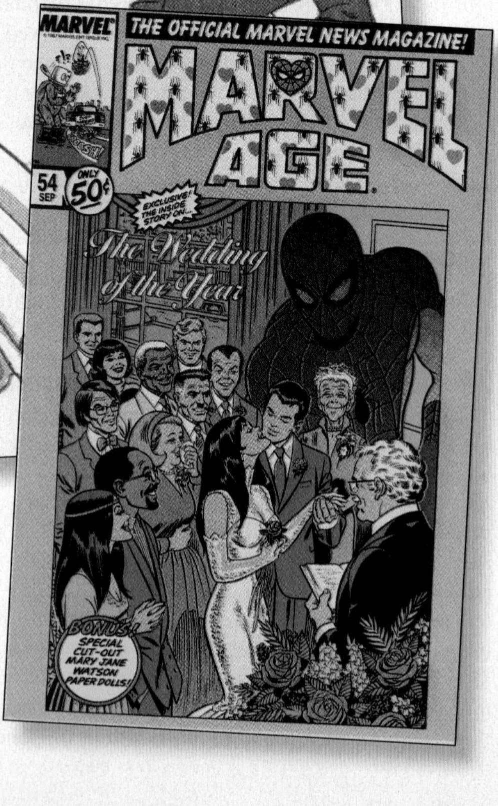
MARVEL
THE OFFICIAL MARVEL NEWS MAGAZINE!
MARVEL AGE
54 SEP
ONLY 50¢
EXCLUSIVE! THE INSIDE STORY ON...
The Wedding of the Year
BONUS! SPECIAL CUT-OUT MARY JANE WATSON PAPER DOLLS!

Marvel Age 54 (right): *The cover may have stated "Wedding of the Year" but as far as comic fans were concerned, the wedding between Peter Parker and Mart Jane Watson was the "Wedding of the Century."* **Marvel Age 54 (above):** *What more could a fanboy wish for? A cut-out paper doll page featuring MJ in a camisole and heels and some stylin' outfits—including her wedding gown designed by real-life designer, Will Smith.*

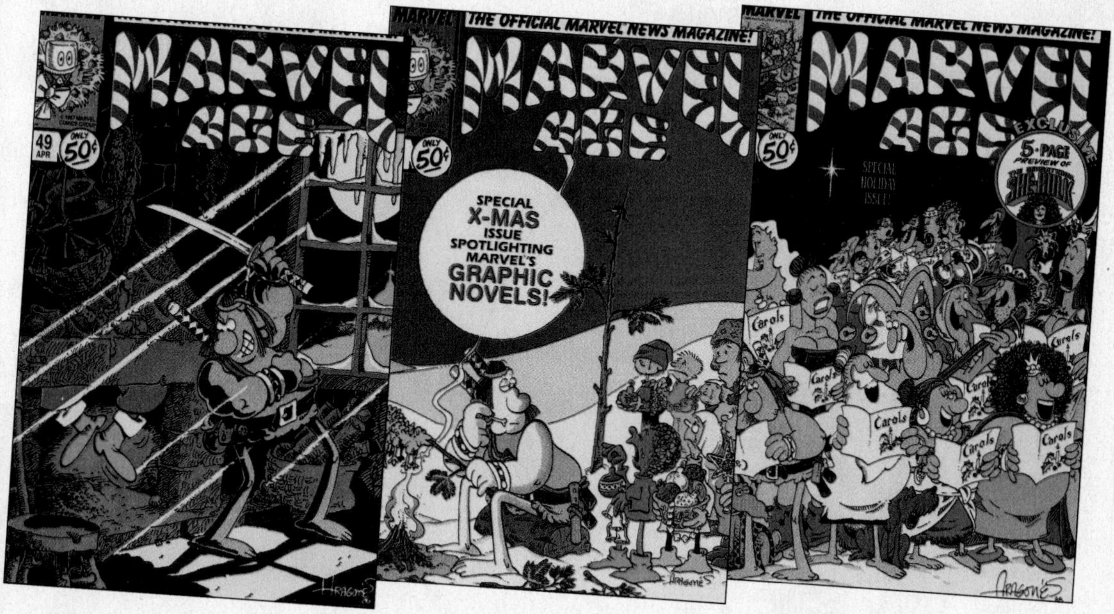
MARVEL AGE
49 APR
50¢
THE OFFICIAL MARVEL NEWS MAGAZINE!
MARVEL AGE
50¢
SPECIAL X-MAS ISSUE SPOTLIGHTING MARVEL'S GRAPHIC NOVELS!
THE OFFICIAL MARVEL NEWS MAGAZINE!
MARVEL AGE
50¢
EXCLUSIVE
5-PAGE PREVIEW OF
Carols

Marvel Age 49, 61, 73 (l-r): *One of the running gags was to feature a candy cane Marvel Age logo and an appearance by Groo on the cover of the holiday issues.*

being available on newsstand everywhere (the newsstand distribution was dropped a few months later). The December 1990 issue (#85), featured the long-running, holiday candy cane Marvel logo complete with Sergio Aragones' *Groo* cover. I don't know what the running gag was in the Marvel office, but Groo sure seemed to show up a lot on the December covers.

Always ahead of his time, cartoonist Fred Hembeck turned in a visually interesting center spread featuring The Li'l Avengers, taking advantage of issue #93 Avengers-themed emphasis. His rendition of Avengers as kids is as timeless and classic as today's Skottie Young's current baby cover variants. (Interesting note, Hembeck has Brother Voodoo stating that his Li'l Avengers had as much chance of getting by the Marvel brass as he did as making the lineup of the grownup Avengers, hmmmm.) This issue also saw the cover blurb change from The Official Marvel Fan Magazine to Official Marvel Zombie Magazine.

Issue #96, the X-Mas issue, once again had the same cover motif with Groo, everyone's favorite barbarian, making yet another appearance. Salicrup's Section takes some time to point out that anyone submitting to Marvel Age's new Talent Department should check out one of his favorite fanzines—the Marvel Zombie Society-APA (Amateur Press Association).

Not many comics make it to the lofty triple digit list, but *Marvel Age* did just that in May of 1991. In the 100th issue Mark Gruenwald delivered an epic 100 "Mark's Remarks," sharing 100 short observations about life, comics, and the universe. Probably one of the most reveling articles written by a Marvel editor without being an interview. Over in the New Talent Department we had an unknown penciler, Leonard Kirk, showing off his skills with a two-page Ghost Rider story. Marvel's Managing Art Director at the time, Steve Geiger, had this to say about Leonard's pencils, "I think Leonard will do just fine, and I wish him the best of luck." (Leonard Kirk broke into comics drawing Malibu Comics *Dinosaurs For Hire* series and continues to work on many high profile comics for DC and Marvel Comics).

The following issue, #101 was special for me as it contained my second piece of writing for Marvel (the first being an Alien Legion piece in *Marvel Age* #96). More importantly, it introduced me to Carol Kalish. Carol was the first editor of *Marvel Age Magazine* and a brilliant sales and marketing person. The article, announcing the Wild Agents of Marvel, was their newest fan club, following in the footsteps of the Merry Marvel Marching Society, Marvelmania, and FOOM. Sadly, Carol passed away at a way-too-young age at the peak of her creativity. I learned a lot from her and appreciated getting to know her, even if it was just via phone conversations.

After editing 99 issue of *Marvel Age*, Salicrup moved on, handing the reigns over to Renee

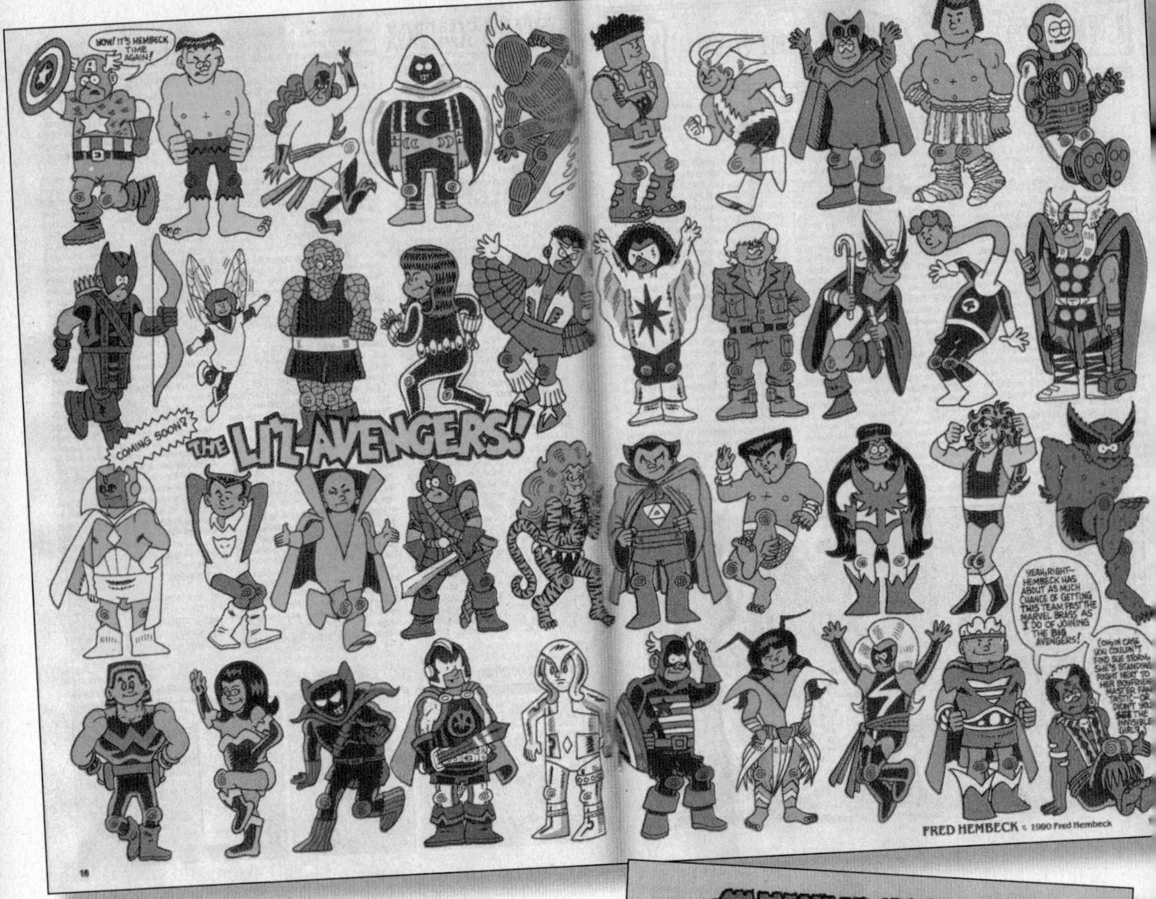
WOW! IT'S HEMBECK TIME AGAIN!
COMING SOON?
THE LI'L AVENGERS!
YEAH, RIGHT— HEMBECK HAS ABOUT AS MUCH CHANCE OF GETTING THIS TEAM PAST THE MARVEL BRASS AS I DO OF JOINING THE BIG AVENGERS!
FRED HEMBECK © 1990 Fred Hembeck
16

Marvel Age 93A: *This issue was a look at all things Avengers with Fred Hembeck delivering one of his best pieces—his rendering of The Li'l Avengers.*

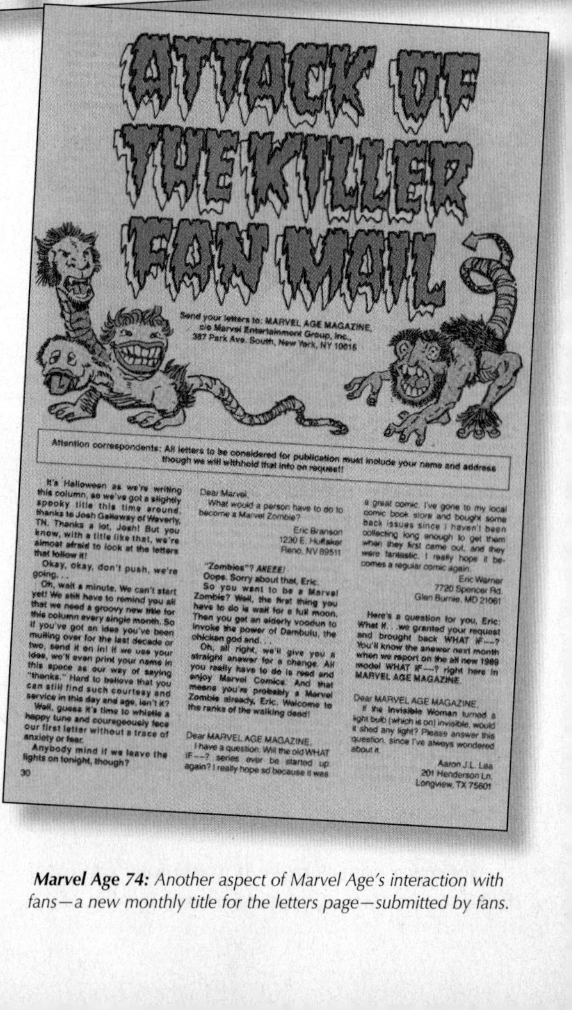
ATTACK OF THE KILLER FAN MAIL

Send your letters to: MARVEL AGE MAGAZINE,
c/o Marvel Entertainment Group, Inc.,
387 Park Ave. South, New York, NY 10016

Attention correspondents: All letters to be considered for publication must include your name and address though we will withhold that info on request!

It's Halloween as we're writing this column, so we've got a slightly spooky title this time around, thanks to Josh Galloway of Waverly, TN. Thanks a lot, Josh! But you know, with a title like that, we're almost afraid to look at the letters that follow it!

Okay, okay, don't push, we're going. . .

Oh, wait a minute. We can't start yet! We still have to remind you all that we need a groovy new title for this column every single month. So if you've got an idea you've been mulling over for the last decade or two, send it on in! If we use your idea, we'll even print your name in this space as our way of saying "thanks." Hard to believe that you can still find such courtesy and service in this day and age, isn't it?

Well, guess it's time to whistle a happy tune and courageously face our first letter without a trace of anxiety or fear.

Anybody mind if we leave the lights on tonight, though?

Dear Marvel,

What would a person have to do to become a Marvel Zombie?

Eric Branson
1230 E. Huffaker
Reno, NV 89511

"Zombies"? AKEEE!

Oops. Sorry about that, Eric.

So you want to be a Marvel Zombie? Well, the first thing you have to do is wait for a full moon. Then you get an elderly voodun to invoke the power of Dambulu, the chicken god and. . .

Oh, all right, we'll give you a straight answer for a change. All you really have to do is read and enjoy Marvel Comics. And that means you're probably a Marvel Zombie already, Eric. Welcome to the ranks of the walking dead!

Dear MARVEL AGE MAGAZINE,

I have a question: Will the old WHAT IF—? series ever be started up again? I really hope so because it was a great comic. I've gone to my local comic book store and bought some back issues since I haven't been collecting long enough to get them when they first came out, and they were fantastic. I really hope it becomes a regular comic again.

Eric Warner
7720 Spencer Rd.
Glen Burnie, MD 21061

Here's a question for you, Eric: What If. . .we granted your request and brought back WHAT IF—? You'll know the answer next month when we report on the all new 1989 model WHAT IF—? right here in MARVEL AGE MAGAZINE.

Dear MARVEL AGE MAGAZINE,

If the Invisible Woman turned a light bulb (which is on) invisible, would it shed any light? Please answer this question, since I've always wondered about it.

Aaron J.L. Lea
201 Henderson Ln.
Longview, TX 75601

30

Marvel Age 74: *Another aspect of Marvel Age's interaction with fans—a new monthly title for the letters page—submitted by fans.*

Witterstaetter effective with issue #105. (Note: Salicrup ended up leaving Marvel to become Editor in Chief of a successful line of comics, including *The X-Files*, *Jurassic Park*, and *Xena Warrior Princess* for the Topps Company. Topps Comics, a wholly owned subsidiary of The Topps Company, went on to become Best New Publisher and Best Small Publisher of the Year as reported by Diamond Comics Distributors).

Another semi-regular feature added in later issues was a wonderful column written by Andy Mangels; "Andy Mangels' Reel Marvel." The column featured a look back at Marvel and their rich history of television and movie adaptations, including cartoon episodes. In-depth and informative, one can only image how much space would be needed to cover all of today's theatrical productions. This issue (#109) also saw the cover banner change from "Official Marvel Zombie Magazine" to "World's Best-Selling Fan Magazine." According to published Statement of Ownership reports, the fanzine/magazine was selling in the range of 60,000 copies monthly. Pretty respectable numbers.

The John Romita Sr. interview issue of *Marvel Age* #111 was notable for a number of reasons,

MARVEL COMICS
OFFICIAL MARVEL ZOMBIE MAGAZINE!
MARVEL AGE
WINNER
$1.00 US
111 APR
JOHN-- WHERE'S THAT MARVEL AGE COVER?
IN THIS ISSUE: JOHN ROMITA SPEAKS

MARVEL Age
RISE OF THE MIDNIGHT SONS
August 1992
TEK WORLD
30TH ANNIVERSARY 1962 1992
THE AMAZING SPIDER-MAN
$1.00 US $1.25 CAN 70p UK
MARVEL III CARDS

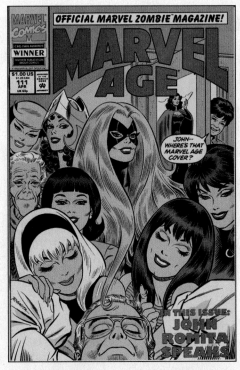

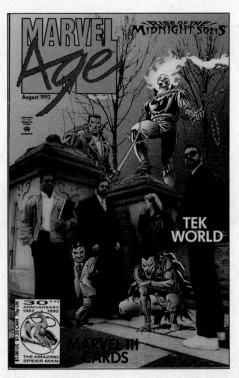

Marvel Age 111 (left): *A John Romita self-portrait graces the cover, complete with a bevy of beauties all created by Jazzy John (John even managed to include his beautiful wife, Virginia, in the piece). The issue included an informative Romita interview.* **Marvel Age 115 (right):** *A new look for Marvel Age as the updated, stylized Marvel Age logo makes its debut.*

first and foremost, an interview with one of the true statesmen of comics, John Romita. The cover, a classic, shows a relaxed, very pleased with himself Romita, surrounded by all of the wonderful women he's drawn over the years—including, of course, Mary Jane and Gwen. A classic Romita cover. The issue also contained a behind the scenes look at "Romita's Raiders," a group of artists that worked diligently to handle corrections and keep production on track. The book also featured one of Hembeck's best, his stylized rendition and salute to the art of John Romita.

After eight issues, Renee Witterstaetter passed the editorial reigns to Steve Saffel. (Renee also went on to become an editor for Topps Comics). After 114 issues, the *Marvel Age* logo was revamped to a new, modernized look, designed to give the magazine a fresh look and a new start. The 120th issue of *Marvel Age Magazine* celebrated ten years of publication with Editor Steve Saffel dedicating the issue to Carol Kalish and Peter David. The issue contained a nice look back at the ten year history of the magazine as well as a look forward at future projects.

Unfortunately, all good things come to an end, as did *Marvel Age*, with issue #140 (September 1994), which featured a painted cover by the Greg and Tim Hildebrandt, featuring Spider-Man 2099. *Marvel Age* also ran four annuals from 1985-1988. Highlights included 48-page issues with original comic content. *Annual* #1 (1985), featured an original tale featuring the Beyonder and just about everyone in the Marvel Universe. Written by Jim Shooter and Kurt Busiek with art by James Fry and Keith Williams, the yarn was entertaining and well-drawn. A comic worthy of annual status. The 1987 *Annual* (#3) featured *The Fred Hembeck Show,* a *Tonight Show* parody written and drawn by Hembeck in which he interviewed just about everyone that existed in the Marvel Universe at the time. Marvel also produced two preview issues in 1990 (48 pages), and a 1992 *Marvel Age Preview* that ran 64 pages.

It really doesn't matter whether you call it a magazine, comic book, or fanzine—the bottom line is that *Marvel Age* will be remembered fondly not only by readers, but also by the plethora of creators, fans, and sales and marketing people that were fortunate enough to work on the publication. At the very least, it will go down as an experiment in the genre of fanzine and sales tools/marketing from a major publisher. But, thankfully for readers, it will be mostly remembered as a wonderful run that was fun to read, visually exciting, and an exciting, behind-the-scenes look at Marvel that made fans feel what it was like to actually work for Marvel Comics.

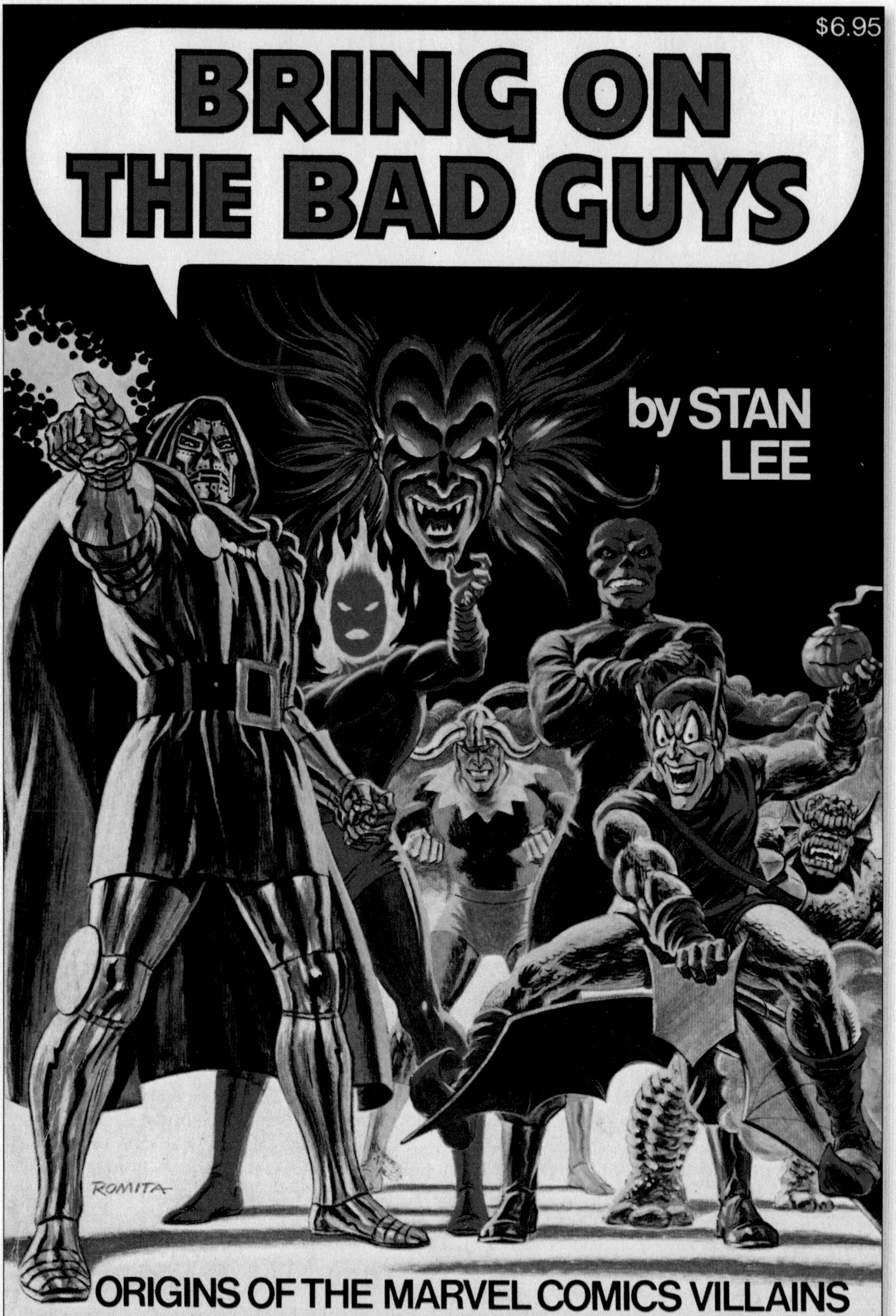
$6.95
BRING ON THE BAD GUYS
by STAN LEE
ROMITA
ORIGINS OF THE MARVEL COMICS VILLAINS

A Slow-Burning Fire:
The Marvel and DC Fireside Books

BY J.C. VAUGHN

In *The Overstreet Comic Book Price Guide* #29, Bob Overstreet made the addition to our listings of the comic book hardcover and soft cover volumes published by Simon & Schuster under their Fireside imprint between 1974 and 1980. At the time, this decision was met with general apathy except for the overwhelmingly positive reaction of the core group who collected the books. As it turned out, they were clearly onto something.

Trade paperback and hardcover collections were already well established in 1998 when the addition was made. DC Comics had distinguished itself as the leader in the emerging market segment with its comprehensive (and comprehensible) publishing program. The beginnings of the robust archival market we enjoy today were well underway.

Both DC's *DC Archives* and Marvel's *Marvel Masterworks* had shown that there was a solid customer base for such programs, but the secondary market for such publications was still in its early stages at that point. One could argue that it still is, at least to some extent.

The Fireside books have always held a special place for a select group of fans. For those in that group, they were among the first hardcover or trade paperback collections of comic books that many of them had ever seen.

THE FORMULAS
Beginning with *Origins of Marvel Comics* and continuing through the numerous follow-ups, the Fireside books presented readers with origin issues and other stories of Marvel's most popular characters. With Silver Age keys already hitting hundreds of dollars – they certainly seemed expensive at the time – these books were providing a great way for new readers to enjoy those issues without having to purchase the originals.

Many copies became dog-eared over time from repeated readings, and this is an important factor to consider when collecting them. Simon and Schuster's line has long been difficult to find in grade, particularly the hardcovers.

As mentioned above, the formula for the Marvel books was simple enough: take the origin story of a key character or group of characters, give it an introduction, and follow it up with a more contemporary story featuring the same character or characters.

Son of Origins, The Superhero Women, and *Bring on the Bad Guys* rounded out the larger volumes. *The Amazing Spider-Man, Captain America, Doctor Strange, Fantastic Four* and *Marvel's Greatest Superhero Battles* were the slightly thinner follow-ups.

Only *The Silver Surfer* (1976) differed. This Stan Lee/Jack Kirby collaboration featured a new take on the Surfer's origin, one which did not feature the Fantastic Four in any way. Not only was it not a reprint (despite being something of a remake), this Bronze Age gem was Marvel's first true graphic novel, well ahead of their series of graphic novels launched in the early '80s.

While clearly not the earliest American graphic novel, this is still a very important piece both historically and by merit of its scarcity. Only now becoming truly appreciated by collectors, it is increasingly difficult to find in grade (again, particularly the hardcover).

The DC Fireside books were theme-based anthologies. *America at War – The Best of DC War Comics, Heart Throbs – The Best of DC Romance Comics,* and *Mysteries in Space* are as difficult to find in grade as their Marvel counterparts, but in reality may actually be significantly more rare. Frequently one can find even experienced dealers who aren't even aware of the DC books.

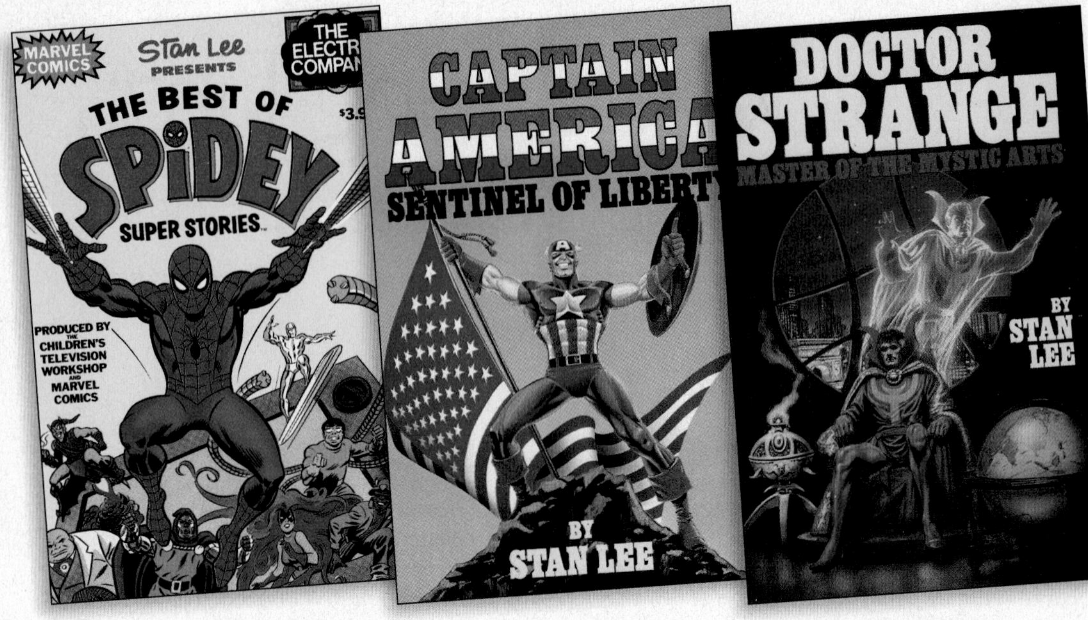
MARVEL COMICS
Stan Lee PRESENTS
THE BEST OF SPIDEY SUPER STORIES
PRODUCED BY THE CHILDREN'S TELEVISION WORKSHOP AND MARVEL COMICS
CAPTAIN AMERICA
SENTINEL OF LIBERTY
BY STAN LEE
DOCTOR STRANGE
MASTER OF THE MYSTIC ARTS
BY STAN LEE

SCARCITY

It's not terribly surprising that grade and printing edition play a huge role in the desirability of the Fireside books for collectors. In all cases, the first printings are in the highest demand with the hardcovers leading the way.

There were multiple printings of some of the books in Simon & Schuster series, and later Marvel issued their own revised editions of some of them. The Marvel reprints of the *Origins* series, it must be noted, have done a great favor for those collectors with the original books in their collections. The more recent editions have contained the same familiar origin stories, but the contemporary (in the late '70s) follow-up stories have been replaced with even more contemporary pieces. If anything, this heightened the perception of the rarity for the original editions.

Skeptical? When was the last time you saw one of these books in a grade that wasn't already in someone's collection?

"We have not sold any, not due to demand, but because we have not had any come in collections. A friend of mine purchased a collection of the hardcovers in 1999. Apart from that particular collection, I have not had the chance to purchase any hardcovers," said Steven Houston of Torpedo Comics. "They are scarce in my opinion and I would price nice condition hardcovers 'through the roof' as they say."

"We've never seen the *Heart Throbs* one or *America at War*! The *Silver Surfer* is always popular, because it's Lee/Kirby," said Ted VanLiew of Superworld Comics. "The hardcovers go for significantly more than the soft covers, as they turn up much less frequently."

Veteran Overstreet Advisor Doug Sulipa reports that demand for the books has been steady, but suggests they're not as "hot" as they were when first listed in the *Guide*. Even with that proviso, though, he believes that the soft cover versions of the post-1976 volumes are significantly undervalued in 2.0, 4.0. 6.0 and 8.0. He reports that they sell as fast as he can find them at 150% to 200% of *Guide*.

"A setter standard spread for the soft covers would be GD=$10; VG=$20; FN=$30; VF=$50; VF/NM=$65; NM-, 9.2 = $80," Sulipa said.

The 1974-1976 soft cover books (*Origins of Marvel Comics*, *Son of Origins*, and *Bring on the Bad Guys*) are slower movers as they are more common, he said, but if listed correctly, noting that they had second and subsequent printings, they sell better. He noted his belief that first printings should be priced 50% higher than later ones.

He said the *Silver Surfer* soft cover, although it is easily found, remains in constant demand as it is the "most important" book in the series. In the original art market, pages from this book have started commanding attention as well.

One volume that had been a sleeper for many years but which has awakened in more recent times is *The Best of Spidey Super Stories*. Sulipa commends it as "by far the scarcest" and suggested its values should be 300% of current *Guide* prices. While that would be a pretty big jump, there is definitely merit to that consideration.

He also noted several other trends.

"*Heart Throbs* is by far the scarcest DC title and should list at 200% of current *Guide* prices, and the 1978-1980 titles focused on one main character are in higher demand than the combo titles," he

FIRESIDE BOOK SERIES Simon and Schuster: 1974 - 1980 (130-260 pgs.), Square bound, color		GD 2.0	VG 4.0	FN 6.0	VF 8.0	VF/NM 9.0	NM- 9.2
Amazing Spider-Man, The, 1979, 130 pgs., $3.95, Bob Larkin-c	HC	7	14	21	48	89	130
	SC	5	10	15	33	57	80
America At War–The Best of DC War Comics, 1979, $6.95, 260 pgs, Kubert-c	HC	10	20	30	64	132	200
	SC	6	12	18	42	79	115
Best of Spidey Super Stories (Electric Company) 1978, $3.95,	HC	9	18	27	57	111	165
	SC	6	12	18	37	66	95
Bring On The Bad Guys (Origins of the Marvel Comics Villains) 1976, $6.95, 260 pgs.; Romita-c	HC	7	14	21	46	86	125
	SC	5	10	15	31	53	75
Captain America, Sentinel of Liberty,1979, 130 pgs., $12.95, Cockrum-c	HC	7	14	21	48	89	130
	SC	5	10	15	33	57	80
Doctor Strange Master of the Mystic Arts, 1980, 130 pgs.	HC	7	14	21	48	89	130
	SC	5	10	15	33	57	80
Fantastic Four, The, 1979, 130 pgs.	HC	7	14	21	46	86	125
	SC	5	10	15	31	53	75
Heart Throbs–The Best of DC Romance Comics, 1979, 260 pgs., $6.95	HC	13	26	39	86	188	290
	SC	8	16	24	56	108	160
Incredible Hulk, The, 1978, 260 pgs. (8 1/4" x 11")	HC	7	14	21	46	86	125
	SC	5	10	15	31	53	75
Marvel's Greatest Superhero Battles, 1978, 260 pgs., $6.95, Romita-c	HC	9	18	27	57	111	165
	SC	6	12	18	37	66	95
Mysteries in Space, 1980, $7,95, Anderson-c. r-DC sci/fi stories	HC	8	16	24	52	99	145
	SC	5	10	15	34	60	85
Origins of Marvel Comics, 1974, 260 pgs., $5.95. r-covers & origins of Fantastic Four, Hulk, Spider-Man, Thor, & Doctor Strange	HC	7	14	21	46	86	125
	SC	5	10	15	31	53	75
Silver Surfer, The, 1978, 130 pgs., $4.95, Norem-c	HC	7	14	21	48	89	130
	SC	5	10	15	34	60	85
Son of Origins of Marvel Comics, 1975, 260 pgs., $6.95, Romita-c. Reprints, covers & origins of X-Men, Iron Man, Avengers, Daredevil, Silver Surfer	HC	7	14	21	46	86	125
	SC	5	10	15	31	53	75
Superhero Women, The 1977, 260 pgs., $6.95, Romita-c	HC	9	18	27	57	111	165
	SC	6	12	18	37	66	95

Note: Prices listed are for first printings. Later printings have lesser value.

said. "Hardcovers are much scarcer and are usually found with dust jackets in FA/GD, GD/VG or VG/FN, usually not higher."

As VanLiew alluded to, the market for the hardcovers remains strong, at least when they actually show up. They don't show up all that often, and when they do, they can command substantial premiums, frequently in the 200-300% of *Guide* range, though sometimes even more than that. In these cases, the dust jackets can become a key component. While they are usually worse for wear even if the book itself is in higher grade, those with high grade dust jackets are rare indeed. It's enough of a consideration that Sulipa offered a formula for pricing the volumes with dust jackets. He suggested

adding 50% of the hardcover book price for its grade to 50% of the book price for the grade of the dust jacket to determine final value in between the two grades.

MARVEL ACTIVITY BOOKS

Fireside also issued a slate of Marvel-based activity, game, and how-to books. The roster included *The Mighty Marvel Superheroes Fun Book* (June 1976), *The Mighty Marvel Comics Strength and Fitness Book* (September 1976), *The Mighty Marvel Superheroes Fun Book #2* (June 1977), *The Mighty Marvel Superheroes Cookbook* (September 1977), *The Mighty Marvel Fun Book #3* (July 1978), *How to Draw Comics the Marvel Way* (September 1978), *Marvel Mazes*

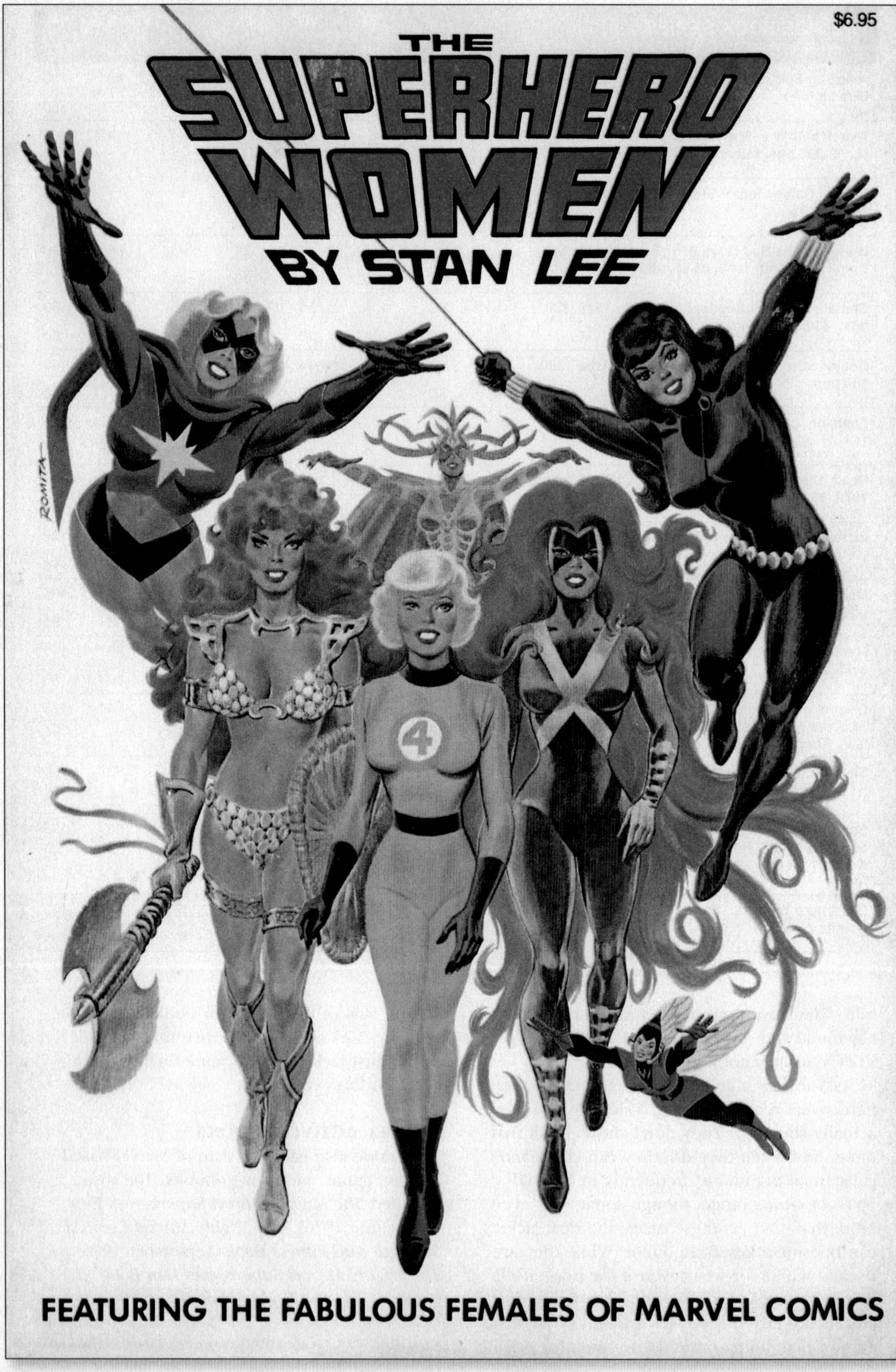
$6.95
THE
SUPERHERO
WOMEN
BY STAN LEE
ROMITA
FEATURING THE FABULOUS FEMALES OF MARVEL COMICS

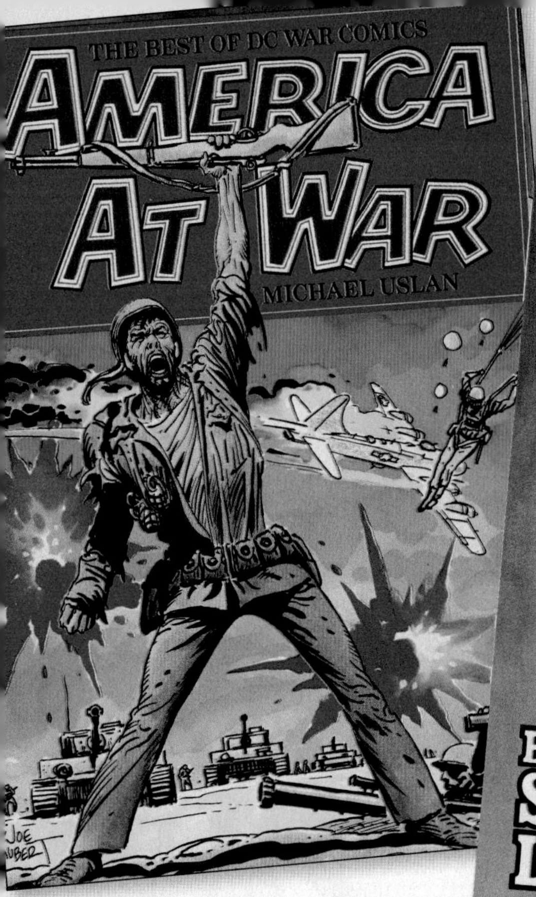
THE BEST OF DC WAR COMICS
AMERICA AT WAR
MICHAEL USLAN

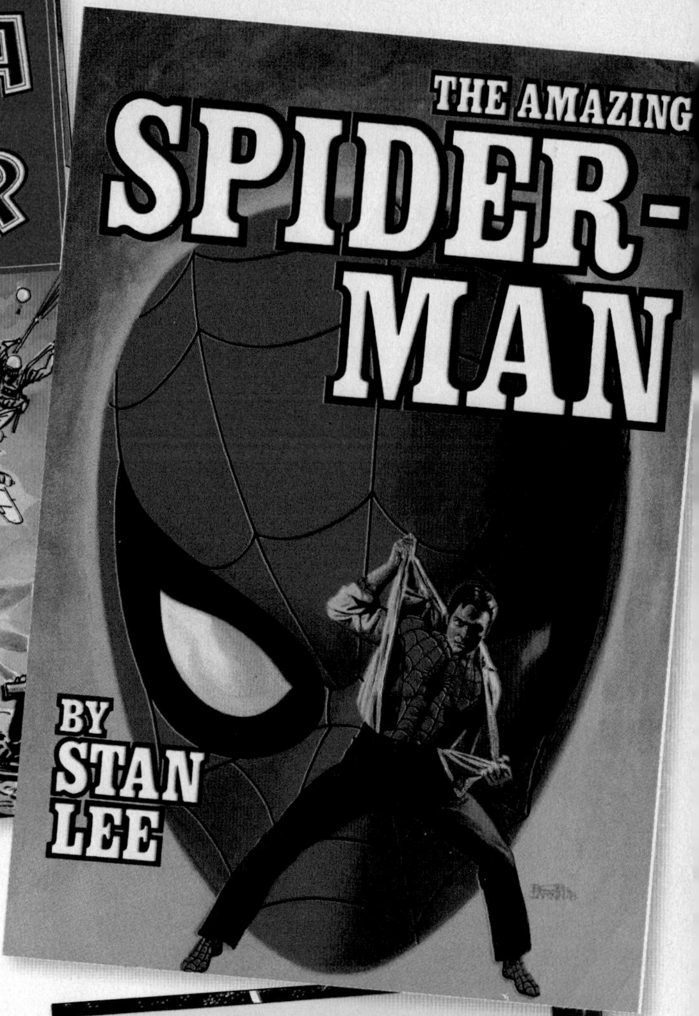
THE AMAZING
SPIDER-MAN
BY STAN LEE

to Drive You Mad (October 1978), *The Mighty Marvel Pin-Up Book* (November 1978), *The Mighty Marvel Fun Book* #4 (1979), *The Mighty Marvel Fun Book* #5 (1979), *Marvel Word Games* (August 1979), and *The Mighty Marvel Jumbo Fun Book* (1979).

The most successful of these, *How to Draw Comics the Marvel Way*, has seen many subsequent printings and a number of updated versions. Both the *Mighty Marvel Comics Strength and Fitness Book* and *Mighty Marvel Superheroes Fun Book* #1 (1976), #2 (1977), #3 (1978), #4 (1978), and #5 (1979) have strong collector demand.

Of *Mighty Marvel Comics Strength and Fitness Book*, Sulipa warns "Beware: most copies have writing inside; marked copies bring 25%-90% less depending on the severity of the marking," and he issued the same caution for the various editions *Mighty Marvel Superheroes Fun Book*. He pegged the 9.2 price at $100 for each of those books.

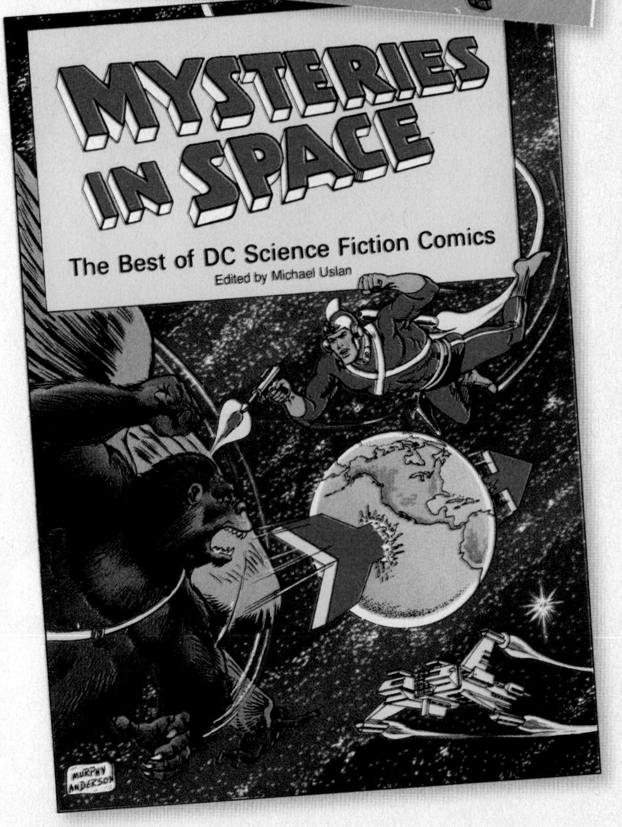
MYSTERIES IN SPACE
The Best of DC Science Fiction Comics
Edited by Michael Uslan

J.C. Vaughn is Gemstone Publishing's Vice-President of Publishing. His well-worn copies of Origins of Marvel Comics *and* Son of Origins *are still close to his desk, just as they have been since the 1970s.*

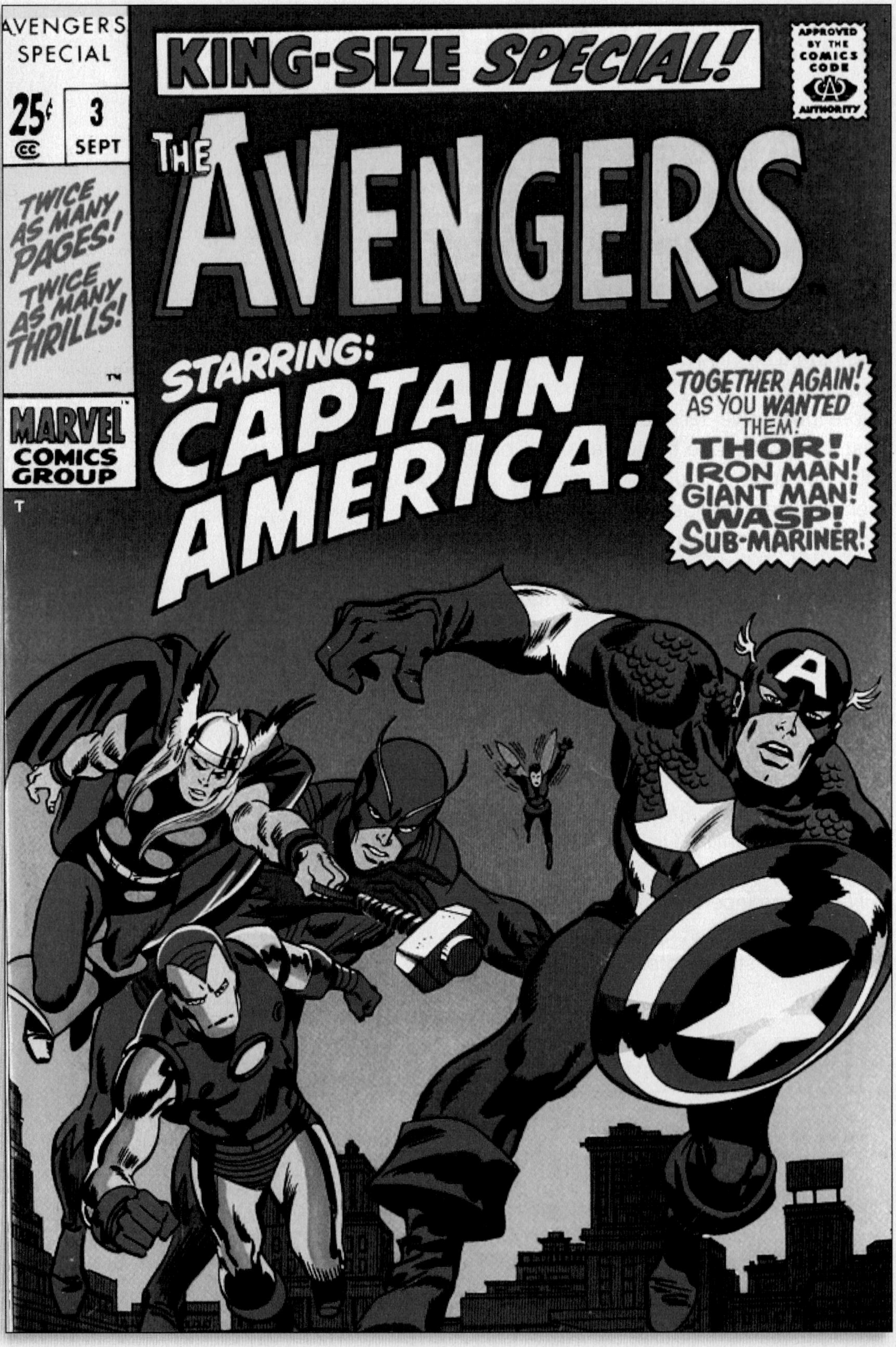
AVENGERS SPECIAL
25¢
3
SEPT
KING-SIZE SPECIAL!
APPROVED BY THE COMICS CODE AUTHORITY
THE AVENGERS
TWICE AS MANY PAGES! TWICE AS MANY THRILLS!
MARVEL COMICS GROUP
STARRING: CAPTAIN AMERICA!
TOGETHER AGAIN! AS YOU WANTED THEM! THOR! IRON MAN! GIANT MAN! WASP! SUB-MARINER!

The Sal Buscema Interview

BY **JASON VERSAGGI**

There are very few "royal families" in the realm of comics, but it's been known for years that the Buscemas are one of them. Sal Buscema, younger brother of "Big John" Buscema, is simply one of the most influential and admired comic creators for so many different reasons. His career at Marvel began in 1968, and he was a huge contributor to the Marvel Universe over the course of five decades.

CBM: Before we get to the art questions, let's get the most important stuff out of the way first. You're from Brooklyn, and I've lived in Brooklyn my whole life. Where is your favorite place to eat in Brooklyn and do you agree that Gil Hodges should be in the Hall Of Fame?
Sal Buscema (SB): My favorite place to eat was the Automat, which you probably don't know about. They've been out of business for years. Yes, Gil Hodges should be in the Hall of Fame. He was a great hitter, and one of the best fielding first basemen of all time. He was also a great manager.

CBM: Aside from your big brother John, and masters like Foster and Raymond, was your early work influenced by anyone else? Even outside the sequential art realm - did you draw any inspiration from film?
SB: The great Renaissance artists and a great American illustrator, Robert Fawcett.

CBM: It seems as if when you started out you were the ultimate utility man artist. Right from the start, your style was a great fit for this medium. Did you ever do any early work penciling or inking that went un-credited? Did you ever ink any of your brother's work when you were just visiting for a barbecue and he hit you up to help him out?
SB: I helped John on numerous occasions when he had deadline problems.

CBM: Your career seems to have several acts. You and your work meant so much to so many fans across different decades. Fans love your *Avengers* work in the late '60s and your *Defenders,* and Hulk, for many, is the definitive example. You have your wildly popular stint on *ROM,* and for me in the '80s and '90s I adored your work on

CAPT. AMERICA
12¢ IND.
115 JULY
CAPTAIN AMERICA
NOW BEGINS THE NIGHTMARE!
MARVEL COMICS GROUP

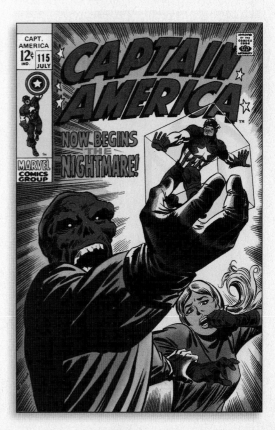

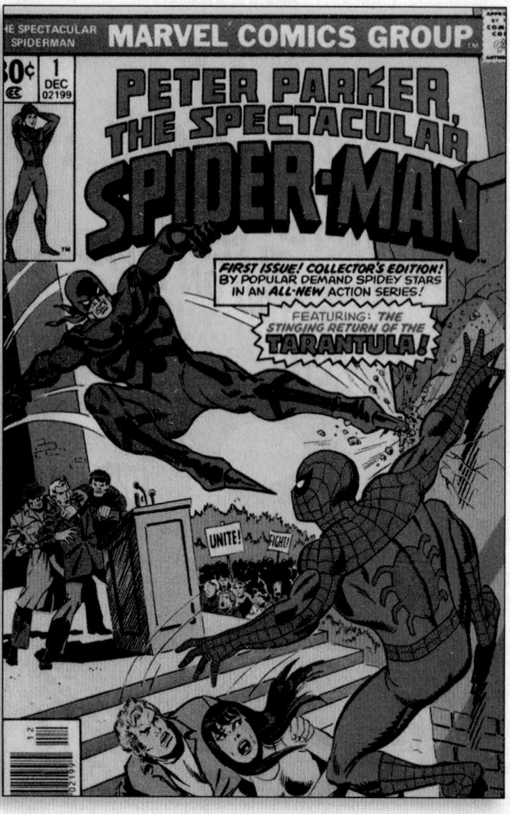
THE SPECTACULAR SPIDERMAN
MARVEL COMICS GROUP
30¢ 1 DEC 02199
PETER PARKER, THE SPECTACULAR SPIDER-MAN
FIRST ISSUE! COLLECTOR'S EDITION! BY POPULAR DEMAND SPIDEY STARS IN AN ALL-NEW ACTION SERIES!
FEATURING: THE STINGING RETURN OF THE TARANTULA!
UNITE!
FIGHT!

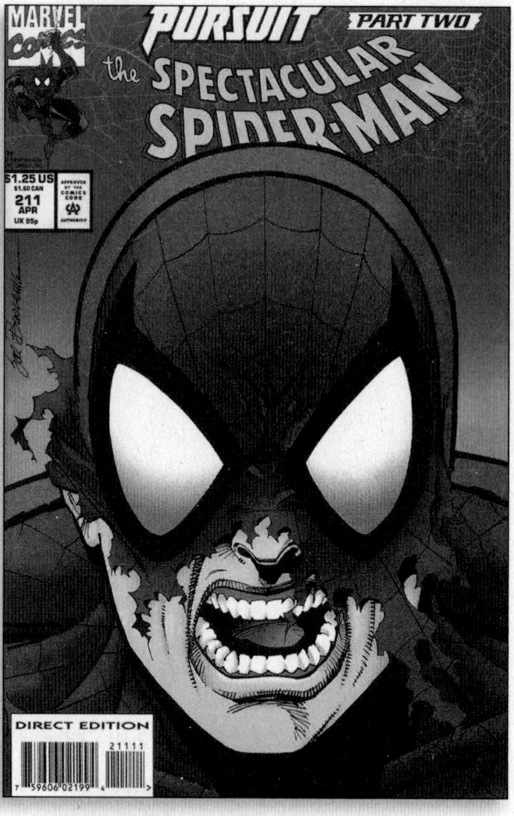
MARVEL COMICS
PURSUIT PART TWO
the SPECTACULAR SPIDER-MAN
$1.25 US $1.60 CAN 211 APR UK 95p
DIRECT EDITION

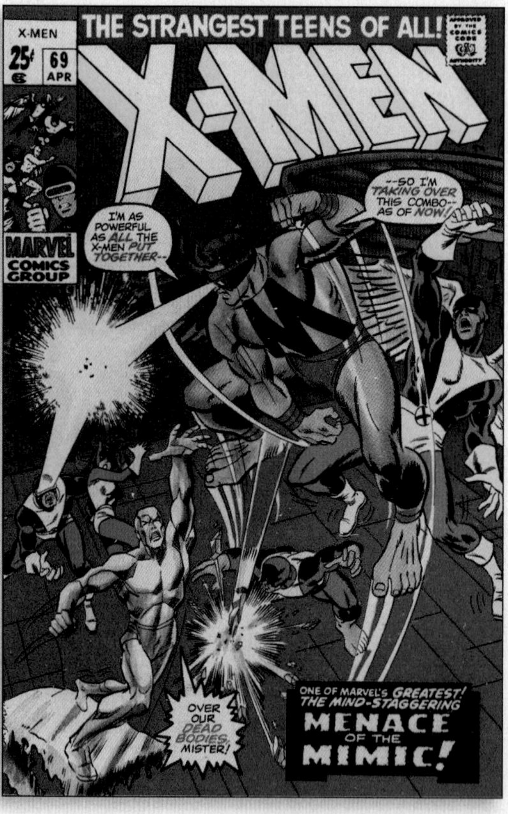
X-MEN
THE STRANGEST TEENS OF ALL!
25¢ 69 APR
X-MEN
MARVEL COMICS GROUP
--SO I'M TAKING OVER THIS COMBO-- AS OF NOW!
I'M AS POWERFUL AS ALL THE X-MEN PUT TOGETHER--
OVER OUR DEAD BODIES, MISTER!
ONE OF MARVEL'S GREATEST! THE MIND-STAGGERING MENACE OF THE MIMIC!

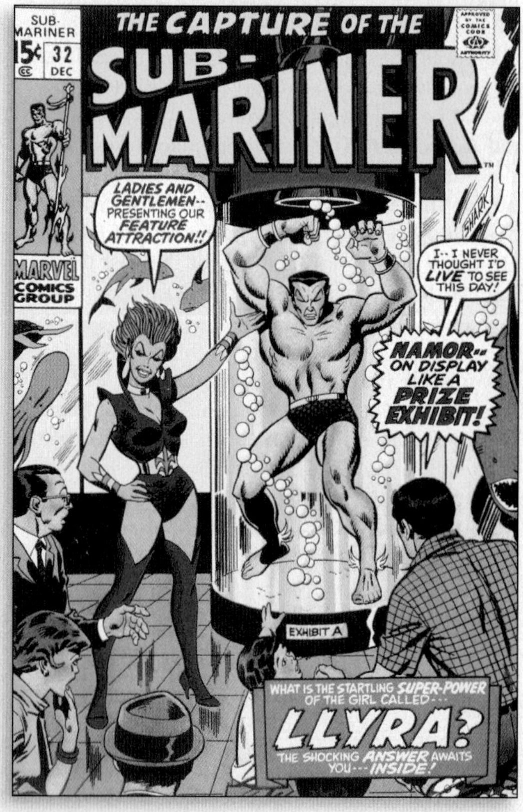
SUB-MARINER
THE CAPTURE OF THE SUB-MARINER
15¢ 32 DEC
MARVEL COMICS GROUP
LADIES AND GENTLEMEN-- PRESENTING OUR FEATURE ATTRACTION!!
I-- I NEVER THOUGHT I'D LIVE TO SEE THIS DAY!
NAMOR-- ON DISPLAY LIKE A PRIZE EXHIBIT!
EXHIBIT A
WHAT IS THE STARTLING SUPER-POWER OF THE GIRL CALLED--- LLYRA?
THE SHOCKING ANSWER AWAITS YOU--- INSIDE!

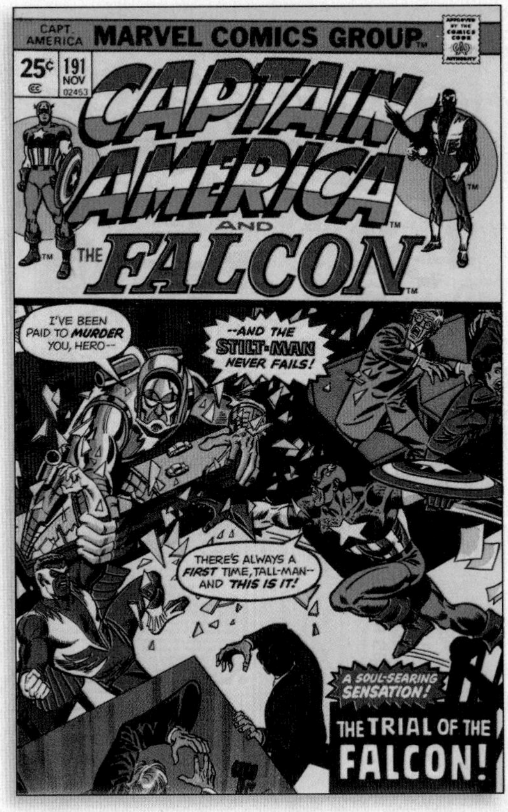
CAPT. AMERICA
MARVEL COMICS GROUP
25¢
191 NOV
CAPTAIN AMERICA AND THE FALCON
I'VE BEEN PAID TO MURDER YOU, HERO--
--AND THE STILT-MAN NEVER FAILS!
THERE'S ALWAYS A FIRST TIME, TALL-MAN-- AND THIS IS IT!
A SOUL-SEARING SENSATION!
THE TRIAL OF THE FALCON!

Spider-Man. Was there an era you enjoyed working in the most? Was there an environment you loved to be enveloped in with your characters?

SB: Loved all of it. Is there a more fun way to earn a living? My all-time favorite is the Hulk. Always will be. By the way, thank you so much for the kind words. They are truly appreciated.

CBM: Not many artists evolve as much as you did. The style that many loved and revered became another style so different that was equally loved and revered. You have said that you enjoyed the work of Bill Sienkiewicz. Was your evolution a conscious decision or did it just happen organically? Pardon me for mixing baseball and comics, but it's like Robin Yount being an All-Star as an infielder, and then later in his career in the outfield.

SB: There are so many wonderful artists in this industry. I learned from all of them. They all helped me to grow in my craft.

CBM: Admittedly any team book presents plenty of difficulty, but was there one character from any of your long runs who you were challenged by to draw? Some artists hate drawing Cap's chain mail or Spidey's costume. Who gave you fits?

SB: You're right. The group books are most difficult. All the characters gave me problems, but Spidey's costume was a pain in the butt.

CBM: Did your brother really not enjoy super hero comics? It's hard to believe that such passion and quality could not come from a great fondness for the source. You seemed to enjoy them more but what were the debates that raged in the Buscema household about which character would win in a fight? Where were your allegiances?

SB: John had a passion for drawing. Not just comics, but drawing in general. He did his best

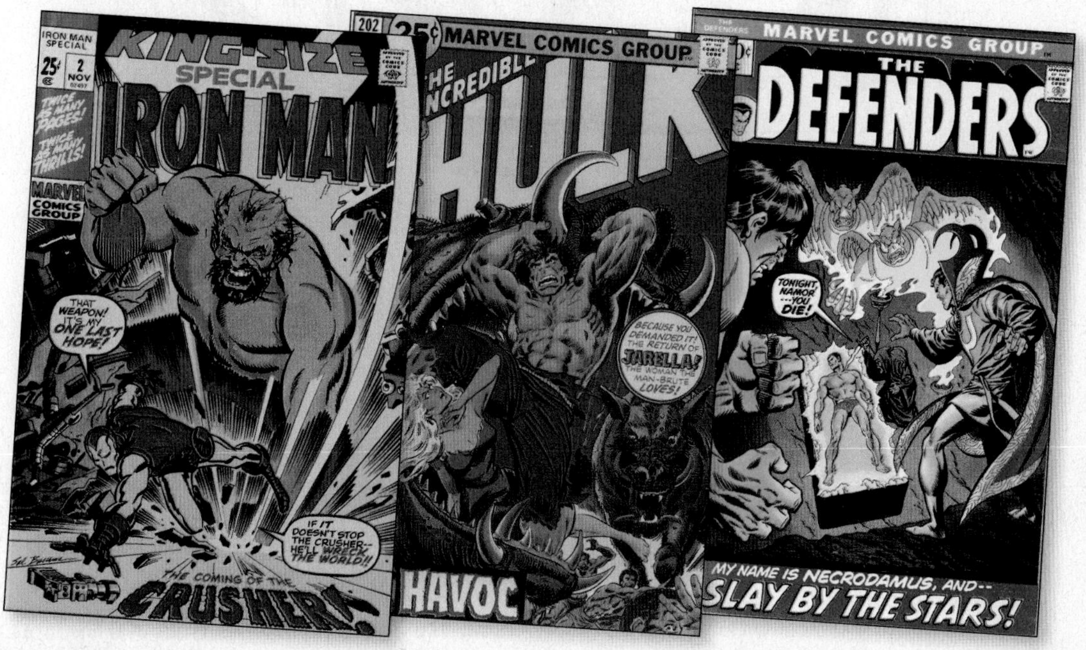
IRON MAN SPECIAL
25¢
2 NOV
KING-SIZE SPECIAL
IRON MAN
TWICE AS MANY PAGES! TWICE AS MANY THRILLS!
MARVEL COMICS GROUP
THAT WEAPON! IT'S MY ONE LAST HOPE!
IF IT DOESN'T STOP THE CRUSHER-- HE'LL WRECK THE WORLD!!
THE COMING OF THE CRUSHER!
202
25¢
MARVEL COMICS GROUP
THE INCREDIBLE HULK
BECAUSE YOU DEMANDED IT! THE RETURN OF JARELLA! THE WOMAN THE MAN-BRUTE LOVES!
HAVOC
MARVEL COMICS GROUP
THE DEFENDERS
TONIGHT NAMOR --YOU DIE!
MY NAME IS NECRODAMUS, AND--
SLAY BY THE STARS!

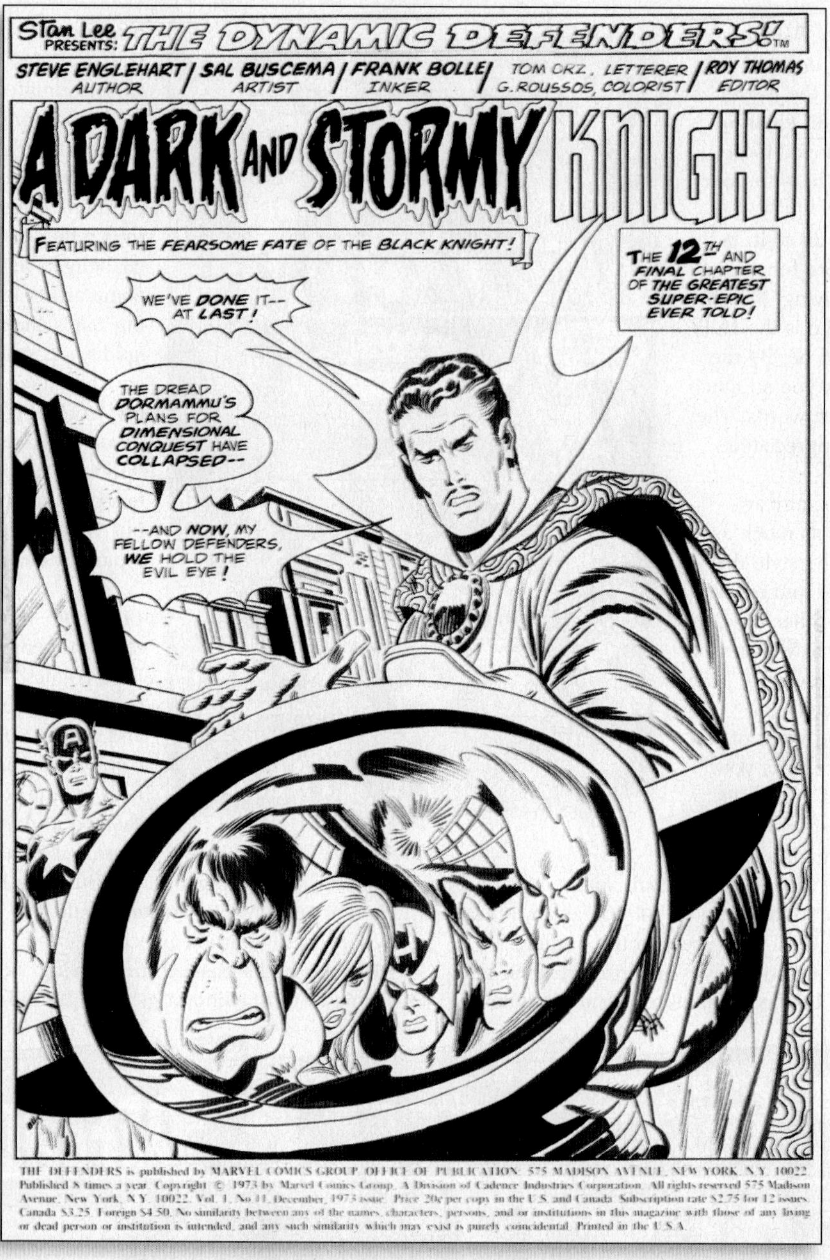
Stan Lee PRESENTS: THE DYNAMIC DEFENDERS!™
STEVE ENGLEHART AUTHOR / SAL BUSCEMA ARTIST / FRANK BOLLE INKER / TOM ORZ, LETTERER G. ROUSSOS, COLORIST / ROY THOMAS EDITOR
A DARK AND STORMY KNIGHT
FEATURING THE FEARSOME FATE OF THE BLACK KNIGHT!
THE 12TH AND FINAL CHAPTER OF THE GREATEST SUPER-EPIC EVER TOLD!
WE'VE DONE IT-- AT LAST!
THE DREAD DORMAMMU'S PLANS FOR DIMENSIONAL CONQUEST HAVE COLLAPSED--
--AND NOW, MY FELLOW DEFENDERS, WE HOLD THE EVIL EYE!
THE DEFENDERS is published by MARVEL COMICS GROUP. OFFICE OF PUBLICATION: 575 MADISON AVENUE, NEW YORK, N.Y. 10022. Published 8 times a year. Copyright © 1973 by Marvel Comics Group, A Division of Cadence Industries Corporation. All rights reserved 575 Madison Avenue, New York, N.Y. 10022. Vol. 1, No 11, December, 1973 issue. Price 20¢ per copy in the U.S. and Canada. Subscription rate $2.75 for 12 issues. Canada $3.25. Foreign $4.50. No similarity between any of the names, characters, persons, and or institutions in this magazine with those of any living or dead person or institution is intended, and any such similarity which may exist is purely coincidental. Printed in the U.S.A.

drawing after a day of work on comics. However, he did love drawing *Conan*. When we talked, it wasn't about comics so much as it was about art.

CBM: What is the single best lesson you could say your brother taught you professionally that is still with you to this day?
SB: John and I agreed that the artist never stops learning. It is a lifetime endeavor.

CBM: You mention "art" as a prevailing topic of conversation with your brother John. You also noted Renaissance masters. Tell me a little about your own painting work. Do you have to change your creative process for that? How do you enjoy painting versus the pencil and inking work of comics?
SB: Painting is a joy, although I don't paint very much anymore. Love black and white art. It's very difficult and challenging. One of the downsides of comics is the repetitive aspect. Especially when you've been doing them as long as I have. But they're still so much fun.
CBM: You have seen the industry grow almost from

WORLD COLOR
THE DEFENDERS
MARVEL COMICS GROUP
20¢
11
DEC
THE DEFENDERS
GUEST-STARRING: THE SILVER SURFER!
BACK, DEFENDERS! ONLY A SORCERER SUPREME CAN HOPE TO STAND AGAINST-- A GOD OF LIVING STONE!

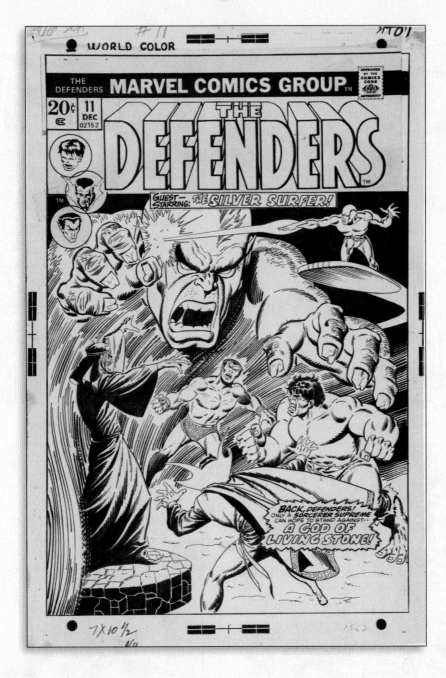

its infancy as a pro. You also got to work on arguably the most important character in the medium in *Spider-Man* and your work on *Spectacular* is an audience favorite. Did you ever think comics would approach the popularity they have achieved and did you think Spider-Man would attain even more global phenomenon status than he had even in the '80s?

SB: Never! The whole thing has blown me away.

CBM: Talk a little about your other work as a professional artist, the commercial art. What was that like in contrast to the comics? How did you like that work?

SB: I worked in commercial illustration and design for 13 years before comics. The difference was deadlines. Sometimes we would work all night to deliver a job the next morning. That seldom, if ever, happened in comics. Plus, the opportunity to work in different mediums was a plus.

CBM: Who are some of the comic creators you have worked with that have impressed you the most as storytellers?

SB: Of course, John. Both Romitas, Ron Frenz;

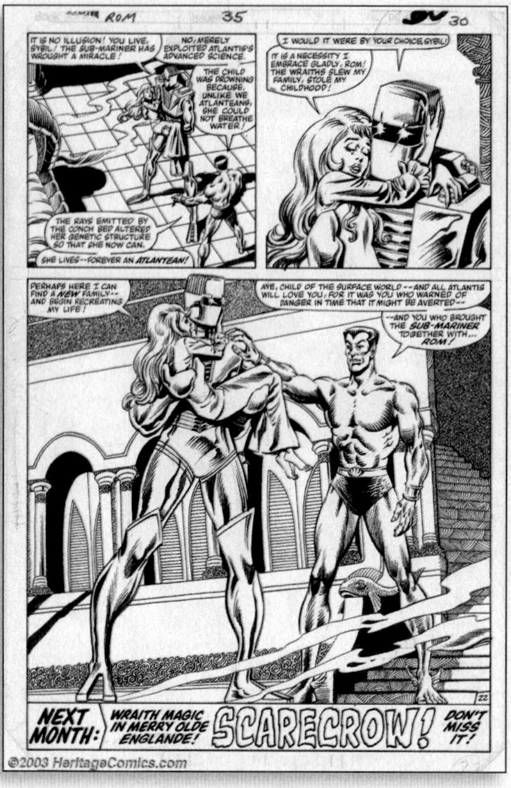
ROM 35 30
IT IS NO ILLUSION! YOU LIVE, SYBIL! THE SUB-MARINER HAS WROUGHT A MIRACLE!
NO; MERELY EXPLOITED ATLANTIS'S ADVANCED SCIENCE.
THE CHILD WAS DROWNING BECAUSE, UNLIKE WE ATLANTEANS, SHE COULD NOT BREATHE WATER!
THE RAYS EMITTED BY THE CONCH BED ALTERED HER GENETIC STRUCTURE SO THAT SHE NOW CAN.
SHE LIVES--FOREVER AN ATLANTEAN!
I WOULD IT WERE BY YOUR CHOICE, SYBIL!
IT IS A NECESSITY I EMBRACE GLADLY, ROM! THE WRAITHS SLEW MY FAMILY, STOLE MY CHILDHOOD!
PERHAPS HERE I CAN FIND A NEW FAMILY-- AND BEGIN RECREATING MY LIFE!
AYE, CHILD OF THE SURFACE WORLD--AND ALL ATLANTIS WILL LOVE YOU; FOR IT WAS YOU WHO WARNED OF DANGER IN TIME THAT IT MIGHT BE AVERTED--
--AND YOU WHO BROUGHT THE SUB-MARINER TOGETHER WITH... ROM!
NEXT MONTH: WRAITH MAGIC IN MERRY OLDE ENGLANDE! SCARECROW! DON'T MISS IT!
©2003 HeritageComics.com

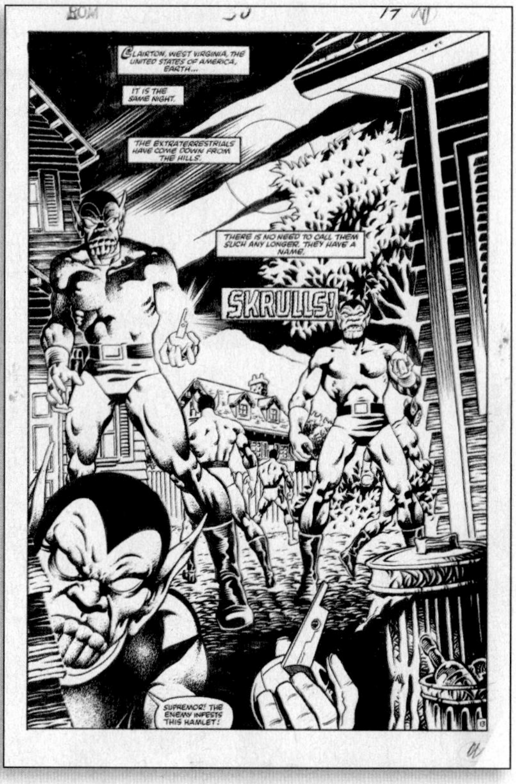
ROM 17
CLAIRTON, WEST VIRGINIA, THE UNITED STATES OF AMERICA, EARTH...
IT IS THE SAME NIGHT.
THE EXTRATERRESTRIALS HAVE COME DOWN FROM THE HILLS.
THERE IS NO NEED TO CALL THEM SUCH ANY LONGER. THEY HAVE A NAME.
SKRULLS!
SUPREMOR! THE ENEMY INFESTS THIS HAMLET!

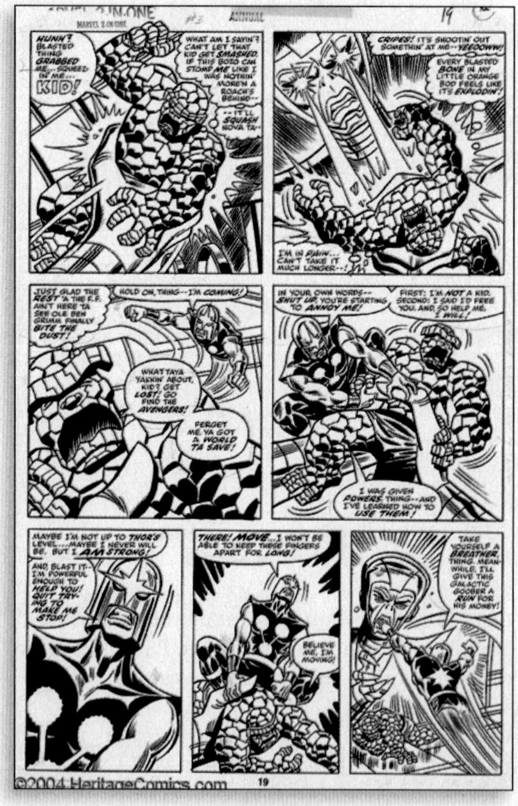
MARVEL 2-IN-ONE #3 ANNUAL 19
HUNH? BLASTED THING GRABBED ME... SQUEEZIN' ME... KID!
WHAT AM I SAYIN'? CAN'T LET THAT KID GET SMASHED. IF THIS BOZO CAN STOMP ME LIKE I WAS NOTHIN' MORE'N A ROACH'S BEHIND--
--IT'LL SQUASH NOVA TA--
CRIPES! IT'S SHOOTIN' OUT SOMETHIN' AT ME--YEEOOWW!
EVERY BLASTED BONE IN MY LITTLE ORANGE BOD FEELS LIKE IT'S EXPLODIN'!
I'M IN PAIN... CAN'T TAKE IT MUCH LONGER--!
JUST GLAD THE REST 'A THE F.F. AIN'T HERE TA SEE OLE BEN GRIMM FINALLY BITE THE DUST!
HOLD ON, THING--I'M COMING!
WHAT TAYA YAKKIN' ABOUT, KID? GET LOST! GO FIND THE AVENGERS!
FERGET ME. YA GOT A WORLD TA SAVE!
FIRST: I'M NOT A KID. SECOND: I SAID I'D FREE YOU. AND, SO HELP ME, I WILL!
IN YOUR OWN WORDS-- SHUT UP. YOU'RE STARTING TO ANNOY ME!
I WAS GIVEN POWERS, THING--AND I'VE LEARNED HOW TO USE THEM!
MAYBE I'M NOT UP TO THOR'S LEVEL... MAYBE I NEVER WILL BE. BUT I AM STRONG!
AND, BLAST IT-- I'M POWERFUL ENOUGH TO HELP YOU! QUIT TRYING TO MAKE ME STOP!
THERE! MOVE... I WON'T BE ABLE TO KEEP THESE FINGERS APART FOR LONG!
BELIEVE ME, I'M MOVING!
TAKE YOURSELF A BREATHER, THING. MEANWHILE, I'LL GIVE THIS GALACTIC GOOBER A RUN FOR HIS MONEY!
©2004 HeritageComics.com 19

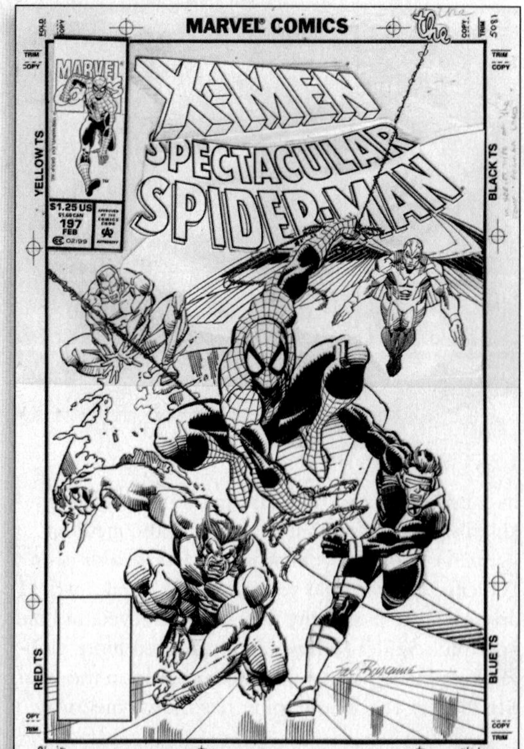
MARVEL® COMICS
the
X-MEN
SPECTACULAR SPIDER-MAN
MARVEL
$1.25 US
197
FEB
YELLOW TS
BLACK TS
RED TS
BLUE TS
TRIM
COPY
FOLD
TITLE SPECTACULAR SPIDER-MAN
NO. 197
MONTH FEB
SCHEDULE
ARTIST SAL BUSCEMA

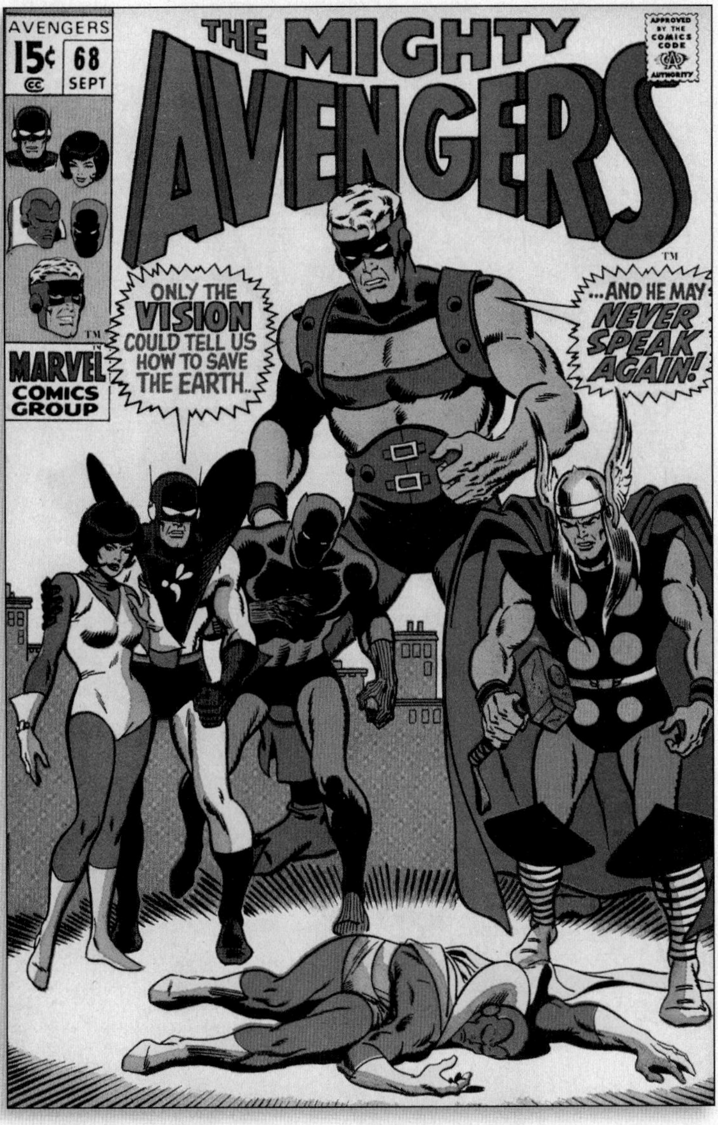
AVENGERS
15¢
68
SEPT
THE MIGHTY
AVENGERS
APPROVED BY THE COMICS CODE AUTHORITY
ONLY THE VISION COULD TELL US HOW TO SAVE THE EARTH..
...AND HE MAY NEVER SPEAK AGAIN!
MARVEL COMICS GROUP

Herb Trimpe is a wonderful storyteller, and of course, the greatest of them all, Jack Kirby. So many others too numerous to mention.

CBM: Who are some creators you would have liked to have collaborated with?
SB: All the ones I've mentioned and of course, right now I have the privilege of working with one of the best, Ron Frenz.

CBM: If there was a character, title or genre you would have loved to work on what would it be?
SB: I would have loved working on full color magazine illustrations back in the '40s, '50s. But I was too young and probably not good enough.

CBM: What are you working on now? What is coming up?
SB: I'm working on a project with Ron Frenz. A superhero called the *Blue Baron* for TV writer Darin Henry. Darin writes, Ron pencils and I ink. Hope you like it.

CBM: Finally, I make no secret about my affection for your *Spider-Man* and I think you are one of the finest Spidey artists ever. A fellow collector – Stanton Singh - recently pointed out an interesting tidbit and I wanted to confirm it with you. Is it true that in almost all of your *Spectacular Spider-Man* covers you hid a Spidey logo? If so, why? Where did that originate?
SB: It wasn't all the covers. It may have been for a couple of years or so. Just a fun thing for the readers to do. Editorial had the idea.

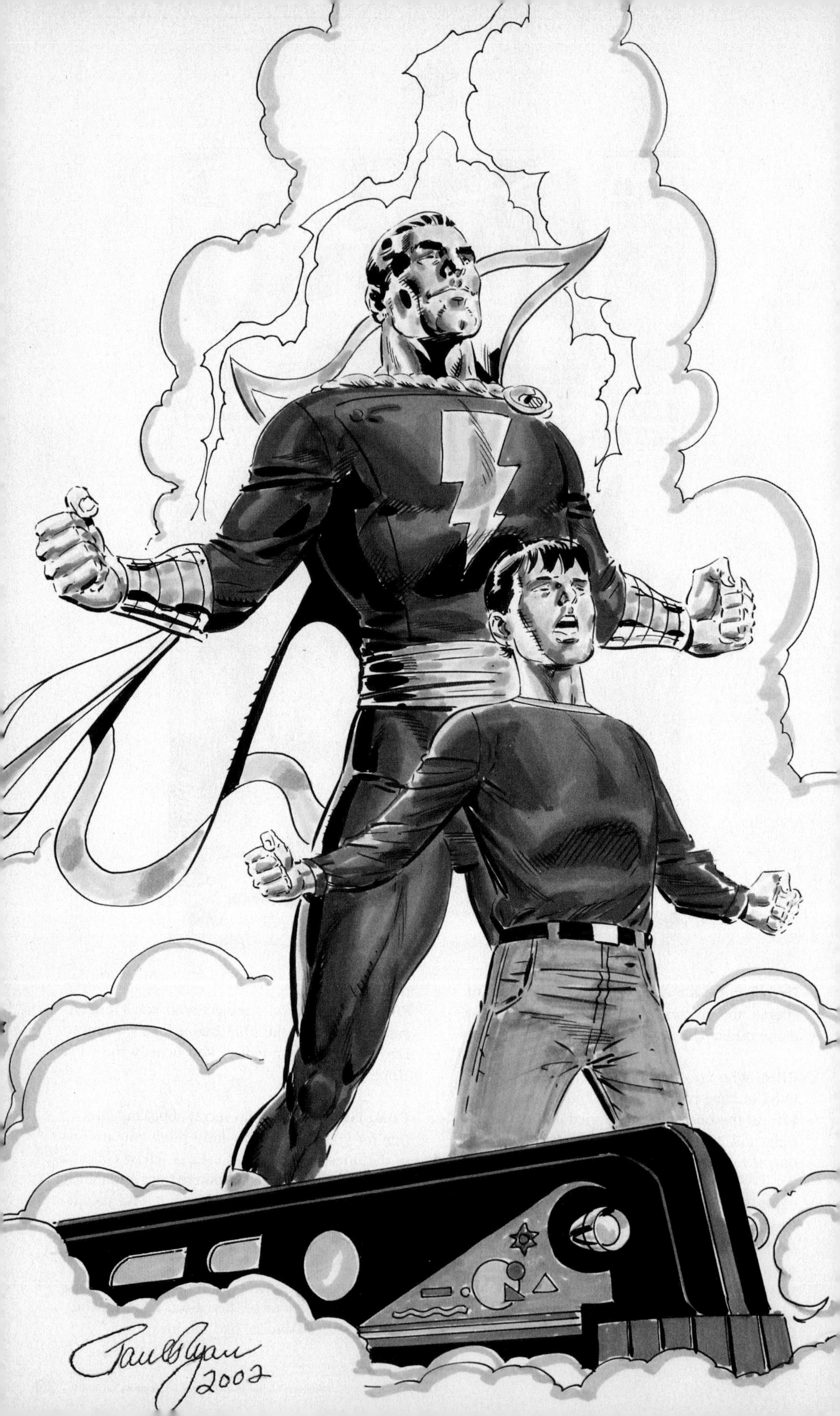
2002

Mr. Dependable:

The Paul Ryan Inteview

BY **JASON VERSAGGI**

Paul Ryan has had a tremendous career in comics, though it didn't start until he was 35. He has that distinct Marvel house style that evolved out of being a true draughtsman in the vein of John Buscema. His run on Avengers *almost felt like a seamless transition from "Big John," almost as a passing of the torch. As we celebrate 30 years since Paul's career with Marvel launched, it's worth noting some major distinctions he has had in his career that no other comic creator can claim. He addresses this amazing achievement, among other topics.*

MARVEL
new universe
D.P.7
75¢
1
NOV
new universe

CBM: First, tell me a little about your training as a comic book artist, both as a fan and more formally.

Paul Ryan (PR): I attended the Massachusetts College of Art from 1967 to 1971, graduating with a Bachelor of Fine Arts degree in Graphic Design. My only formal training in comics came around 1983-1984 working as Bob Layton's assistant.

CBM: Was a career in sequential art or comics storytelling something you longed to do? At what point did you decide you had what it took to make a childhood passion your profession?

PR: I had been drawing little one-page, multi-panel stories since grade school. Never had any thought of a career. Heck, I was only nine. I just loved comics and was inspired to make my own.

In 1983, I heard about a deal offered by Charlton Comics for aspiring comics artists. Charlton would publish your work in a new, dedicated title for amateurs, called *Bullseye*, copyright any character you created in your name and give you 50 copies of the printed piece. There was no pay offered, but it sounded like a good place to start. I sent them copies of the first five penciled pages to get their reaction. I still have the letter they sent me stating that it looked good and to continue. *That's* when I thought I might have a chance to break into the industry.

CBM: You were partly there in Marvel's second Golden Age in the '80s. What was it like really breaking into comics at such a high level in your thirties? Were you more prepared for dealing with the industry or were there things that shocked you?

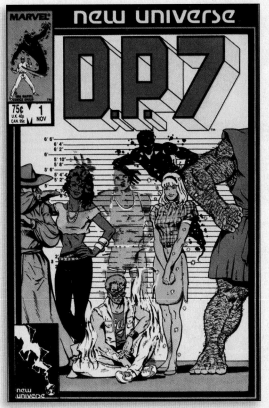

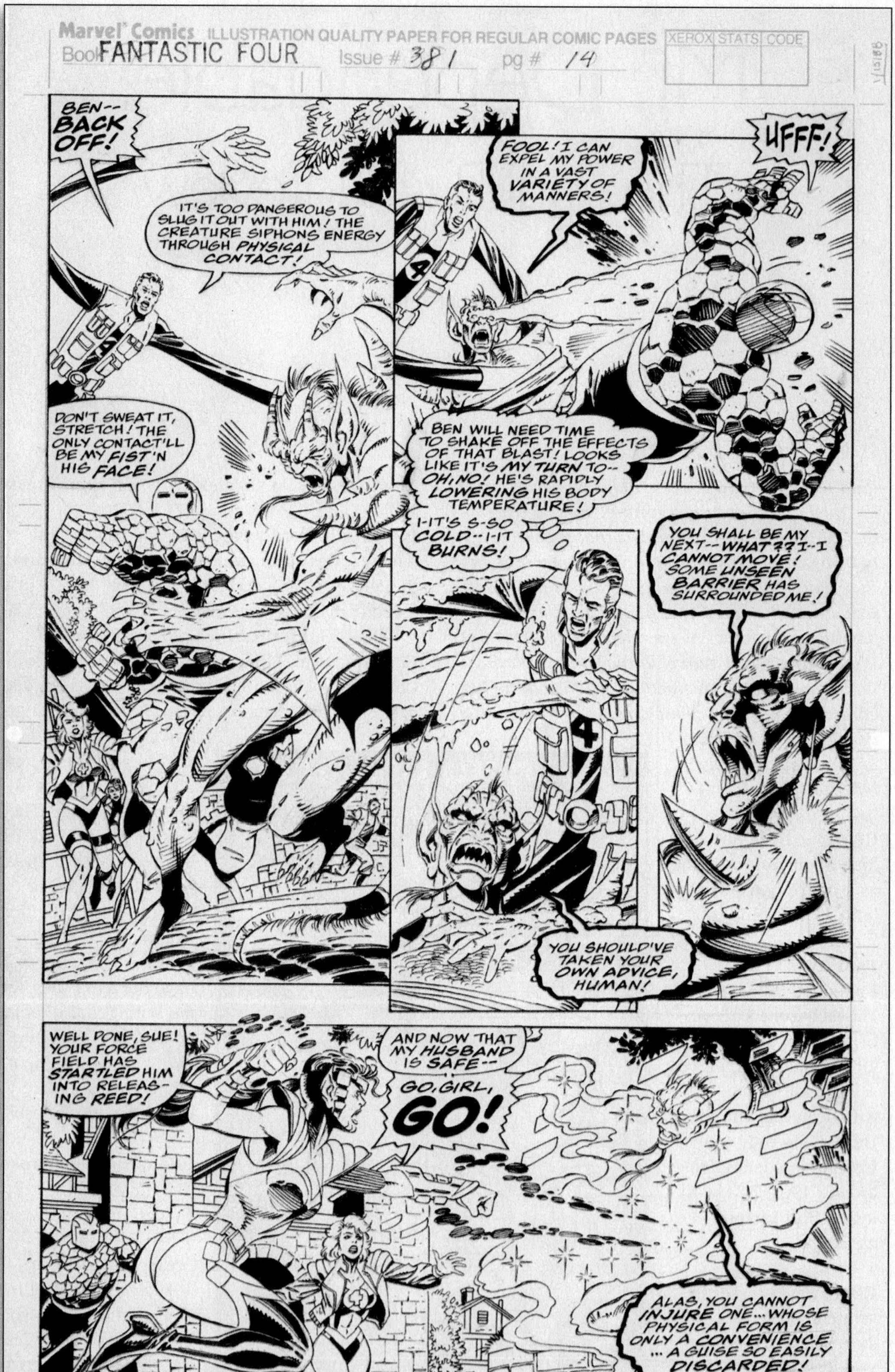

Marvel Comics ILLUSTRATION QUALITY PAPER FOR REGULAR COMIC PAGES
XEROX STATS CODE
Book FANTASTIC FOUR Issue # 381 pg # 14
BEN-- BACK OFF!
IT'S TOO DANGEROUS TO SLUG IT OUT WITH HIM! THE CREATURE SIPHONS ENERGY THROUGH PHYSICAL CONTACT!
DON'T SWEAT IT, STRETCH! THE ONLY CONTACT'LL BE MY FIST'N HIS FACE!
UFFF!
FOOL! I CAN EXPEL MY POWER IN A VAST VARIETY OF MANNERS!
BEN WILL NEED TIME TO SHAKE OFF THE EFFECTS OF THAT BLAST! LOOKS LIKE IT'S MY TURN TO-- OH, NO! HE'S RAPIDLY LOWERING HIS BODY TEMPERATURE!
I-IT'S S-SO COLD-- I-IT BURNS!
YOU SHOULD'VE TAKEN YOUR OWN ADVICE, HUMAN!
YOU SHALL BE MY NEXT-- WHAT?? I--I CANNOT MOVE! SOME UNSEEN BARRIER HAS SURROUNDED ME!
WELL DONE, SUE! YOUR FORCE FIELD HAS STARTLED HIM INTO RELEASING REED!
AND NOW THAT MY HUSBAND IS SAFE--
GO, GIRL, GO!
ALAS, YOU CANNOT INJURE ONE... WHOSE PHYSICAL FORM IS ONLY A CONVENIENCE ... A GUISE SO EASILY DISCARDED!
14

PR: I was pretty naive even at 35. I couldn't believe that I was really walking around the halls at Marvel and talking to adults about comics like they really mattered. I thought that some editors hated me, some tolerated me and a couple liked me. Tom DeFalco scared the crap out of me. The first words he spoke to me were, "So...why should we hire you?" delivered like one of the Bowery Boys. Jim Shooter, for all his size and imposing presence, was very supportive.

CBM: Aside from the influences of Jack Kirby, were there any other creators whose work you felt inspired your own?
PR: Yes, Jack Kirby was indeed the King. I loved his work on Marvel's monster titles and westerns in the late 1950s. His *Fantastic Four* just blew me away. But for other artists, I would have to include. Sy Barry, Dan Barry, John Cullen Murphy, Hal Foster, Alex Kotzky and Leonard Starr for comic strip artists; Curt Swan, Joe Kubert, Carmine Infantino, Murphy Anderson, Steve Ditko, Wally Wood, John Buscema, Don Heck and Gil Kane for comic book artists.

CBM: Your career has some prominent distinctions and one of them is enjoying the third longest tenure on *Fantastic Four*. What did it mean to you personally to work on the title that started it all for Marvel? Did you take away any highlights from that run?
PR: It was very exciting to be offered Marvel's flagship title. Exciting and not just a little intimidating. People had asked me what direction [I wanted] to go with the series. What innovations I might have in mind. My only thought was, "Don't screw up... don't break it!" Luckily, Tom DeFalco knew what he was doing, so we were fine. Yes, that same Tom DeFalco that terrified the newbie in 1985 was my collaborator for nearly five years on the *Fantastic Four* and still remains a dear friend.

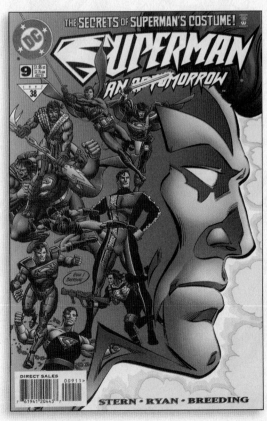

THE SECRETS OF SUPERMAN'S COSTUME!
SUPERMAN MAN OF TOMORROW
DIRECT SALES
STERN • RYAN • BREEDING

CBM: Another of those famous accomplishments you are known for is being the only artist to work on both the *Superman* and *Spider-Man* wedding issues. As we close in on the 30th anniversary of *Amazing Spider-Man Annual #21* in 2016, what was it like getting to contribute to that historic issue?
PR: Okay, you will, undoubtedly, notice that a certain recurring theme is going to run through this interview. *I was terrified*! Excited, but knowing the historic and financial significance of this story for Marvel Comics, I couldn't help but be a little nervous. Considering that I had only been in the business a minute and a half I should never have been given that assignment. Jim Shooter really took a chance with me. He asked. I accepted. He handed me the plot. I hope I didn't disappoint him.

CBM: You were also present for what some might consider one of the most polarizing chapters of Superman's history - the *Superman Red and Blue* concept after his return. At a time when the weddings, death and return of Superman was generating some of the earliest mainstream media buzz for comics, how did that affect you and your work?
PR: One of the greatest thrills I experienced working in comics was to be allowed to draw Superman. To me, he was the first, best hero. I was the only kid on my block to have the official, authorized Superman costume. Although looking back I'm pretty sure my parents never expected that I would run around the neighborhood wearing the official, authorized Superman costume. I think my sisters told everyone I was adopted. As for the Electro Superman, I just drew the stories I was given, hoping he would eventually return to his familiar powers and costume.

CBM: Describe a little bit about your creative process when you are laying out a book. Do you prefer to ink your own pencils?

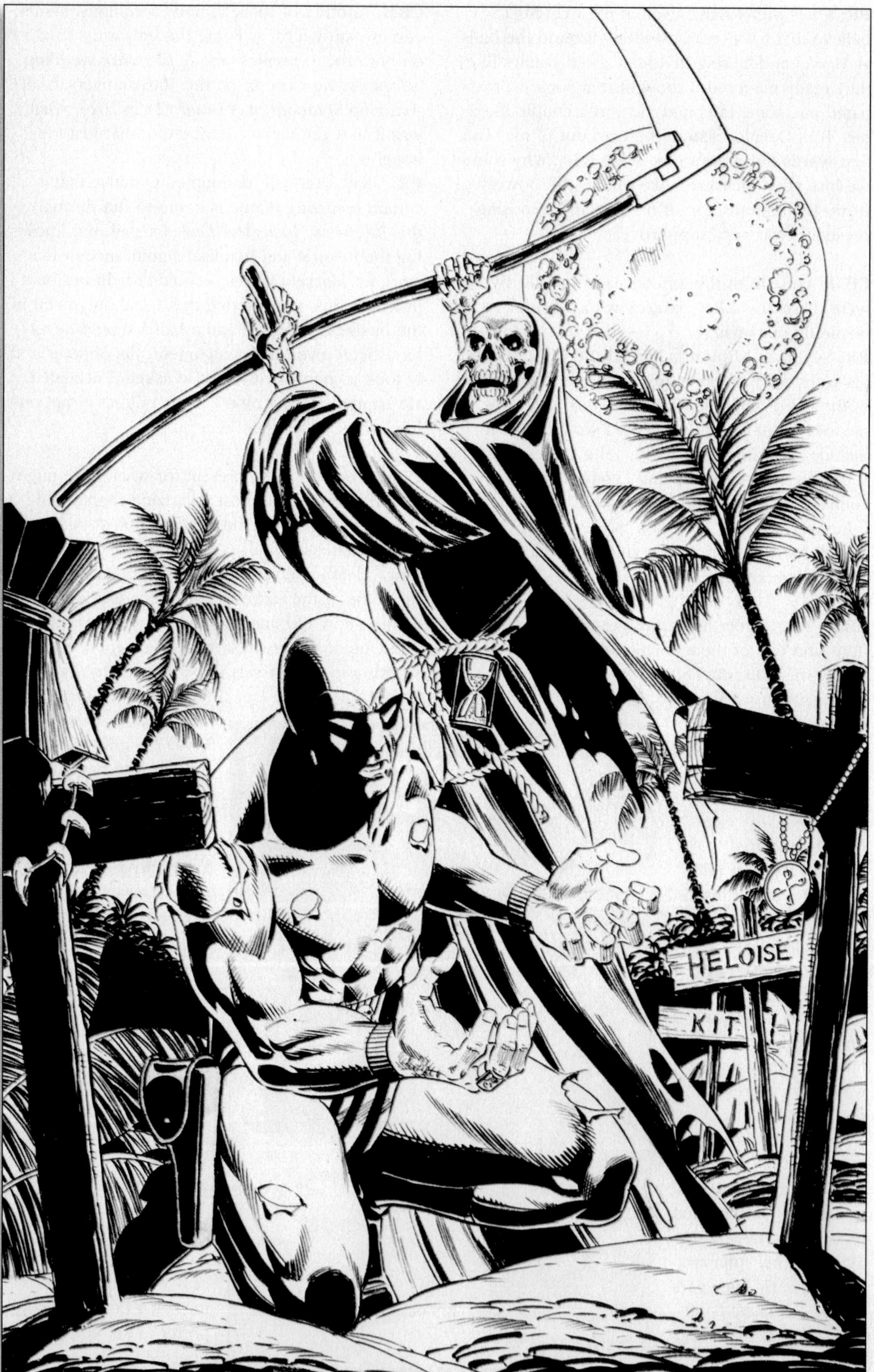
HELOISE
KIT

PR: The creative process is generally not something that happens on a conscious level. I read the stories and "see" what it should look like in my mind, do a thumbnail sketch of the picture in my head and then go to full size drawing paper. Yes, I do prefer to ink my pencils. I have worked with some amazing inkers. Some inkers made my work look better than it was. Some other inkers... not so much. When I ink my pencils, the readers get to see what I can do. What my vision - no pun intended - was for this or that piece. So, for better or worse, it's me.

CBM: Let's talk collaborations. Who are some artists you have enjoyed inking? Conversely, who are some guys you have liked to ink.
PR: I have only a little experience inking other artists' penciled art, but John Byrne does stand out in my memory. It was on *West Coast Avengers.* John asked me to take on the inking chores on that title. His pencils were so finished and complete you could have scanned them and dismissed the inker. It took me about two hours of fretting over his work before I got up the courage to put ink to paper. I think we did well for the four issues we shared before John moved on.

CBM: Your runs on *Fantastic Four* and *Avengers* were high watermarks for me as a fan on those titles since you've left them. Your draft work seemed to seamlessly transition from the end of John Buscema's stints on those books in the '90s. What character or title would you have loved to have another long run on?

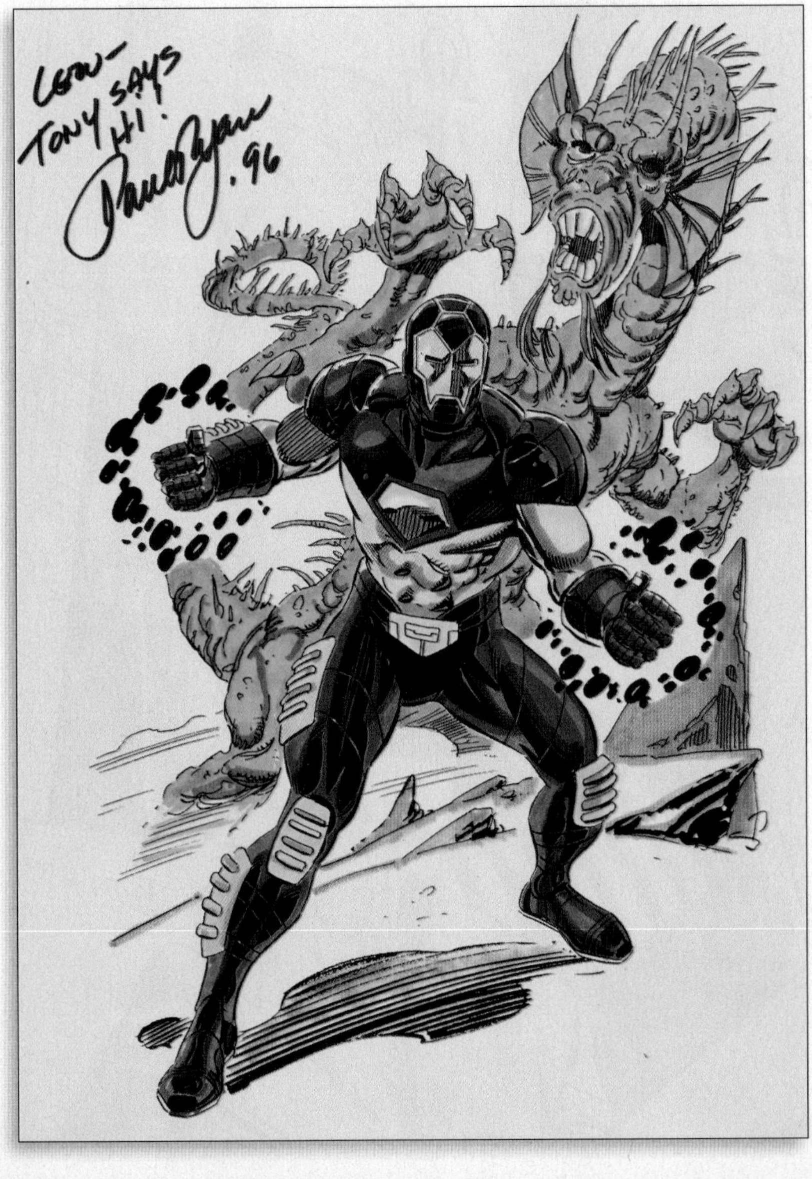
Lew—
TONY SAYS HI!
'96

PR: Thanks, that's kind of you to say. I enjoyed working on both titles. They were favorites of mine as a kid. John Buscema was one of the biggest influences on my work - I had bought and devoured *How to Draw Comics the Marvel Way* by Stan and John when I was younger - and with Tom Palmer doing finishes, our issues had a passable John Buscema look. I think I was on *Avengers* for a year before anyone knew that Big John had left.

CBM: It's now been officially 30 years since you started working for Marvel. What was your favorite creative moment from your time there?
PR: Favorite creative moment - that's an easy one. Sitting down with Mark Gruenwald and coming up with the look for *DP7.* At Mark's direction we "cast"

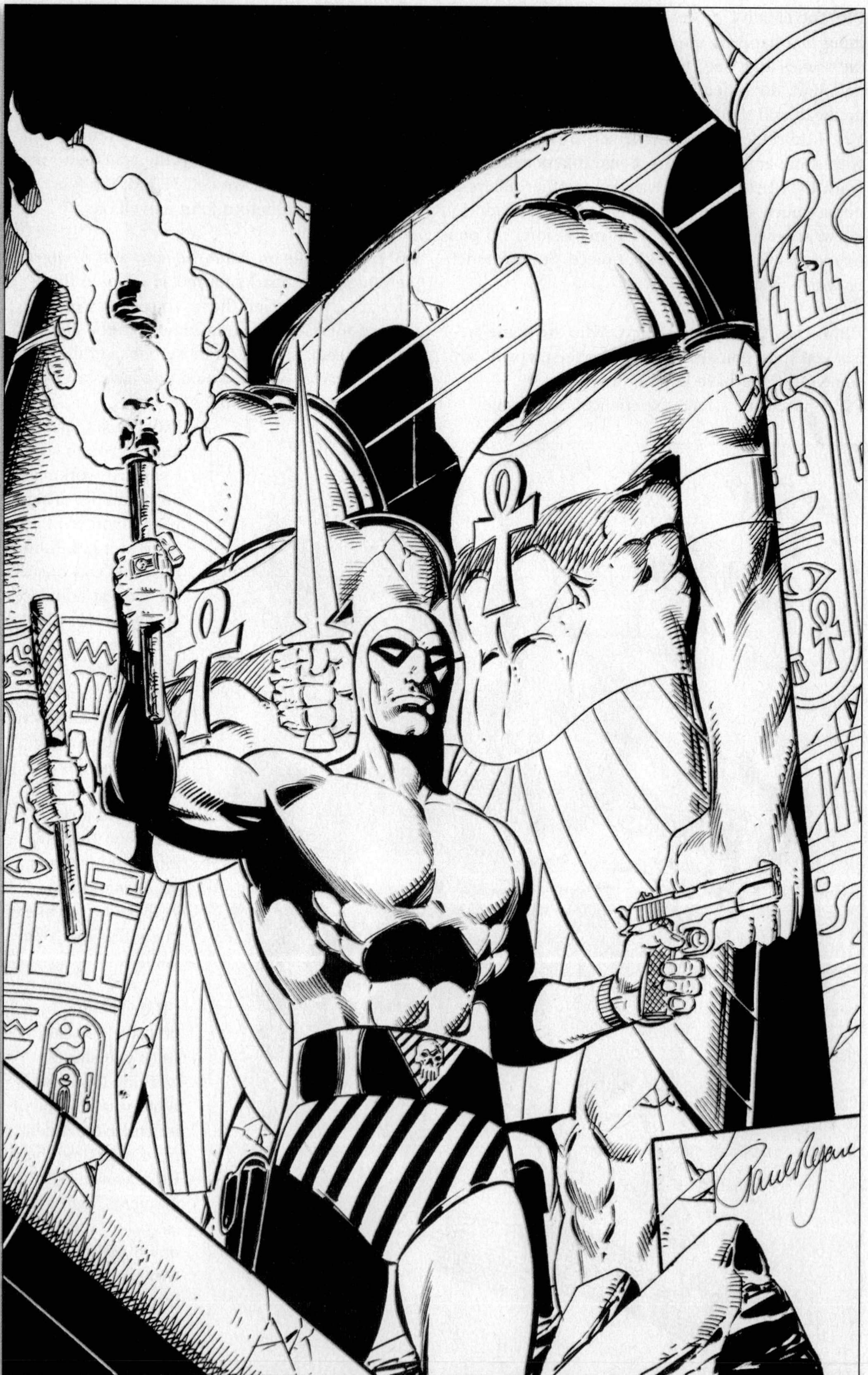

our characters based on real people. This is something that I still do when confronted with new characters. When given a description of a character by the writer I look through various magazines for just the right look.

CBM: How did you become involved with *The Phantom*?

PR: I was running an eBay auction back in 2001 and received an email from a prospective bidder named Jonas Vesterlund from Sweden. He was a fan of my work and asked if I ever considered working for a comics company outside the U.S. In his younger days he was an intern at Egmont Publishing, which produces *The Phantom* – *Fantomen* – comic in Sweden. I told him I was interested. He gave me contact information, I sent a cover letter and some Marvel and DC comics I had penciled to Editor in Chief Ulf Granberg. He wrote back and asked if I would draw some model sheets to see how I would handle the Phantom and the supporting cast. I guess he liked what he saw. He signed me on to Team Fantomen and we collaborated for five years. It was this experience with the Ghost Who Walks that put me in a pretty good position when George Olsen retired from the daily *Phantom* strip. King Features Editor Jay Kennedy asked me to take on the dailies. That was almost 10 years ago. I also handled the Sunday strip from 2007 to 2011.

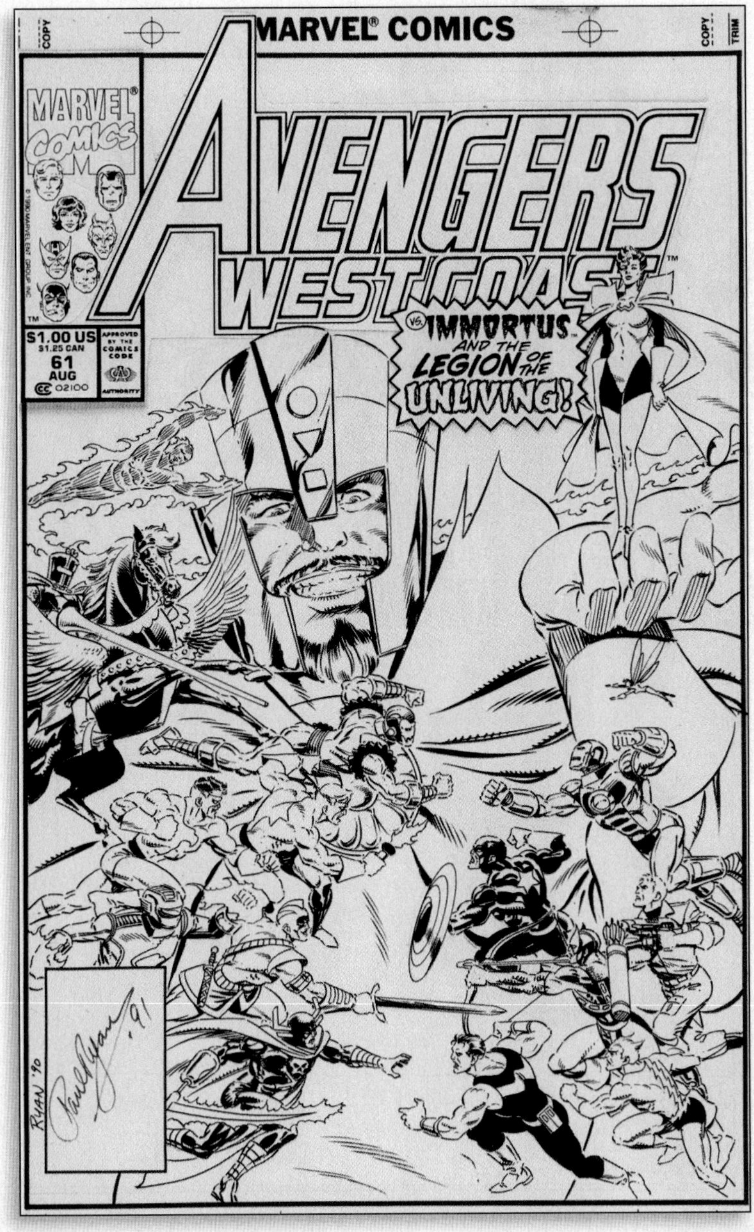
MARVEL COMICS
AVENGERS
VS. IMMORTUS AND THE LEGION OF THE UNLIVING!
$1.00 US
$1.25 CAN
61
AUG
RYAN '90

CBM: What upcoming projects do you have? Where can fans see you and your work in 2015 and beyond?

PR: Sorry, but the only project I have coming up is to participate in a three day cattle drive in Montana. No.... not kidding. [I] always wanted to be a cowboy. I get to live the cowboy life with my wife, Linda, every summer in Melville, Montana surrounded by the Crazy Mountains.

CBM: Finally, *Guardians of the Galaxy* was a massive hit at the box office and with fans. There was one character in particular who stood out to me among the "Ravagers." The pirate with the reddish locks and one bionic eye - he reminded me of your creation, Ravage 2099. Any word from the producers if this was a nod to your hero?

PR: Really?! I will have to check *Guardians* again when it comes out on Blu-ray. I don't remember that character. If such a nod was intended, it never reached me. Producers don't call me. Editors don't call me. My cats don't call me. Luckily the lovely Linda does call. It's all good.

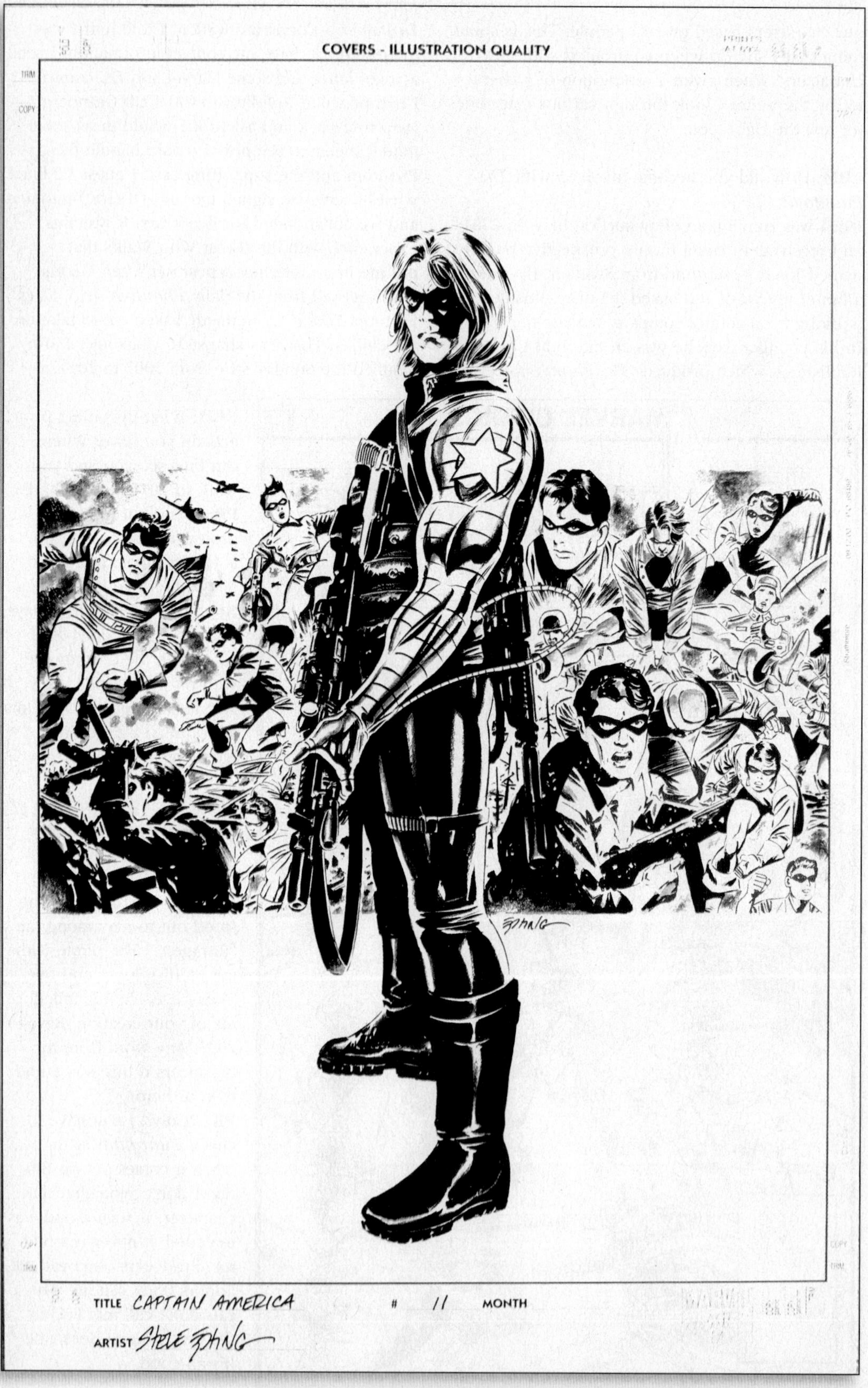
COVERS - ILLUSTRATION QUALITY
TITLE CAPTAIN AMERICA
11
MONTH
ARTIST STEVE EPTING

The Steve Epting Interview: A Decade of Captain America & the Winter Soldier

BY **JASON VERSAGGI**

Time. Pink Floyd warned about wasting it. Jim Croce tried to bottle it. Musically, Cyndi Lauper, The Foo Fighters, Foreigner, The Chambers Brothers and others all have invariantly been warning us of its passage. Time has also been known to fly and it has definitely flown in the 10 years – yes, 10 – since the game-changing Captain America *run by Ed Brubaker and Steve Epting.*

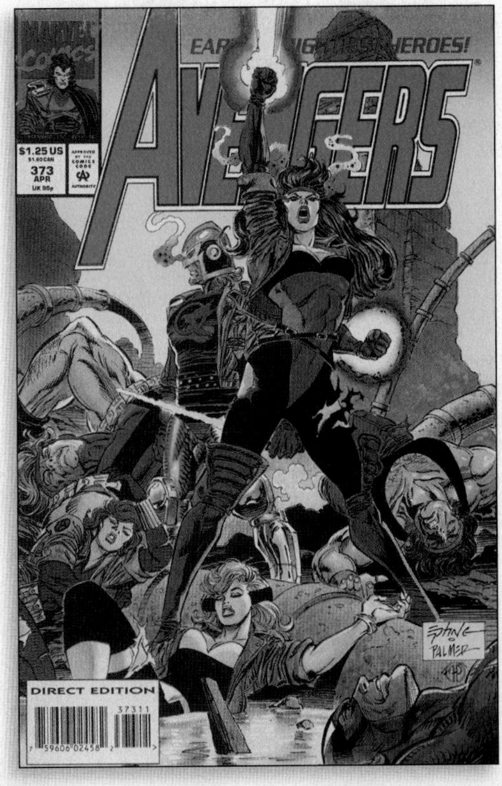
$1.25 US
373
APR
DIRECT EDITION

A highly influential and perhaps seminal comics run in a time when circumstances seem to disdain the long play, consider the pop culture contributions of the Brubaker-Epting tenure on the series. It introduced, or rather revived, one of the most significant Marvel heroes since Wolverine debuted over 40 years ago, The Winter Soldier (or Bucky Barnes).

In doing so, it went against tradition and strident public opinion, and yet it succeed brilliantly. The first two Captain America *movies – collectively earning over $1 billion worldwide – owe much of their source material to this extended story.*

And finally, it presented the re-elevation of The Falcon, who would not only be an integral part of Captain America: The Winter Soldier, *but also replaced Steve Rogers as Captain America in late 2014.*

As an artist, Epting's work first came to our attention in 1989 when he illustrated the Judah The Hammer *back-up stories in First Comics'* Nexus. *A three-year stint on* The Avengers, *followed by turns on various* X-Men *titles, time at DC on* Superman *and* Aquaman, *a 25-issue run on CrossGen's* Crux, *and six issues on their* El Cazador *before landing* Captain America. *Since that time, he's worked on* Fantastic Four *and most recently on* Velvet *from Image Comics.*

Epting was interviewed by Jason Versaggi to mark the 10-year anniversary of the Winter Soldier *story.*

CBM: You were just coming off doing the covers for a wonderful final arc on *Thor* - the *Ragnarok* storyline - (with some of the finest *Thor* cover work in years at that point). When was the new *Captain America* series brought up to you? How did you land that gig?

Steve Epting (SE): I had been working at

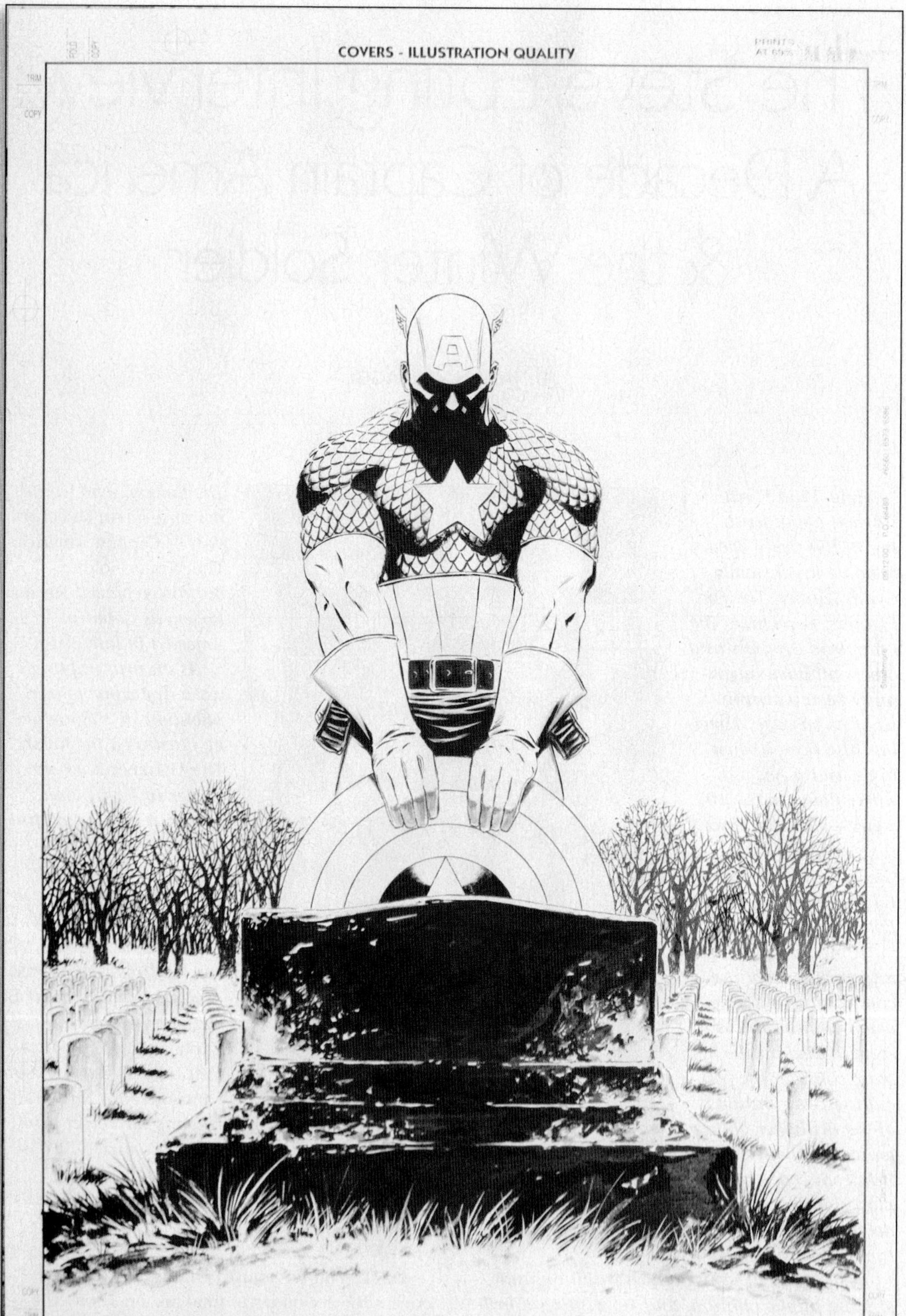
COVERS - ILLUSTRATION QUALITY
TITLE CAPTAIN AMERICA
4
MONTH
ARTIST

CrossGen for the previous four years and as things began to wind down there I reached out to Tom Brevoort about doing some work at Marvel. I had a working relationship with Tom prior to my work at DC and CrossGen and hoped to work with him again at Marvel. The timing was right because at that point Marvel was preparing to relaunch several of their series, including *Captain America, Iron Man*, and a couple of others that escape me at the moment. Tom eventually offered the Cap relaunch to me, which I gladly accepted. Ed still had a month or two left on his DC contract so Tom kept me busy with the *Thor* covers and *Avengers Finale* while we waited until we could get started on Cap.

CBM: You were already acquainted with Captain America, having done a fantastic run on *Avengers*, offering another consistently high-caliber run a la Paul Ryan right before you. How did your approach to your character design change for this series versus your *Avengers* work?
SE: Cap's costume had evolved a bit when I returned to Marvel, largely due to John Cassaday's work on the previous volume of *Captain America*. Across the line most artists had adopted Cassaday's distinctive look for the cowl and scale mail, as well as adding military pouches on the belt. For consistency's sake, I followed this trend at the beginning, but over the course of the series I gradually began to return Cap to his more traditional look, although the pouches stayed for the duration.

CBM: What were some of the things going through your mind, seeing Ed Brubaker's scripts and being privy to the details beforehand, such as the Red Skull shocker in first issue, and of course the return of Bucky?
Steve Epting: Before I actually started drawing the book, I read Ed's outline for the first 12 issues, so I knew that Bucky was going to be returning as the Winter Soldier from the very beginning. I remember telling Ed that everyone was going to hate us for bringing Bucky back from the dead, and I think when the word started spreading the reaction to the idea was very negative. As the story unfolded and more people actually read it, their opinions changed.

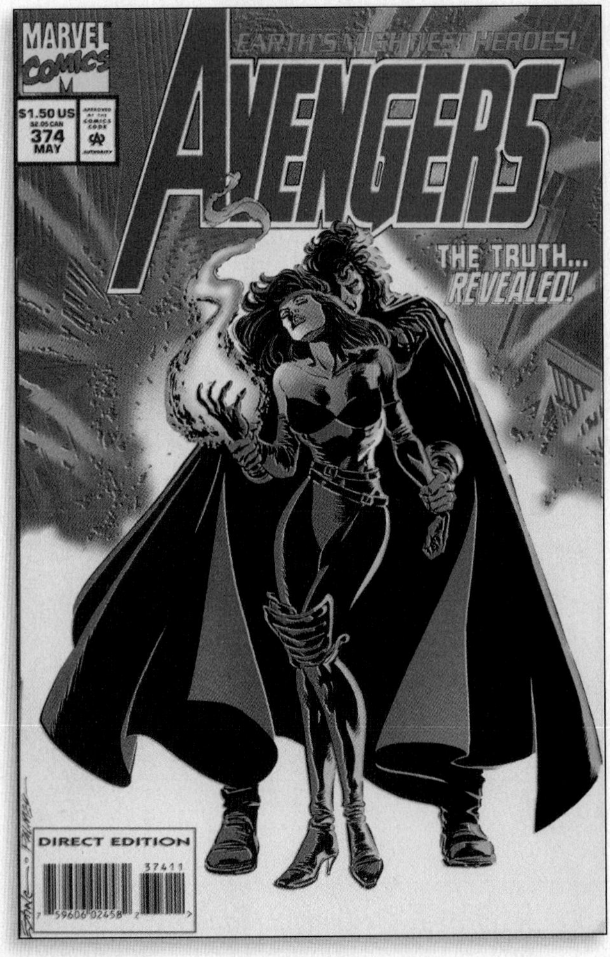

MARVEL COMICS
EARTH'S MIGHTIEST HEROES!
AVENGERS
$1.50 US
374
MAY
THE TRUTH... REVEALED!
DIRECT EDITION

CBM: There was some very slick design that went into the Winter Soldier design but what made you settle on the final look of the character? Where were you drawing inspiration from? Why the bionic arm and whose idea was that?
SE: The arm was Ed's idea from the beginning, and he tied it into the story where Bucky "died" by having the arm blown off when the buzz bomb exploded. Beyond that, the design was originally a commando/soldier type outfit with a red star incorporated. Joe Quesada wanted some more superhero elements, which led to a more spandex-type look on his arm and legs. I designed the tunic to sort of mimic Bucky's double breasted shirt from his Golden Age costume, and of course the domino mask was there for the same reason.

CBM: With so many classic villains and supporting characters on the seminal *Captain America* series, were there any favorites you got to play with? Anyone you wished you could have worked into the series?
SE: I really don't think so. I was lucky in that Ed and I shared a fondness for the same things when it came to Cap

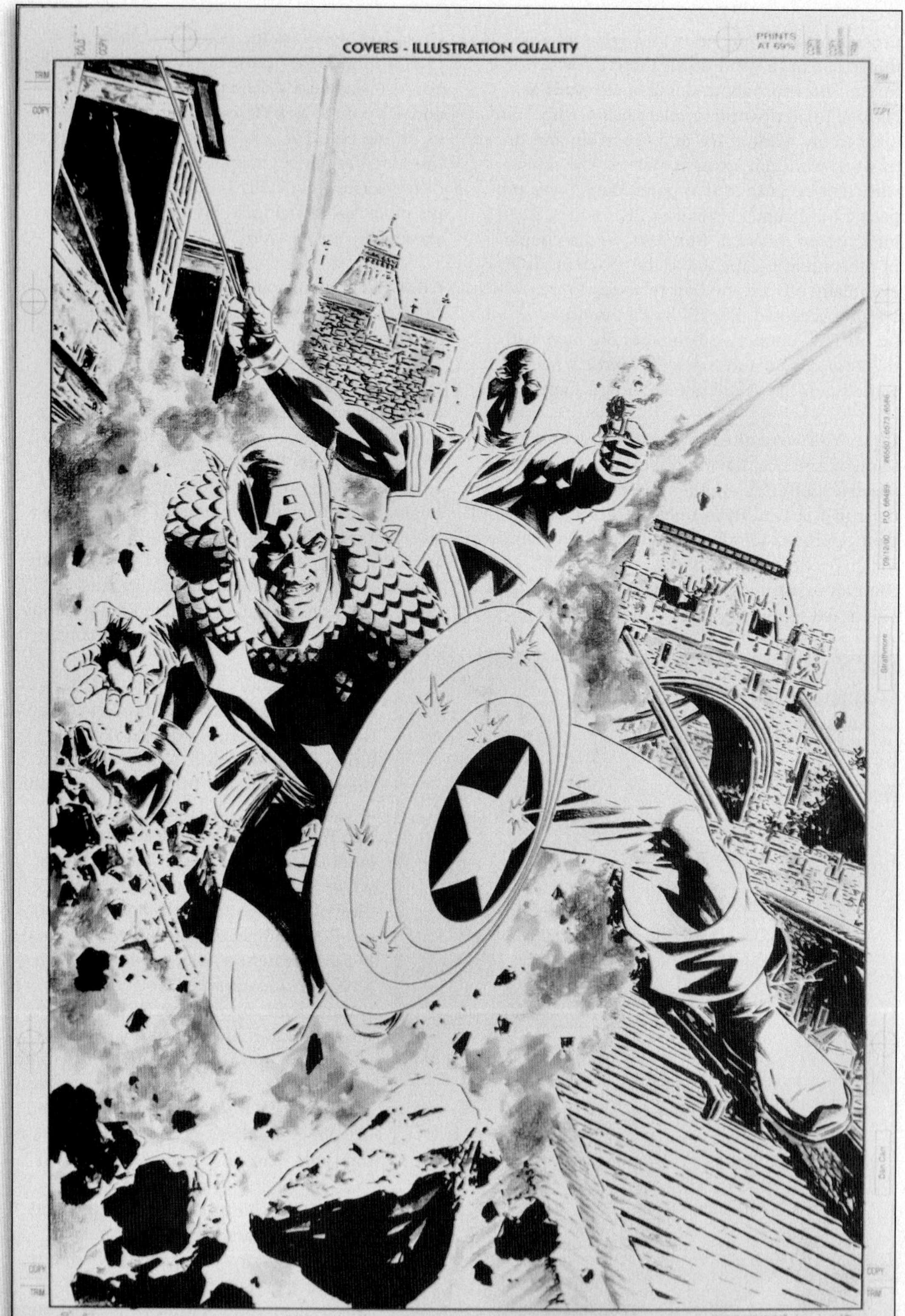
COVERS - ILLUSTRATION QUALITY
TITLE CAPTAIN AMERICA
19
MONTH
ARTIST

and I can't think offhand of anything he left out. Maybe Madame Hydra? I was especially glad that S.H.I.E.L.D. and Sharon Carter were both part of the series.

CBM: Your run on the title was not the longest by an artist, but it seemed like a throwback performance to how comic stories used to be told, and it has already achieved legendary status. What was it like creatively turning in so many covers and pages that seemed to all be part of one long serial? When comics now have seemed to go the way of the four-part arc, was it refreshing for you to get to be part of such an epic?
SE: I always prefer to have a longer run when possible. My first assignment at Marvel was *The Avengers* and I drew that book for three years, so this wasn't my first extended run on a book. I drew *Crux* for 25 issues at CrossGen, and when I took over *Fantastic Four* from Dale Eaglesham, I stayed through the end of Hickman's run, which was a couple of years. So actually, the short arcs are not the norm for me.

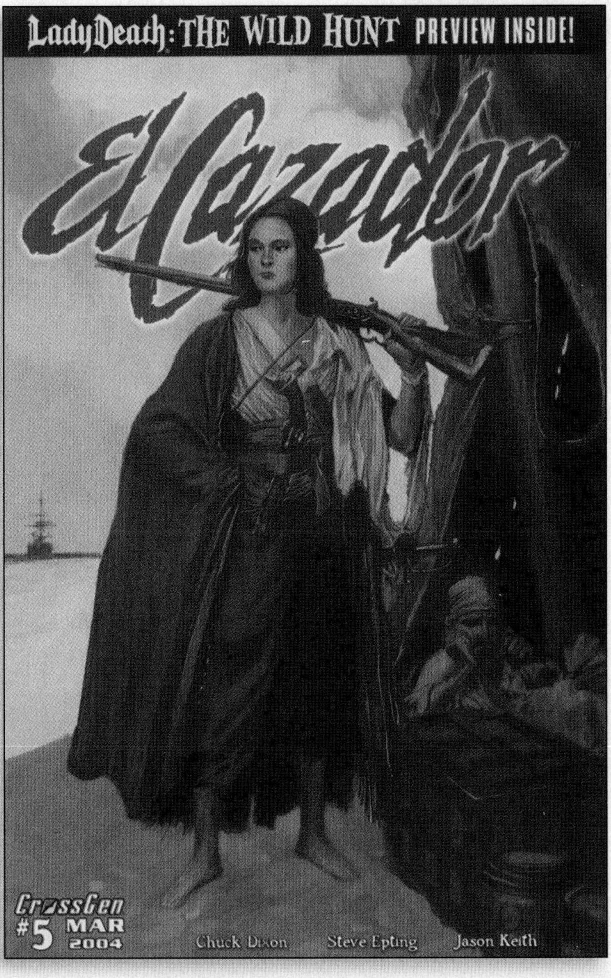
Lady Death: THE WILD HUNT PREVIEW INSIDE!
El Cazador
CrossGen
#5 MAR 2004
Chuck Dixon
Steve Epting
Jason Keith

CBM: The collaboration of the other artists on this title seemed to only enhance the ambiance of the book and the environment you all created. What was it like working collectively with creators like Michael Lark, Butch Guice, Mike Perkins, and Frank D'Armata?
SE: We all shared common influences which I think helped to make it all work together without being jarring. The glue that really held it all in place was Frank D'Armata. His colors really did a lot of the work establishing and maintaining the look of the book. I think he colored every single issue of Ed's run with the exception of #10, which was the *House of M* crossover and not part of the regular continuity. It also helped that I worked with Butch, Mike, and Frank at CrossGen for several years and we are actually friends instead of just collaborators.

CBM: Ed Brubaker told me that the image you created which would ultimately be the cover for the *Captain America Omnibus*, collecting your first 25 issues, was the first piece of art you created for the series and that it was held back. Why was that? What's the story behind that image?
SE: That piece was assigned to me as promo art that would accompany an article for *Wizard* magazine in the run up to the launch of the book. As far as I know that's exactly what it was used for and that was to be the end of it (I never actually saw the issue of *Wizard* that it ran in, by the way). I'm not sure what it would have been held back for, unless Ed means it was held back from the *Wizard* article. I thought it ran as intended so I don't know. In any event, I suppose someone decided it would be good to use for the *Omnibus* and the rest is history. Incidentally, that particular piece was colored by Laura Martin.

CBM: With the global hit that *Winter Soldier* became on the silver screen, did you ever imagine 10 years ago that a title you had such a huge role in creating would impact so many people around the world?
SE: I never would have imagined it, but then again, I would never have imagined any of the dozens of comic book movies being so popular. I mean, imagine telling someone 10 years ago that *Guardians of the Galaxy* would be a global phenomenon. This is a golden age for superhero

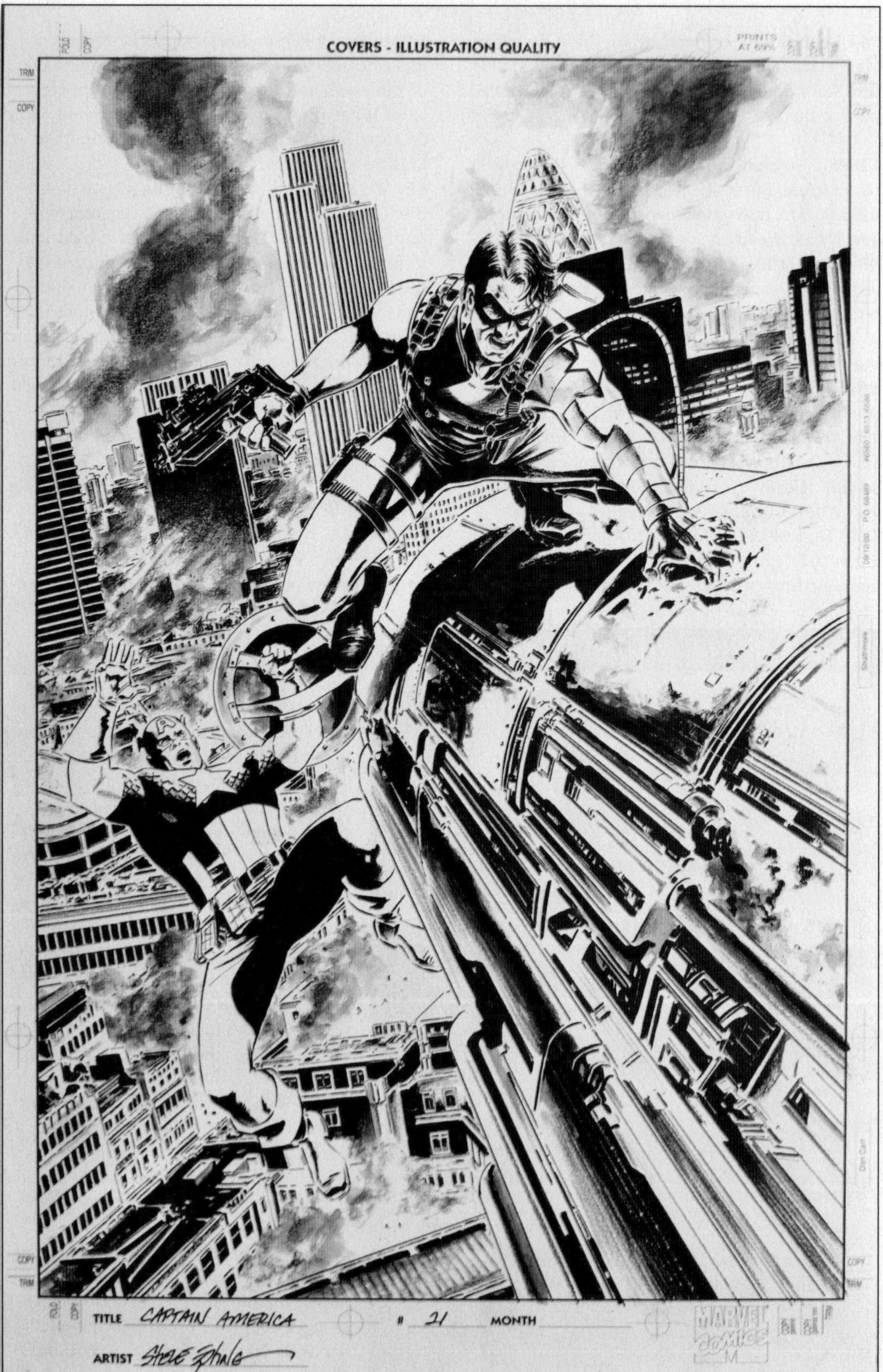
COVERS - ILLUSTRATION QUALITY
TITLE CAPTAIN AMERICA
21
MONTH
ARTIST Steve Epting

movies and of course I'm thrilled that one based on our work was so popular!

CBM: One would think that with Ed Brubaker jockeying for a role in the *Winter Soldier* film as Hydra scientist he would have been able to at least get you cast as a S.H.I.E.L.D. agent. What happened to your cameo?
SE: Well it was a little easier for Ed since he lives in LA! I was there on the set when they were filming Cap and Winter Soldier's final fight aboard the helicarrier, and as you know, there was no one else in that scene, so I guess even if they wanted to try to squeeze me in there was no way to do it. Ed said he didn't get to see any of the action scenes being filmed though, so at least I got that!

CBM: What projects are you working on now or that are coming up that you can share?
SE: I'm currently working with Ed on *Velvet*, our creator-owned book published by Image. It's sort of a mix of James Bond and Modesty Blaise, featuring a middle aged secretary working for a global intelligence agency in the early '70s. What no one knows is that she used to be one of the deadliest spies in the world, and circumstances force her back into that role after 15 years sitting at a desk, all against the backdrop of the Cold War.

CBM: Will there ever be a return to *Captain America* for you? Is there another Marvel character you'd like to reinvent like what you did for Cap?
SE: Never say never, but I don't really think it's a good idea to return to a book that you left your mark on previously. The run we did is fondly remembered and it really was a product of a specific time and place. It's almost impossible to capture that lightning in a bottle twice and I think we would almost certainly fall short. I'm not sure I can think of any examples where someone returned to a book and matched the success of a previous run that is considered classic, so I think it's just best to move on and do new things.

As for another character, I would love to do with Spider-Man what we did with Captain America. Spider-Man was what made me want to draw comics. Ed and I even discussed doing Spider-Man after Cap but we couldn't work it out with Marvel. Who knows, maybe one day I'll get a run on the book, but I have a feeling that it's very unlikely.

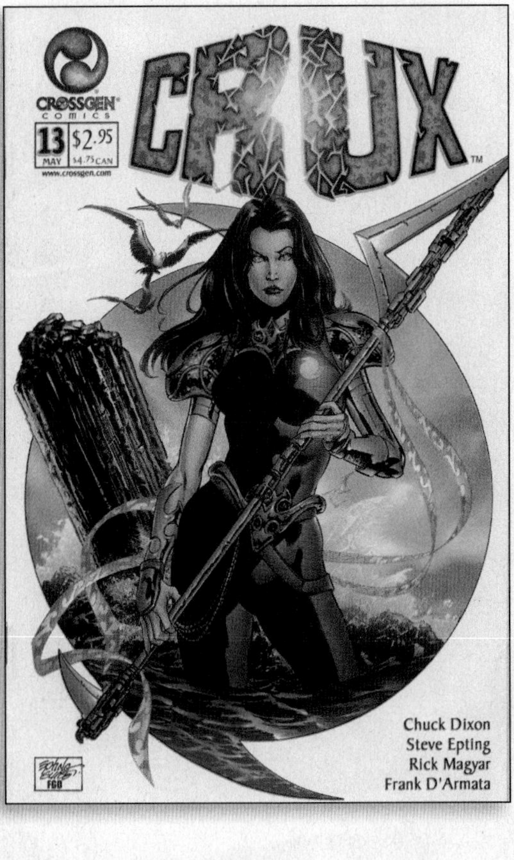
CROSSGEN COMICS
CRUX
13 $2.95 MAY $4.75 CAN
www.crossgen.com
Chuck Dixon
Steve Epting
Rick Magyar
Frank D'Armata

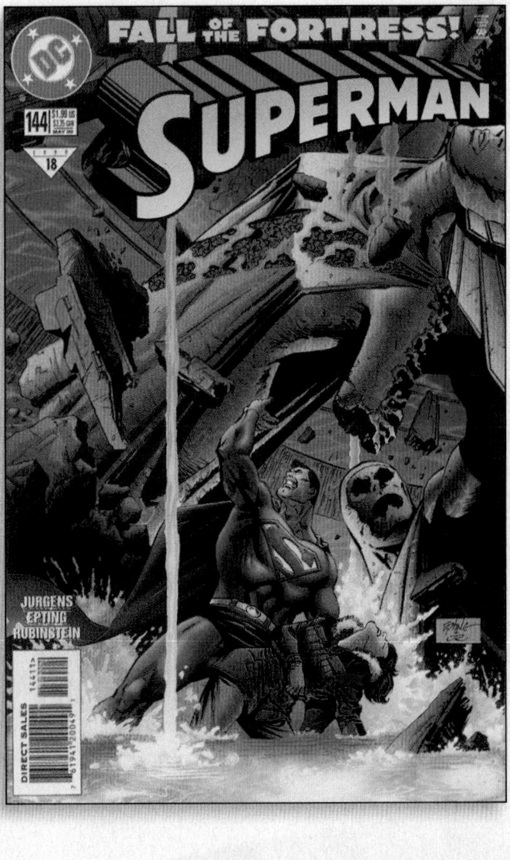
FALL OF THE FORTRESS!
DC
SUPERMAN
144
18
JURGENS
EPTING
RUBINSTEIN
DIRECT SALES

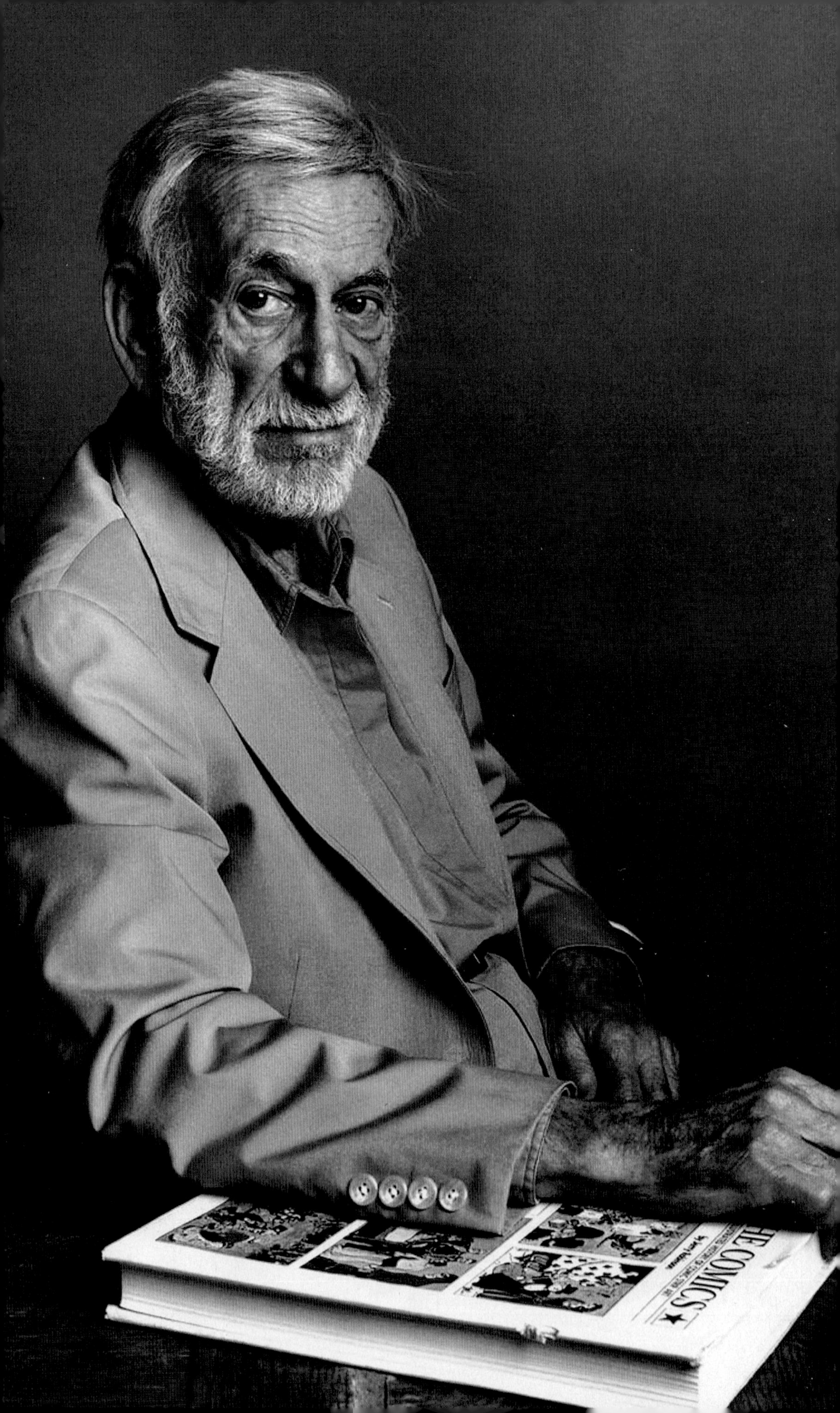
HE COMICS

Batman & Beyond: Jerry Robinson

BY **J.C. VAUGHN**

Jerry Robinson was a Columbia University student when he met and began working for Batman creator Bob Kane in 1939. He started out working on backgrounds and lettering, teamed with Kane and writer Bill Finger. He quickly became the main inker for the character. When Kane and Finger discussed adding a sidekick for Batman while preparing for Detective Comics #38, *Robinson suggested Robin, drawing inspiration from N.C. Wyeth's illustration of Robin Hood. In time for* Batman #1, *he (along with Finger) is unofficially credited with creating the Joker as well.*

After working for Kane, then on staff at DC and illustrating comic books for others, Robinson had a highly successful career in newspaper comic strips and editorial cartooning. He served as President of the National Cartoonists Society and the Association of American Editorial Cartoonists, founded the Cartoonists & Writers Syndicate. He, along with Neal Adams and others, championed the cause of Superman creators Jerry Siegel and Joe Shuster receiving royalties for their creation.

He passed away December 7, 2011 at the age of 89.

In 2007, not long after the NCS awarded him the Milton Caniff Lifetime Achievement Award, he spoke with Gemstone's J.C. Vaughn in an interview for our Scoop *email newsletter. It was later printed in* Comics Spotlight, *but has never appeared in a Gemstone print publication until now.*

CBM: How did you start out in illustration as a youngster?
Jerry Robinson (JR): I just liked to draw naturally. I don't remember being inspired by anything in particular. There weren't any artists in the family, though one of my older brothers drew cartoons for his college yearbook, but I wasn't even aware

of it. He's 17 years older than me and I didn't even see any of it until I was actually an adult. I just liked to draw. I was always encouraged to, and I liked to do it. I never studied it. I don't know how it is now, but in high school they didn't give any credits for art classes. There were so few that it wasn't meaningful enough. I just drew for the school paper and on my own time.

CBM: Were you inspired by any comic strips of the day?
JR: No, I really wasn't. I enjoyed reading the comics. I grew up in Trenton, New Jersey, and at the time, the *Philadelphia Inquirer* and the *Record* had the largest comics section. I remember trying to get those Sunday editions, but I wasn't drawing anything like comic strips.

CBM: What were you drawing?
JR: When I was very young, like, as a kid in first grade, I would draw an elephant on top of a mountain. Ridiculous things. Later, I would do some portraits. I would lie on the floor and draw my family sitting around talking. My grandfather, I remember, was a favorite subject. That was when I was seven or eight. I really didn't draw much again until I was in high school.

CBM: When you were in high school, what did you draw?
JR: I just drew cartoons for the school paper. Humor stuff. I was also an editor and wrote humorous pieces and did some reporting. That's where I was going. My ambition was to study journalism.

CBM: Were you going to Columbia University or about to when you met Bob Kane?

JR: I met Bob the summer I graduated high school. I was 17. I had sold ice cream all that summer to make enough money for my first year's tuition. At that time it was done with a cart on the back of a bicycle. I was given the outer-most territory of Trenton to cover, being just a kid signing up. I think I would net about $17 a week. At the end of the summer, my mother insisted that I take 25 hard earned dollars, which I was loathe to do, and go to a resort to fatten up. She thought I'd never survive the first year of college. I think I was down to about 89 pounds. So I went to this resort. My favorite sport has been tennis all my life, as it was with my three eldest brothers, who were all city champions or college players. So I grew up with tennis, and the first thing I did at this resort was to go out to find a partner and to see their tennis facilities. I was wearing a jacket - many people have asked me for this jacket. I wish it still existed - it was a white painter's jacket with a lot of pockets. It was a fad at that time; we used to decorate them with our own cartoons, graffiti, what have you. That's because Princeton University was close by and that was a fad at Princeton. So, when you're in high school, you're trying to copy the collegiate... So I felt a tap on my shoulder and someone asked me, "Who did the drawings on your jack-et?" I thought I was going to be arrested or some-thing. I turned around and it was Bob. He had just started Batman, and I think the first issue was out. This was the summer of '39.

CBM: Let's go back to the jacket for a minute. What was on it? Was it just doodles, your own characters or famous characters?
JR: You know, I can't remember all the things that I put on it. They were just gags as I recall, probably something about the school. There might have been caricatures of students or teach-ers, things like that.

CBM: So Bob sees this jacket and he's impressed by it enough to ask you about it. Batman's just come out. What's the next step in your meeting with him?
JR: He asked me if I knew anything about Batman. I'd never heard of it. Of course it had just come out and I didn't know anything about it or even Superman. We walked down to the local village. He wanted to show me a copy of it, which I saw, and frankly at the time I wasn't ter-ribly impressed. The art that I admired - that I saw in newspapers, was Prince Valiant and Milton Caniff. So, he said that if I came to New York I could join the Batman team. At that time there was just him and Bill Finger, the writer.

Even at that stage he needed more than the two of them.

As I said, I was interested in journalism. Just coincidentally I had applied to Syracuse University, Columbia, and Penn. Fortunately I was accepted at all three. I had decided to go to Syracuse for no particular reason except it sound-ed more collegiate. Columbia didn't sound right to me - a college in the middle of a big city. I was used to something like Princeton. Same thing for Penn in Philadelphia. I was all set to go to Syracuse, but Bob said, "If you come to New York, you can join the team on Batman."

I told him I'd see if my application was still good at Columbia, which it was. I called Syracuse and told them I wasn't coming, and I went right from that resort to New York. I started at Columbia and moonlighted on Batman in the beginning at the ripe old age of 17.

CBM: Did you go to the DC offices or did you work at Bob's studio?
JR: He had a studio in his own apartment. He lived with his folks at the time and had his own room and studio. I took a room nearby. I did my work in my room for the most part. Once and a while we'd do something at his place, but for the most part we worked independently because I worked much different hours since I was going to school at the same time. I was really burning the candle at both ends for a couple years.

CBM: Did your schedule necessitate you working quickly?
JR: It necessitated *learning* quickly. [Laughter]

CBM: Did you go into the DC offices and meet people there?
JR: Not for some time.

CBM: How long before you did that?
JR: I would say maybe a year, year and a half.

CBM: They worked through Bob then?
JR: Just through Bob. It was the same for Bill Finger. Later we opened an office in the Times Building downtown, just a studio, and we hired George Roussos to help. He did backgrounds and lettering. Up until that time I was doing complete inking, figures, backgrounds and lettering. And I began to pencil stories as well. Bill Finger and I were given a lot of offers from other publishers because Batman quickly became a success.

CBM: What was the first issue you contributed to?

JR: I don't think it was the second, it was probably the third. In any event, I started in the fall of '39. So, Bill and I were about to leave for greener pastures and DC heard about it. The other publishers didn't want us so much as anybody connected with Batman and its success. Bill and I were prime targets since Bob was tied up with DC. When they heard about it they made us a good offer to stay. They took over the feature and it was no longer through Bob. That's when we went to DC and actually worked there or in my studio.

CBM: What were the DC offices like in those days?

JR: It was a very exciting place in retrospect. We all were quite young. There was Siegel and Shuster, Joe was at the next table and Jerry would come in and write scripts. Jack Kirby was there. I had two friends I had made after I came to New York, who worked downtown at MLJ. They were great, so I took them to our editor, Whit Ellsworth, he hired them and they joined the staff. That was Mort Meskin and Bernie Klein. Fred Ray was also on the staff. He did most of the great Superman covers. For a period, everyone worked there at DC. Then there were some who weren't there and did things at home. It was pretty loosely structured. It was really a very exciting time. Sometimes we worked on each other's projects or were influenced by each other. It was pretty harmonious. I made lifetime friends there like Kirby, Siegel and Shuster, Fred Ray. Bernie was one of my best friends, and with Mort Meskin we had an apartment together and a studio together later.

CBM: Were you still going to school at this point?

JR: I continued for about two and a half years until the burden became too much and I had to make a decision. By that time I saw a future in writing and drawing, which I hadn't anticipated. When I first started on Batman I thought of it as a way of earning my way through college. Then I had to make a decision. Batman got very popular. We had to do a lot more work. *Batman* #1 came out, and I was inspired to create the Joker because we needed more stories instantly.

CBM: This seems like a good time to talk about the origin of the Joker. There were some card players in your family, including your mother?

JR: There was a lot of card playing in my family. My brother played Contract Bridge, tournament playing. My brother was a champion. He once won 17 in a row. My mother was an expert, though not on that level. And my father loved to play all sorts of games. I saw a lot of cards for recreation during my childhood, so that came in when I was trying to think of the visuals for the Joker. But first I named him. Names are quite important, and it established in my mind the persona of the character. I was studying journalism at the time and had literary classes at Columbia, and I had started to study the great masters. I didn't want this character to be one-dimensional as most of the villains were at that time. They were ordinary crooks or embezzlers. The crime period, the Prohibition era, Pretty Boy Floyd, John Dillinger, etc., were the precursors of the villains in the strips. They were pretty flat. I think in the newspapers before us they did a better job with things like *Dick Tracy*, who had a whole plethora of great, bizarre characters. If there was any influence, it might have been Tracy. I think it might have been more of an influence on Bill Finger as a writer than me at the time.

So that's why we had better stories. They grew out of the characters. So, I wanted to create a larger-than-life villain; I started out with that. I thought that was the greatest thing lacking in Batman, particular when I was studying literature and every great hero had a protagonist, from The Bible through Sherlock Holmes and Moriarity, etc. I thought it a very interesting contradiction in terms would be a villain who had a sense of humor. I love to write humor, by the way. A lot of the pieces I wrote for the high school paper were satirical pieces. I used to submit them occasionally to *Colliers*. I never got accepted, of course, but I used to prize the rejection slips. I'm sure I was well intended, but I didn't have the experience in high school to be writing for them. So, I had that ambition, and I loved the stories of Edgar Allen Poe, the bizarre, the twists of Mark Twain.

CBM: How long was it between the time you came up with the name and concept for the character and the time when you had an illustration of him?

JR: It was all in one night. We met at Bob's, Bob, Bill Finger and I. We were notified that they wanted to put out *Batman* #1 with four Batman stories. We were dead just doing one a month at thirteen pages, plus some smaller, other features. Bill was on that kind of schedule. Bill was the best writer in the business at that time, but he was not a natural writer. He worked very hard. He slaved over his scripts. So we knew right away that he was going to have difficulty coming up with four scripts in such a short time. They wanted to get this out almost immediately. I think we had one story in the bank. So I said okay, I'll do

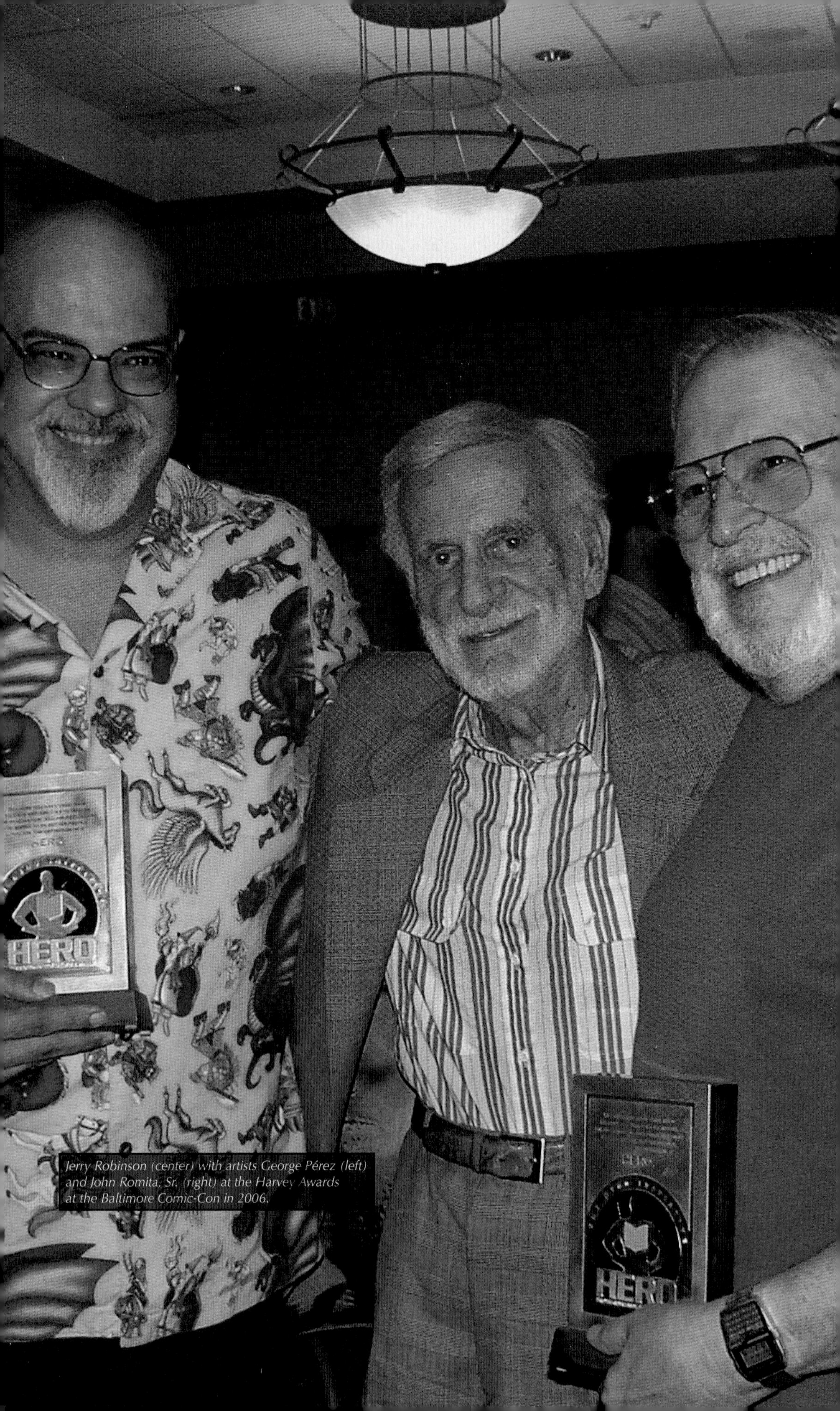
HERO
HERO

Jerry Robinson (center) with artists George Pérez (left) and John Romita, Sr. (right) at the Harvey Awards at the Baltimore Comic-Con in 2006.

one, which I was very happy to do. I thought it would do double duty. I could hand it in for my creative writing class at Columbia and get credit for and get paid for it, too. Bill was pleased with that and we discussed other ideas. That night I went home very excited. I'd been writing creative pieces for Columbia, and so this was going to be a showcase piece for me. It was actually going to be published. I sat down to analyze what I wanted to do with Batman. I wanted the villain to be more than one dimension, to be somebody unusual that had some contradiction in terms. I immediately thought of a villain that had a sense of humor. I'm sure, talking about where these things come from, this was from the fact that I enjoyed writing humor. I enjoyed the comics, not just the adventure strips, but also the humor strips. Then came the name. Searching for a name, I wrote down many, many things until I hit on Joker. I immediately made the association of the playing card of the Joker. I remember searching frantically for a deck of playing cards that night to see if I could find that Joker image I had in mind. Luckily, there it was. I found a deck. It had that classic court jester image of the Joker, and that's what I based the visual on. He was a joker, he would leave a joker playing card as his calling card, and that was the inception of it. That was all in one night.

CBM: How long did it take for that first story to be finished?
JR: I didn't finish the first story. I couldn't wait to get in the next day to see Bill and Bob and tell them what my story was going to be about, and the new character, The Joker. Unfortunately it was too good because Bill immediately wanted to write it. Bob really wanted me to write it, but he knew that Bill was the writer. This would have been my first story. He really had to persuade me. It was like giving up my baby. I was only 18 and literally had tears in my eyes, but I had to agree that Bill would do the best job. I had to describe the character and the things he would do.

CBM: Since you then had to put it in someone else's hands, how close did it come out to what you had intended?
JR: It was very close because I had done the sketches of the figure of the Joker, and I had worked with Bob to flesh it out.

CBM: How about in terms of the writing?
JR: Yes. I just had the broad outline of the story, that he was to be a master criminal, he would not murder anybody, he would outwit Batman and be a real test of Batman's skill, and being a joker he would flaunt to Batman that he couldn't catch him.

CBM: What was the reaction of the people at DC when they saw the story?
JR: Everybody who saw it knew it was going to be great. They immediately put it as the first story in *Batman* #1. Other stories had already been done. It was instantaneous. Nobody questioned it.

CBM: Did that blunt the feeling of not being able to write it yourself?
JR: Well, in a way, I guess. I wish I was a little older and had a little more experience at the time, where I would have put a copyright on it. [Laughs] Oh, well, you know, young and foolish. But anyway, this helped form the foundation of my career. I illustrated 30 books, I've been a political cartoonist, I founded a syndicate, so I never regretted it.

CBM: Your career has had a lot of turns to it, even just in the period we've covered so far. You could have left Batman with those offers right after the initial success. For that matter, you could have not worn that jacket and never met Bob...
JR: That's true. I would have pursued primarily, I think, a journalist writing career, but who knows, maybe I would have ended up drawing something I wrote later on.

CBM: How were you involved with the origin of Robin?
JR: The three of us really lived, ate, slept, dreamed about Batman. It was all encompassing, all absorbing. We rarely went out to dinner or lunch where we weren't thinking of ideas for characters. So, Robin was initially thought of by Bill. He came in said it would be great to add a boy. Bill was really the best read at the time. I was getting my education in college. Bill didn't have any formal education, but he was extremely well read. He went to all the foreign films. That's how we got really into the German expressionist films. He was really my cultural mentor at that time. He created all the other characters. He was a product of the pulps and early radio. He was very inventive. All the other characters were Bill's initial concept. One day he came in with this idea of a boy. Bob and I liked it. Bill, first of all, thought it would expand the story potential. You could have more complicated stories with the two of them. And on another level the kids at that time mostly identified with Batman, but most of them were 10 or 12 on up. By adding a boy, it

gave the younger readers someone to identify with. It was just obvious that it was a great idea.

It's been written about a number of times, but I named Robin and helped design his costume. It was really a collaborative effort. We were all sitting around, and we made a list of about 30 names and none of them seemed to fit. None of them grabbed us. And so finally I suggested Robin. It came from my background and youth. My favorite stories were of Robin Hood. And Robin Hood held a special fascination for me because the books I was given were the original N.C. Wyeth books of Robin Hood. I think I still have one or two from my youth. I didn't have to look at it. They were indelibly pressed in my mind. I instantly liked it myself - I thought of it after all [laughs] - because it was human. We were thinking of names like "Mercury," about mythological things, something to go with Batman. The name Robin wasn't universally accepted at first, but I began to argue for it. We each argued for our own thing, and they finally came around. If you look at his costume, the original sketch, it came from my memory of the Wyeth costumes of Robin Hood.

CBM: During this conversation when you were talking about the characters, did someone say "Batman and Robin" out loud?
JR: Once we got to Robin, yes.

CBM: At this point, it's difficult to imagine hearing it fresh for the first time, but it still has a natural ring to it.
JR: That's it. It was Bill who dubbed them the Dynamic Duo. He came up with all those things.

CBM: That's another great phrase. Was that during the same meeting?
JR: No, that was probably during the script that he fleshed out once we were done. All those things were really Bill's. Some stories later said that I had named Robin after myself - you know, Robinson - but that couldn't be further from the truth. The idea never entered my mind. I wouldn't have been so presumptuous at the ripe old age of 18 or 19, whatever I was at the time. The other thing came up with was "The Boy Wonder." They were always kidding me once Robin started, saying "Robinson the Boy Wonder." I was the youngest of the crew. It was a very young field. All of them were maybe in their early 20s. Siegel, Shuster, Kirby, all of them. But I hated that when they would call me that. When you're that age, you want to be older. But now

you can call me the Boy Wonder and I won't object. [laughs]

CBM: The comics moved very rapidly away from the stereotyped gangster villain into some of the really eccentric characters, didn't they?
JR: Exactly. That was the thing. Of course we didn't anticipate that The Joker would be a continuing character, but we had the idea of a sequel right away. He was going to be killed off, but by that time he was much too good, and so the story was changed where we didn't kill him. And he's still with us today.

CBM: It's often said that comic strip artists in those days looked down at comic book artists.
JR: I didn't know many comic strip artists in those days. [laughs] I think maybe the reverse was true, that maybe we looked up to the more successful comic strip artists. Not only for their creativity and ability, but also we knew they were making tons of money. I never had a great desire at that point to become a comic strip artist. In fact, I turned down a couple of opportunities.

CBM: When Batman was taking off and you were working at DC, there were all these great characters being created and you're in this creative atmosphere, did you have any involvement in how the characters were licensed or did you work on any of the non-comic book stuff?
JR: No. Well, maybe once and a while we'd have a piece of art for some licensing, but not very often. We just did it as an extra assignment. That wasn't done in any organized way.

CBM: Who was running the offices at DC in those days?
JR: My editor was Whit Ellsworth. That's who I would report to. Above him was Jack Liebowitz. And Donenfeld was kind of a mysterious figure. I didn't have much to do with him. There were other editors there on different features, but dealt with Whit Ellsworth more than the story editors like Jack Shipp and Mort Weisinger.

CBM: Were you friendly with them or was it strictly a business relationship?
JR: No, it was a unique period. Today there aren't many bullpens with the artists all working together. We were very friendly. As I mentioned, Mort Meskin, Bernie Klein and I had an apartment together not far from DC Comics. And we'd have parties. Whit Ellsworth would come down, the other artists, Siegel and Shuster, Fred Ray, and other friends and girlfriends and whatnot. We'd

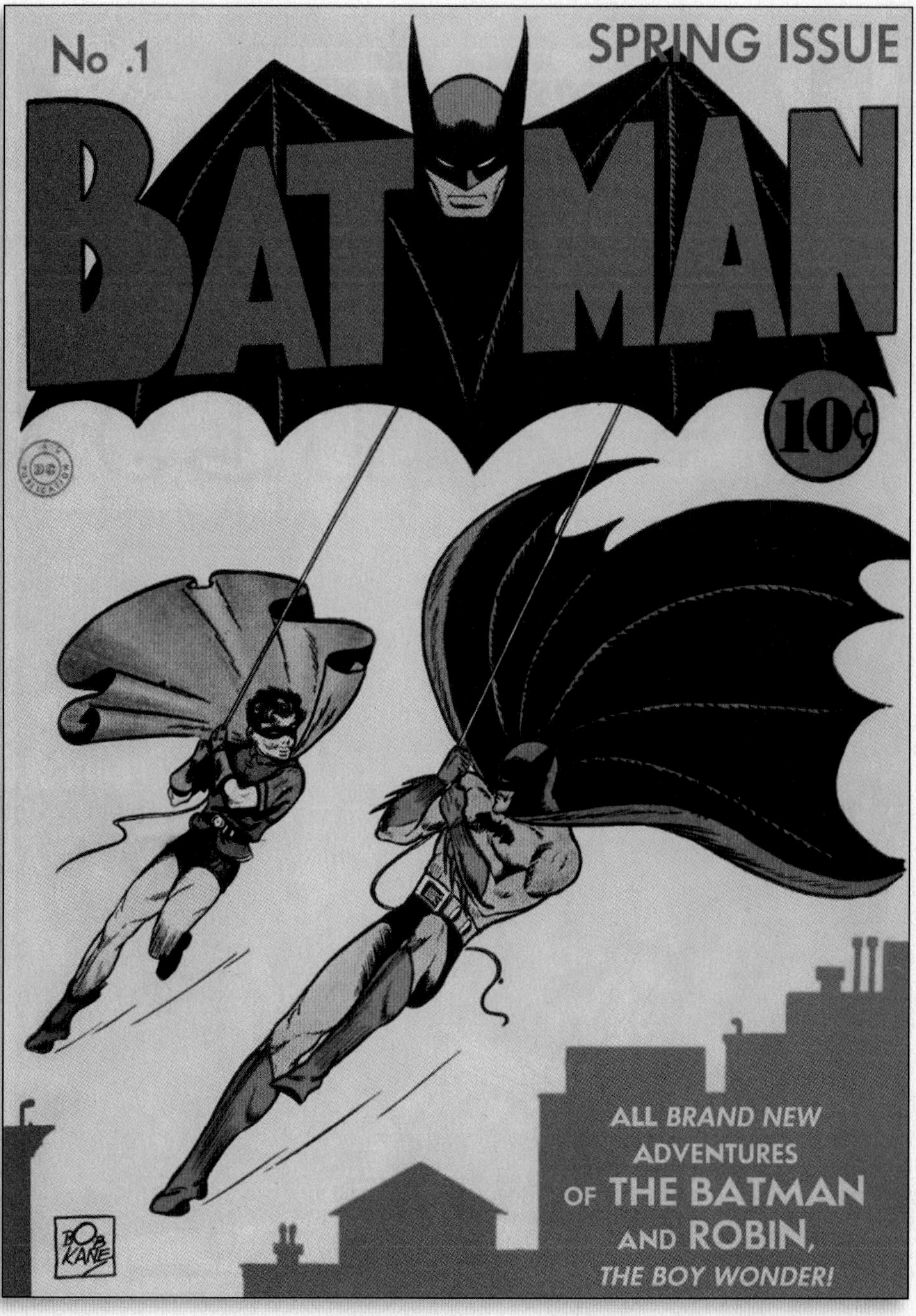
No .1
SPRING ISSUE
BATMAN
10¢
ALL BRAND NEW
ADVENTURES
OF THE BATMAN
AND ROBIN,
THE BOY WONDER!
BOB KANE

sit around the floor, drinking beer, and we'd have cartoons pasted all over the walls.

CBM: In those days, were the guys who created the characters the top paid people on the creative teams? For instance, was Bob making more than everyone else?

JR: Well, in the beginning he certainly was because he signed the contract with DC and we didn't even go down there. I've gone onto other careers and Batman was great, and the Joker credit and all that, but I did Batman for seven years and then I left. I didn't like doing the same things over and over. But Bill stayed in the business, and he was really the co-creator of Batman. I know that they did the initial concept together. It should have been like Joe Shuster and Jerry Siegel. Unfortunately Bill never got the credit nor the money. That was the greatest tragedy. He died broke and unappreciated until recent years when

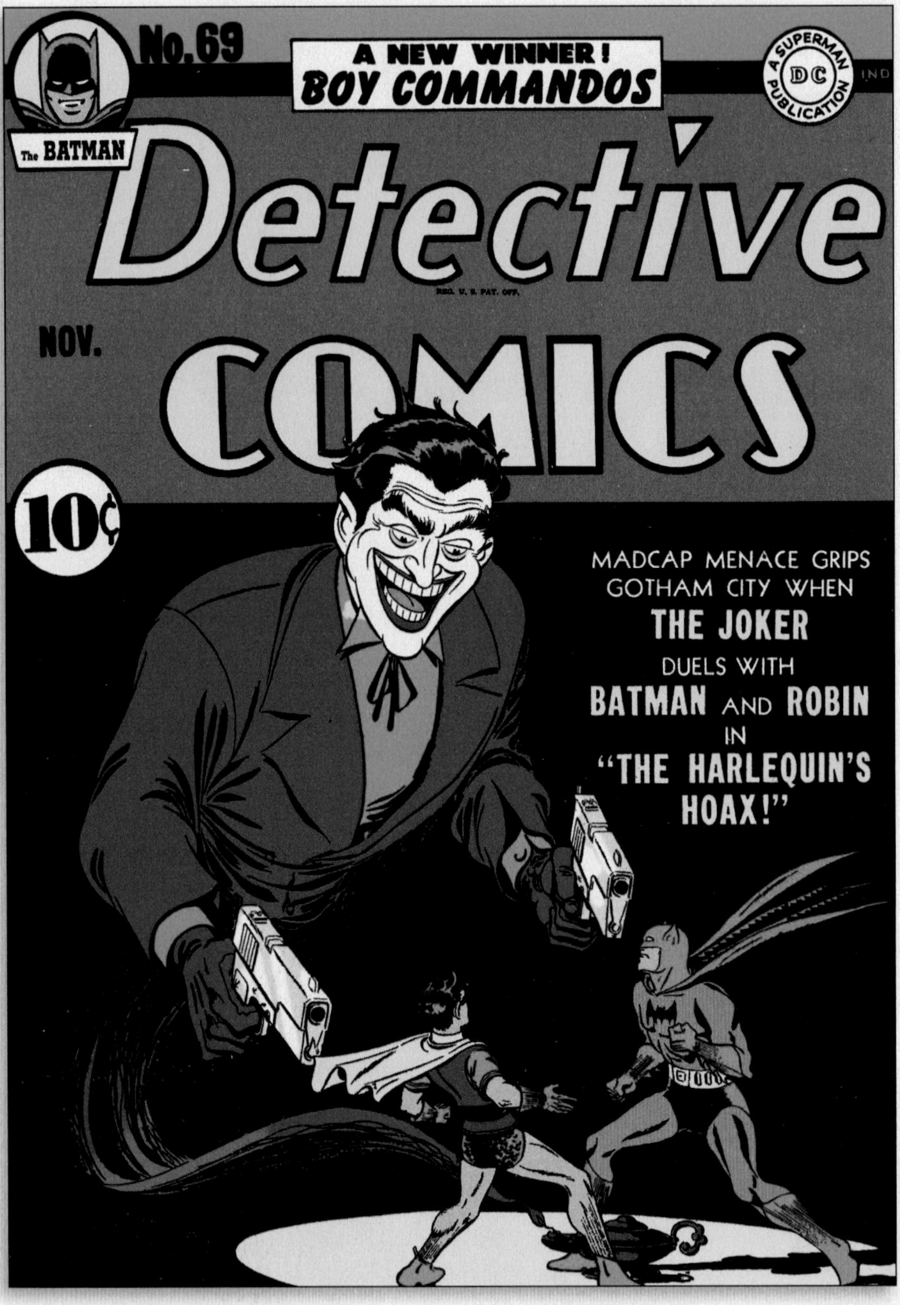
No. 69
A NEW WINNER!
BOY COMMANDOS
A SUPERMAN DC PUBLICATION
The BATMAN
Detective
NOV.
COMICS
10¢
MADCAP MENACE GRIPS
GOTHAM CITY WHEN
THE JOKER
DUELS WITH
BATMAN AND ROBIN
IN
"THE HARLEQUIN'S
HOAX!"

his role, due to the fans and historians, came to light. That's not to lessen Bob, who was a very good creator and visualizer himself.

CBM: For a lot of people of certain ages, the first they heard of Bill Finger was when Frank Miller mentioned him in *Batman: The Dark Knight Returns.*

JR: He had begun to be mentioned before that, though. I think Bob had made a mistake in a couple interviews by saying he wrote everything. Some writers or artists, I don't know who it was, took umbrage at this and wrote different fan magazines, etc.

I was at a convention as a guest just about the time that *Dark Knight* came out. A fan came up and was very excited about Miller's work, which at that point I didn't know at all. So I started to read it. Bruce Wayne walks through Robinson Park, and I didn't think anything of it, and then past the Finger memorial or something like that.

Then I realized it was kind of his homage to some of the early Batman and I was rather taken. Then I saw that the book was dedicated to several of us.

It was very nice of him. I didn't even know him at the time. He is an exceptional creator and I thought that was a very fine piece of work.

CBM: When you left Batman, what did you do next?
JR: I did a slew of other comics for a lot of publishers. I did Vigilante and Johnny Quick. I did the Black Terror, Fighting Yank and I did Lassie for... I hated that dog. I used to invent ways how not to draw the dog. If he had to run across a field to save a burning barn, which he was always doing, I'd have him run through a field of tall grass or hay and you'd only see the tail. He was always putting out fires. So I handed in a script one time where at the end of the story it was revealed that Lassie was really the arsonist. [laughs] For some reason they didn't me publish that one.

After that I did a lot of advertising. It paid very well. From there I went into book illustration and writing. I did about 30 books for most of the major publishers. But all this while I was seething inside. The thing I hadn't done, that I really longed to do, was commentary and social satire. So, one day I sat down and drew up samples to syndicate. It was called *Still Life*. It won the NCS Award later on. I did it for 17 years, and then we changed the name to *Life With Robinson*. So I did political and social satire for about 32 years, one every day. That was a lot of pressure, but it was very satisfying.

CBM: So within the niche of comics, you're considered a landmark figure for Joker and Robin and all your work on Batman and other comics, but that's only a small portion of your career?
JR: Well, looking back, yes. Most of the time I was a political cartoonist, but I did other things while I did that.

CBM: What led you to found your own syndicate?
JR: With *Still Life*, I was syndicated at that time by the *Chicago Tribune* - New York News Syndicate. A lot of cartoonists always feel their syndicate isn't doing enough for them. They'd promote you a year or two, then they'd find someone new and you'd be on a certain plateau. Since then I've learned the economics of the business and that's usually true. If it doesn't become an instantaneous success like a *Peanuts* or *Garfield*, strips

remain at a certain level. One reason for starting my own syndicate was to handle the strips more individually. I remember working for newspapers. I thought I was a journalist, yet I never visited a newspaper. I just handed my work into the syndicate. There was a disconnect between the cartoonist and the public. The second factor was that by this time I had served as President of the National Cartoonists Society, had been invited to juries around the world, had entertained our soldiers around the world, and I met artists all over. It really opened my eyes to these great artists we knew nothing about. That was my other idea with the syndicate, to syndicate the work of foreign cartoonists who weren't known but who were great. It took about two years to put together the first group of cartoonists - about 18 or 20 from 12 countries. We sent out the promotion for the feature, which we named "Views of the World," and it was conceived as showing American readers what the political or social views were by the top artists from papers around the world. The next day after we sent it out the *Los Angeles Times* signed up and they've been our client since, over 20 years. That expanded to other features. What it did was add another dimension. It wasn't just a dog strip or family strip or whatever. This hadn't been done elsewhere. It provided something new for the editors.

We were able to publish work by artists from the Iron Curtain countries. We were able to bring royalties to artists who were starving, and the American dollar was like gold to them. I remember once I had to smuggle in $5,000 to artists in Moscow, under the Soviet Union before the break-up. I couldn't bring it in legally because they'd take like 90 percent of it. So I took a chance and smuggled it in. I was never stopped. I figured if I was, they wouldn't object as much to me bringing money in as if I was trying to take it out. One of the artists had a party for me at an apartment. The artists that we were selling their work for and others came. During the evening I took out the royalties. They were in different envelopes. This one made $500, this one $1,000, and so on. They told me that I couldn't imagine what it meant to them. "I could live of this for four years with my family," one said. That was maybe six or seven hundred dollars.

CBM: Was that one of the most exciting times in your life?
JR: That was one of them, yes. No question about it. Seeing what it actually means to these artists, aside from the credit. To be published outside of their own country was quite a prestige. I think

No.12
TEN CENTS
BATMAN
AUG. SEPT.
WAR SAVINGS BONDS AND STAMPS KEEP 'EM ROLLING!
U.S.A.
ANNIVERSARY ISSUE

No. 70
BATMAN & ROBIN CHALLENGE "MAN WHO COULD READ MINDS"
Detective
DEC.
COMICS
10¢

No. 29
ON THE AIR
IN THE MOVIES
GREEN HORNET
COMICS

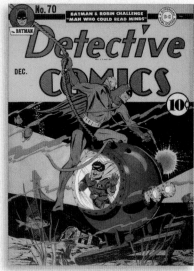

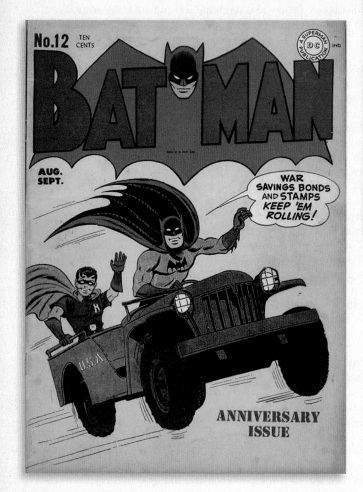

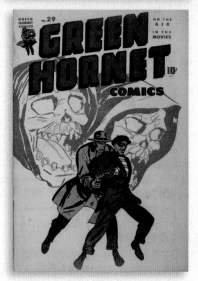

the only thing that compared to it was we worked a couple of years to get an artist who had been jailed and tortured out of jail in Uruguay. Nothing can be as satisfying as something like that.

They say one thing leads to another. Traveling with the syndicate, contacts with the other artists, meeting people and so on, I was able to be effective in that regard when I was working to try to get the rights for Siegel and Shuster and get some settlement for them. We were able to orchestrate articles and pressure.

CBM: Out of all the awards that you've won, is there one that means more to you?
JR: I guess I'd have to say the Milton Caniff Lifetime Achievement Award from the National Cartoonists Society, particularly because it was named after Milt, whose work I have so long admired. I got to know him very well when I served as President of NCS. He was the dean of past Presidents. He sat in on my board meetings, so we became friends. Later on, during the years he lived in New York, we played poker with a group of cartoonists. Mostly with his wife, because he would be working most of the time. We had a good relationship.

Oddly enough, he was the first strip cartoonist that I met when I came to New York. I was still doing *Batman*. I was very young, maybe 18-19. I had already started to draw a feature of my own, something I thought I'd do on the side. I never did do that feature for some reason, but I read in the paper that Milt was giving a speech at some Museum uptown. I put my portfolio under my arm just like a beginner, which I really still was, and I went to see his speech. It was very crowded. I came in late and was in the back, standing. I was just in awe, fascinated to hear him talk. He

No. 76
BOY COMMANDOS
BATMAN
Detective
JUNE
COMIC
10¢

AMAZING WORLD OF
DC COMICS
★ COMICS ★ MOVIES ★ ANIMATION ★ NEWS AND REVIEWS ★ BEHIND THE SCENES ★ JAN. 1975 ★ $1.50
SPECIAL BATMAN ISSUE

THE OFFICIAL OVERSTREET
No. 19
BATMAN 50 Years
COMIC BOOK
PRICE GUIDE
Robert M. Overstreet

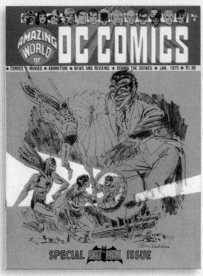

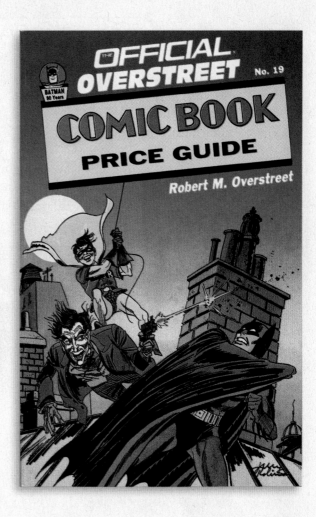

was a great speaker. After his speech they all crowded around. I saw I'd never get a chance to talk to him or show him anything. All of sudden the crowd broke up because he had to leave for an appointment. As he passed me, he saw me standing there with my portfolio. I didn't say a word. And this is so indicative of Milt... his kindness. He said, "Did you want to show me something?" He thought I was probably a young artist wanting to show his work. I said, "Yes." He said, "Well, I have an appointment downtown. If you want to drive down in the car with me, I'd be glad to look at it." That was our first meeting. He took me in his limousine. I still remember some of the critique he gave me on the pages. That was our first meeting. Many years later, you can imagine when he was sitting in on my board meeting, how I felt.

CBM: Are there any other areas you really wanted to work in that you haven't done yet?
JR: I'd like to do more in some areas. I've done some painting during summers I spent at Cape Cod, but I never really had the time put aside to say, "I'm going to paint." I'd like to set aside a year and just paint. I have done a lot of photography and had a couple photography shows. I always loved photography and I'd like to spend more time with that. My daughter's now a photographer. I'd certainly want to have pursued my tennis career. [laughs] The furthest I ever got was the semi-finals in a 13-year-old city tournament and was defeated by the champion. That was the high point. [laughs] I've been playing all my life and I really enjoy it. For years I played once a week in a group with Mike Wallace and a *60 Minutes* group. Fiercely competitive, as you might imagine. That I enjoyed.

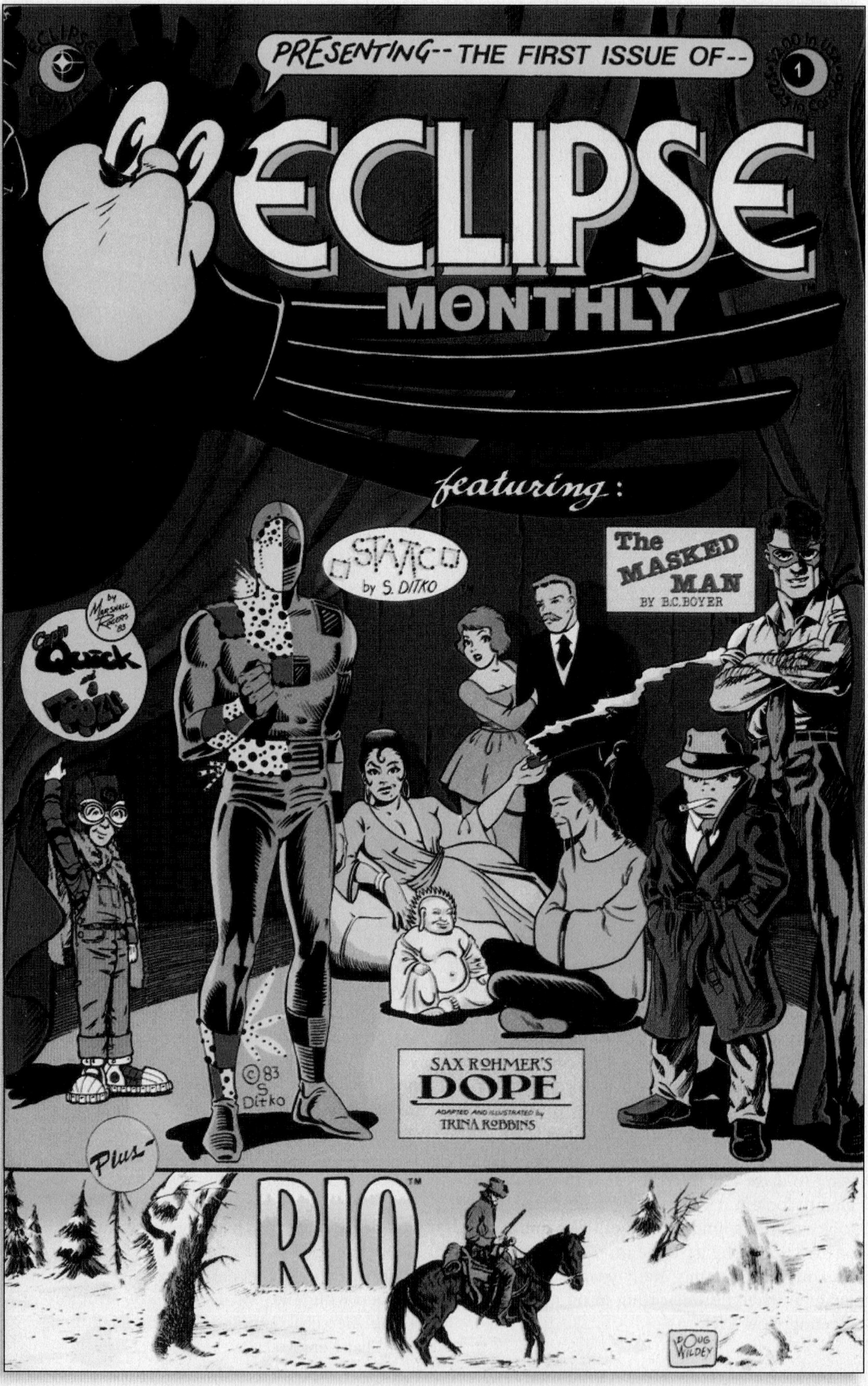
PRESENTING-- THE FIRST ISSUE OF--
ECLIPSE
MONTHLY
featuring:
STATIC by S. DITKO
The MASKED MAN BY B.C.BOYER
Cap'n Quick and a Foozle
SAX ROHMER'S DOPE ADAPTED AND ILLUSTRATED by TRINA ROBBINS
©83 S. Ditko
Plus-
RIO
DOUG WILDEY

Looking Back into the Eclipse

BY **DAVID ALLEN**

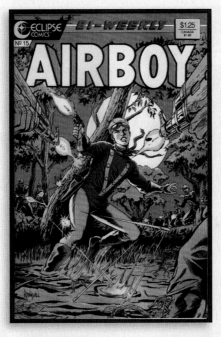

Eclipse Comics was there at the dawn of the direct market and had more than a moment in the sun. The independent publisher lasted more than 15 years, from 1978 to 1994, until market forces and an ill-fated co-publishing deal snuffed it out.

ECLIPSE COMICS
BI-WEEKLY
$1.25
Nº 15
AIRBOY

Before the sun set on Eclipse, the company pioneered graphic novels, creator-owned characters, royalties, quality paper stock, manga and bi-weekly publication. It was the third-largest publisher in the direct market after Marvel and DC, at its peak releasing 20 titles per month. Eclipse attracted such talents as Alan Moore, Neil Gaiman, Jack Kirby, Steve Ditko, Bruce Jones, Steve Englehart, Marshall Rogers, Jim Starlin, Paul Gulacy and Steve Gerber, who broke away from the mainstream to seize the opportunity for fewer creative restrictions and ownership of what they produced.

"They really were the first independent publisher to do creator-owned work," scripter Marv Wolfman said earlier this year. "Mike Friedrich (of *Star Reach*) did it first, but he had one book. Eclipse had a whole line, across the board."

In the spirit of full disclosure, I worked in the Eclipse office in 1986 and stayed friends with its principals until the end, and beyond. In 1988, after going into newspapers, I wrote a 10th anniversary piece on the company for the *Comics Buyer's Guide*. Some of those interviews are used in this *Comic Book Marketplace Yearbook* piece.

Founder Dean Mullaney took more than a decade off after Eclipse's painful end in bankruptcy and auction of its assets. He returned in 2007 with the Library of American Comics, an imprint of IDW, which publishes collections of classic newspaper comics. In 2014, his work was awarded three Eisners.

Mullaney was always one to look forward, not back, but his return to comics, and the warm words of the current generation of indie publishers who tell him Eclipse was a model for them, make him reflective. "It's a nice legacy to have," he admitted.

His name may not have rivaled Stan Lee's, but Mullaney was known to sharp-eyed readers of Marvel Comics as a prolific contributor to its letters pages in the mid-1970s. From his childhood home at 81 Delaware Street in Staten Island, NY, Mullaney pumped out letters to a wide range of titles, from the most mainstream to the ones that seemed to be the product of singular visions. Through those letters and attendance at conventions, Mullaney met and befriended some of those iconoclastic creators, among them Don McGregor, Doug Moench, Steve Gerber and P. Craig Russell.

Mullaney was a 22-year-old accountant on Wall Street when he visited McGregor's Bowery apartment in 1977 and noticed a drawing by Paul Gulacy pinned on a wall. Known for his Steranko-influenced art on Marvel's *Master of*

Kung Fu, Gulacy in this case had drawn a Jimi Hendrix-like hero with bandoliers across his bare chest. McGregor explained that it was a new character the writer had come up with: Sabre.

"Four hours later," Mullaney said, "I left deciding that I was going to try to get the money together to publish it."

"I had no idea that Dean even wanted to start a comic book company," McGregor said a decade afterward. "Dean gave me a call a couple of days later and asked if he could publish Sabre. I was looking for a place where I could do a character and strip where I wouldn't have to face the restrictions that were in the traditional comics market," said McGregor, who was best known for writing the impassioned *War of the Worlds* and *Black Panther* for Marvel.

He pressed Mullaney for copyright ownership and for the final say on creative decisions. Mullaney agreed.

Gulacy and Marvel letterer Annette Kawecki were brought in. McGregor said Gulacy deserved a page rate higher than Marvel paid him because, with the fledgling Eclipse, "he was working for a company that didn't exist." For his part, McGregor took a pay cut in exchange for a larger royalty percentage. It was a risk — McGregor was living on $3,000 a year — but one he hoped would pay off.

Mullaney borrowed money from his brother, Jan, a professional musician, and made him partner in the venture. Their company was called Eclipse Enterprises. Why? "Because I hoped we would eclipse the established system of creative servitude, bad printing and lack of creative spark," Mullaney recalled.

Under the philosophy "ask the man who does it," Mullaney sought advice from underground publisher Denis Kitchen and magazine publisher and former comics artist Jim Steranko. He visited a printing plant to watch the process and ask questions.

Sabre was published in August 1978 as a "graphic album." It was printed in black and white on heavy paper, using metal plates instead of the then-common plastic, and saddle-stitched. The retail price was $6. At that point, the most expensive publication from Marvel or DC may have been $1.50 treasury editions, which were in full color.

ECLIPSE COMICS
BI-WEEKLY
$1.25
CANADA $1.80
Nº 9
AIRBOY
BIGGER AND BETTER THAN EVER!

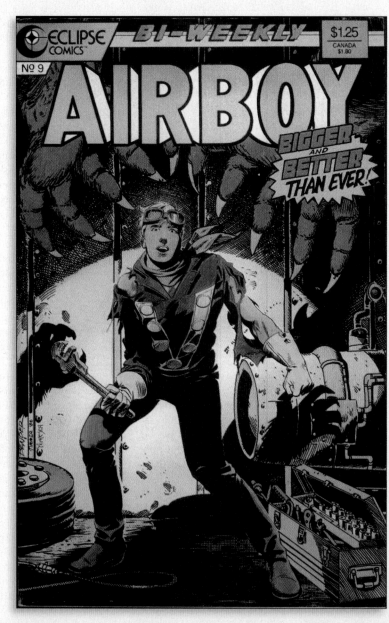

Mullaney had shown the art to Phil Seuling, owner of Seagate, the major East Coast distributor, for his reaction. "No one's going to pay $6 for a comic book!" Seuling had yelled. "I don't care how beautiful the art is!" But when *Sabre* came out, Seuling placed an order, as did Bud Plant, a West Coast mail-order retailer. Without their support, Mullaney said, the project would have failed.

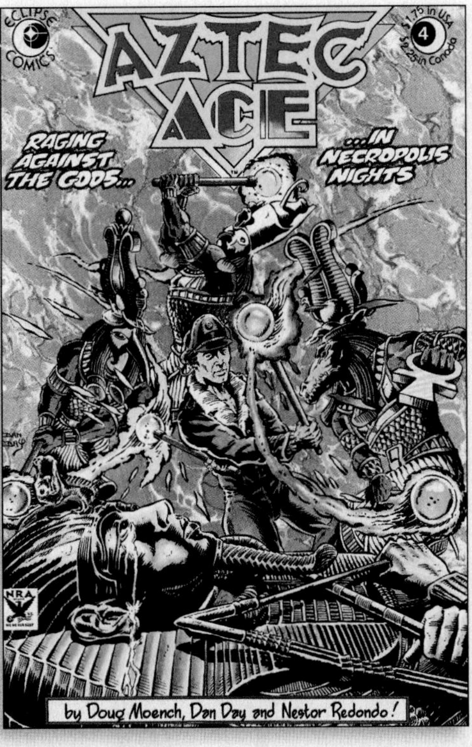

ECLIPSE COMICS
4
$1.75 In USA
$2.25 in Canada
AZTEC ACE
RAGING AGAINST THE GODS...
...IN NECROPOLIS NIGHTS
by Doug Moench, Dan Day and Nestor Redondo!

Sabre sold out its 5,000-copy run in three months, plus as a 3,000-copy second printing. It was sold in a half-dozen European countries, was reprinted in color comics form in 1982 and then became an ongoing series until 1985, all issues written by McGregor. A 10th anniversary edition of the album was issued in 1988.

McGregor said at the time that *Sabre* was ground-breaking in several ways. The lead character was a swashbuckling hero in a future ravaged by nuclear war and ruled by a totalitarian government — and he was African-American. "Putting Sabre in an Errol Flynn-type role was another way of breaking down barriers," McGregor said.

As for Mullaney, he said he was confident of success. He felt he knew what readers wanted. And on the other side of the coin, he knew what creators wanted.

"I knew they were getting shafted by the major companies at the time. Their work was getting butchered editorially, they were getting their copyrights taken away from them, and their work was being printed on toilet paper," Mullaney said.

While *Sabre* had been envisioned as a shot across the bow of corporate comics, not to be repeated, Mullaney discovered that he liked publishing it. He decided to keep going.

After putting out a collection of fan Fred Hembeck's humorous cartoon essays about comics, Mullaney published four more graphic albums from 1979 to 1981: *Night Music*, a collection of Russell's science fiction and Symbolist stories ("Do whatever you want and we'll publish it," Russell said Mullaney told him); *Detectives, Inc.*, a contemporary and gritty urban tale by McGregor and Marshall Rogers, an artist highly regarded for his run on Batman for DC's *Detective Comics*; *Stewart the Rat*, by *Howard the Duck* creator Steve Gerber and frequent *Duck* artist Gene Colan; and *The Price*, a science fiction story written and drawn by Marvel "cosmic" artist Jim Starlin.

With *Night Music,* Eclipse had a new and permanent colophon, designed by *X-Men* letterer Tom Orzechowski, supplanting the original by Mark Gruenwald, a Marvel editor and long-time friend of Mullaney's.

Colan's involvement in *Stewart the Rat* was a coup. The artist had been associated with Marvel for more than a decade, on such titles as *Daredevil, Tomb of Dracula* and *Dr. Strange,* and was under exclusive contract. But Jim Shooter, the company's editor-in-chief, gave Colan permission to draw the novel by former Marvel compatriot Gerber, because Marvel wasn't then publishing any competing graphic novels. "Dean and I about fainted," Gerber recalled in 1988.

Starlin's graphic novel preceded the first Marvel graphic novel, 1982's *The Death of Captain Marvel*, which he wrote and drew. The experience with Eclipse apparently emboldened him on behalf of himself and fellow creators.

"Jim used the negotiations with us on 'The Price" to get himself a better deal with Marvel on the graphic novel contract," Mullaney said, "forcing them to concede on a lot of points they hadn't formerly conceded to creators."

After five graphic albums, Mullaney decided to publish a periodical. The result was *Eclipse, the Magazine,* a magazine-sized, black-and-white anthology that sold for $2.95. The first issue, in 1981, had stories by Starlin, Englehart and Rogers (reuniting the former *Detective Comics* team on *Coyote,* later an Epic series), Russell, underground cartoonists Trina Robbins (adapting a Sax Rohmer novel, *Dope*), and more, under a cover by Gulacy and logo by Orzechowski. The first issue sold 25,000 copies.

Also in that first issue was *Ms. Tree*, a serial starring a female private eye, by crime novelist Max Allan Collins and artist Terry Beatty. The character appeared in all eight issues of the magazine, then in an Eclipse color comic for nine issues — before moving to Aardvark-Vanaheim (publisher of *Cerebus*) and, later, Renegade Press and DC. It was the first independent comic to prove its independence by switching publishers.

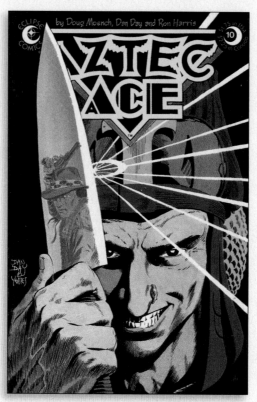

by Doug Moench, Dan Day and Ron Harris
10

Subsequent issues of *Eclipse* featured work by Harvey Pekar, Hunt Emerson, Charles Vess, Gerber and Val Mayerik (who had first drawn Gerber's Howard the Duck in Marvel's *Fear*), and a McGregor and Colan continuing feature, the semi-autobiographical *Ragamuffins*, about a boy's 1950s childhood. It was the first time art had been reproduced from Colan's pencils without an inker, an approach employed on several later Colan projects from various publishers, including DC, to better showcase the subtleties of his art.

The magazine was converted into a 48-page color comic, an anthology modeled on Golden Age comics with recurring series, although readers didn't embrace the format. Steve Ditko, co-creator of Marvel's Spider-Man, drew a new hero, Static, for two issues before an editorial disagreement led to a parting of the ways. Mullaney had suggested shortening dialogue and Ditko had refused. (In one small panel, the face of the character speaking is almost obscured by the windy dialogue.) Mullaney published the story as Ditko submitted it but declined further installments. While he characterized that outcome, in a letters page reply to criticism by yours truly, as a win for the creator-owned approach, it also showed the limits of his patience.

Eclipse had already dipped its toe into color comics. The first was *Destroyer Duck*, a benefit done without profit to Eclipse or the creators. The beneficiary was Gerber, who was suing Marvel over the rights to Howard the Duck. Published in 1982 with a script by Gerber and art by Jack Kirby and Alfredo Alcala, *Destroyer Duck* #1 had as a backup story the first appearance of Groo the Wanderer by Sergio Aragonés. It sold 80,000 copies and enabled Gerber to, in his words, "continue the lawsuit to a successful settlement" that, while not returning rights to the character, did give him creator credit on future Howard appearances.

Gerber knew Kirby from their work together at Ruby-Spears animation studio yet was nervous about asking the co-creator of many of Marvel's top series to essentially draw a 20-page story for free. But he said Kirby's response was a cheerful "Gee, that sounds like fun."

Kirby sent a handwritten letter to Mullaney in 1988 expressing his appreciation for the company's existence and its "support for many good causes," signing off, "Your friend, Jack Kirby."

Kirby wasn't the only veteran from comics' Golden Age to contribute to Eclipse. Jerry Siegel, the co-creator of Superman who later waged a long fight with DC over the rights, also winning credit for himself and artist Joe Shuster, wrote *The Starling,* a Siegel-owned superhero feature in the back of *Destroyer Duck*, thus neatly pairing two aggrieved comics creators in one package.

In a 1988 letter of congratulations to Mullaney on the company's 10 years, Siegel wrote in part: "Eclipse Comics does not seek to subvert and undermine the cartoonist's goal with crafty, unethical contracts intended to deprive the cartoonists of their creators' rights and moral rights. Thanks, Eclipse Comics, for your historic pioneering efforts to bring ethics, common decency and economic justice to a cut-throat industry, where to stand up for your rights could get you fired and blackballed."

Destroyer Duck, Sabre, Ms. Tree and *Eclipse Monthly* were Eclipse's color series, employing paper and coloring superior to newsstand comics. The price, $1.50, was also above other comics.

DNAgents became Eclipse's first superhero series, although like the company's other comics, its rights stayed with creator Mark Evanier. He spun off one character, Surge, into a miniseries and another, Crossfire, into his own series. *Crossfire*, set in Hollywood, began in color and switched to less-expensive black and white to keep the comic, drawn by veteran Dan Spiegle, afloat. "They stuck with it at a time when I don't think any other publisher would have," Evanier later said.

Eclipse had been based in Staten Island, but changes in Mullaney's personal life saw him relocate to an unlikely place for the city boy: rural Missouri.

Catherine Yronwode was a longtime comics fan and fellow letter hack who was writing a news and reviews column for *The Buyer's Guide to Comic Fandom*, *CBG*'s predecessor, when she met Mullaney and they fell in love.

Jan Mullaney had been publisher, with his brother as editor-in-chief, but with his music career taking more of his time, the guitarist took a step back. Dean took over as publisher and Yronwode became editor-in-chief. They had already moved in together, in Columbia, Missouri, in 1982. They relocated to California, living and working in Guerneville, a small town 90 miles north of San Francisco with an alternative vibe and a redwood forest.

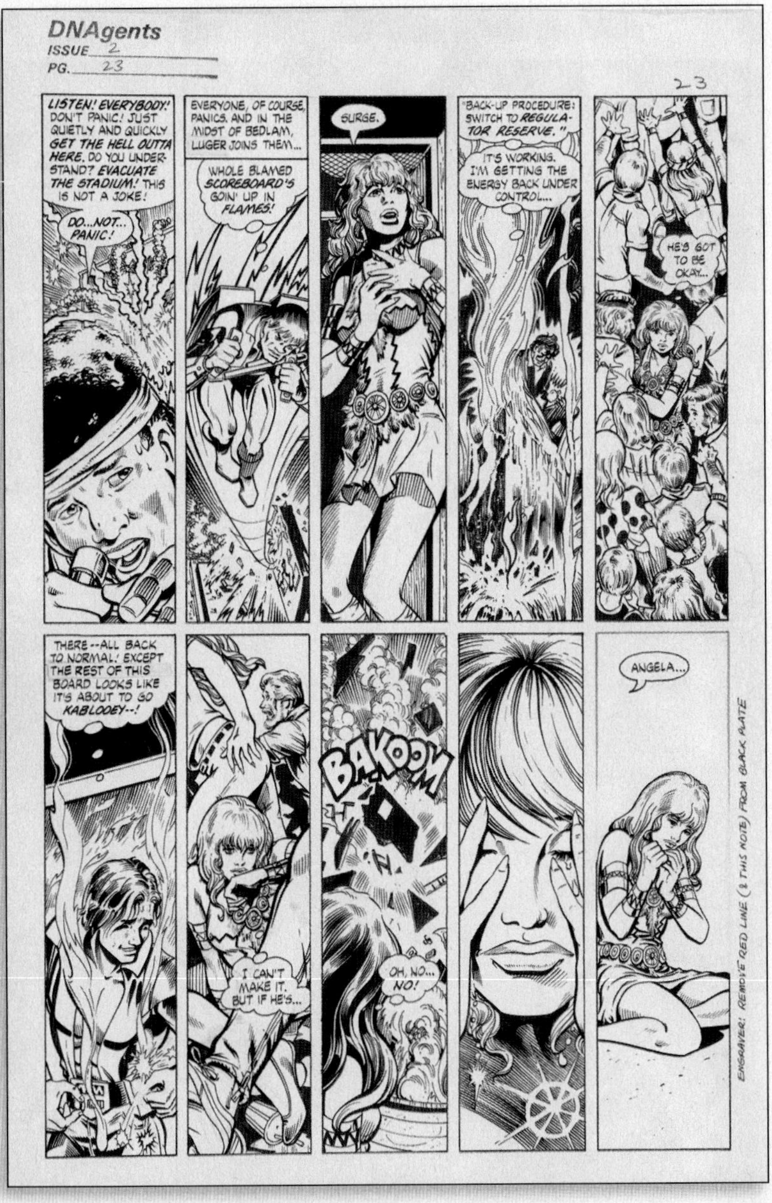
DNAgents
ISSUE 2
PG. 23
23
LISTEN! EVERYBODY! DON'T PANIC! JUST QUIETLY AND QUICKLY GET THE HELL OUTTA HERE. DO YOU UNDERSTAND? EVACUATE THE STADIUM! THIS IS NOT A JOKE!
DO...NOT... PANIC!
EVERYONE, OF COURSE, PANICS. AND IN THE MIDST OF BEDLAM, LUGER JOINS THEM...
WHOLE BLAMED SCOREBOARD'S GOIN' UP IN FLAMES!
SURGE.
"BACK-UP PROCEDURE: SWITCH TO REGULATOR RESERVE."
IT'S WORKING. I'M GETTING THE ENERGY BACK UNDER CONTROL...
HE'S GOT TO BE OKAY...
THERE--ALL BACK TO NORMAL! EXCEPT THE REST OF THIS BOARD LOOKS LIKE IT'S ABOUT TO GO KABLOOEY--!
I CAN'T MAKE IT. BUT IF HE'S...
BAKOOM
OH, NO... NO!
ANGELA...
ENGRAVER: REMOVE RED LINE (& THIS NOTE) FROM BLACK PLATE

Unfortunately, the town also lay by a river. In February 1986, several days of rain swelled the Russian River to overflowing. Mullaney, Yronwode and Sean Deming, their assistant editor, evacuated to a Red Cross shelter and were carried out by National Guard helicopters to nearby Santa Rosa, along with other residents. When the water receded, the trio returned to find they'd lost not only many of their personal possessions, but Eclipse's back-issue stock and research material for a Steve Ditko retrospective and biography.

While the flood was a setback, Eclipse continued growing. The company had already expanded its output considerably, in part due to the travails of another publisher.

Pacific Comics, a San Diego-based comics distributor, was also the publisher of Dave Stevens' *Rocketeer*, the Bruce Jones-written anthology titles *Alien Encounters* and *Tales of Terror*, and others. In 1984, it was an open secret that Pacific, roughly the same size as Eclipse, was in financial trouble. Mullaney called publisher Steve Schanes and offered to buy material that was ready to go but which Schanes didn't have the resources to publish.

Mullaney grabbed his checkbook and flew to Los Angeles, where he met with Stevens and signed him to continue *Rocketeer*, then continued to San Diego to meet with Schanes. By midnight, they had a deal that doubled Eclipse's output.

That deal also included American rights to *Marvelman*, a United Kingdom superhero revival by Alan Moore, who due to his work on DC's *Saga of the Swamp Thing* was arguably the first comics writer since Stan Lee whose name, in a field where artists' work was collected, not writers', meant more to fans than whoever was drawing his scripts.

The first issue of the redubbed *Miracleman* was published in 1985 by Eclipse. It was priced at 75 cents, only 15 cents more than Marvel and DC then charged. The series began by reprinting the original British stories by Moore and Garry Leach and became Eclipse's best-selling series.

The series continued with new stories, first by Moore and then, with issue 17, Neil Gaiman, another Brit whose DC series *Sandman* was making an even bigger mainstream splash than Moore's *Swamp Thing* had. Yet deadline problems not only persisted but worsened.

"It was exciting and it was never on time," Mullaney recalled with a rueful chuckle when asked about the title. "It could have been the breakout book that sold in huge numbers. The creative talent just could not deliver the book on time." The title lasted 24 issues, published fitfully over eight years.

Marvel is now reprinting the series, relying on Eclipse's film negatives, stats and original scripts, archived along with much of the rest of Eclipse's output at Michigan State University. "I'm glad to see it reprinted because it's great work," Mullaney said.

Eclipse turned to the distant past to revive characters published in the 1940s and '50s by Hillman, notably Airboy, Valkyrie and the Heap, that had fallen into the public domain. *Airboy*

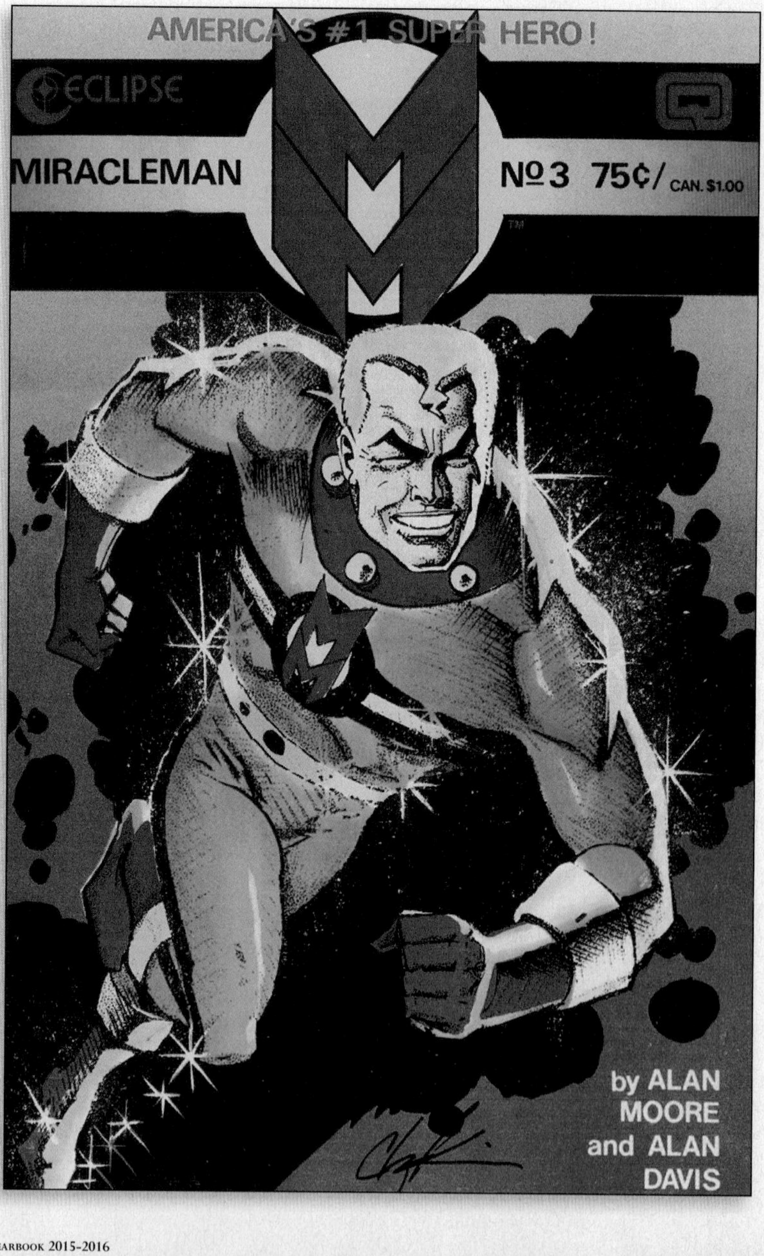
AMERICA'S #1 SUPER HERO!
ECLIPSE
MIRACLEMAN
Nº3 75¢/ CAN. $1.00
by ALAN MOORE and ALAN DAVIS

AMERICA'S #1 SUPER HERO
ECLIPSE
MIRACLEMAN
Nº5 95¢ CAN $1.25
The MYSTERY of EMIL GARGUNZA— The SECRETS of "THE VISITOR"— The ORIGIN of MIRACLEMAN— REVEALED!

was published bi-weekly, a novel schedule — even more novel because Eclipse's other comics were so often late. *Airboy* and *The New Wave*, a modern but generic superhero title that was also published bi-weekly, made every deadline.

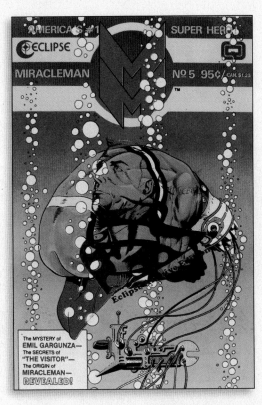

Artist Tom Yeates on several occasions bailed out Eclipse in a pinch. The Kubert School graduate who drew for DC had relocated from New Jersey to Jenner, a town a 20-minute drive up the coast from Guerneville. Mullaney and Yronwode invited him to use their photocopier whenever he liked before he mailed off his art. That led to friendship and occasional assignments.

While Yeates never drew a regular series for Eclipse, he penciled or inked various issues and covers, and he made corrections in the Eclipse office once or twice on art by others. Perhaps his most unusual Eclipse assignment was drawing *Captain Eo*, an oversized 3-D magazine done at Disney's behest and featuring Michael Jackson as a science fiction hero, tying in with a short 3-D film shown in Disney theme parks. For Yeates, his photo-realistic art proved to have its drawbacks where the King of Pop was concerned.

"I had to redraw the faces," Yeates recalled earlier this year with a chuckle, "based on his latest face-lift."

Yeates was involved in *Brought to Light*, Eclipse's return to graphic novel publishing, along with Alan Moore, Bill Sienkiewicz and Joyce Brabner. It was an anthology of political nonfiction stories about the CIA's involvement in Central America.

"I liked them," Yeates said of Mullaney and Yronwode. "They were fellow leftists. We had similar politics. They hated Reagan. They had the nerve to publish stuff like that. It took an enormous amount of courage to do that. Nobody else would have done it. It was real incendiary stuff. I respect those guys."

Eclipse had relatively straightforward comics like Tim Truman's *Scout*, a post-apocalyptic adventure series starring a Native American warrior, and more experimental heroes like *Aztec Ace*, a 23rd century time traveler created by Doug Moench, an established Marvel and DC writer whom Mullaney and Yronwode both admired. "When they heard I was leaving Marvel," Moench recalled in 1988, "they called me up and said, 'Why don't you write something for us?'"

One of Eclipse's most fondly remembered series is *Zot!* Its creator, Scott McCloud, was a newcomer to comics. His optimistic, manga-inflected space opera lasted 36 issues, and McCloud went on to produce *Understanding Comics*, an acclaimed book about the visual language of comics. "Eclipse guaranteed me the right to have creative control over my work. Cat as my editor gave me a lot of good input," McCloud said in 1988, "but she never restricted me in any way. They've kept their word absolutely right down the line when it comes to that."

The company took chances on many commercially marginal series. *Tales of the Beanworld* was perhaps the strangest, a minimalist series about anthropomorphic legumes that drew from world mythologies and ecology for its themes. Creator Larry Marder went on to oversee Image Comics. *Beanworld* was Yronwode's favorite series and one of Eclipse's most celebrated.

Eclipse forged unique partnerships with creators, some of whom, like Marder or Matt Feazell, were proudly producing mini-comics on their own, "printed" with photocopiers and folded or stapled. By publishing their work in standard B&W comics form, Eclipse allowed them to reach a larger market in a fashion that involved little risk on the company's part.

Rather than pay a page rate, Eclipse would share profits after publication, sometimes 50-50, sometimes 80-20 in the creator's favor, depending on the comic. Although these were technically Eclipse comics, with the company logo and house ads, Eclipse acted more as a distributor than a publisher. "I like a wide variety of material," Mullaney explained. "We had the distributor pipeline. We could include all these cartoonists in it." Image Comics today uses a similar approach, he said.

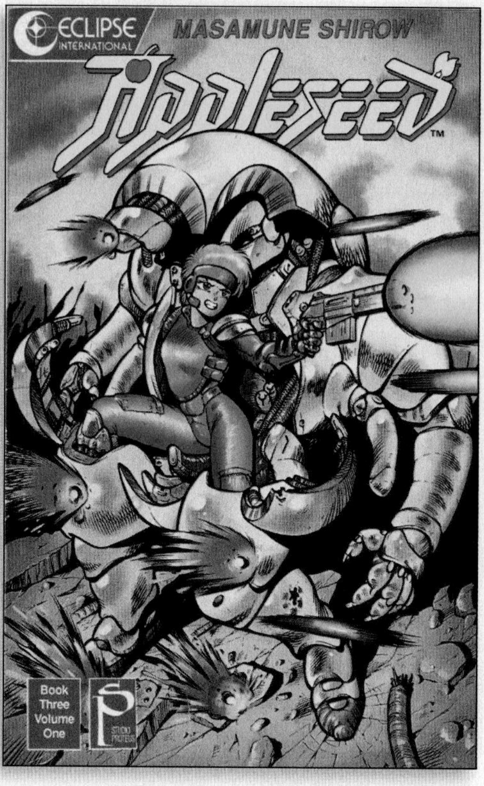
ECLIPSE
INTERNATIONAL
MASAMUNE SHIROW
Appleseed
TM
Book Three Volume One

The first comics work by Chris Ware was published in one of these low-key releases during the B&W boom. 1988's *Floyd Farland: Citizen of the Future* collected a serialized science fiction strip from the University of Texas student paper, which had been seen by Texas student and sometime Eclipse editor Fred Burke. He championed it to a bemused Mullaney and Yronwode, who nevertheless agreed to publish it as a one-shot with some redrawn art by Ware. It's a footnote in the career of Ware, now celebrated for *Jimmy Corrigan* and *Building Stories.*

Manga was another unusual publishing line. In the mid-1980s, Japanese comics were little-known in the United States. A Japanese publisher, Viz, wanted to test the waters across the ocean by partnering with a West Coast publisher. At the time, Eclipse was the only publisher that fit the bill.

The result was *Mai the Psychic Girl*, *The Legend of Kamui*, *Area 88*, *Xenon* and *Appleseed*, published in 1987-88.

"We published the first line of manga in the U.S.," Mullaney said. "People think we must have sold millions." In reality, sales began at about 50,000 copies each and dwindled to 12,000 by the end.

"The market wasn't really ready yet. Manga was a cult item then," Mullaney said. "It didn't become popular until many years later."

To mark its 10th anniversary in 1988, Eclipse took a cue from Marvel and DC: a multi-character crossover miniseries. *Total Eclipse* was scripted by Marv Wolfman, who had written DC's mega-popular *Crisis on Infinite Earths.* This one, however, threw together creator-owned characters, all with their creators' permission. (Evanier, who said he was opposed to crossovers, declined to participate and Eclipse obliged him by leaving out *DNAgents* and *Crossfire.*)

Wolfman believes the series was a mistake. "It was a stupid idea done badly," he said earlier this year. "Because it was an independent company, all the concepts had not been in the same universe. *Beanworld* — which I read — should not have been in the same universe as *Skywolf.* But I liked the guys, I liked Cat and Dean, very much. They were hoping it would help them." He added: "I didn't have a passion for the material."

Mullaney disagrees about the concept's merit, and after all it was his company. He wasn't a purist. "It was a celebration. To see *Beanworld* and *Miracleman* in the same piece of art, it was worth it just for that," Mullaney said. He pointed to 2015's *Archie vs. Predator* as a later "weird crossover" that made little formal sense.

"There were no rules. We made up the rules as we went along. We were going by our instinct and having a lot of fun," Mullaney said.

By then, Mullaney and Yronwode, who had married, had moved a few miles east to the still-secluded Forestville, where they bought nearly two acres that included a barn and a fruit orchard. Mullaney used his carpentry skills to restore the 1886 home to its original look. They operated the company out of a low-slung outbuilding on the rambling property. Yronwode tended the landscaping and planted a garden. The company had a local staff of seven as well as a sales representative, Beau Smith, who worked from his home in West Virginia.

Speaking in 1988, Yronwode recalled that she realized Eclipse was big when it dawned on her and Mullaney that their 15 titles a month was a greater number than Marvel had published in the mid-1960s. They were publishing 20 per month by 1988 — superhero, adventure, fantasy, science fiction, manga, humor and more — and selling a half-million copies per month. Eclipse was the third-largest publisher, after sales behemoths Marvel and DC. As Yeates put it recently, "There was a big gap between No. 2 and No. 3, but they were No. 3."

The couple was happy to be able to achieve all that on their terms, in an almost agrarian setting a world away from New York, where Marvel and DC were based. Mullaney and Yronwode dressed in vintage clothes, listened to old-time music and outfitted their kitchen with an antique stove and icebox.

"The people who work for us tend to see it our way," Yronwode said then. "Tim Truman draws in his basement. That's the best of 20th century decentralization. Marv Wolfman has a computer and he can send us a script on his modem. When I come in to work in the morning, there's a script from Marv. I don't have to burn up commute hours on the freeway, and neither does he."

As Mullaney put it at the time, "We can publish what we choose to publish. We don't have to justify ourselves to a board of directors."

Chuck Dixon was another mainstream talent that found a kinship with Eclipse's iconoclastic ways. He wrote *Airboy* and *Strike!* for the company while also scripting for Marvel and First. His adaptation of *The Hobbit* for Eclipse, with art by Dave Wenzel, was the company's all-time best-seller, coming out in three prestige-format comics and then as a softcover in the U.S. and U.K., ultimately selling 300,000 copies. Twenty years later, the creative duo still see "substantial royalties" due to subsequent reprints, Mullaney said.

ECLIPSE COMICS
Nº 17
MONDAY: THE ELIMINATOR AND
$1.75
CANADA $2.50
SCOUT
--TOGETHER!
KEY TO THE HIGHWAY
WITH AN UNEXPECTED GUEST APPEARANCE BY LARRY MARDER'S "BEANWORLD!"

"My relationship with Eclipse is special," Dixon said in 1988. "Cat changes more of my stuff than any other editor, and I mind the least. You can call Eclipse and tell them any idea you have and they won't laugh at you. They'll find a way to make it work. They've taken it on the chin a couple of times with my stuff, but they've never complained. I always think of them when I create something new."

Eclipse also found a niche in producing trading cards. Some were political, about the Kennedy assassination, the savings and loan scandal and Iran-Contra hearings, and *Friendly Dictators,* about tyrants backed by the U.S. Another highlighted ballplayers from the Negro Leagues. (Perhaps ironically, given

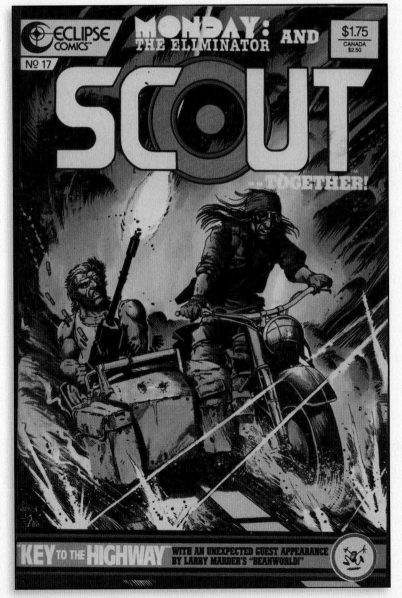

Eclipse's political leanings, images of the Negro Leagues cards were used in a vintage baseball exhibit in 2014 at the Reagan Library.) The most notorious, *True Crime,* included serial killers, and in the wake of news about Jeffrey Dahmer, who was hurriedly added to the set, the cards received national publicity, most of it of the how-dare-they variety. Ironically, the publicity only spurred sales of what would otherwise have been a quiet product. "We ended up selling 9 million cards," Mullaney said. "It was a helluva lot of fun."

Eclipse's undoing was no fun at all. It was a deal with HarperCollins to co-publish graphic novels and distribute them in bookstores. Eclipse got a $100,000 advance and set about commissioning material. They began with adaptations of genre fiction by Clive Barker, Dean Koontz and Anne McCaffrey and hoped to expand to literary fiction once the market was ready.

But the market wasn't ready. Eclipse spent the advance and, with no sales dollars coming in, burned through its financial reserves to keep the material flowing. But bookstores and the sales force were resistant. Twenty years ago, graphic novels were not yet reviewed in the New York Times and there were no Best Comics of the Year hardcover anthologies.

"I knew it was a risk. I went in with my eyes wide open. But I was willing to take it because I wanted to see graphic novels in bookstores," Mullaney said. He joked: "Now there are graphic novel sections, but they're filled with 5 million Marvel and DC books."

Mullaney said Dick Giordano, then the publisher of DC, once told him he envied Eclipse's nimbleness: Mullaney could come up with an idea overnight and implement it the next day; with DC's bureaucracy, a brainstorm might require nine months of vetting to launch. Mullaney, for his part, told Giordano he envied DC's resources, because Eclipse was fundamentally a shoestring operation.

The shoestring snapped. Besides the HarperCollins deal, the comics market changed in the early 1990s with variant covers and gimmicky concepts fueling a speculators' market, with Marvel and DC crowding other publishers out of the marketplace. Sales rose to unsustainable heights, and then the bubble burst.

Mullaney saw the end coming. He began selling off the company's stock of back issues, which had constituted up to 25 percent of its monthly profit, at wholesale prices. When Eclipse declared bankruptcy, in 1995, "we didn't owe a dime to any creator," Mullaney said proudly. "Distributors and retailers got burned, unfortunately." The intellectual property rights to Eclipse properties were acquired by Image co-founder Todd McFarlane.

ECLIPSE
FIRST ISSUE!
NO.1
$1.00
Sabre
by Don McGregor & Paul Gulacy
The most explosive hero in comics!

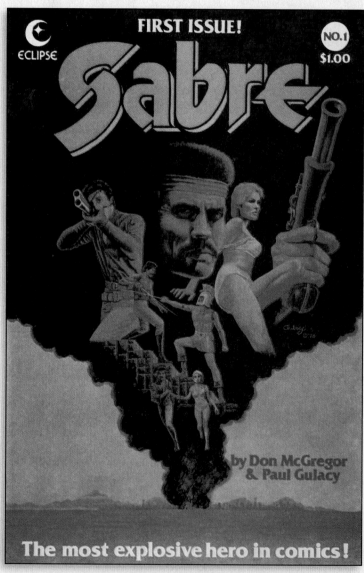

ECLIPSE COMICS
THE MOST EXPLOSIVE HERO IN COMICS!
ONE DOLLAR 3 $1.25 in Canada
Sabre
NO, MELISSA! PUT THE KNIFE DOWN, PLEASE!
YOU'RE A POET OF DECEIT, SABRE!
I'M GOING TO KILL YOUR FLOWERY VERSES OF HONOR, MY LOVE--
IT STARTS HERE, COLLECTORS!
THE SHOCKING BEGINNING TO THE FIRST ALL-NEW SABRE EPIC IN FOUR YEARS!

Mullaney and Yronwode divorced and he ended up in Key West, Florida, where he started a new career as owner of a graphic design business and a sign-making shop. He stayed in touch with McGregor, and later with me, but otherwise kept a low profile. Many friends, like Yeates, didn't know where he was.

"I missed being in comics every day," Mullaney said.

He found a way back in. He had long wanted to publish a definitive edition of Milton Caniff's *Terry and the Pirates,* his favorite comic strip, which had seen a murky black-and-white reprint in the 1980s from NBM. After selling his businesses, he created an imprint, the Library of American Comics, in 2007, under IDW Publishing, which is owned by Ted Adams, a former Eclipse employee. After a six-volume reprinting of the complete *Terry,* the imprint has gone on to produce more than 120 books, among them volumes of *Little Orphan Annie, Dick Tracy, Secret Agent X-9* and *Steve Canyon.*

Without the business headaches of being a publisher, Mullaney said, "I'm playing in the sandbox much more than I ever was at Eclipse."

Some current projects have roots stretching back to the 1980s. Mullaney is publishing Hugo Pratt's *Corto Maltese,* with plans to bring out Carlos Gimenez' *Paracuellos,* both of which he had hoped to do with Eclipse. He's also working on a reprint of Alex Toth's graphic novel *Bravo for Adventure,* which Toth's estate has authorized; the cantankerous artist never gave Mullaney an answer to earlier entreaties. A *Ragamuffins* collection, with an unpublished 20-page McGregor-Colan story, is on tap for 2016.

"Eclipse lives on in some of the projects I'm doing now," Mullaney said.

Its anti-establishment philosophy may have came and went. Creators' rights, an Eclipse hallmark and a rallying cry from the late 1970s into the Image era of the early 1990s, are almost an afterthought today. Creators are better paid and receive royalties at Marvel and DC, a change Mullaney said might never have taken place if not for the pressure applied by defections to Eclipse. But neither company, after earlier experiments, publishes much creator-owned work. And these days the Big Two are bigger and more corporate than ever under ownership by Disney, in Marvel's case, and Warners, in DC's.

"All the battles we had over creator rights, in some respects, they paid off. In other respects, it's not even an issue," Mullaney lamented.

That said, Eclipse was and is admired. In a 1988 statement on Eclipse's anniversary, distributor Bud Plant wrote in part: "Publishing unique non-superhero comics and initiating the graphic novel were high-risk undertakings at the time, but Eclipse's enthusiasm and admiration for the comic medium motivated them to explore the boundaries of what comics can offer...and to go beyond them."

Looking back, Mullaney said his timing was excellent in entering the publishing world at the dawn of the direct market, when retailers were hungry for material to sell, but poor in pushing too hard for bookstore sales before that world was ready to accept comics. He's proud he got to publish Kirby, Ditko and Siegel, and the last book of Caniff's work in the artist's lifetime. He's surprised and thrilled to be back in comics.

"I count my blessings every day that I have a second career in comics at 60," Mullaney said. "Those were the days — but these are the days now, too."

Eclipse lives on in another way. Mullaney's new imprint, EuroComics, under which Pratt, Gimenez and perhaps others will be published, has a logo that looks almost identical to Eclipse's.

"It's just a little nod to the Eclipse days. EuroComics, Eclipse Comics. It works," Mullaney said brightly. "Those who are too young may think it's just a cool design, and the old farts can look at it and say, 'I remember that.'"

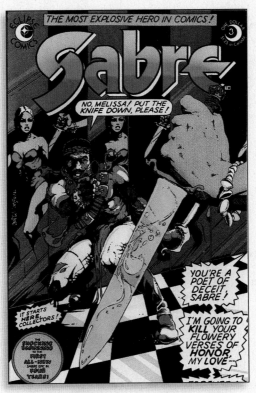

Truman's Scout

BY **SCOTT BRADEN**

From the pages of Starslayer, Grimjack *and his graphic novel* Time Beavers *at First Comics to the reboot of DC Comics' Hawkman mythos with* Hawkworld, *writer-artist Timothy Truman has offered readers hard-boiled action and no small amount of grit. While his career has been distinctly varied, it was at Eclipse in the 1980s that Truman created and launched what is perhaps his signature character and title,* Scout. *As he prepares to reintroduce the world he invented in* Scout: Marauder, *Truman talked with CBM about the character and the story.*

TIMOTHY TRUMAN'S
SCOUT
ECLIPSE COMICS
FIRST ISSUE!
No. 1
$1.75
Plus: FASHION IN ACTION

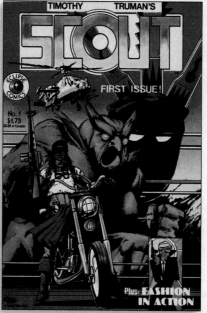

CBM: What's the story behind the creation of *Scout*?

Timothy Truman (TT): I'd always been interested in Native American culture when I was growing up. My great-grandmother on my father's side was a full-blooded Cherokee, and I'm sure that played a part in it. In college, the interest intensified and I started reading a lot of scholarly studies and histories about various Native American tribes. Finally, my wife Beth purchased a big, thick book by a historian named Arthur Haley called *Apaches: A Culture and History Portrait* and gave it to me for my birthday. That book really set the scene for coming up with *Scout*. I became intensely interested in Apache culture.

It was the Reagan era, so, as an unrepentant leftist, I saw things going on around me that concerned me quite a bit. So I speculated about what might happen if these things were allowed to progress and eventually pictured this bleak future where America had basically become an impoverished third-world nation. It seemed to me that the only person who might have any sort of hope of existing in such a future would be someone with these old school traditional Apache cultural ideals that I was reading about. So before I knew it, the whole scenario for the *Scout* series appeared.

CBM: What can you tell us about the huge popularity of the series?

TT: To give a bit of background, the original series was published by Eclipse Comics in two series, *Scout* and *Scout: War Shaman*. A one-shot *Scout Handbook* and a couple of spin-off titles were also published. The story takes place in the near-future in a sort of ravaged, impoverished, dystopian United States. The country has split off into various smaller states or governments, the main one being centered in the American Southwest, called New America.

The star of the series is an Apache named Emanuel Santana who is AWOL from a special Army training program. Scout learns, or at least thinks, that he is the reincarnation of the mythical Apache hero, Child of Water, and that it's his mission to destroy the Four Monsters of Apache legend. The monsters have taken the form of

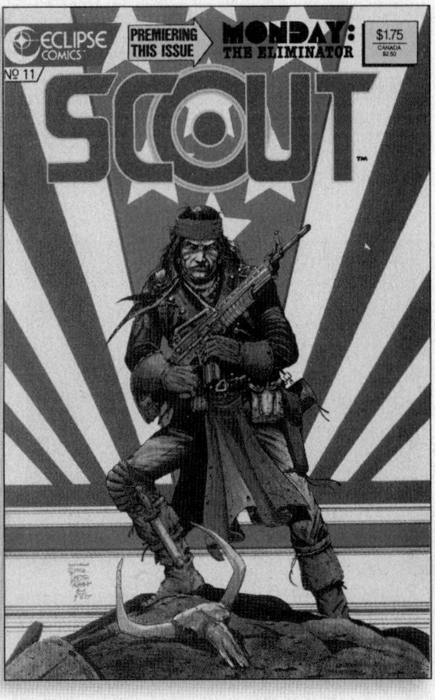
ECLIPSE COMICS
PREMIERING THIS ISSUE
MONDAY: THE ELIMINATOR
$1.75
№ 11
SCOUT

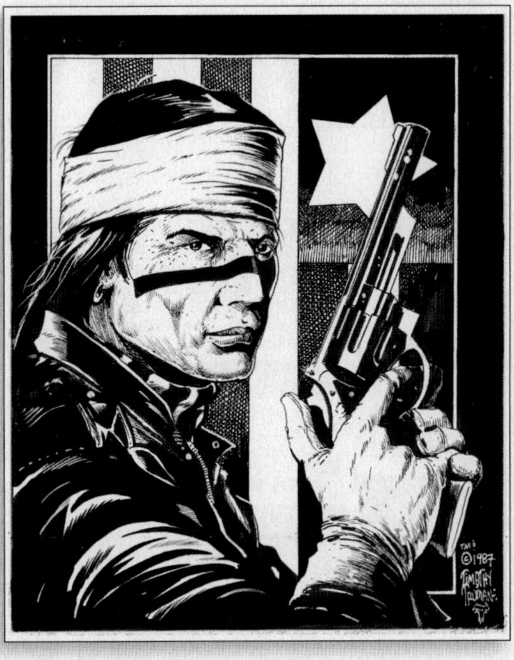

four businessmen and statesmen aligned with acting President, Jerry Grail – himself a former pro-wrestler. The reader never knows whether or not the Monsters are real or just a figment of Santana's imagination.

The second series, *Scout: War Shaman*, takes place about a decade or so after the first series, chronologically, during which time Scout married and had two small children, Tahzey and Victorio. After his wife dies, he and the boys set out on a trek across the southwest. Most people were really taken with the second series - the fact that you have this outlaw who has been branded a terrorist by the government who is on the run and must worry about the welfare and safety of his two small children. In what was a pretty dramatic step for the time, at the end of the series, Scout dies. One boy, Tahzey, is adopted by one of Santana's allies, a militant missionary named Rev. Sanddog Yuma. However, the fate of the youngest boy, Victorio, is uncertain. When we last see him, he's very much alone, hiding in some rocks. Keeping his fate uncertain was a deliberate move on my part, as readers will hopefully discover in *Scout: Marauder*.

I'm very proud of what the series accomplished, especially for the way it was accepted by Native American readers who followed it. I studied Apache culture and tradition quite intensely and tried to be respectful of Apache beliefs and traditions. In his book, *Native Americans in Comic Books: A Critical Study* author Michael A. Sheyahshe noted that "*Scout* is presented in a respectful and genuine manner with tribally specific cultural ties."

The series was used in several Native literature classes as an example of a positive portrayal of Native American characters. The series represents some of my earliest writing and drawing, when I was just finding my footing, but the respect it garnered from the Native American community is a thing I'm very, very proud of. Before *Scout*, Native Americans in comics were represented as some sort of single, pre-fabricated, generic, mythological, feather-and-fringe wearing tribe. *Scout* was the first comic series to focus on the traditions and cultures of a single tribe - the Apaches of the southwest.

So I was very serious about the research I did. I think the series helped comics readers realize that there are actually several different Native American tribal groups in the U.S., and that each tribe can be as distinct from one another as, say, the Irish are from the Chinese.

In addition to working on Scout: Marauder, *Truman has provided several illustrations for the* Robert E. Howard's Conan *role-playing game, the script for the next* King Conan *miniseries that he and Tomas Giorello are doing for Dark Horse Comics, a big poster for a big live presentation of the classic David Bowie album* The Rise and Fall of Ziggy Stardust *that a popular local band will be doing in Lancaster, Pennsylvania in October. For updates and more information about his work, his website is www.timothytruman.com.*

Look for more coverage of Scout *in our weekly email newsletter,* Scoop, *and in our Free Comic Book Day issue of* Comic Book Marketplace.

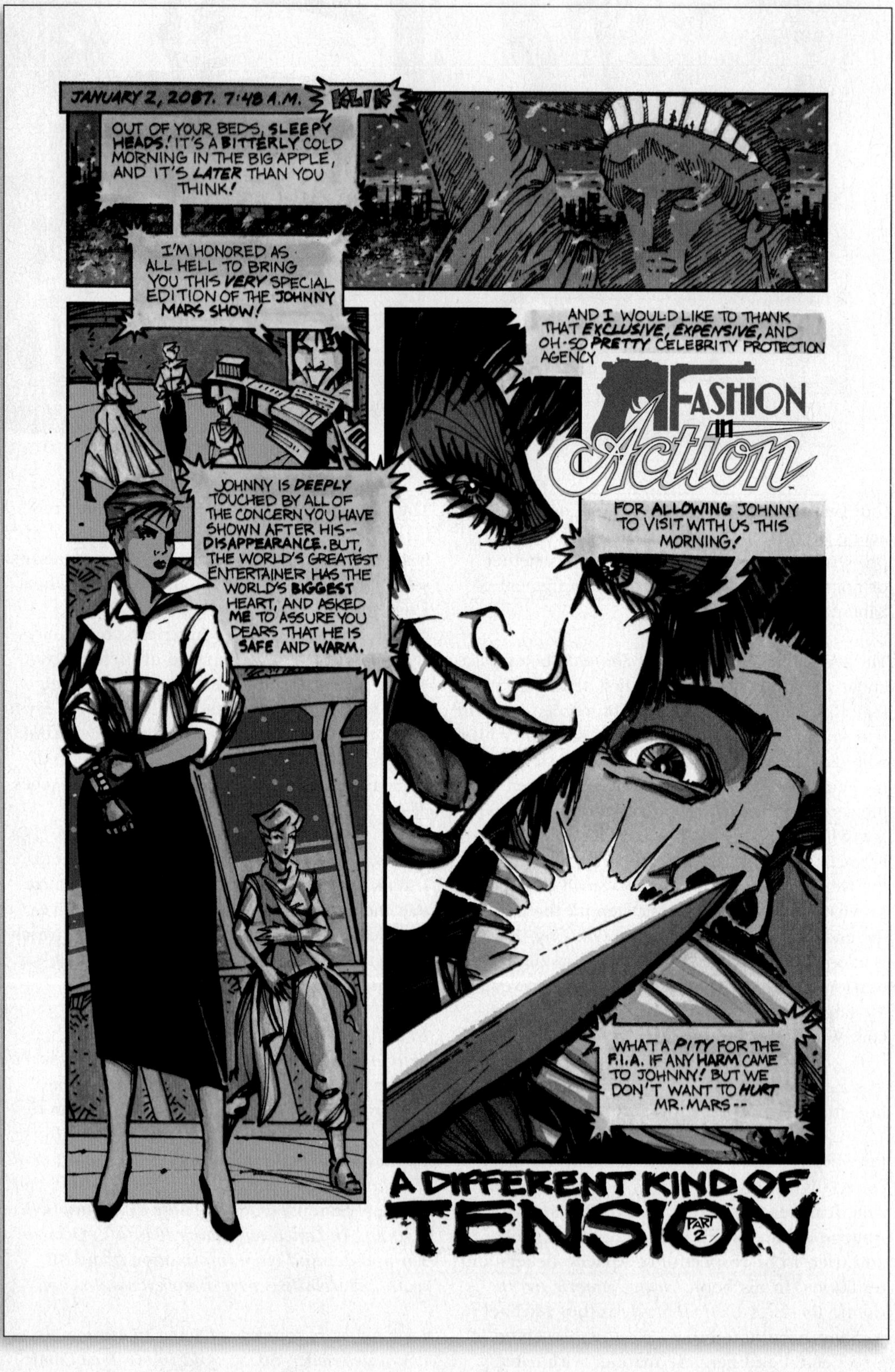

JANUARY 2, 2087. 7:48 A.M.
KLIK
OUT OF YOUR BEDS, SLEEPY HEADS! IT'S A BITTERLY COLD MORNING IN THE BIG APPLE, AND IT'S LATER THAN YOU THINK!
I'M HONORED AS ALL HELL TO BRING YOU THIS VERY SPECIAL EDITION OF THE JOHNNY MARS SHOW!
AND I WOULD LIKE TO THANK THAT EXCLUSIVE, EXPENSIVE, AND OH-SO PRETTY CELEBRITY PROTECTION AGENCY
FASHION in Action
FOR ALLOWING JOHNNY TO VISIT WITH US THIS MORNING!
JOHNNY IS DEEPLY TOUCHED BY ALL OF THE CONCERN YOU HAVE SHOWN AFTER HIS-- DISAPPEARANCE. BUT, THE WORLD'S GREATEST ENTERTAINER HAS THE WORLD'S BIGGEST HEART, AND ASKED ME TO ASSURE YOU DEARS THAT HE IS SAFE AND WARM.
WHAT A PITY FOR THE F.I.A. IF ANY HARM CAME TO JOHNNY! BUT WE DON'T WANT TO HURT MR. MARS--
A DIFFERENT KIND OF TENSION PART 2

Fashion in Action
The Pioneering Female Action Hero Team

BY J.C. VAUGHN

When writer-artist John K. Snyder III's *Fashion in Action* debuted in the pages of Tim Truman's *Scout* from Eclipse Comics, it was like nothing else on the market. These days, the revolutionary nature of *FIA* might be overlooked because it's no longer as uncommon for a team of non-super-powered women to be the focus of comic book stories. Back in 1985, it was groundbreaking.

Fashion in Action centers on the exploits of an all-female celebrity protection agency owned and run by the enigmatic Frances Knight. Set in the late 2080s, FIA's assignments to protect high-profile clients often result in well-dressed political intrigue and world-saving adventures.

"There had been a news story about concert-goers being attacked by gangs leaving a free show in Central Park in the summer of 1983, and that got me thinking about the concept of a futur-istic bodyguard service. Combined with numerous drawings in my sketchbooks that reflected my interest in music, art-deco, music videos - a grow-ing medium at the time - noir films, and the design work that was being done in the movies in that era, *Blade Runner, Alien, Escape from New York* – there was a lot to draw from and be inspired by in the late '70s/early '80s. Plus it was a very rocky time economically and politically," Snyder said of the concept's origin.

In a market in which *Danger Girl* has been around since 1998 and *Buffy the Vampire Slayer* has lived on in comic book form after the show's demise, it's easy enough for the pioneering status of his work to be overshadowed, but how deliber-ate was Snyder's decision to create the first action-hero series with an all-female main cast?

"There had been other kinds of all-female super-hero teams, but nothing that was like what I was aiming for, more of a femme fatale group of all types, not just one body form, and a variety of per-sonalities, with an emphasis on individuality. And

no superpowers," he said.

Prior to starting work on his own project, Snyder had worked with Truman on his *Time Beavers* graphic novel for First Comics. That led to *FIA* becoming a back-up feature in *Scout*.

"I had spent a month with Tim and his fam-ily while we worked on *Time Beavers*, during that period Tim had expressed interest in what he saw in my sketchbook, and urged me to fine-tune the rough ideas to be presented as a back-up for *Scout*," he said.

Once he had the concept for the team, he said it came together quickly. "I had so many ideas, it didn't take long to put together a proposal and submit it to Cat Yronwode and Dean Mullaney at Eclipse," he said.

Unlike many second features, it received cover blurbs and imagery. Following its run in Truman's title, Eclipse published two *FIA* specials.

"The interest in *Fashion in Action* had grown to the point where Eclipse was ready to give the series a shot with the specials. I was quite taken with the positive response to the series, very heart-felt letters from readers who really appreciated the representation of the female characters as more than stereotypes and 'got' the tongue-in-cheek style of the series," he said.

There were a lot of changes going on in comics at the time, and Snyder said his favorite part of that was being in the thick of it and having the luck to start out with his own creator-owned series.

"It was an exciting time, certainly for a newcom-er like me. I felt that I was encouraged to go with the material in any direction I wanted to with con-tent and style, there was a real sense of freedom there," he said.

Snyder is currently completing work on an adap-tation of a best-selling classic of detective fiction for a major publisher and says he has a few other surprises planned for the year ahead.

Mai the Psychic Girl

Manga in America

BY **CARRIE WOOD**

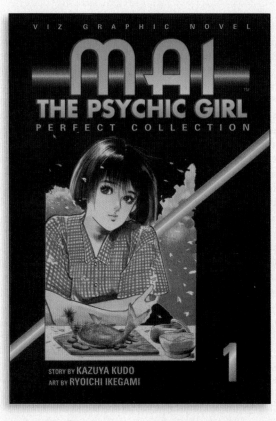

While anime and manga are now as dominant a force in pop culture as nearly anything, it wasn't always that way. The medium only slowly trickled into North America; first with anime series such as Astro Boy, Voltron *and* Speed Racer, *and then followed by manga. The first manga series to be officially translated and released in the American market were published in a partnership between Viz Media and Eclipse Comics. These series included* Area 88, The Legend of Kamui, *and* Mai the Psychic Girl.

Mai *in particular saw success thanks to its artwork by Ryoichi Ikegami, which was neither "too Japanese" nor "too American."*

VIZ GRAPHIC NOVEL
MAI
THE PSYCHIC GIRL
PERFECT COLLECTION
1
STORY BY KAZUYA KUDO
ART BY RYOICHI IKEGAMI

Mai the Psychic Girl *follows the story of Mai Kuju, a 14-year-old who realizes that she has powerful psychic abilities and is forced to go into hiding while being pursued by the Wisdom Alliance, a group bent on controlling the world. She must deal with not simply her powers, but how they have affected her family and friends; along the way Mai meets other children with similar powers who have been tasked with taking her down and bringing her to the Alliance.*

Dean Mullaney, currently the Creative Director of both The Library of American Comics and EuroComics imprints of IDW Publishing, was a co-founder of Eclipse Comics as well as its publisher. We spoke with him about his reflections on Mai the Psychic Girl *and its lasting impact on manga and comic books.*

CBM: Why was *Mai the Psychic Girl* chosen to be the first manga to officially be brought to North America?

Dean Mullaney (DM): When Shogakukan decided to enter the American market, it used Viz as its U.S. subsidiary and although they were publishers of long-standing in Japan, they knew very little about the American specialty comics market. They wanted a U.S. partner to guide them and Eclipse was the largest independent comics publisher of the time. After a series of negotiations, the decision was made for Eclipse and Viz to co-publish the new line. I created the "Eclipse International" imprint for these titles, an imprint that I also used for reprints of South American and Italian adventure comics.

Viz brought expertise and knowledge of manga, while Eclipse brought expertise in promotion, printing, and distribution. Viz chose the initial three titles, and I thought *Mai* should be the flagship series because I believed *Mai* was the most accessible to an American audience that was just beginning to appreciate manga. You have to remember that this was the first line of manga to be published in the U.S. Other publishers had tried individual titles or books, but not on this scale. So it was new to most of our audience. Kazuya Kudo created a character who readers could identify with; in many ways, it's a coming of age story told in a rich fantasy world. And Ryoichi Ikegami's art is just amazing.

VIZ GRAPHIC NOVEL
MAI
THE PSYCHIC GIRL
PERFECT COLLECTION
2
STORY BY KAZUYA KUDO
ART BY RYOICHI IKEGAMI

MAI
THE PSYCHIC GIRL
PERFECT COLLECTION
3
STORY BY KAZUYA KUDO
ART BY RYOICHI IKEGAMI

CBM: The series was presented in a "flipped" format, reading left-to-right instead of the original right-to-left. Did you run into any art issues by flipping everything?
DM: Sure! It was a tremendous amount of work, more having to do with reshaping word balloons than anything else.

CBM: Was there ever an argument for leaving the book in its original right-to-left format?
DM: Not that I recall.

CBM: What was the initial reaction from readers to the publishing of *Mai*?
DM: Readers loved it! That is, the readers who bought it. Again, manga was new to most American readers. While artists such as Scott McCloud were espousing the joys of manga to U.S. comics fans, most American comics readers knew more about anime than they did manga. It should also be pointed out that during this time there was a chasm separating readers' thoughts about color comics versus black-and-white comics; many American fans wouldn't even try a black-and-white comic.

CBM: The other two manga series that were published by Eclipse at that time were *Area 88* and *The Legend of Kamui*. How does *Mai* stand out from the others?
DM: While I enjoyed all three series, *Mai* stood out to me personally because I found the story enthralling. In terms of sales, the three series did about the same, although if memory serves me correctly, *Area 88* sold best, although none of the manga approached the sales levels of Eclipse's top series such as *Miracleman* and *Airboy*. A smart move Viz made was to choose three completely different types of series to start the line—basically, a "something for everyone" approach. All three series had their merits, as did *Xenon*, the fourth title.

CBM: The success of *Mai* and the other early titles opened the door for Eclipse to publish more manga, such as *Appleseed*, before the company shut down in '93. Were there plans for any other manga titles to release before the shutdown?
DM: No. *Appleseed*, by the way, ended up the best-selling manga we published.

CBM: *Mai the Psychic Girl* was published in a partnership between Eclipse and Viz. With Viz now being one of the most dominant anime and manga distributors in North America, how significant of a part did *Mai* play in the company's development?
DM: I'd say that it was *very* significant. I knew from the start that our partnership was temporary. Shogakukan made it clear that they wanted to learn the ropes from Eclipse, and I fully expected that they would go out on their own as soon as they felt comfortable with the American distribution system.

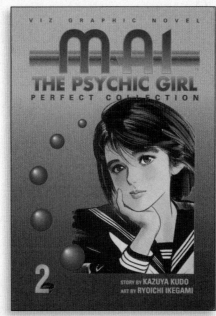

Winterworld:

Chuck Dixon and Jorge Zaffino on Ice

BY **J.C. VAUGHN**

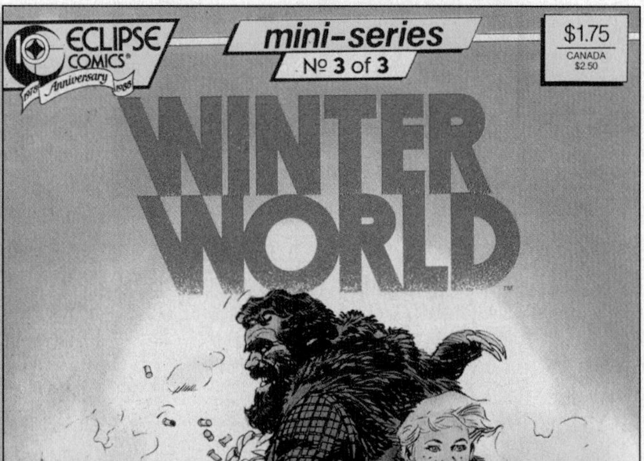
ECLIPSE COMICS
mini-series
№ 3 of 3
$1.75
CANADA $2.50
WINTER WORLD
DIXON ZAFFINO

In 1985, writer Chuck Dixon – these days better known as the creator of Batman's Bane, among many others – had gotten the gig writing Eclipse's Airboy. *After delivering on that biweekly comic, he approached the company's Dean Mullaney and Cat Yronwode with his concept for* Winterworld, *a post-apocalyptic tale of the struggle for survival on a near future, nearly frozen Earth.*

Illustrated by the late Jorge Zaffino, it became a three-issue mini-series; the comic attracted a strong following and then disappeared, seemingly forever. Operative word: seemingly.

Dixon and IDW Publishing revived the title with a hardcover collecting the original mini-series and a previously unpublished Epic Comics second story, Wintersea, *in 2011 (with a second printing last year), followed by a new* Winterworld *series in 2014.*

Chuck Dixon has said (and written) that *Winterworld* came about pretty quickly after he saw Jorge Zaffino's artwork for the first time.

"His work had the raw vibrant quality of Joe Kubert with the attention to detail of Russ Heath. For me, that was an irresistible combination. Looking at his portfolio, my mind ran over various genres that I'd like to see him on. A dystopic survival story leapt out at me from the pages," Dixon said.

"I had been looking to do something in that sub-genre with no firm plans. When I saw Jorge's work it came together in an instant. A post-apocalypse saga where weather played a part," he said. "I was showing the samples and treatment to other publishers who were kind of ho-hum about it. Dean saw what I saw in Jorge's work."

The Eclipse era was still the early days for creator-ownership in American comics, and Dixon described the working relationship with the publisher as organic.

"There was nothing corporate there. That's not to suggest that it was an unprofessional outfit. It was a smooth operation driven by enthusiasm and sold through guerilla marketing. I've met very few people smarter than Dean in this business. And their creator-owned contract was iron-bound, bullet-proof and the best, the most fair, of any I've signed," he said.

Dixon and Zaffino clicked as a team.

"Despite a language barrier - we were both monolingual - we really got each other. In one script I had a character close a scene by saying 'f--- you' to someone as he walks away. The publisher felt uncomfortable with that so I took it out of the script and had the character walk away silently. Jorge never saw that first draft and yet, when the art came back, the character was giving the other guy the finger as he walked away," he said.

After the end of *Winterworld*, there was about eight years before Carl Potts asked Dixon if he'd be interested in continuing the series for Epic.

"I had a trilogy in mind beforehand. *Winterworld*, *Wintersea*, *Winterwar*," Dixon said. Before it could come to pass, though, came the 1990s market implosion and Potts' departure from Marvel.

The artwork sat on a shelf there for a few years before eventually being returned to Zaffino. In the interim, Dixon and Zaffino collaborated on two Punisher graphic novels for Marvel, *Kingdom Gone* and *Assassin's Guild*, and the Conan story "The Horned God" for the publisher's *Savage Sword of Conan*. Both completed many other stories independent of each other as well.

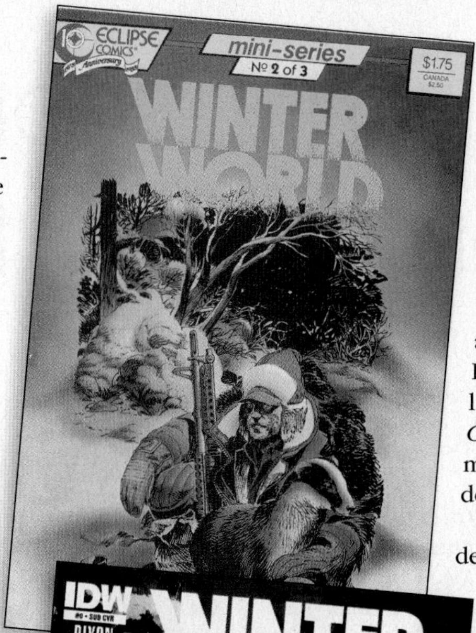
ECLIPSE COMICS
mini-series
No 2 of 3
$1.75
WINTER WORLD

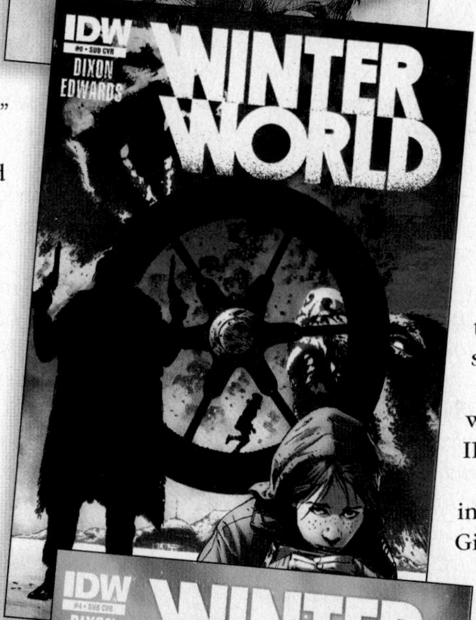
IDW
DIXON
EDWARDS
WINTER WORLD

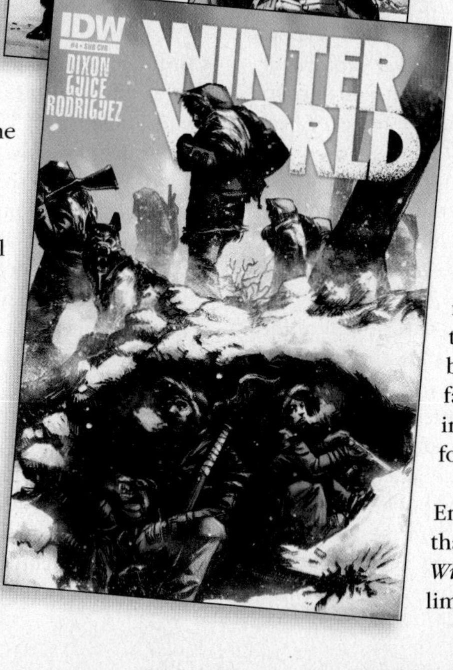
IDW
DIXON
GUICE
RODRIGUEZ
WINTER WORLD

Zaffino passed away suddenly due to a heart attack at age 43 in 2002.

When Zaffino died, Dixon didn't foresee bringing it back.

"For me it always felt 'too soon.' It was a property tied to Jorge in my mind. After a while I began to think about returning to it. But only if I could have top art talent [on it]," he said.

And that's what happened with the new material from IDW.

Butch Guice penciled and inked the first arc, Tomas Giorello handled the second one, and Esteve Polls drew the *Winter Fleet* arc, and Tommy Lee Edwards illustrated *Winterworld* #0. Zaffino's son, artist Gerardo Zaffino, has contributed covers.

In addition to the hardcover/soft cover black-and-white collection of the original series and *Wintersea*, there are two trade paperbacks and a prose novel thus far, and the next trade will include *Wintersea* in color for the first time.

In April 2014, IDW Entertainment announced that they are developing *Winterworld* as a live-action limited series.

Beau Smith's Journey From Fan to Pro

BY SCOTT BRADEN

One of the many great things about the funny book business is that the fans have a voice in what transpires in their favorite books, as well as the chance – with the right guidance, the right story ideas, and the right contacts – to creatively participate in the four-color process of making comic books. Take veteran creator Beau Smith, for example. In his West Virginia-based Flying Fist Ranch and thereabouts, he first entered comics as a prolific letter column writer – which in turn helped him become a fan-favorite comic book scribe for DC Comics' Guy Gardner: Warrior *and his creator-owned* Wynonna Earp, *among other projects. Yeah, we know what you're thinking — if all he did was write to comic book publishers, then what was the secret of his success? Read on and find out.*

CBM: As a fan, you were a prolific letter column writer. How did you decide which comic books to write to?

Beau Smith: Back in the late 1970s, before I began my professional writing career, before the internet, before fax machines and other sources of communication technology, I figured that the only way an aspiring writer was going to make any connection with Marvel and DC comics was to write letters to the editors. The letter columns in the back of the comic books were the focal point of fan/reader communication. That was where I was going to do my networking. I decided that I would write a letter of comment to

each comic book that I bought each week, and that put me at about 10 letters a week. I only wrote to the comic books that I liked and read. I wasn't going to waste my time and money writing to comic books that I didn't enjoy. I knew then I had to market myself differently from the other folks writing letters, so I signed my full name, Stephen Scott Beau Smith. I also made sure that I did my best to make each letter entertaining as well as constructive. I must have done something right because from 1978 through 1986 I had over 300 letters printed in comics. It also helped when I attended conventions and introduced myself to editors. I'd usually get the "Hey! I know you! You're the guy with four names that writes me all the time!" Well, it worked. Pretty soon editors were sending me advance copies of upcoming series so that I would write letters for their letters pages. Relationships were built and soon the editors asked me to send in pitches and story ideas. I'm sneaky like that.

CBM: Did your letter column writing introduce you to other future comic book creators?

Beau Smith: Yup! There were other guys that were doing the same thing I was during that time period. We would sometimes exchange letters and shared opinions. Some of the other creators that were writing letters during that time period were Mark Waid, Todd McFarlane, Chuck Dixon, Kurt Busiek, Kevin Dooley, just to name a few. In fact, if my faded memory serves me right, there was an issue of *Supergirl* that had letters from me, Todd McFarlane and Mark Waid in the same letters page. Before I started writing letters of comment to comics I remember growing up reading the printed letters of future comic book creators such as Dave Cockrum, Marv Wolfman, Len Wein, Tony Isabella, Gerry Conway, Frank Miller, Gary Groth, Dean Mullaney, and many others. I made some really great lifetime friends from the letter columns.

CBM: Did your letter column writing introduce you to editors?

Beau Smith: Yeah, it did. I met DC editors and creators Alan Gold (*Blue Devil*), Ernie Colon (*The Flash*), Murray Boltinoff, (*G.I. Combat*), Robert Kanigher (*Sgt. Rock*), Joe Kubert (*Sgt. Rock*), and Marvel Editors and creators Jim Shooter, Walt Simonson, Louise Simonson, Tom DeFalco, and Roy Thomas. All of them were super helpful in getting me started in writing comic books in one way or another. Walt Simonson sent me plot proposals to learn from, Joe Kubert gave me advice on how best to write for an artist, and Robert Kanigher became a very good friend and taught me hours and hours of story-telling lessons. I couldn't ask for a better foundation for my career.

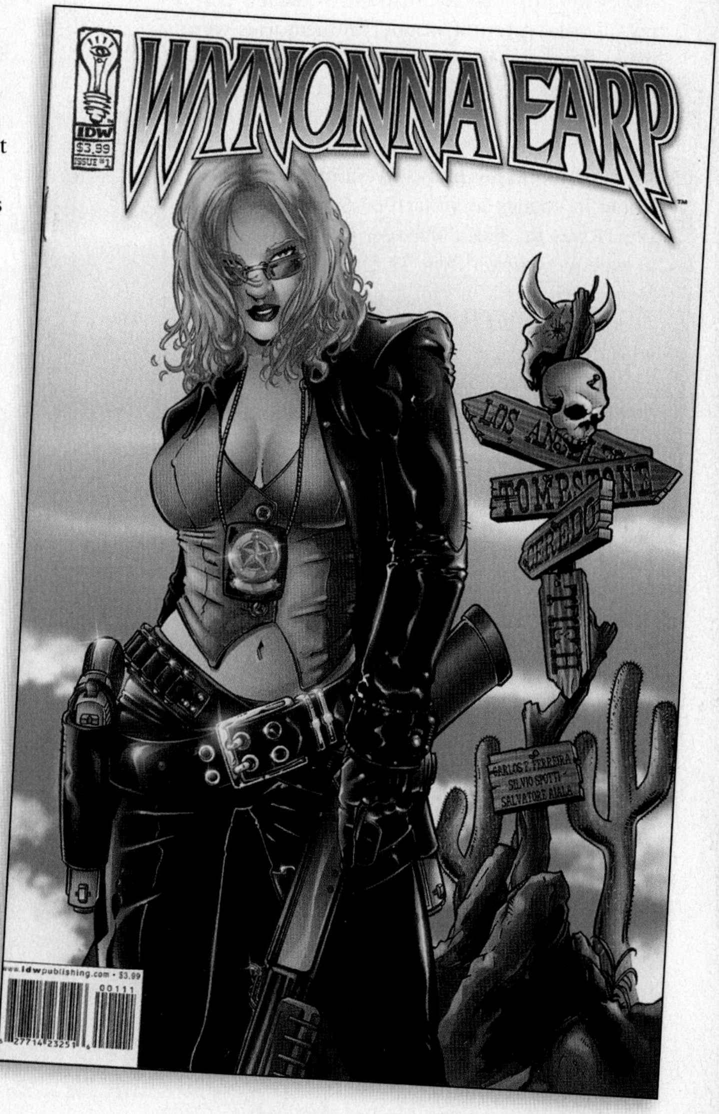
WYNONNA EARP
IDW
$3.99
ISSUE #1
TOMBSTONE
CARLOS E. FERREIRA
SILVIO SPOTTI
SALVATORE AIALA
www.idwpublishing.com • $3.99

CBM: Which editors did you first work with as a young comic book writer?

Beau Smith: My first editor was Cat Yronwode at Eclipse Comics where my writing career began. Cat was a tough, but fair editor. She put my grammar-poor butt through boot camp and I thank her for that. I needed it badly. She pretty much left me alone with my story ideas and characters, giving me the freedom to create and I appreciated that. At DC Comics, Kevin Dooley was my first editor there on my *Green Lantern Quarterly* story. Kevin was a huge help in the fact that he trained me on how to work with DC Comics and long established characters. He and his then-assistant editor, Eddie Berganza, were wonderful sounding boards on creative ideas and character traits. Tight bonds were made.

Tim Truman was my player/coach at Eclipse Comics when I started out. He knew the creative ropes and how much slack or how tight they needed to be. We was an immense help in forming the way I write and see a story. I also have to mention, even though he was not an editor of mine, early on, writer Mike Baron took me under his wing and taught me a lot about writing by sending me his layout scripts from *Nexus* and *The Badger*. I still have them today. My friend Chuck Dixon also taught me a lot with his scripts that help me crawl through the mine field of how to pitch an editor.

CBM: As a comics pro, which conventions did you first go to when you were starting out?

Beau Smith: Living in Huntington, West Virginia, I didn't really have much access early on to conventions. Before he went to work for Marvel Comics in promotions, Steve Safeel, a Huntington native, worked with Marshall University in putting on a sci-fi convention here in Huntington. That was my first one back in 1983. Ron Frenz was the comic book guest there. We struck up a lifetime friendship there. The next year I was sent to my first really major convention, Chicago Con. I was sent there via Westfield Comics to give a reader's report to their subscribers in the *Westfield*

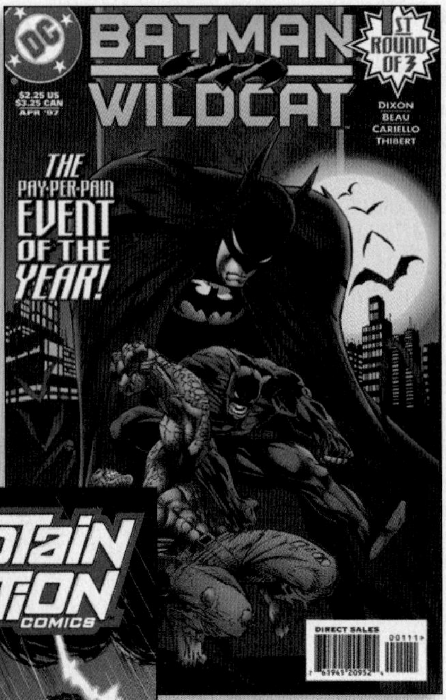
DC
BATMAN
WILDCAT
1ST ROUND OF 3
$2.25 US
$3.25 CAN
APR '97
DIXON
BEAU
CARIELLO
THIBERT
THE PAY-PER-PAIN EVENT OF THE YEAR!
DIRECT SALES

Newsletter. To this day, that 1983 Chicago Con is my favorite. A ton of wonderful memories were made there and it still seems like a dream to me in my mind. It was there I met such creators as Sergio Aragonés, Mike Grell, Jim Shooter, Peter David, Robert Greenberger, John Romita, Sr. and so many more. My first convention as a professional in comics was the 1987 San Diego Comic Con. I was the Sales Manager for Eclipse Comics as well as writing "Beau La Duke's Tip For Real Men" in the back of Tim Truman's *Scout* comics. That con also doubled as a honeymoon for my wife, Beth and me. An amazing time was had. This was before San Diego had remodeled the downtown and Gas Lamp area. In fact, now that I think about it, this summer celebrates my 25 years working in comics!

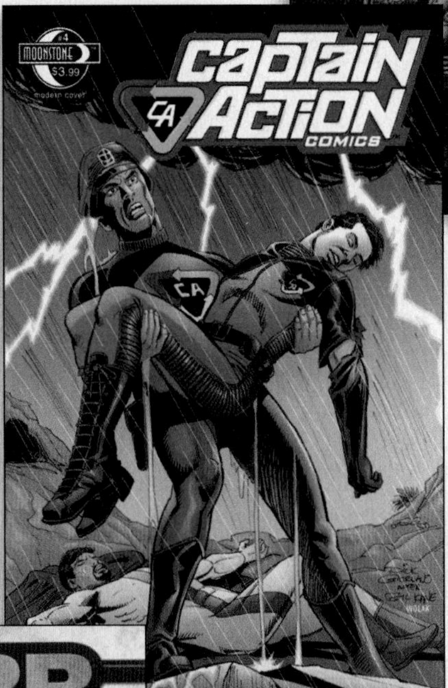
#4
MOONSTONE
$3.99
modern cover
Captain Action
CA
COMICS

CBM: How did you enter the business and become a comics pro?

Beau Smith: It was during that 1984 Chicago Con that I met Tim Truman for the first time. Tim was doing *GrimJack* at First Comics. We hit it off through our mutual West Virginian accents. We talked a long time about our West Virginia roots and remained in contact from that con forward. In 1987 Tim contacted me and told me that Eclipse Comics was looking for a Sales Manager. I was working in sales and marketing at that time for a local audio/video chain here in Huntington. Tim suggested that I apply for the job with Eclipse publisher, Dean Mullaney. The ABA (American Bookseller's Association) was being held in Washington, D.C. that year, so Dean flew me in to meet and work the show with him, Tim and Chuck Dixon. That was also my first meeting with Diamond Comics Distributors, Eclipse's biggest distributor at the time. I had a good meeting with Steve Geppi and Bill Schanes, once again, more lifetime friends in comics. Dean offered me the job, my only stipulation was that I wouldn't have to move. That was no problem since most of my work would be done by phone and traveling to the various conventions, distributor meetings and retail stores. I loved it and worked for Eclipse until 1994. Today, all these years later, I am once again working for Dean Mullaney at The Library of American Comics through IDW Publishing.

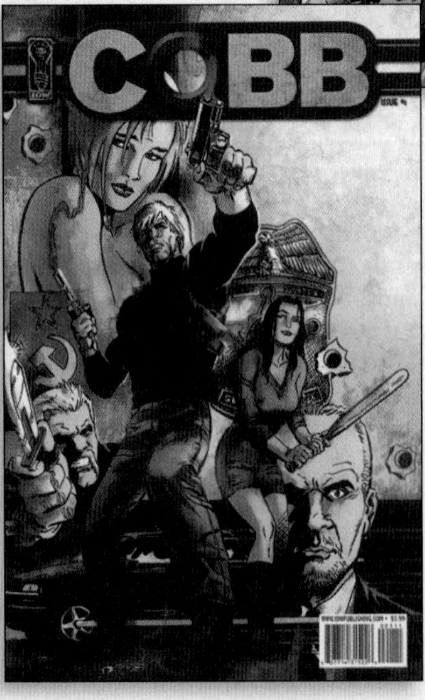
COBB
ISSUE 4

CBM: You worked with many different companies as a comics pro. Which of those companies did

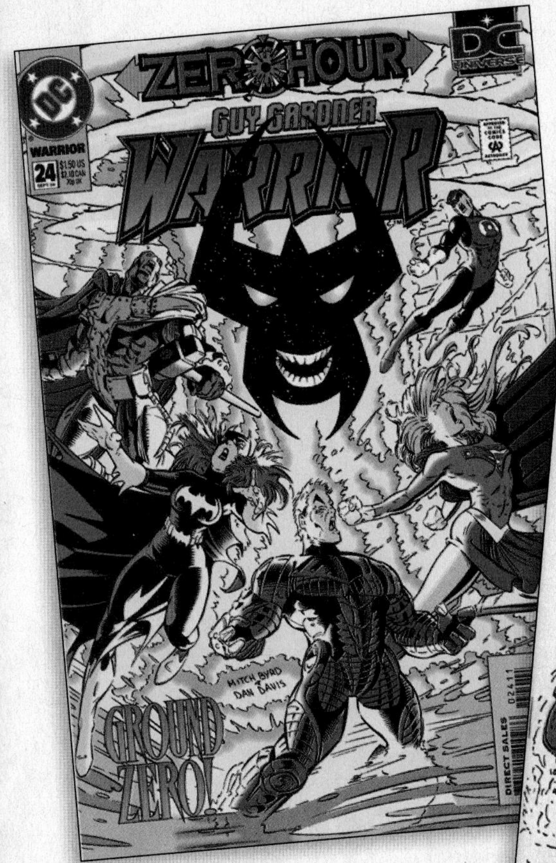
ZERO HOUR
DC UNIVERSE
GUY GARDNER
WARRIOR
24
GROUND ZERO!

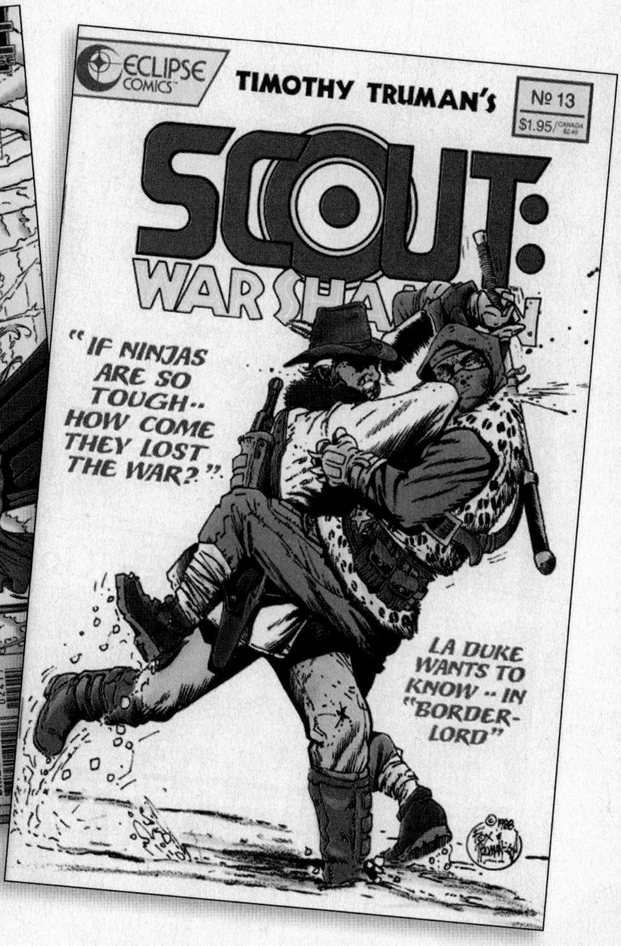
ECLIPSE COMICS
TIMOTHY TRUMAN'S
№ 13
SCOUT: WAR SHAMAN
"IF NINJAS ARE SO TOUGH.. HOW COME THEY LOST THE WAR?"
LA DUKE WANTS TO KNOW .. IN "BORDER-LORD"

you enjoy working for the most?

Beau Smith: As I mentioned, I think I enjoyed working for Eclipse Comics the most, as they say, your first is always retains the fondest memories. My time as VP of Marketing for Image Comics, Todd McFarlane Productions and McFarlane Toys was without a doubt the wildest. I got to be a part of something brand new from the start and work with it to make it one of the biggest creative changing forces in comics. It was the wild frontier in many ways, no rules, no boundaries and sometimes just flat out crazy. I enjoyed my years as VP at IDW Publishing a lot in the sense that I once again got to work for another friend and former Eclipse alumni, Ted Adams. IDW was without a doubt the smartest run company I have ever worked for. Ted Adams is the best business mind in comics today bar none. Just look at where the company has gone in such a short time. Its foundation is rock solid and its future is amazing.

CBM: What projects have you been working on lately?

Beau Smith: Currently on the business end, I'm the director of marketing for The Library Of American Comics. On the writing end, I'm working on a creator-owned western project of mine for Dark Horse called *200 People to Kill.* Originally the artist was my friend Eduardo Barreto, but since Eduardo passed away, and unfortunately so did artist and friend, Enrique Villagran. I am currently looking at new submissions for the project. Earlier this year, I had my creation *Wynonna Earp* optioned and greenlit for a new live-action TV series on SyFy, that I am very stoked about. It will air in April of 2016. For the future, I'm working on new plots for my *Cobb* series and another *Wynonna Earp* series. As always, I am the columnist for my long running pop culture column Beauology 101 for Westfield Comics (www.westfieldcomics.com). I am always seeking out new opportunities as a writer and on the marketing end of comics, so the phone rings and I take the calls. I hope the next 25 years turn out to be as much fun as the first.

This updated story appeared in different form in The Overstreet Guide To Collecting Comics.

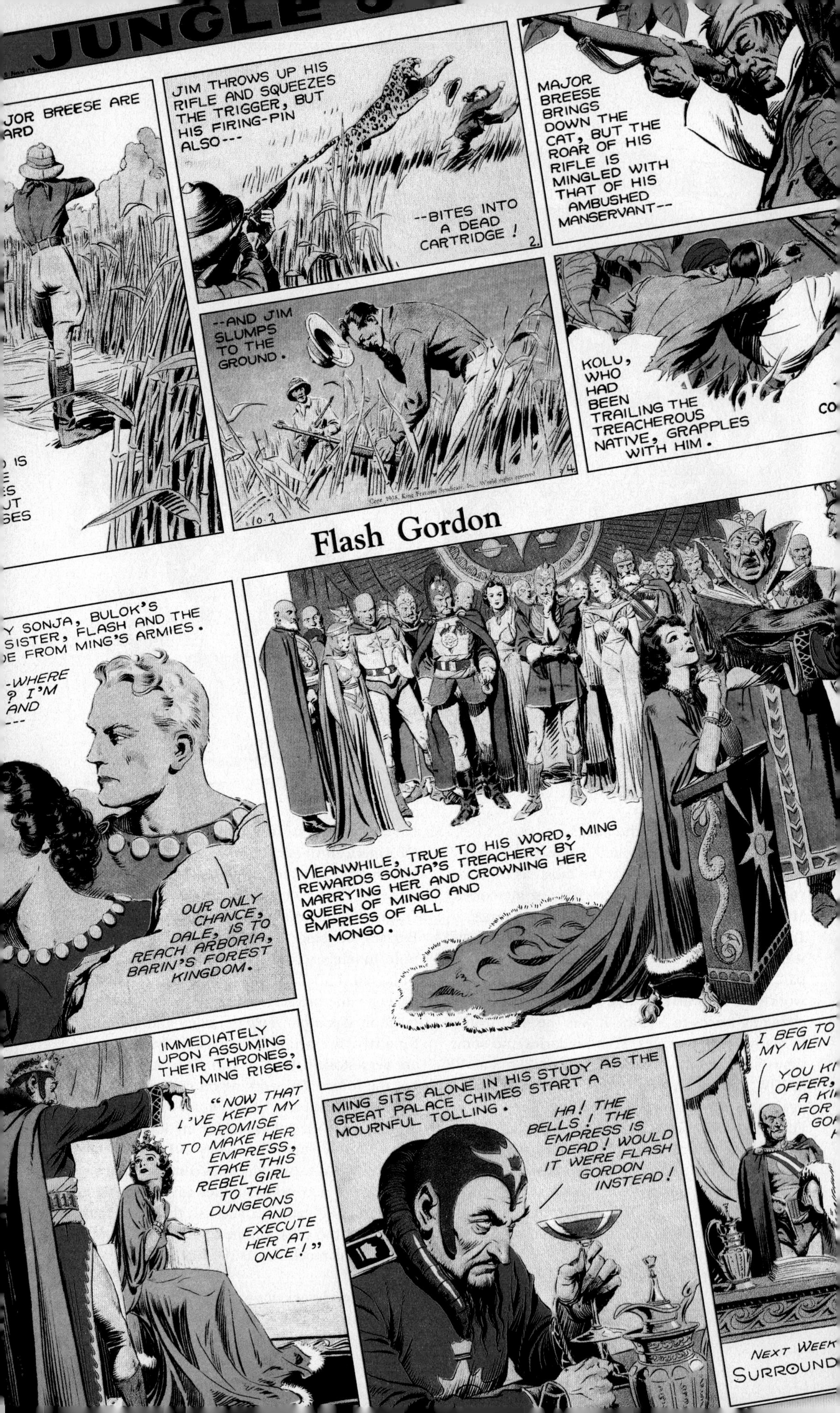
JUNGLE
JOR BREESE ARE
ARD
) IS
E
ES
UT
SES
JIM THROWS UP HIS RIFLE AND SQUEEZES THE TRIGGER, BUT HIS FIRING-PIN ALSO---
--BITES INTO A DEAD CARTRIDGE !
2.
MAJOR BREESE BRINGS DOWN THE CAT, BUT THE ROAR OF HIS RIFLE IS MINGLED WITH THAT OF HIS AMBUSHED MANSERVANT--
--AND JIM SLUMPS TO THE GROUND.
Copr 1935, King Features Syndicate, Inc., World rights reserved
KOLU, WHO HAD BEEN TRAILING THE TREACHEROUS NATIVE, GRAPPLES WITH HIM.
CO
Flash Gordon
Y SONJA, BULOK'S
SISTER, FLASH AND THE
DE FROM MING'S ARMIES.
-WHERE
? I'M
AND

OUR ONLY CHANCE, DALE, IS TO REACH ARBORIA, BARIN'S FOREST KINGDOM.
MEANWHILE, TRUE TO HIS WORD, MING REWARDS SONJA'S TREACHERY BY MARRYING HER AND CROWNING HER QUEEN OF MINGO AND EMPRESS OF ALL MONGO.
IMMEDIATELY UPON ASSUMING THEIR THRONES, MING RISES.
"NOW THAT I'VE KEPT MY PROMISE TO MAKE HER EMPRESS, TAKE THIS REBEL GIRL TO THE DUNGEONS AND EXECUTE HER AT ONCE!"
MING SITS ALONE IN HIS STUDY AS THE GREAT PALACE CHIMES START A MOURNFUL TOLLING.
HA! THE BELLS! THE EMPRESS IS DEAD! WOULD IT WERE FLASH GORDON INSTEAD!
I BEG TO
MY MEN
YOU K
OFFER,
A K
FOR
GO
NEXT WEEK
SURROUND

Head Librarian:

Dean Mullaney & The Library of American Comics

BY **J.C. VAUGHN**

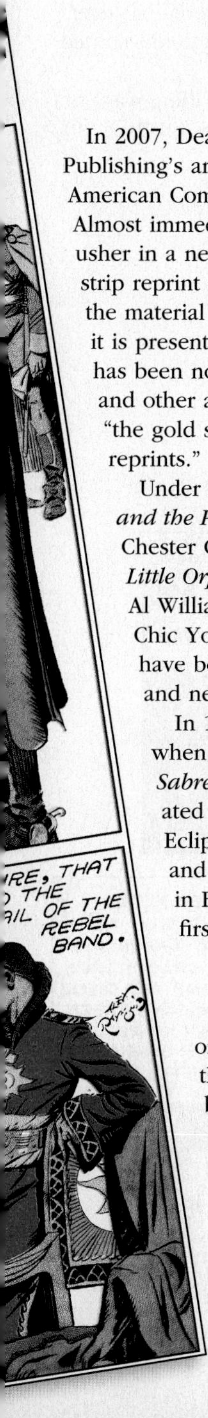
OF THE
REBEL
BAND.

In 2007, Dean Mullaney created IDW Publishing's archival imprint, The Library of American Comics, which he edits and designs. Almost immediately, his efforts began to usher in a new Golden Age of classic comic strip reprint collections, significant in both the material itself and the manner in which it is presented. In its first four years, LOAC has been nominated for nine Eisner awards and other accolades, and it has been called "the gold standard for archival comic strip reprints."

Under his guidance, Milton Caniff's *Terry and the Pirates*, Alex Raymond's *Rip Kirby*, Chester Gould's *Dick Tracy*, Harold Gray's *Little Orphan Annie*, Archie Goodwin and Al Williamson's *Secret Agent Corrigan*, Chic Young's *Blondie* and other strips have been showcased for seasoned fans and new readers alike.

In 1978, he launched Eclipse Comics when he published Don McGregor's *Sabre*, the first graphic novel created for the comics specialty market. Eclipse championed creator ownership and the first line of Japanese manga in English translations, and had the first digitally-colored comic book.

– *The Overstreet Hall of Fame*

Dean Mullaney might have originally been best known as the founder of Eclipse Comics, but for the past eight years The Overstreet Hall of Fame member has been staking a whole new claim to comic book history with his imprint The Library of American Comics (LOAC), which has released a prodigious number of archival collections through IDW Publishing.

From Alex Raymond's *Rip Kirby* to Archie Goodwin and Al Williamson's *Secret Agent Corrigan* and from Chic Young's *Blondie* to Cliff Sterrett's *Polly and Her Pals*, the Library of American Comics has offered either chronological presentations (most of the line) or "best of" selections (like *Bringing Up Father*) and they've won a number of awards doing so. *Little Orphan Annie*, *King Aroo*, *Dick Tracy*, and *Bloom County* have all found new magic in these collections, which have generally provided the best reproductions the material has ever seen.

The line kicked off with Milton Caniff's *Terry and the Pirates*, which ended up running six volumes, all of which are still kept in print.

"There's no better comic strip to inaugurate The Library of American Comics than Milton Caniff's masterpiece," Mullaney said at the time, and the acclaim LOAC and IDW received for the book was merely a harbinger of things to come. Multiple award nominations and wins have characterized the intervening years.

In addition to the strip reprint books, Mullaney, Associate Editor Bruce Canwell, Art Director Lorraine Turner, and company have also produced impressive career retrospective books, including *Scorchy Smith and the Art of Noel Sickles*, the *Genius* trilogy by Alex Toth (*Genius, Isolated*, *Genius, Illustrated*, and *Genius, Animated*), and *Caniff: A Visual Biography*.

The line has included insightful histories such as *What Fools These Mortals Be* (the story of *Puck* magazine), *The Dream That Never Was* (the story of Chuck Jones' mostly ill-fated *Crawford*), and the *King of Comics: 100 Years of King Features* (a 100-year retrospective of the syndicate's output).

Their roster includes a few surprises, too. While *Rip Kirby* by Alex Raymond was a natural, the series has continued with collections of the work of John Prentice, who took over the strip when Raymond died. The *Secret Agent Corrigan* collections, which featured the collaboration of Goodwin and Williamson, now includes a volume of the work by George Evans, who succeeded them, and they've also put out a volume with the complete *Secret Agent X-9* originals by Dashiel Hammett and Alex Raymond, which began the strip.

The volumes in the *LOAC Essentials* line have reprinted a year's worth of dailies of George Herriman's *Baron Bean* (two installments), Cliff Sterrett's *Polly and Her Pals*, Harry J. Tuthill's *The Bungle Family*, Sidney Smith's *The Gumps*, V.T Hamlin's *Alley Oop*, and Edgar Rice Burroughs' *Tarzan* (illustrated by Hal Foster and Rex Mason).

The other offerings range from *Archie* and *Amazing Spider-Man* to *Skippy* and Russ Manning's stint on *Tarzan*.

LOAC does not stand alone as archival publishers. Fantagraphics and Hermes Press, among others, have also released outstanding volumes that capture and preserve key elements of comics history.

By combining a historian's eye for detail, a fan's passion for celebrating the best material, and a journalist's drive to put things in context with the best reproduction the material has ever received, LOAC has time and again demonstrated that they know what they're doing.

And even with that they keep finding ways to surprise us. (Continues on Page 98)

Walt Disney's
DONALD DUCK
THE COMPLETE DAILY NEWSPAPER COMICS VOLUME 1 • 1938-1940

STEVE CANYON
by MILTON CANIFF
GEE, MR. CANYON, MR. ROMULUS BRANDYWINE HAS BEEN A LONG TIME CONFABING WITH THE BOSS OF THOSE FIGHTER PLANES WHICH FORCED US TO LAND AT THIS REBEL AIR FIELD...
YEAH, REED--- I WANTED TO EASE IN ON THAT CHINFEST, BUT BRANDYWINE WAVED ME AWAY - HE MUST HAVE PLENTY OF GUMPTION - OR NO BRAINS
LISTEN

TERRY AND THE PIRATES
by MILTON CANIFF
MASTER KLANG, FOR MUCH TIME WE BATTER THE VILLAGE OF THE DRAGON LADY WITH BOMB AND SHELL! FOR TWO DAYS THERE HAS BEEN NO REPLY FROM THE GUNS ON THE CLIFF!

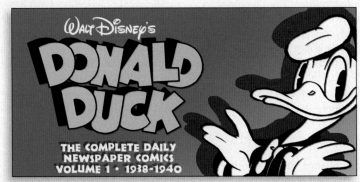

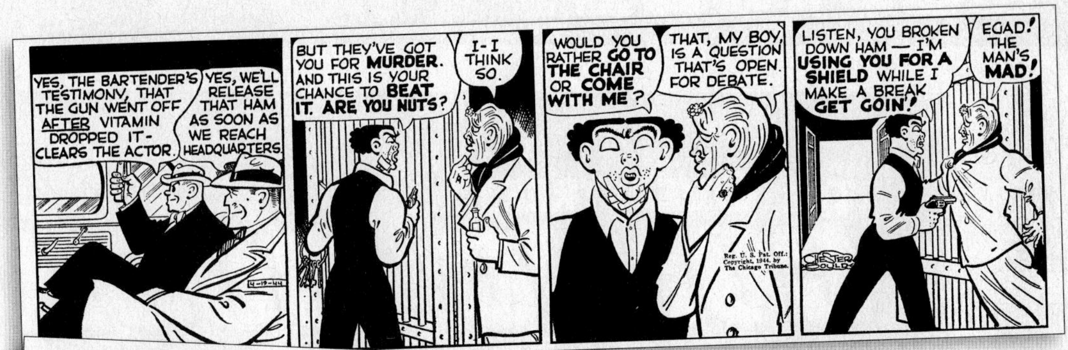
YES, THE BARTENDER'S TESTIMONY, THAT THE GUN WENT OFF AFTER VITAMIN DROPPED IT- CLEARS THE ACTOR.
YES, WE'LL RELEASE THAT HAM AS SOON AS WE REACH HEADQUARTERS.
4-19-44
BUT THEY'VE GOT YOU FOR MURDER. AND THIS IS YOUR CHANCE TO BEAT IT. ARE YOU NUTS?
I-I THINK SO.
WOULD YOU RATHER GO TO THE CHAIR OR COME WITH ME?
THAT, MY BOY, IS A QUESTION THAT'S OPEN FOR DEBATE.
Reg. U. S. Pat. Off.: Copyright, 1944, by The Chicago Tribune.
LISTEN, YOU BROKEN DOWN HAM — I'M USING YOU FOR A SHIELD WHILE I MAKE A BREAK GET GOIN'!
EGAD! THE MAN'S MAD!
CHESTER GOULD

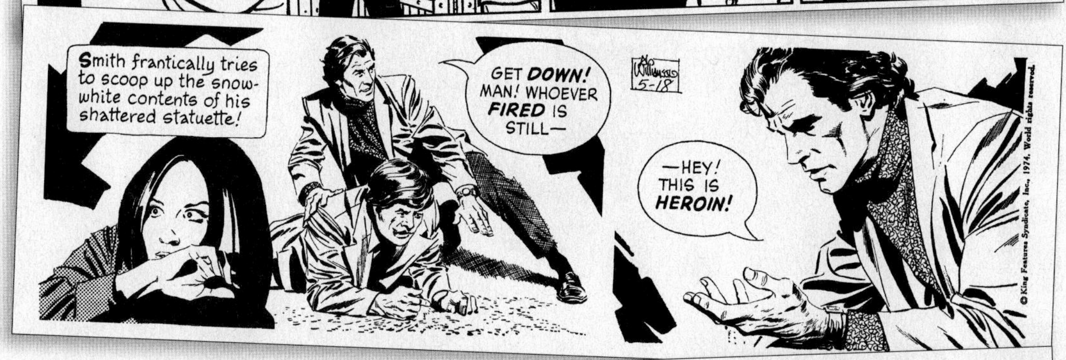
Smith frantically tries to scoop up the snow-white contents of his shattered statuette!
GET DOWN! MAN! WHOEVER FIRED IS STILL—
5-18
—HEY! THIS IS HEROIN!
© King Features Syndicate, Inc., 1974. World rights reserved.

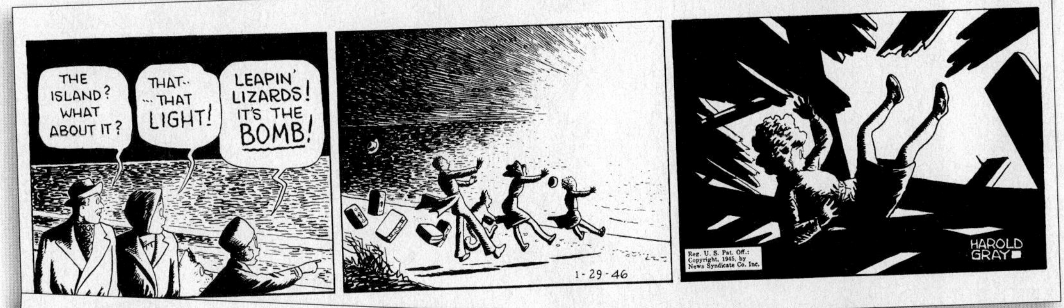
THE ISLAND? WHAT ABOUT IT?
THAT.. ..THAT LIGHT!
LEAPIN' LIZARDS! IT'S THE BOMB!
1-29-46
Reg. U. S. Pat. Off.: Copyright, 1945, by News Syndicate Co. Inc.
HAROLD GRAY

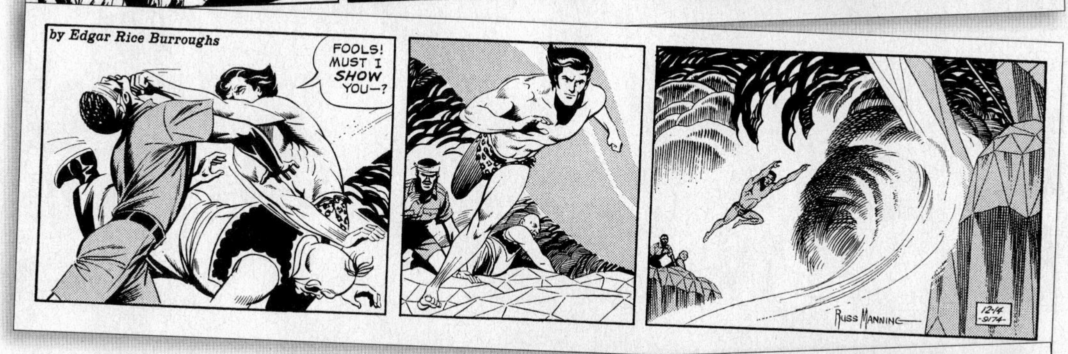
by Edgar Rice Burroughs
FOOLS! MUST I SHOW YOU—?
RUSS MANNING
12-14 -9/74-

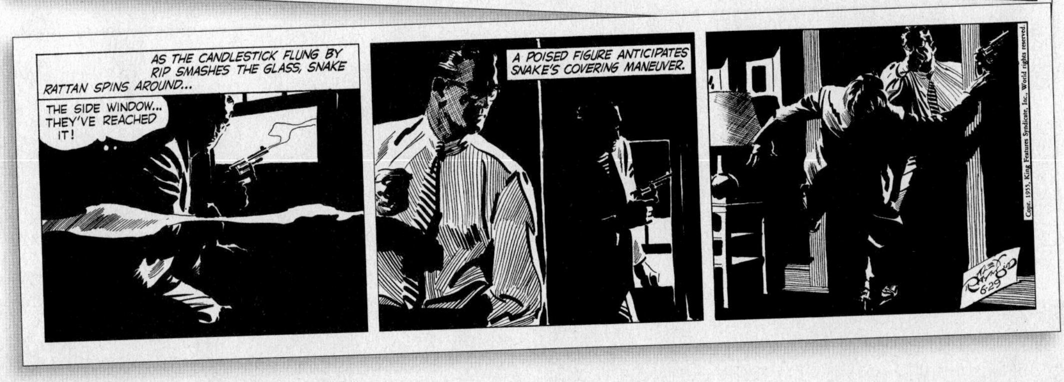
AS THE CANDLESTICK FLUNG BY RIP SMASHES THE GLASS, SNAKE RATTAN SPINS AROUND...
THE SIDE WINDOW... THEY'VE REACHED IT!
A POISED FIGURE ANTICIPATES SNAKE'S COVERING MANEUVER.
Copr. 1955, King Features Syndicate, Inc., World rights reserved.
6-29

GEMSTONE
PUBLISHING

SINCE 1970,
THE OVERSTREET COMIC BOOK PRICE GUIDE
HAS BEEN THE GO TO DESTINATION
FOR SERIOUS COMIC BOOK ENTHUSIASTS,
DEALERS AND HISTORIANS!

- **Full Page Color ads start at $2,500!**
- **Full Page B&W ads start at $900!**
- Save 10% when you take **three** or more ads
  of the same size & type!
- **Save 10% with our Early Bird rates!**
- **Save 20% with both discounts!**

For additional rates, specs or technical information, contact

Carrie Wood
Assistant Editor
(443) 318-8468
wcarrie@gemstonepub.com

Early Bird Deadline   **Standard Rate Deadline**
December 2, 2015   **March 4, 2016**

Keep it up, Dean!

COMMENTARY BY **MAGGIE THOMPSON**

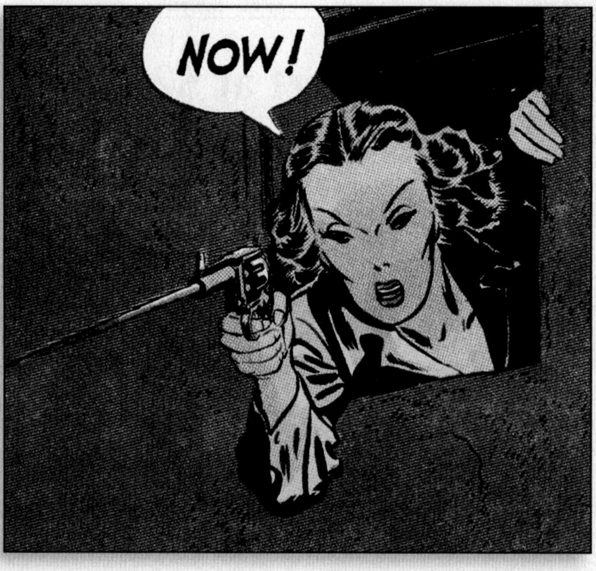
NOW!

The first time I talked with Dean Mullaney was (I think) in 1982; that was pretty much typical of many interactions in the world of comics in the 20th century. By that point, he'd already co-created Eclipse with his brother, published the trail-blazing *Sabre*, and, indeed, developed that company into pioneering the expansion of what the direct market had to offer the world of comics.

Within a year of that first meeting, my late husband, Don, and I were editing *Comics Buyer's Guide*, a weekly newspaper for comics collectors—and the interaction with Dean continued, eventually bringing Eclipse to our pages as a regular advertiser running its own one-page mini-newspaper.

When Eclipse went into bankruptcy in 1995... Well, I saw Dean now and then, but it was a "Hey, hi!" situation.

Then, years later, as the creative director of IDW's The Library of American Comics, Dean asked me to write an introduction for the first volume of its collection of *Archie* comic strips. It was because, he said, he wanted coverage of how a pulp-magazine publisher had turned to comic books, once the pulps began to fail.

And I said no, thanks, because...

Well, because I didn't know *Archie*'s publisher had ever published pulps in the first place.

And Dean assured me that (a) there were pulps in *Archie*'s past and (b) he was sure I could do the job, if I'd just do the research.

So (a) Dean was right and (b) Dean was right.

When it comes to the ongoing delights of The Library of American Comics from IDW, I don't have the details of how the concept was developed, whose idea it was, how its projects are chosen, or how much work each and every volume has involved. I'm sure I could find out some of that information, if I'd just do the research.

But, frankly, it doesn't matter to me.

What *does* matter to me is that, in the course of my work, I learned a huge amount about a major aspect of the world of pulps. (Did you know that "M" and "L" of Archie's "MLJ" publishing company [Maurice Coyne and Louis Silberkleit] worked with "Father of Science Fiction" Hugo Gernsback?) I learned that the MLJ comics publications were simultaneous with the pulps. And that comics won the economic battle to survive.

And I learned that Dean Mullaney had the talent of motivating me to learn more about the history of our field.

And IDW and Dean made it possible for me

SUCCESS...THE HANDSOME ONE GUESSED WISELY! WE HAVE CUT KLANG'S FORCE BY MANY MEN...
YEAH – BUT THERE'S NOT EVEN A SANDWICH IN THEIR PACKS! AND I'M HUNGRY ENOUGH TO EAT ANYTHING WITH SOME MEAT ON IT!

to read—at last—comic strips that had never before been compiled for a general readership.

And the volume in which I participated was only one of many, many such publications.

Because Dean Mullaney matters.

And has mattered for decades.

Keep it up, Dean!

I want to learn more. And so do the others who treasure your projects.

Maggie Thompson co-edited Comics Buyer's Guide *for 30 years, now participates in the Comic-Con International: San Diego Toucan blog and Gemstone Publishing's* Scoop *newsletter, and wrote "From Pulp to Pep" for* Archie Volume 1: 1946-1948.

Scorchy Smith and the Art of Noel Sickles

IDW Publishing; $49.99

We're somewhere between speechless and babbling, and let's just get this out of the way right now: yes, this book is *that* good. While the rest of us sit around and ponder just how we knew next to nothing about Noel Sickles previously, Dean Mullaney and Bruce Canwell can enjoy the fact that they have put together one of the best definitive volumes on an artist we've seen in a long time, or maybe ever.

The "ever" part comes in because most have never heard of Noel Sickles, and this book is easily going to put him back on the radar of discerning fans. Even in-the-know artists who have been aware of his major contributions to the world of comic strip storytelling are going to be blown away by the scope of this book, which is one part career retrospective and one part collection of Sickles' all too brief years on the *Scorchy Smith* strip.

Starting with an introduction by artist Jim Steranko, the book details his approach to art, his long friendship with *Terry and the Pirates* creator Milton Caniff, and his avoidance of self promotion, which is part of why many don't know his work even if they've been influenced by it.

Scorchy Smithy and the Art of Noel Sickles would be a steal at double the price. Our congratulations, and thanks, to Mullaney, Canwell, and the folks at IDW Publishing for this tremendous piece of history. No library of comic strip collections will be complete without it.

SCORCHY SMITH
AND THE ART OF
NOEL SICKLES

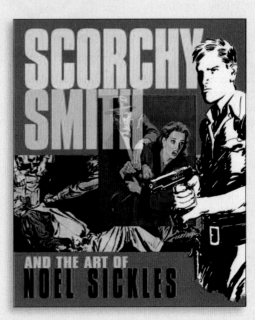

EuroComics:
Bringing Europe's Best to America

BY **SCOTT BRADEN & J.C. VAUGHN**

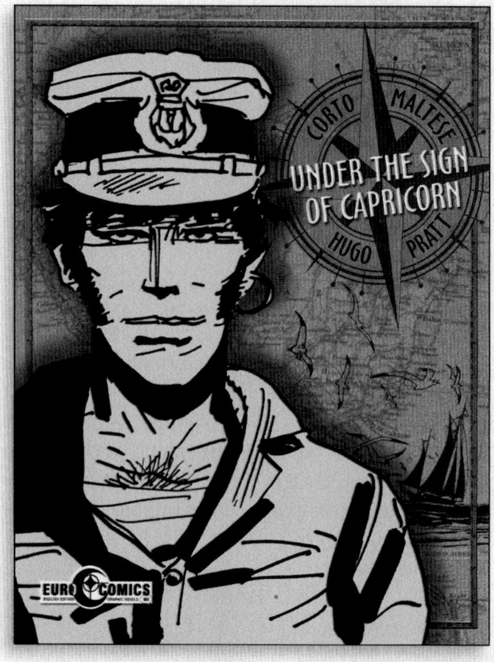
CORTO MALTESE
UNDER THE SIGN OF CAPRICORN
HUGO PRATT
EURO COMICS

After launching The Library of American Comics in 2007 and seeing its success, Dean Mullaney created the EuroComics imprint specifically to publish a complete English-language edition of *Corto Maltese*. It was something he'd wanted to do a long time, even if very few people had been aware of it.

"I first saw Corto in a French edition in the 1970s. I couldn't read French, but the art and storytelling simply blew me away. I actually tried—unsuccessfully—to get the rights in the early 1980s. My idea was to serialize Pratt's 20-page stories in *Eclipse Magazine*, alongside *Coyote* by Steve Englehart and Marshall Rogers, *Ragamuffins* by Don McGregor and Gene Colan, etc.," Mullaney said.

"Flash forward 30 years and I still wanted to be able to read *Corto Maltese*, but no comprehensive English-language editions have been available. So I pitched the complete *Corto Maltese* in English to Patrizia Zanotti, Pratt's long time colorist and partner, who manages all of his work. It turned out that she loved LOAC's Milton Caniff and Alex Toth books, so we met at a Greenwich Village coffee shop, hit it off, and agreed to a deal on the spot," he said.

Although Hugo Pratt hasn't necessarily been a household name among American comics fans, he's long been a favorite of North American comics writers and artists. Mullaney said that part of his impact has to do with his sheer drawing ability and his sense of composition.

"Pratt created images that stay with us forever. He's very much like Caniff and Toth in that regard—you learn simply by looking at what he does," Mullaney said.

"The other influence Pratt's had is in the honesty and truthfulness of his storytelling. His personal history, living through various events in many parts of the world, gave him a first-hand perspective on culture and history and an empathy for oppressed people that is reflected in his stories. The *Corto Maltese* stories are not juvenile fiction. Kim Thompson said it succinctly: '*Corto Maltese* was the first European strip to advance a mature, artistically serious sensibility within the traditional adventure format.' And that's saying a lot. Europe in the 1970s led the way in comics innovation. Pratt helped show American creators what was possible when creators are given freedom to create without corporate restraint," he said.

Although he was confident that he and Simone Castaldi had produced a drop-dead translation and thought that they had the finest possible reproduction of Pratt's art in a luxurious format, Mullaney said he couldn't help be concerned that it would live up to fans' expectations.

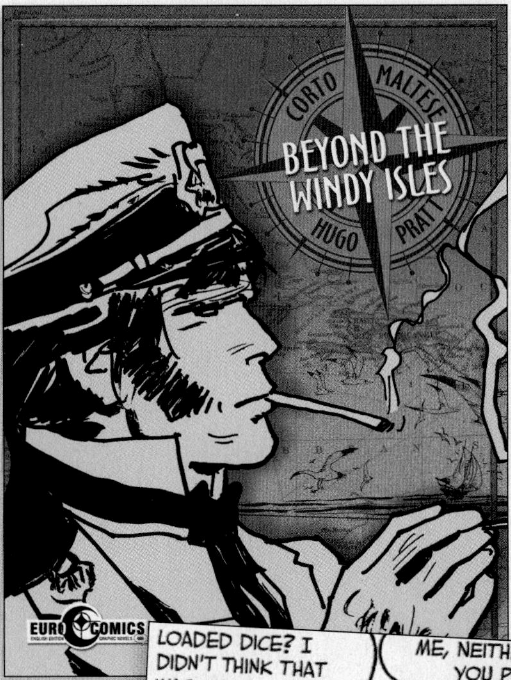
CORTO MALTESE
BEYOND THE WINDY ISLES
HUGO PRATT
EURO COMICS

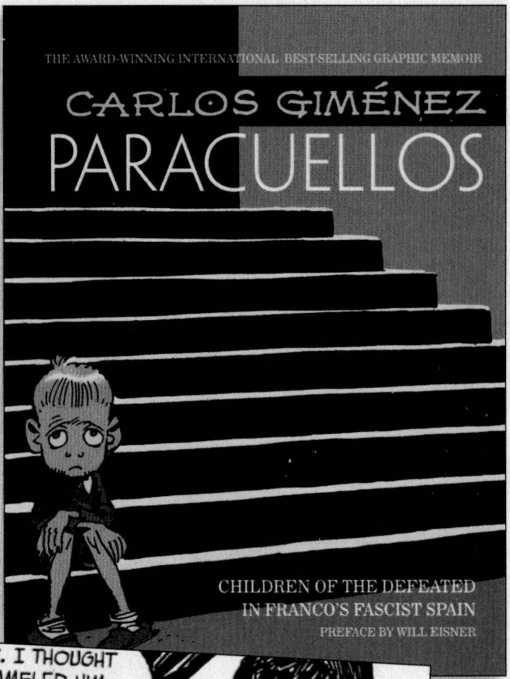
THE AWARD-WINNING INTERNATIONAL BEST-SELLING GRAPHIC MEMOIR
CARLOS GIMÉNEZ
PARACUELLOS
CHILDREN OF THE DEFEATED IN FRANCO'S FASCIST SPAIN
PREFACE BY WILL EISNER

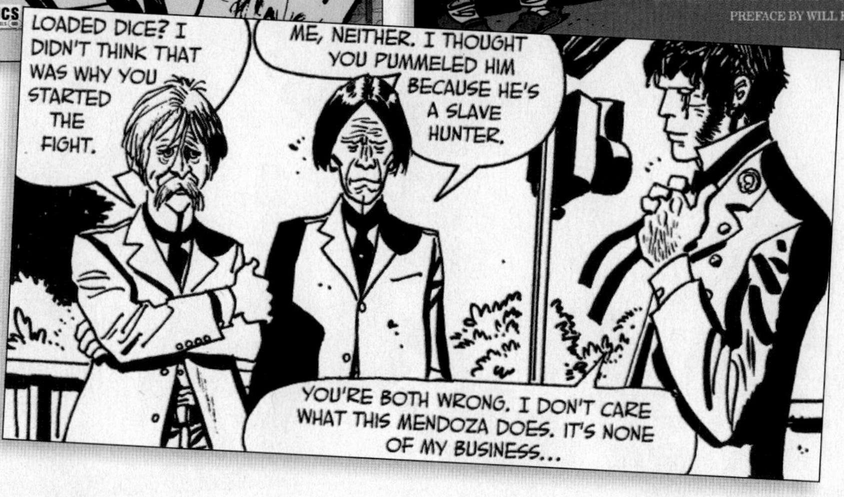
LOADED DICE? I DIDN'T THINK THAT WAS WHY YOU STARTED THE FIGHT.
ME, NEITHER. I THOUGHT YOU PUMMELED HIM BECAUSE HE'S A SLAVE HUNTER.
YOU'RE BOTH WRONG. I DON'T CARE WHAT THIS MENDOZA DOES. IT'S NONE OF MY BUSINESS...

"Thankfully, reaction has been uniformly positive," he said. "Great reviews, great sales, and perhaps the best indicator—non-stop emails from readers asking if we can release new books faster!"

Beginning in January 2016, EuroComics hopes to release three *Corto Maltese* books per year, but Hugo Pratt's most famous creation is not the imprint's only project. Once the decision was made, and after consulting with IDW's Ted Adams, Mullaney said it was a no-brainer to include other European series and graphic novels.

In March, they will release *Paracuellos*, Carlos Giménez's poignant stories of being forced to grow up, along with thousands of other "children of the defeated," in church-run "orphanages" in Franco's fascist Spain. *Paracuellos* has won virtually every comics award in Europe, including "Best Album" at the 1981 Angoulême Festival, and the "Heritage Award" at Angoulême in 2010.

In May, EuroComics will issue the complete *Dieter Lumpen* by Jorge Zentner and Rubén Pellejero, winners of the "Best Foreign Album" award at Angouléme.

"Fans may remember several episodes from the pages of *Heavy Metal*. This omnibus edition brings a complete translation into English for the first time. No having to wait for the next episode, you get the complete series—including all five graphic novels—in one book," Mullaney said.

Also being translated is the complete (in two books) *Alack Sinner* by José Muñoz and Carlos Sampayo, another Angouléme winner, considered one of the best hard-boiled series created in any language. The first volume will be in stores mid-summer.

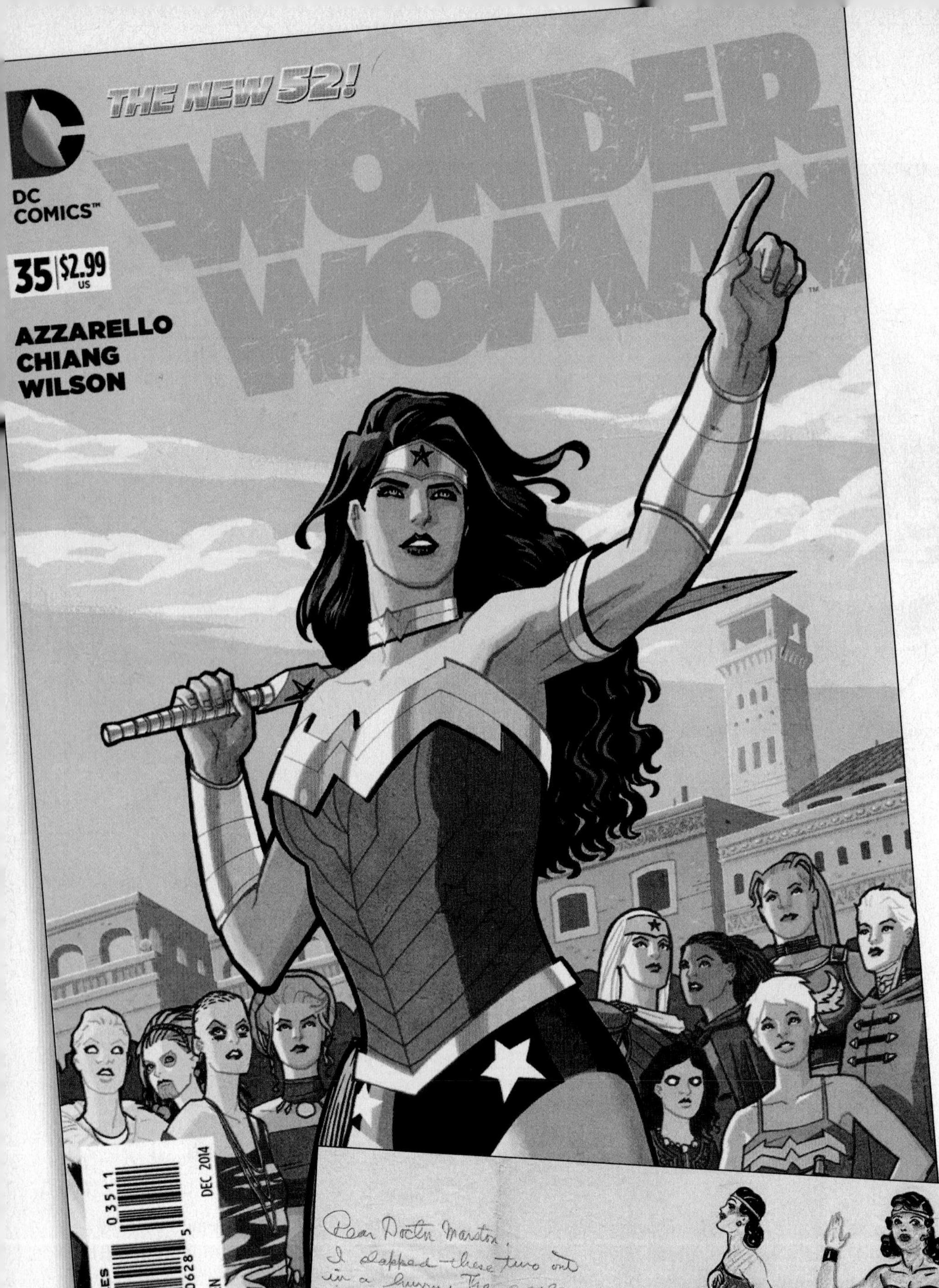

THE NEW 52!
DC COMICS™
WONDER WOMAN™
35 $2.99 US
AZZARELLO
CHIANG
WILSON
DIRECT SALES
RATED T TEEN
DEC 2014

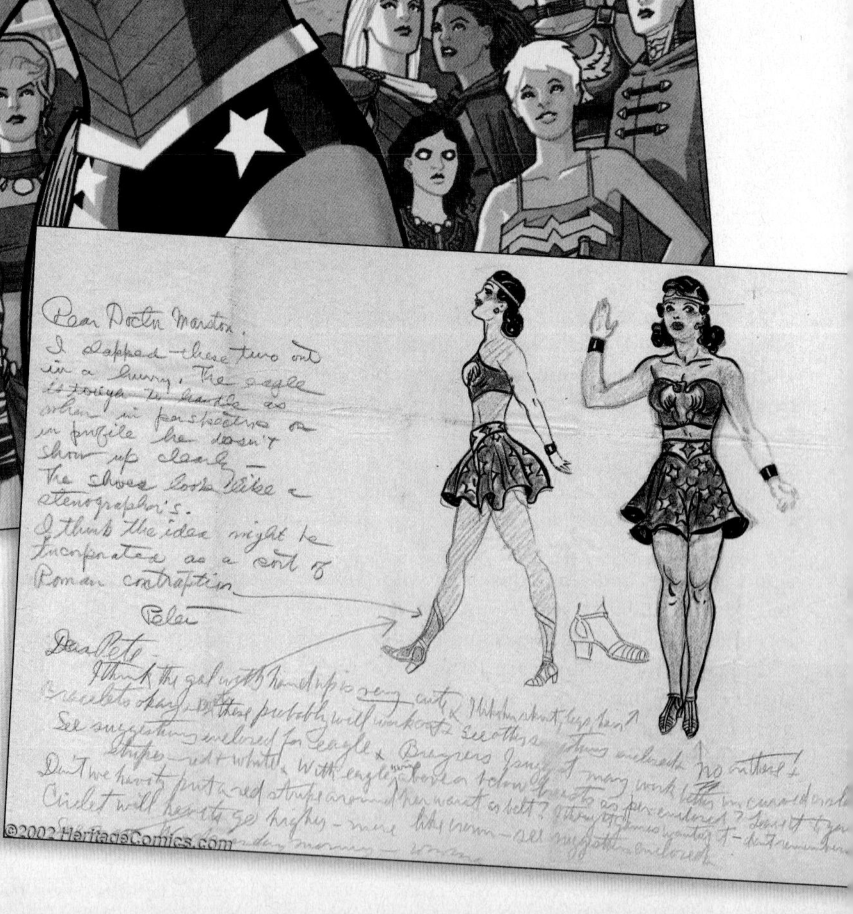

Dear Doctor Marston,
I slapped these two out in a hurry. The eagle is tough to handle as when in perspective or in profile he doesn't show up clearly —
The shoes looks like a stenographer's.
I think the idea might be incorporated as a sort of Roman contraption
Peter
Dear Pete —
I think the gal with hand up is very cute
©2002 HeritageComics.com

Wonder Woman at 75

BY **CARRIE WOOD**

All the world was waiting for her (and the wonders she could do), and in December of 1941, she arrived – Wonder Woman. The Princess of Themyscira, Wonder Woman has gone from a World War II hero to a feminist icon over her 75 years in comics, a fact that should not come as a surprise to anyone who's read her tales.

Wonder Woman was created by William Moulton Marston, a psychologist, who had caught the attention of publisher Max Gaines via an interview in which Marston discussed the then-unfulfilled potential of comic books. Gaines hired Marston on as a consultant for All-American Publications (a company which would later merge into DC Comics), and thanks to some influence from Marston's wife Elizabeth, Wonder Woman was born. As the story goes, Marston wanted to make a hero that triumphed with love rather than force, and Elizabeth responded by saying "Fine, but make her a woman."

Wonder Woman's trademark weapon – the Lasso of Truth – was also influenced by Marston's life, as he was instrumental in developing the technology used in polygraph machines.

Our heroine made her debut in *All Star Comics* #8; a member of the tribe of Amazons native to Paradise Island (later changed to Themyscira), the princess Diana encounters the plane wreck of Captain Steve Trevor. Diana not only nurses him back to health, but quickly falls in love with him and longs to leave the island. After winning a competition put on by her mother, Queen Hippolyta, Diana is deemed worthy enough to deliver Steve back to man's world and fight for justice. Upon arriving in America, she discovers a nurse who wishes to leave for South America but is unable to, due to lack of funds. Wonder Woman gives her the funds necessary, but also is able to assume the nurse's identity – Diana Prince – creating Wonder Woman's alias.

During her Golden Age appearances, Diana mostly fought alongside Steve Trevor against the likes of Nazis, though supervillains such as the Cheetah and Doctor Psycho also made their first appearances during this period. During this time she starred as the lead feature in *Sensation Comics*. By the time the Silver Age started, most of her ties to WWII were severed, and her ties to Greek mythology were strengthened in their place. For a period of time in the late 1960s to 1973, she quit being Wonder Woman entirely and instead fought crime as a powerless Diana Prince; her traditional star-spangled jumpsuit was replaced with the mod fashion that was popular at the time.

While many other heroes have had their personalities fluctuate over the many years they've been around, Diana's have been remarkably consistent by comparison. While she has experienced moments of stubbornness and naiveté, her unrelenting compassion – given without discrimination – has been what's set her apart over the years. Her powers – which have included super-strength that rivals Superman's, near-invulnerability, and flight – have put her ahead of many of her male counterparts when it comes to sheer ability.

Wonder Woman's cultural impact has been significant, to say the least. Besides proving that a woman could be just as powerful as a man could be, Diana has gone on to star in a multitude of media outside the comic book pages. The most successful of these thus far has easily been the 1970s live-action television series that starred Lynda Carter in the lead role. Since then, another television project was planned, and flopped – but with Gal Gadot to feature prominently into 2016's *Batman v. Superman: Dawn of Justice* as Diana before starring in a solo film, it's as obvious as ever that Wonder Woman is as significant as she's ever been. We look forward to seeing her powerful presence in pop culture for at least another 75 years or so!

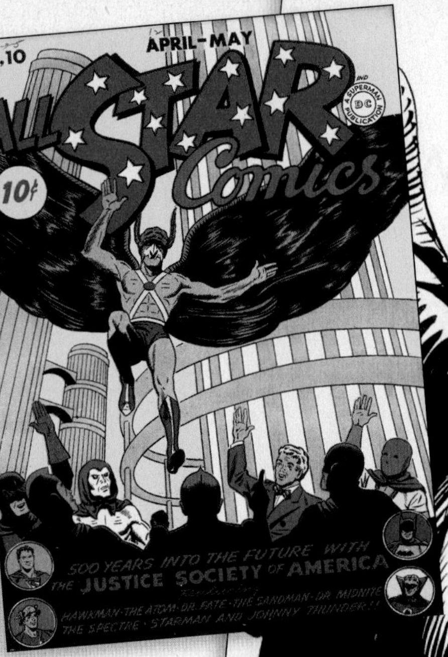
APRIL-MAY
NO.10
ALL STAR Comics
A SUPERMAN DC PUBLICATION
10¢
500 YEARS INTO THE FUTURE WITH THE JUSTICE SOCIETY OF AMERICA
HAWKMAN·THE ATOM·DR. FATE·THE SANDMAN·DR. MIDNITE
THE SPECTRE·STARMAN AND JOHNNY THUNDER!!

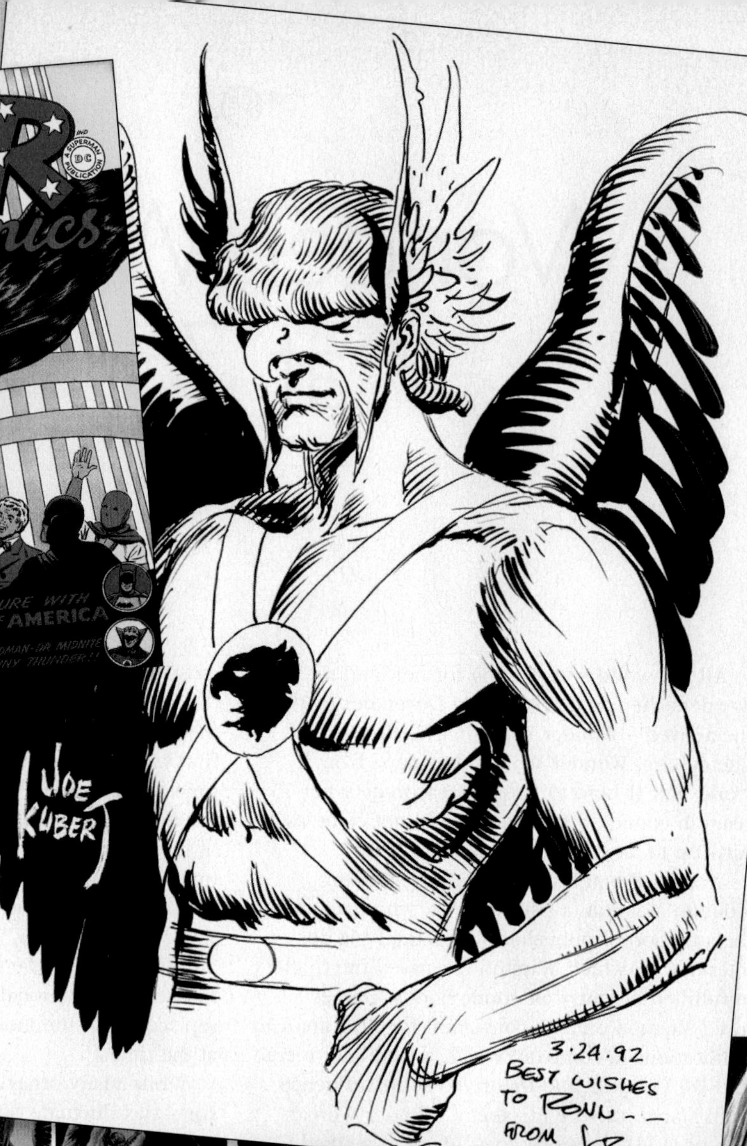
JOE KUBERT
3·24·92
BEST WISHES
TO RONN--
FROM JOE

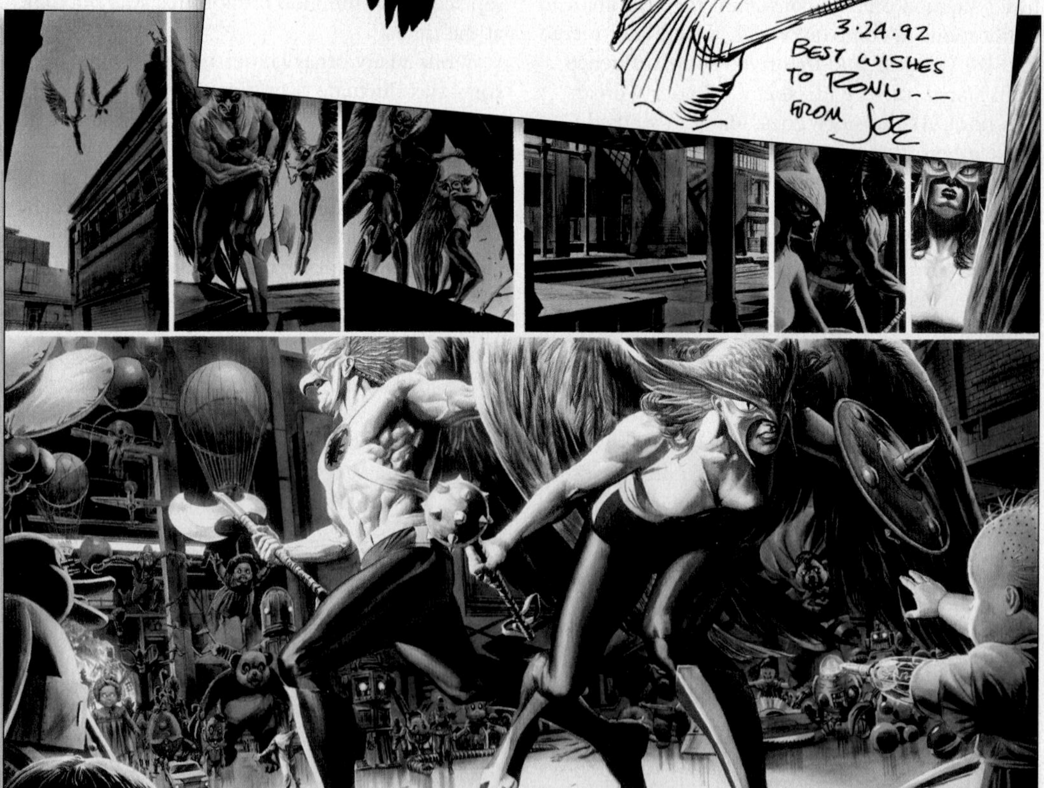

Hawkman at 75

BY CARRIE WOOD

When *Flash Comics* #1 hit the stands in 1940, it introduced the first Flash, Jay Garrick, to the world – but he wasn't the only one making his debut. A man who could fly with bird's wings and wielded a dangerous mace also soared into public view in that same issue: Hawkman.

Like many of DC's heroes, there have been multiple versions of the Hawkman character over the last 75 years, but the first was Carter Hall. Carter, an archeologist, is the reincarnation of the ancient Egyptian prince, Khufu, who was killed by his rival, the priest Hath-Set. Khufu wasn't the only one reincarnated, however, as Hath-Set was reborn as the scientist Anton Hastor and Carter's girlfriend Shiera Sanders was the reincarnation of his past self's consort, Chay-Ara.

Carter regains the memories of his past self upon discovering the knife that Hath-Set had used to kill him. He uses the "Nth metal" to create his gravity-defying outfit as he takes on the identity of Hawkman, and defeats Hastor who had kidnapped Shiera. Shiera shortly thereafter took on the Hawkgirl persona and fought alongside Carter for much of the 1940s.

When the Justice Society of America was founded, Hawkman was a founding member and later became its chairman. In fact, he was the chairman when, in 1951, the JSA was investigated by the "Joint Congressional Un-American Activities Committee" for communist ties and ended up disbanding and retiring for most of the 1950s.

As with many other characters, the Silver Age ushered in a new version of Hawkman – Katar Hol, a policeman on his home planet of Thanagar. Along with his wife Shayera Thal, they were sent to Earth to capture the shapeshifting criminal Byth, and after capturing him elect to stay on Earth. They take on aliases – Carter and Shiera Hall – and fight crime as Hawkman and Hawkgirl.

Many heroes saw their backstories and ultimate fates change with 1985's *Crisis on Infinite Earths*, and Hawkman was no exception. While he did survive *Crisis* intact, Hawkman's continuity became somewhat convoluted with retcons via 1989's *Hawkworld* series, which rebooted his backstory. Since then, others have used the "Hawkman" name, including the Thangarian spy Fel Andar, and Charley Parker. Parker had previously been a member of the Teen Titans as Golden Eagle, but when Carter Hall was presumed dead, Parker took over the mantle of Hawkman for a short period of time. As it actually turned out, Parker was the son of Fel Andar – and Andar was the one responsible for Hall's demise. Andar is eventually defeated, Carter reclaims his title, and Parker returns to the name of Golden Eagle.

The Hawkman most recently seen in DC's New 52 line is closer to the Silver Age incarnation – Katar Hol, going under the identity of Carter Hall. Despite attempting to rid himself of the suit and the responsibility of being Hawkman by burying the armor in a forest, the Nth metal re-bonds with him and does not allow him to escape his fate. This version of Hawkman also came from Thanagar, though unlike those around him, did not seek battle and was instead a total pacifist. After being blamed for the king's death, he flees to Earth and ends up fighting crime as Hawkman.

Despite having played a large part in the Justice League and Justice Society within the pages of the comic books – plus featuring in many of the Justice League animated television series – Katar seems to have been relegated to the sidelines recently, with no plans yet to introduce him into DC's rapidly expanding film universe. But the winds of change have seemingly always carried Hawkman into the future, and if the last 75 years are any indication, he's just getting started.

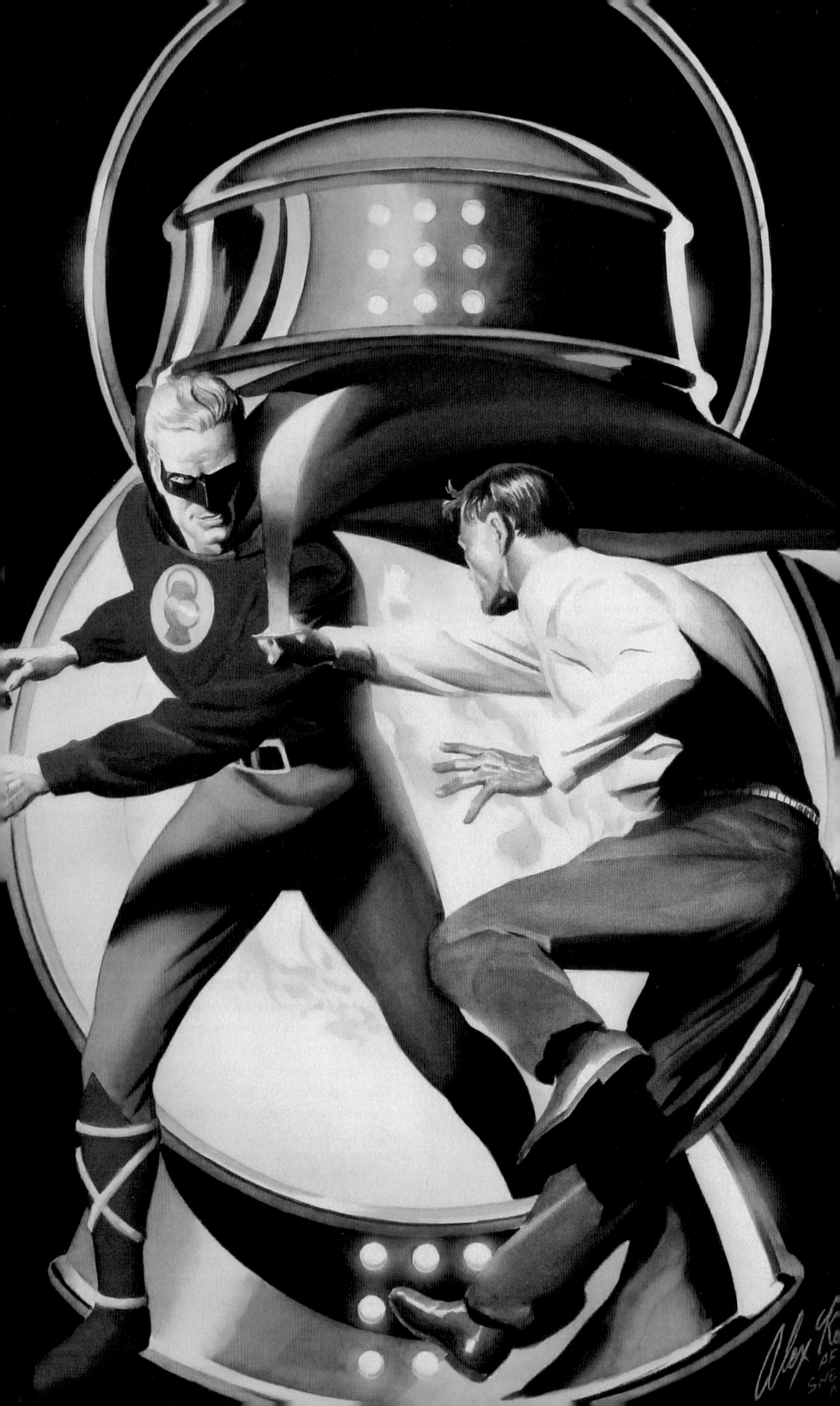

Green Lantern at 75

BY **CARRIE WOOD**

"And I shall shed my light over evil, for the dark things cannot stand the light, the light of the Green Lantern!" Sound familiar? No? Well, it's the Green Lantern Oath, of course – the original one, recited by Alan Scott, the first of many Green Lanterns to appear in the pages of DC comics and who happens to be celebrating his 75th anniversary this year.

While subsequent Lanterns have enjoyed significantly more popularity, Alan Scott made his debut in July of 1940 in *All-American Comics* #16 and left behind a lofty legacy. Alan was created by Martin Nodell, a struggling artist who drew inspiration from the opera *The Ring of the Nibelung* and wanted to create a superhero that could draw power from a magical ring. After presenting the idea to publisher M.C. "Max" Gaines, Nodell received approval to start working on the story.

The design for the first Green Lantern would end up differing significantly from later iterations of the character; rather than the now-typical green bodysuit, Alan Scott wore a red top with the Lantern emblem on it, green pants, and a purple and green cape.

Alan Scott enjoyed popularity in the 1940s – so much so that he was not only given his own book, *Green Lantern*, but was a founding member of the Justice Society of America, a group that was featured in *All Star Comics*. However, like many superheroes, his popularity waned after World War II, and his comic book was canceled in 1949. It would be more than a decade before Alan Scott made another appearance, and by then, a new Lantern had taken the spotlight.

Hal Jordan arrived in *Showcase* #22 in October of 1959, where he gained the Green Lantern Power Ring by the dying alien, Abin Sur. This new storyline also introduced the concept of the Green Lantern Corps as an organization seen throughout the galaxy, of which Hal was simply one of many members. In comparison to the Alan Scott stories, Hal's tales were significantly more science-fiction-oriented. Hal remains easily the most recognizable version of the Green Lantern even to this day (in a similar way to how Barry Allen remains the most notable Flash) and has been seen most often in television and in film; he's appeared in *Super Friends*, plus starred in *Green Lantern: The Animated Series*, and was portrayed in the 2011 live-action film by Ryan Reynolds.

While Hal Jordan, for many remains *the* Green Lantern, many others have taken on the responsibility of reciting the oath and protecting the Earth from extraterrestrial threats. Most notable among these was John Stewart, who became DC's first black superhero when he debuted in 1971. Stewart had replaced the first Bronze Age Lantern, Guy Gardner, who had fallen into a coma after the power battery exploded in his face. Stewart's popularity has so far been the only to rival that of Hal Jordan's – he is the primary Lantern in the DC Animated Universe on shows such as *Justice League* and *Justice League Unlimited*.

The most recent additions to the seemingly ever-expanding Green Lantern Corps have been Kyle Rayner (who became a White Lantern after mastering all of the other seven Lantern rings) and Simon Baz (who is the first Middle Eastern-American member of the Corps). Both Rayner and Baz played large roles in DC's *New 52* line, which managed to actually show nearly every Lantern – including Alan Scott. While the person wearing the ring (and the oath that goes along with it) may have changed a few times over the years, DC's continued focus on the Green Lantern Corps has proved that there will be someone behind the mask continuing to protect the Earth for years to come. *Beware their power – Green Lantern's light!!*

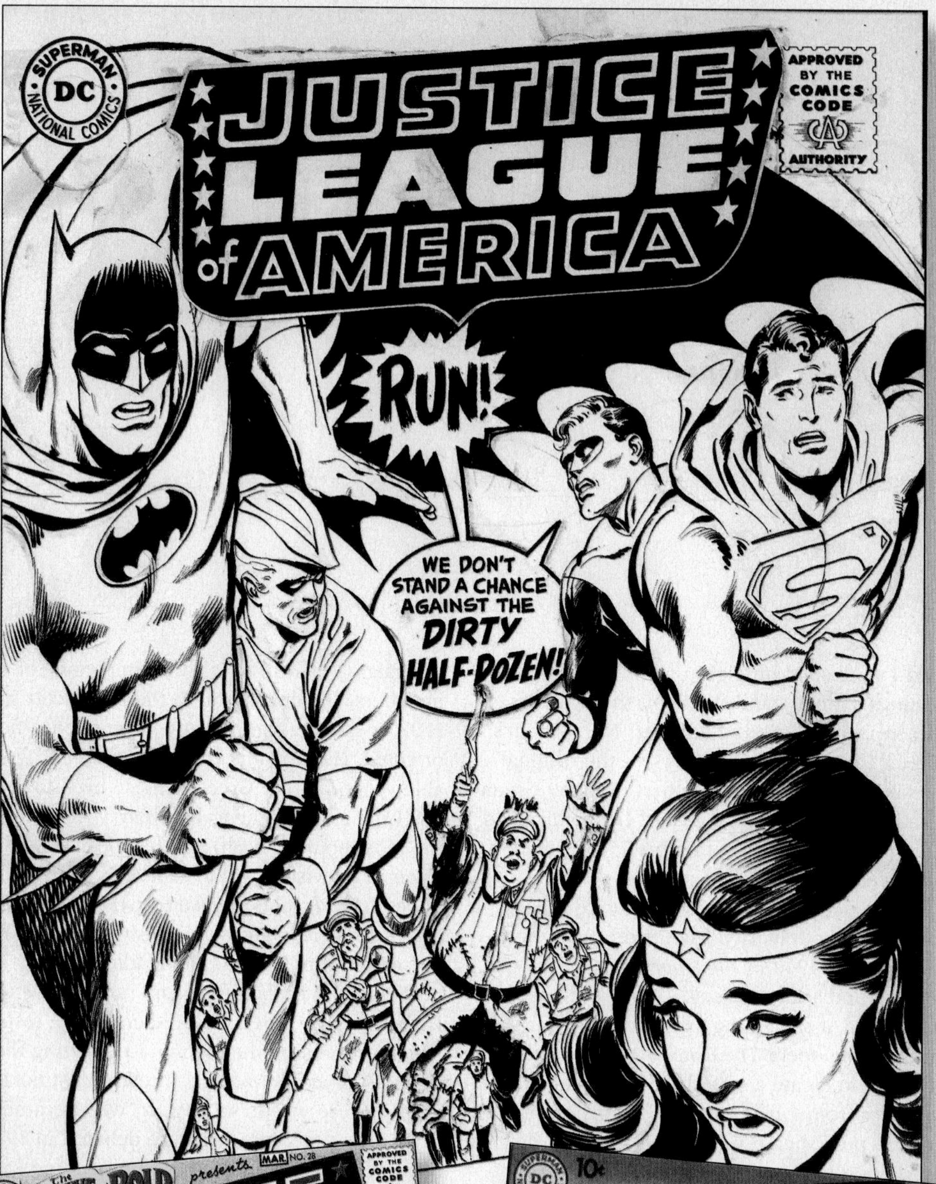
SUPERMAN DC NATIONAL COMICS
JUSTICE LEAGUE of AMERICA
APPROVED BY THE COMICS CODE AUTHORITY
RUN!
WE DON'T STAND A CHANCE AGAINST THE DIRTY HALF-DOZEN!

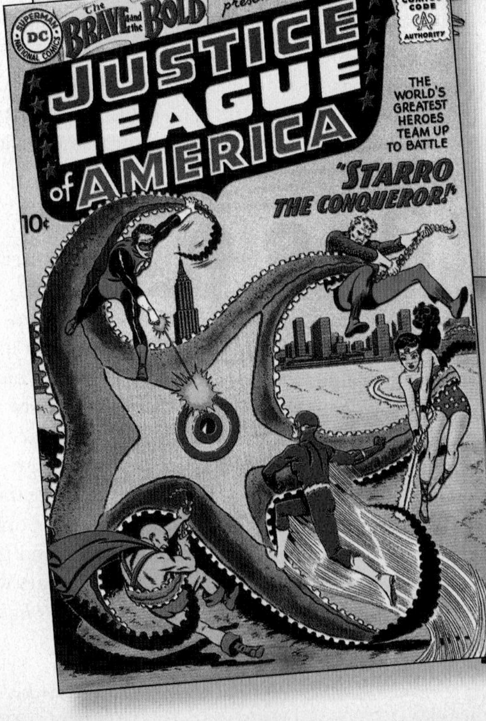
SUPERMAN DC NATIONAL COMICS
The BRAVE and the BOLD presents
MAR. NO. 28
APPROVED BY THE COMICS CODE AUTHORITY
JUSTICE LEAGUE of AMERICA
THE WORLD'S GREATEST HEROES TEAM UP TO BATTLE
"STARRO THE CONQUEROR!"
10¢

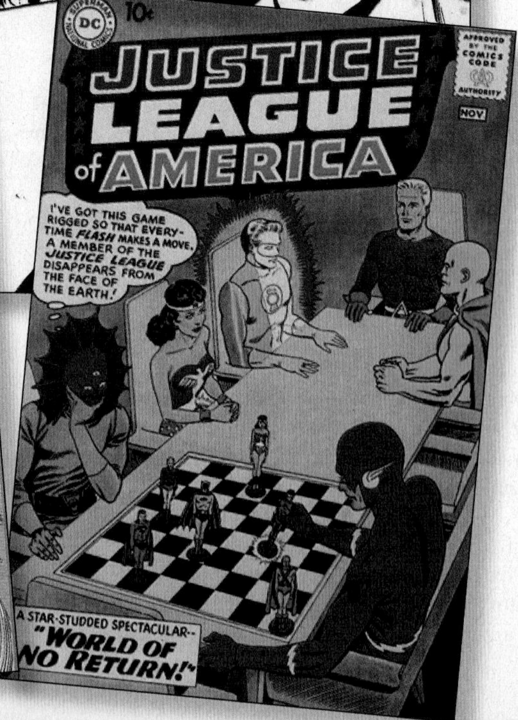
SUPERMAN DC NATIONAL COMICS
10¢
APPROVED BY THE COMICS CODE AUTHORITY
JUSTICE LEAGUE of AMERICA
NOV
I'VE GOT THIS GAME RIGGED SO THAT EVERY-TIME FLASH MAKES A MOVE, A MEMBER OF THE JUSTICE LEAGUE DISAPPEARS FROM THE FACE OF THE EARTH!
A STAR-STUDDED SPECTACULAR-- "WORLD OF NO RETURN!"

The Justice League of America at 55

BY **CARRIE WOOD**

Superhero teams have become so common that it's hard to imagine a time without them. And while there are many popular teams in comics today, the one that started the modern era trend is the Justice League.

Though the Justice League's predecessor, the Justice Society of America, had been popular throughout the 1940s, the team vanished from the public eye into the '50s. In the late 1950s, many of the characters that disappeared when the Justice Society titles ended publication began to return, such as The Flash and Green Lantern. DC editor Julius Schwartz went to acclaimed writer Gardner Fox and tasked Fox with bringing back the Justice Society.

However, Schwartz – liking the sound of baseball's National and American Leagues – instead opted to change the name of the team to the Justice League. The Justice League of America made its debut 55 years ago, in *The Brave and the Bold* #28 in 1960. They remained in the pages of that book for a couple of more issues before quickly starring in their own title.

The first *Justice League of America* book hit the stands in November of 1960. That issue's lineup is still the most classic – Superman, Batman, Aquaman, Wonder Woman, the Flash, Green Lantern, and Martian Manhunter. However, despite being immensely popular on their own, Batman and Superman didn't appear in many stories, leading to the addition of Green Arrow, the Atom, and Hawkman within a few years. The team took on missions and fought a variety of villains as they operated from a secret cave in the fictional town of Happy Harbor, Rhode Island.

One of DC's earliest crossover events – and the company's first use of the word "Crisis" to refer to them – was *Crisis on Earth-One!* with the follow-up *Crisis on Earth-Two!* This story was the first time the Silver Age's Justice League and the Golden Age's Justice Society would team-up, where they fought against the likes of Chronos, Dr. Alchemy, the Icicle, the Wizard, the Fiddler, and Felix Faust. The villains

end up jailed on their respective Earths; the Fiddler makes note of the fact that there must be an Earth-Three somewhere, alluding to the multiverse that was established. Earth-Three would be explored and saved in *Crisis on Earth-Three*, with the JLA and JSA fighting the Crime Syndicate of America.

By the end of the 1960s, Wonder Woman and Martian Manhunter had left the team, replaced with Black Canary. And in the early '70s, the JLA moved their headquarters to a satellite orbiting around the planet, where they were soon joined by the Elongated Man, the Red Tornado, Hawkwoman, Zatanna, and Firestorm, plus saw the return of Diana Prince.

The Justice League of America was headquartered… well, in America, but the Justice League itself soon saw expansions into other parts of the world in the 1980s. The team was spun off into *Justice League International* in 1987, *Justice League Europe* in 1989, *Justice League Task Force* in 1993, and *Extreme Justice* in 1994; all of these spinoffs were cancelled by 1996.

Recently, the JLA returned to comics as simply *Justice League* in DC's New 52, with *Justice League Dark* also starting in 2011. The Dark team handled situations deemed a little too unseemly for the traditional team, and consisted of John Constantine, Deadman, Shade, Zatanna, the Changing Man, and Madame Xanadu. The "traditional" Justice League saw many of the usual faces within its ranks and also happened to relocate to Canada for a while before the title was relaunched as *Justice League United* in 2014.

The original superhero team has clearly had a massive impact on comics (including influencing the initial decision to even create the Fantastic Four at Marvel) and has enjoyed enduring popularity over the last five and a half decades. The team has starred in cartoons, video games and feature films and with Warner Bros. planning out the DC film universe it's become obvious that the JLA will be seen everywhere for at least another few decades or so.

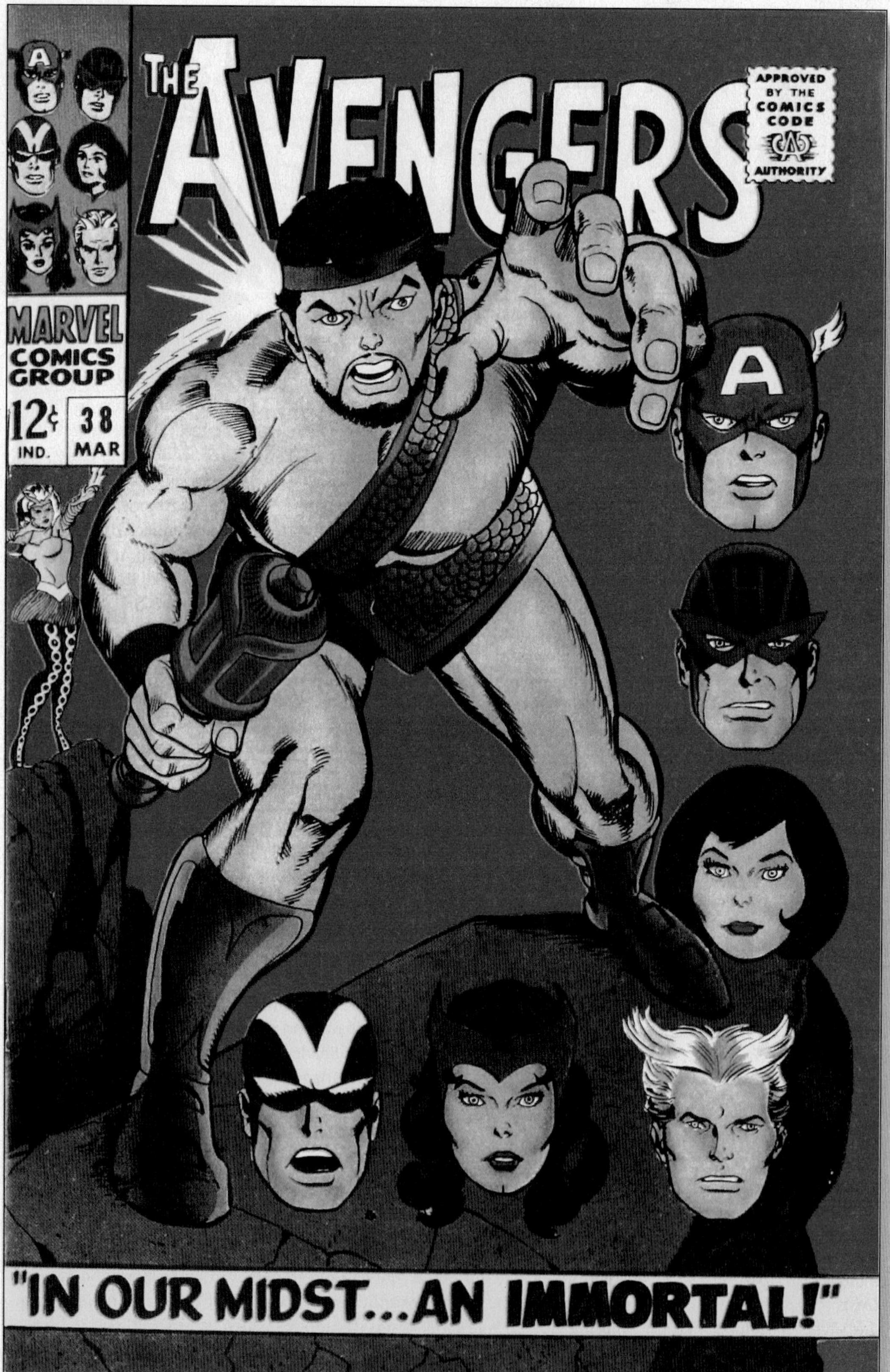
THE AVENGERS
APPROVED BY THE COMICS CODE AUTHORITY
MARVEL COMICS GROUP
12¢ IND.
38 MAR
"IN OUR MIDST...AN IMMORTAL!"

Hercules at 50

BY **CHARLES S. NOVINSKIE**

If you're going to make a big splash in the Marvel Universe, why not do it by tackling the Norse God of Thunder, Thor? After all, crossing the lines between Greek, Roman, and Norse mythology is the perfect way to stir things up— Marvel style. Hercules made his first appearance in the Marvel pantheon of heroes – a fairly misunderstood hero – by taking on Thor in *Journey Into Mystery Annual* #1 back in 1965.

Hercules' star continued to glow brighter following numerous appearances with the Avengers, Thor, and then *Tales to Astonish* #79, where he encountered the Incredible Hulk. With two high-profile slugfests with the likes of Thor, then the Hulk, it was apparent that Hercules was climbing the list of Marvel strongmen. While banished from Asgard by Zeus, Hercules spent time adding some muscle to the Avengers lineup before becoming a permanent member of the team in *Avengers* #45.

Looking for a change of scenery, Hercules headed to the west coast to form the Champions (*Champions* #1-17), a group of loosely-connected superheroes including the Angel, Black Widow, Ghost Rider, and Iceman. Hercules, along with his teammates, battled against the machinations of Olympians Pluto and Hippolyta. Following up on Hercules' exile from Olympus, the Prince of Power starred in two limited series titles that featured a 24th-century Hercules in space.

Hercules' return to Earth was short-lived as he once again teamed up with the Avengers to take on the High Evolutionary in the *Avengers Annual* #17. Taking on another cosmic threat, Hercules and the Avengers go up against the Collector in *Avengers* #334. Hercules continued to thwart cosmic baddies as a reserve Avenger, taking on the likes of Korvak, Maelstrom, Terminus, Nebula, Immortus and Kang the Conqueror. During the *Civil War* storyline, Hercules sided with the opponents to the Superhuman Registration Act (SRA). Hercules took on the alias of Victor Tegler in order to escape registering for the SRA.

Following the events of the World War Hulk storyline in which Hercules played a prominent role, the Hulk comic went through a significant change. *The Incredible Hulk* series was transformed to *Incredible Hercules* starting with issue #113.

Among Hercules' most recent stories was a series of adventures with Amadeus Cho, a teenage genius and sidekick. The series concludes with the "Assault On New Olympus" storyline in *Incredible Hercules* #141, followed by the launch of a new series, *Hercules – Prince of Power*.

During the *Dark Reign* storyline, Cho and Hercules form a new team of Avengers, enlisting the aid of U.S. Agent, Hank Pym, Vision, Stature, Quicksilver and Jocasta in *Mighty Avengers* #21. Hercules and the new team collaborate to defeat the Elder God Chthon and to defeat the Chaos Cascade. The Mighty and New Avengers, along with Herc, teamed up to prevent Hera from destroying and remaking the universe with a device known as the Continuum in *Assault On New Olympus Prologue*.

Hercules can be found throughout the Marvel Universe, including being exposed to a bug bite that provides him with spider-like powers during the *Spider-Island* storyline in *Hercules* #7. Cured of his spider-infliction by Peter Parker, Hercules then ran a Greek bar in Brooklyn and helped fight crime with an array of weapons, including a magical sword called the Sword of Peleus, the Shield of Perseus (an unbreakable shield that turns anyone who looks at it to stone), arrows that can penetrate any substance, and a helmet of invisibility. Hercules also applied his unique talents as a guest teacher at the Avengers Academy in *Avengers Academy* #30.

Moving forward, Hercules continues to serve as a prominent—and powerful—figure in the Marvel Universe.

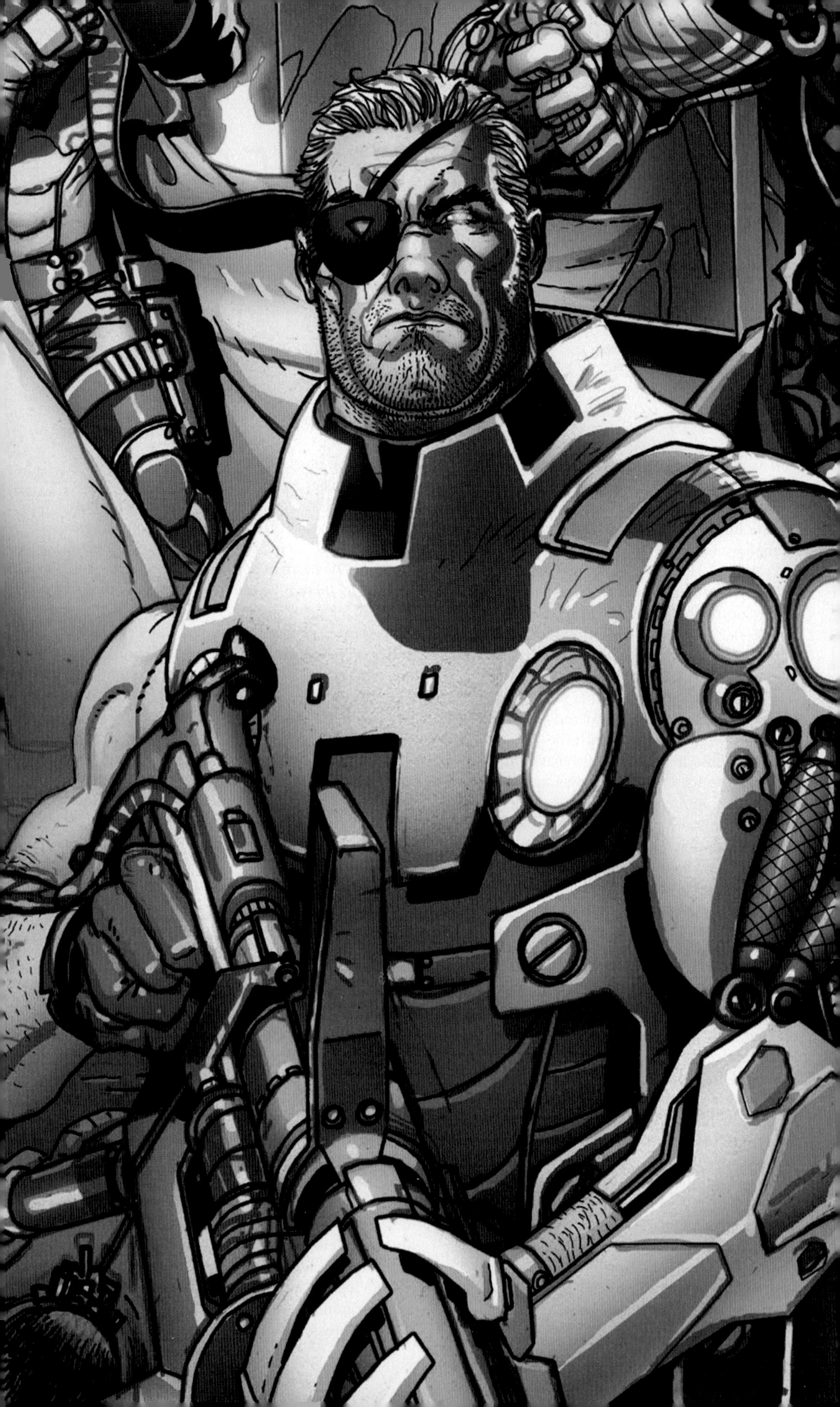

Cable at 25

BY **CARRIE WOOD**

A glowing eye, a few scars, a metal arm, and plenty of pockets; thanks to a popular cartoon series, mutants enjoyed incredible popularity in the 1990s, but few of them perfectly nailed the '90s look like Cable. Though his alter-ego Nathan Summers had been introduced a few years prior in the January 1986 issue of *Uncanny X-Men*, it wasn't until March 1990 that the fully-powered Cable emerged on the scene in *New Mutants* #87.

THE NEW MUTANTS
WATCH OUT MUTIES!!
HERE COMES THE MAN CALLED-- CABLE!!

As the son of Scott Summers/Cyclops and Madelyne Pryor (a clone of Jean Grey), Cable is imbued with powerful telekinetic and telepathic abilities; however, somewhat tragically, he is unable to fully use these abilities in combat due to the fact that they must be constantly used to protect his life and his body from the "techno-organic" virus that constantly ravages it. In fact, the reason that he appears to be so much older than he should for the time period in which he appears in is because his parents sent him to the future in an attempt to cure the virus. Despite this, he's still an absolute force to be reckoned with due to the fact that he's a master marksman and has expert fighting skills.

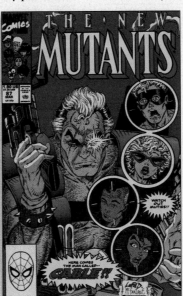

Cable was first seen in conflict with the Mutant Liberation Front, the U.S. government and the Freedom Force – the New Mutants assisted him in his war against Stryfe, and he ended up becoming their de facto leader and reorganizing them into the X-Force. *New Mutants* ended with issue #100, with Cable, plus Domino and other members of the New Mutants team appearing in the following month's *X-Force* #1.

After that, Cable would star in his own series, which began in 1993 and would run for 107 issues until September 2002. Following the end of his solo run, he was paired with Deadpool in 2004's *Cable & Deadpool*; both Cable and Deadpool were creations of Rob Liefeld in the early 1990s. This "buddy" team balanced the humor seen in Deadpool's character with the stark seriousness of Cable's personality and ran for four years, until 2008. The series ended with #50 and both Cable and Deadpool returned to solo series. Cable has since been seen acting alone, most notably in the "Messiah War" storyline, and alongside a reformed X-Force team.

Though the 1990s saw a boom in the mutant population in Marvel's comics, it's been pretty apparent since then that he's enjoyed significantly more popularity than some of the other characters created around that time. He's appeared in a number of video games, including as a playable fighter in *Marvel vs Capcom 2* and as a supporting figure in the 2013 *Deadpool* game. While he has yet to make an appearance in the *X-Men* film franchise, an *X-Force* film is currently in the works and it has been announced that Cable will be a part of that team.

For many, it seems as though the 1990s were just yesterday, but Cable's evolution over the years has helped mark the time. He's gone from a typical cryptic antihero to a fan-favorite gun-toting mutant over the last 25 years and in that time has proven that he's got the same staying power as the Magnetos, Nightcrawlers and Jean Greys. Many products of the '90s have faded – boy bands, frosted tips and grunge are all out of vogue – but Cable? He's not going anywhere. Thankfully for him, the "big guns and lots of pockets" look still works.

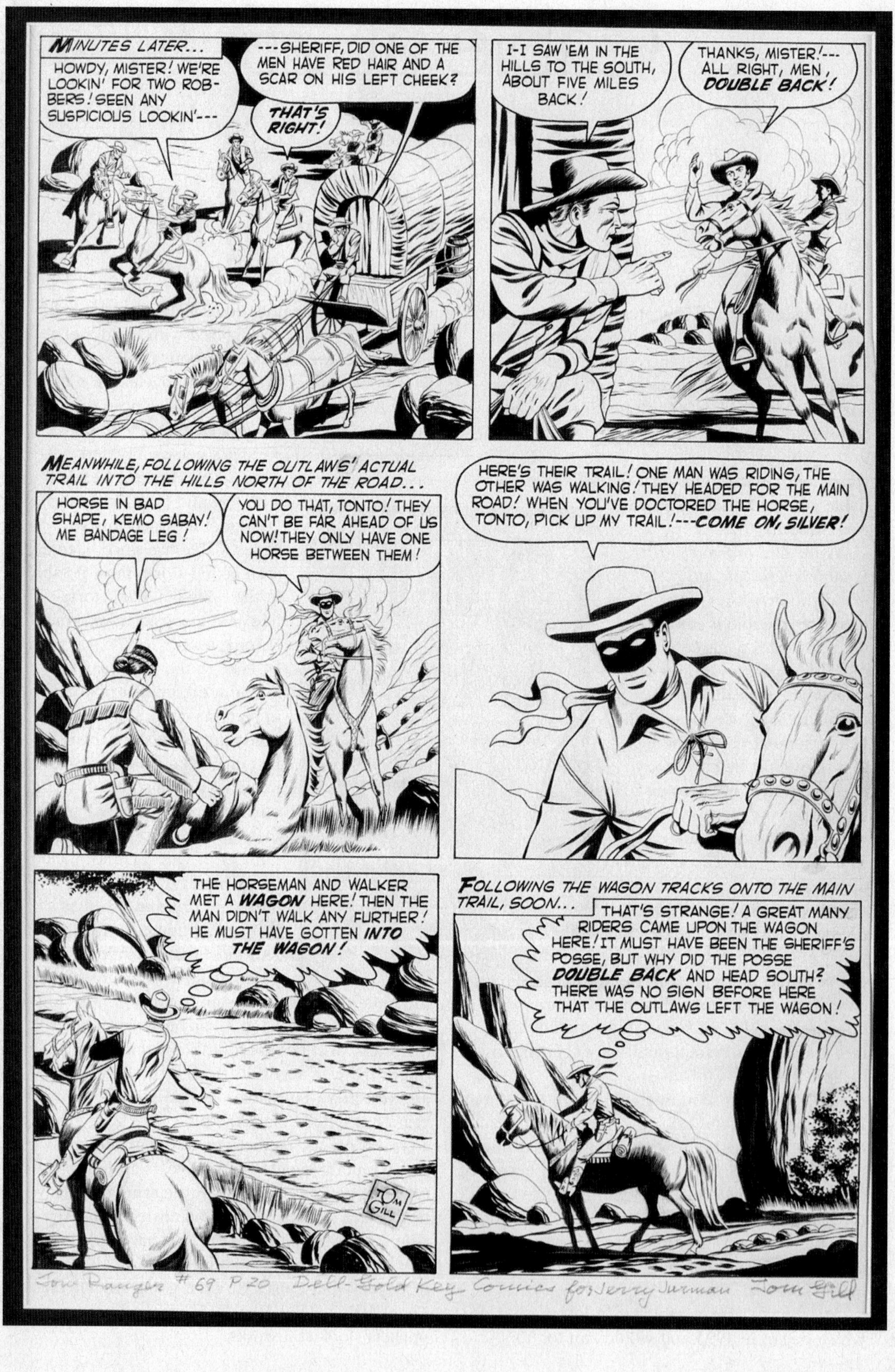
MINUTES LATER...
HOWDY, MISTER! WE'RE LOOKIN' FOR TWO ROBBERS! SEEN ANY SUSPICIOUS LOOKIN'---
---SHERIFF, DID ONE OF THE MEN HAVE RED HAIR AND A SCAR ON HIS LEFT CHEEK?
THAT'S RIGHT!
I-I SAW 'EM IN THE HILLS TO THE SOUTH, ABOUT FIVE MILES BACK!
THANKS, MISTER!---ALL RIGHT, MEN, DOUBLE BACK!
MEANWHILE, FOLLOWING THE OUTLAWS' ACTUAL TRAIL INTO THE HILLS NORTH OF THE ROAD...
HORSE IN BAD SHAPE, KEMO SABAY! ME BANDAGE LEG!
YOU DO THAT, TONTO! THEY CAN'T BE FAR AHEAD OF US NOW! THEY ONLY HAVE ONE HORSE BETWEEN THEM!
HERE'S THEIR TRAIL! ONE MAN WAS RIDING, THE OTHER WAS WALKING! THEY HEADED FOR THE MAIN ROAD! WHEN YOU'VE DOCTORED THE HORSE, TONTO, PICK UP MY TRAIL!---COME ON, SILVER!
THE HORSEMAN AND WALKER MET A WAGON HERE! THEN THE MAN DIDN'T WALK ANY FURTHER! HE MUST HAVE GOTTEN INTO THE WAGON!
TOM GILL
FOLLOWING THE WAGON TRACKS ONTO THE MAIN TRAIL, SOON...
THAT'S STRANGE! A GREAT MANY RIDERS CAME UPON THE WAGON HERE! IT MUST HAVE BEEN THE SHERIFF'S POSSE, BUT WHY DID THE POSSE DOUBLE BACK AND HEAD SOUTH? THERE WAS NO SIGN BEFORE HERE THAT THE OUTLAWS LEFT THE WAGON!
Lone Ranger #69 P 20 Dell-Gold Key Comics for Jerry Jurman Tom Gill

The Lone Ranger:
The Men Behind the Mask

BY **TIM LASIUTA**

Based on the character developed by James Jewell, Fran Striker and George Washington Trendle in the early 1930s, the Lone Ranger first appeared in the long lasting radio drama produced by WXYZ, sending "thrilling adventures of yesteryear" into the aether until 1957. As groundbreaking as the Lone Ranger was on radio, his comic strip ran from 1939 to 1971, and comic book adventures based on the comic strip began in 1941 and are still ongoing today from Dynamite. The success of the Masked Man was due in part to the men behind the mask: those who picked up pen, ink and brush to illustrate the now iconic character.

While the artists behind the masked man included Charles Flanders, Jose Delbo, Jack Davis, Russ Heath, Ed Kressy, Sergio Cariello, Jack Kirby, Hank Hartman, Don Spaulding, H.J. Ward, Vatche Mavilan, Esteve Polls, Francesco Francavilla, Rey Villegas, Alex Ross, John Cassiday, Gil Kane, Carmine Infantino, Tim Truman, Bruce Minney, Pete Kuhlhoff and Henry Vallely, Croton-on-Hudson artist Tom Gill stood the tallest. From 1948 to 1971, Gill illustrated the Lone Ranger in comic books, on advertising art and in the newspapers, ghosting for Charles Flanders during his frequent illnesses.

Gill's reputation as an artist was built on the foundation of his work on the Lone Ranger titles, which was done during a period when he taught at the School of Visual Arts in New York and quickly became his trademark.

Gill's success was due to his innate talent, but also a stable of art assistants from his classes in continuity at the SVA, or the Cartoonists and Illustrators School, as it was first called.

He cut his artistic teeth at the *New York Daily News* as an errand boy who eventually moved up to staff artist. Gill was among the first teachers at the new art school started by Silas Rhodes and Burne Hogarth. He developed a successful freelance art career in the fledgling comic book industry and had created and sold the daily comic strip *Flower Potts* in 1946 to the *News*, but his growing account list, which included Timely, St, John Comics, Fox Comics and Dell Western required eager hands looking to learn the craft and get paid. His students were more than willing to oblige. Among his first assistants was an artist named Norman Steinberg.

"Steinberg was in the Battle of the Bulge and he suffered from what we would call Post-Traumatic Stress Disorder today," said Joe Sinnott, who worked with Gill during his school years. "He was so great and he could draw horses beautifully. Later on, he worked with Syd Shores on books for Timely."

Steinberg worked mainly on war features such as *Battle, War Comics, Battlefield, Battle Brady, Red Warrior* and *War Combat* for Timely/Atlas until 1957 when he disappeared from the comic book industry.

Sinnott started his schooling in New York in 1948 and was soon asked by Gill to join his studio while still studying at the SVA.

"Tom gave me my start, paying me very well, and helped me break into the comic book industry. With his help, I landed my first published work in *Mopsy* #12 on a five-page story in my first year of school for which I was grateful," Sinnott said. "There were so many kids just out of the service looking for a way to make a living and they thought maybe they could do it by drawing comic books or cards. A lot of them could draw well but the odds were against them."

Sinnott remembered working with Gill as a young man.

"It got so I was doing all his work, and at first he would say, 'Joe, I want to do the heads so it looks like my work,'" Sinnott said. "I would do the pencils and the inks and he would draw the heads on *Red Warrior, Kent Blake of the Secret*

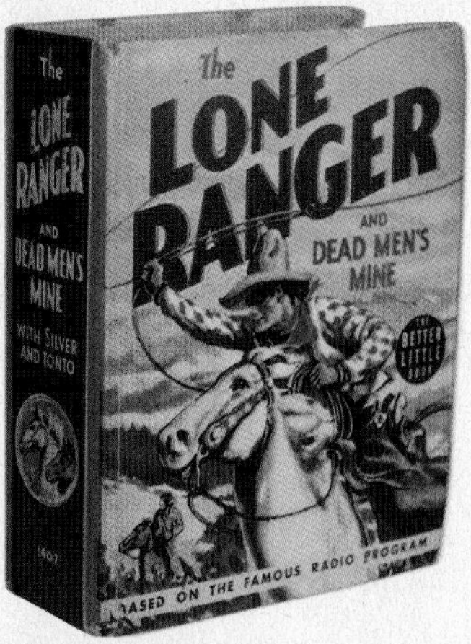
The
LONE RANGER
AND
DEAD MEN'S MINE
BETTER LITTLE BOOK
BASED ON THE FAMOUS RADIO PROGRAM
The LONE RANGER AND DEAD MEN'S MINE WITH SILVER AND TONTO
1407

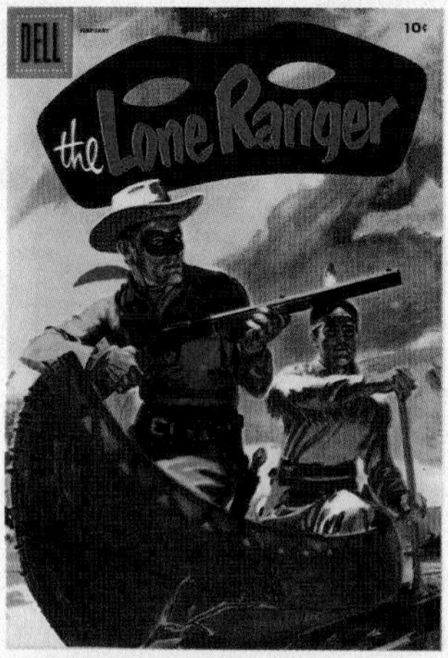
DELL
10¢
the Lone Ranger

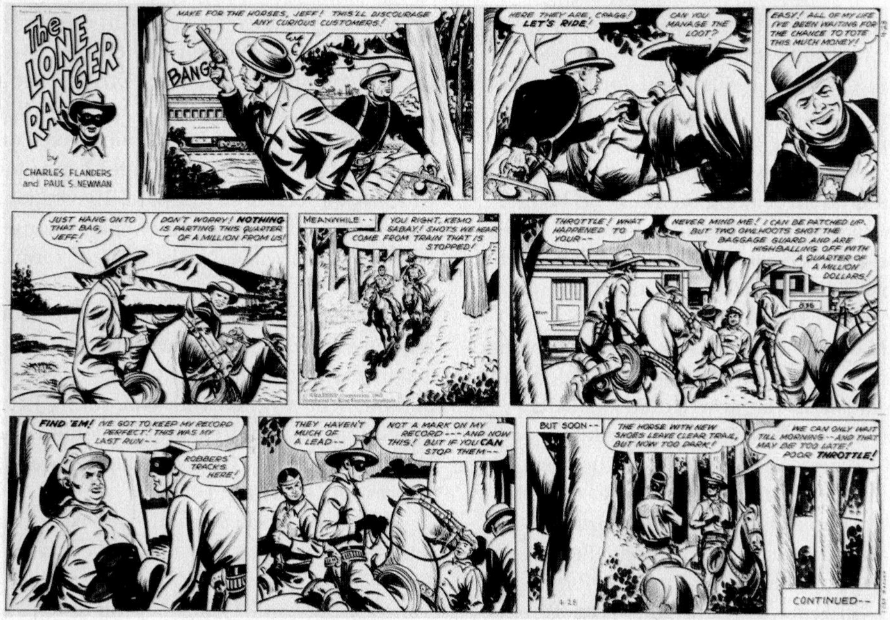
The LONE RANGER
by
CHARLES FLANDERS
and PAUL S. NEWMAN
MAKE FOR THE HORSES, JEFF! THIS'LL DISCOURAGE ANY CURIOUS CUSTOMERS!
BANG
HERE THEY ARE, CRAGG! LET'S RIDE!
CAN YOU MANAGE THE LOOT?
EASY! ALL OF MY LIFE I'VE BEEN WAITING FOR THE CHANCE TO TOTE THIS MUCH MONEY!
JUST HANG ONTO THAT BAG, JEFF!
DON'T WORRY! NOTHING IS PARTING THIS QUARTER OF A MILLION FROM US!
MEANWHILE--
YOU RIGHT, KEMO SABAY! SHOTS WE HEAR COME FROM TRAIN THAT IS STOPPED!
THROTTLE! WHAT HAPPENED TO YOUR--
NEVER MIND ME! I CAN BE PATCHED UP. BUT TWO OWLHOOTS SHOT THE BAGGAGE GUARD AND ARE HIGHBALLING OFF WITH A QUARTER OF A MILLION DOLLARS!
FIND 'EM! I'VE GOT TO KEEP MY RECORD PERFECT! THIS WAS MY LAST RUN--
ROBBERS' TRACKS HERE!
THEY HAVEN'T MUCH OF A LEAD--
NOT A MARK ON MY RECORD---AND NOW THIS! BUT IF YOU CAN STOP THEM--
BUT SOON--
THE HORSE WITH NEW SHOES LEAVE CLEAR TRAIL, BUT NOW TOO DARK!
WE CAN ONLY WAIT TILL MORNING--AND THAT MAY BE TOO LATE! POOR THROTTLE!
CONTINUED--

Service and other books. It wasn't long before he said, 'Joe, you can do the heads because you can draw enough like me,' so I did. That was how I took over all of Tom's Timely work on *Red Warrior, Kent Blake* and the other little incidental characters. I did that for about nine months."

After Sinnott's marriage to Betty Kirlauski in August of 1950, he joined the growing ranks of Timely's artists, illustrating stories by Stan Lee and Hank Chapman.

Sinnott went on to become one of Timely's most dependable artists along with developing a lucrative freelance career. During the collapse of the comic book industry, Sinnott found steady work illustrating *Treasure Chest,* but soon Marvel came calling one more time.

"I got a call from Stan (Lee) and I went onto ink Jack Kirby on *Fantastic Four* #4," said Sinnott, who went onto establish the Marvel style in the 1970s and 1980s. "I'm still working with Stan on *Spider-Man*, 65 years later!"

After the departure of Sinnott and Steinberg, Gill found another talented artist in his classes: John Calnan.

"I graduated high school in 1950, and then went to the School of Visual Arts, which at that time was the cartoonists and illustrators school where I met Tom Gill and inked *The Lone Ranger* and *Cheyenne*," said Calnan, who also worked on *Classics Illustrated* titles.

Calnan, who turned to advertising art moonlighted on horror comics for titles such as *House of Mystery,* eventually took over penciling *Batman* in the 1970s (around *Batman* issue 300) and titles such as the *Superman Family.* He discussed working on the classic "Around the World in 80 Days" in Gill's studio with other artists in the mid-1950s.

"We each worked on a little part of the book," he said. "I do know that my work

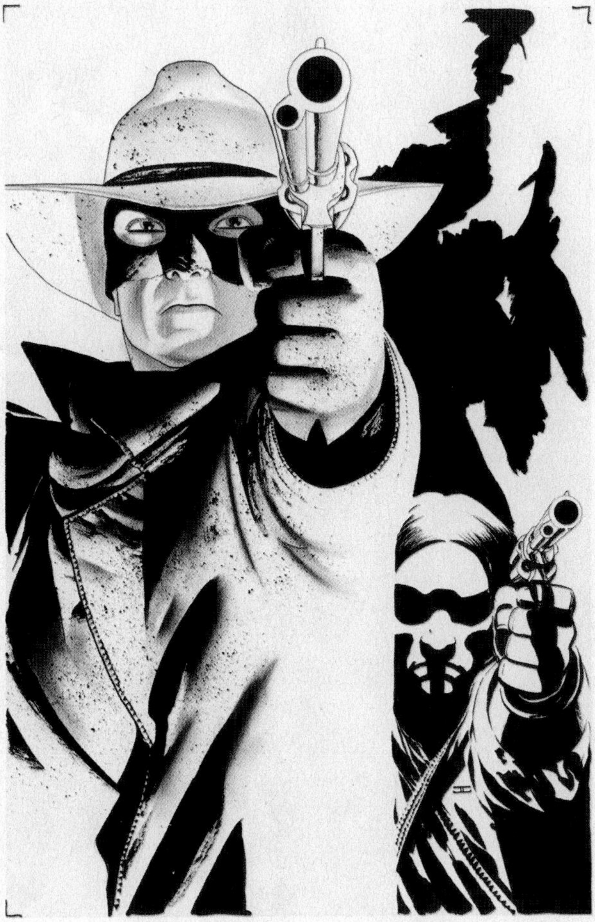

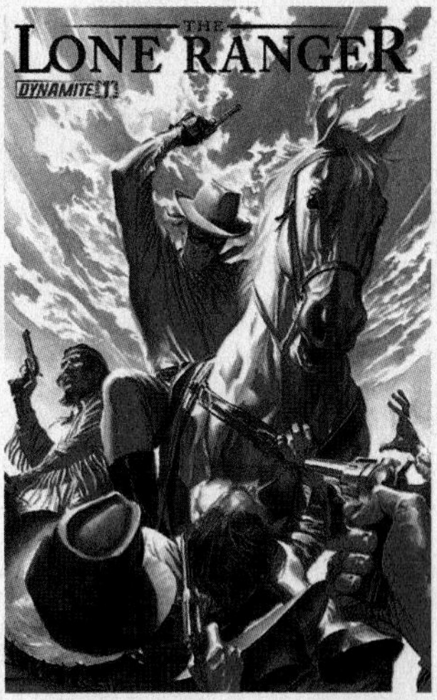
THE
LONE RANGER
DYNAMITE

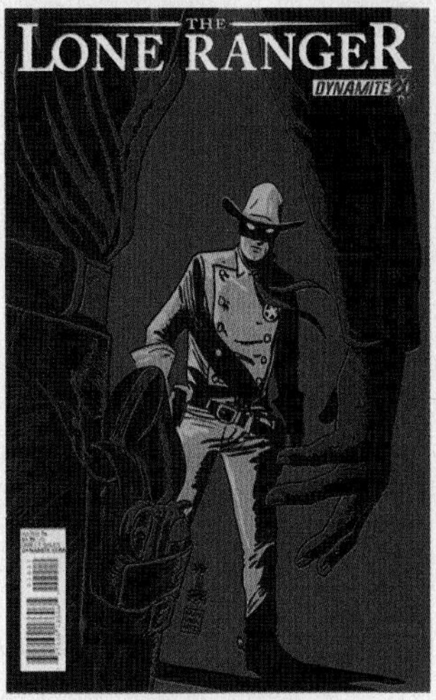
THE
LONE RANGER
DYNAMITE

preceded the *Lone Ranger* movie book in 1956 but that is all I can tell you, it was a long time ago. We were never given credit, but it was valuable experience for a young artist. Tom would pencil the faces and we would do the rest over his layouts."

Herb Trimpe attended the art school starting in 1957, Gill needed a student to "ink his backgrounds and stuff," Trimpe said.

"That's how I started at Dell Comics," said Trimpe. "I was mostly doing westerns and licensed books, like the adaptation of the movie *Journey to the Center of the Earth*. I had a long career in comic books and without Tom, it would not have happened."

The Marvel connection continued with John Verpoorten who worked with Gill in the early 1960s prior to his start in the bullpen in 1967. Like Trimpe, he and Gill worked on the Ranger and other Dell titles. Verpoorten rose to the position of production manager in 1970 and passed away in 1977.

Jimmy Christiansen and artist Mac L. Pakula were two other art assistants to the teacher/artist who also attended the SVA. Christiansen worked on the Ranger and eventually developed a lifelong friendship with Gill. He eventually went onto a career in design.

The Timely/Atlas connection for Gill was strong into the mid-1950s, with cartoonist and sculptor Mac L. Pakula contributing to their war, spy, horror and western comic books. Pakula, who passed away in 2013, worked with Gill for several months on *Lone Ranger* in addition to his school work. The well-regarded artist studied with Norman Rockwell at the SVA, eventually forming a friendship with the legendary painter, and developing a remarkable career in the process.

While Gill received the credit for the *Lone Ranger* art over his 107-issue run and the other titles his studio produced, he recognized the talent of his students and mentored them into successful careers in corporate artwork and the comic book industry for more than 40 years.

Hi Ho Silver, Away!

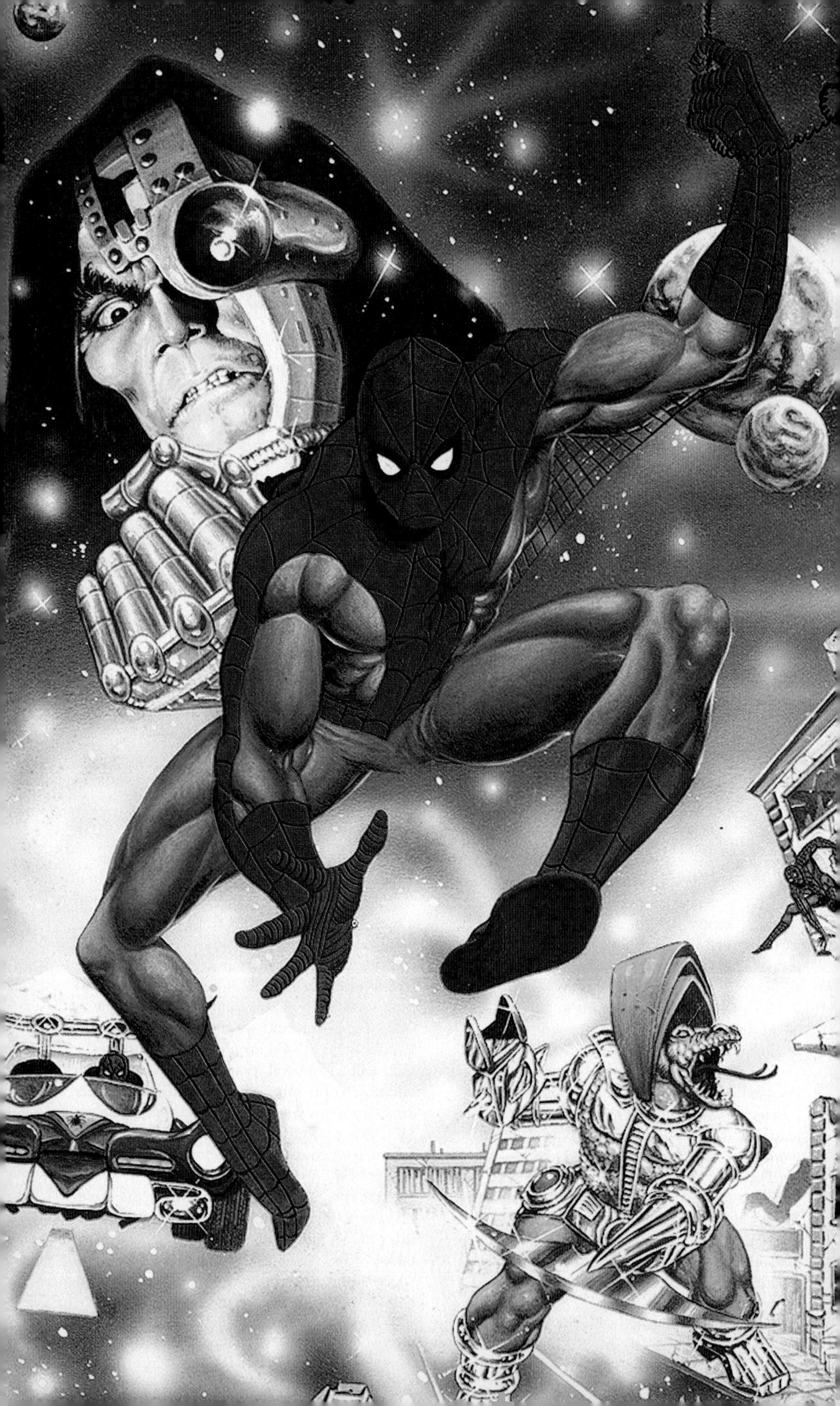

Coming to America:
Japan's Spider-Man

BY **CARRIE WOOD**

In January of 2015, Marvel brought back a character many never thought would ever hit the pages of a comic book – the Japanese Spider-Man, Takuya Yamashiro. In *The Amazing Spider-Man* #12, which was part of the "Spider-Verse" event; "Spider-Verse" had previously brought several other Spider-Men, such as Spider-Man 2099 and Spider-Man Noir, into the same universe to fight an evil threatening all of them. But Takuya's most striking feature as Spider-Man isn't simply his place of origin, but rather, his enormous fighting robot, Leopardon. While some readers may have thought this to be a *Power Rangers*-inspired addition, it was actually quite the opposite, as Japan's Spidey debuted back in 1978.

This live-action adaptation of *Spider-Man* was produced by Toei, a company probably best known for their "tokusatsu" shows. Tokusatsu is a term that literally translates to "special filming," so the genre encompasses any film or live-action show that uses a lot of special effects. While tokusatsu series are immensely popular in Japan, very few have achieved the same sort of success elsewhere; *Power Rangers* (based on *Super Sentai*) and *Godzilla* are likely the best-known tokusatsu series in the United States.

Though giant monster battles had been popular since the debut of Godzilla in 1954, thanks to the success of *Kamen Rider* and similar series, the "masked hero" sub-genre of tokusatsu had taken off. *Spider-Man* effectively combined a "masked hero" with the giant monster battles, and helped set a standard that would later be used in *Super Sentai*.

One of the most successful tokusatsu series of all time is *Kamen Rider*, which got started in 1971. *Kamen Rider* features a masked hero (the titular character) who fights against the evil organization known as Shocker while wearing a suit that gives him a grasshopper-like appearance. The *Kamen Rider* franchise has since spawned 25 different series, but it clearly had an impact on *Spider-Man* as well; both main characters

ride a fancy motorcycle, and both have an accessory they wear constantly that allows them to transform (a belt in the case of Kamen Rider, a bracelet in the case of Spider-Man). The success of Kamen Rider's insect-like appearance may have also spurred Toei into pursuing Spider-Man as their main character, rather than other Marvel properties they had access to.

Toei's *Spider-Man* series featured a character that only lined up with the original version of the character in so much that he had the same suit and superhero name. There's no Peter Parker here. Takuya Yamashiro is the main character – a motorcycle racer who gains the powers of Spider-Man after investigating a UFO crash. He sees the ship land, and goes after his father, Dr. Hiroshi Yamashiro, who wants to see what it is. Unfortunately, Hiroshi is killed during his investigation by members of the evil Iron Cross Army, an alien group led by Professor Monster that has spent 400 years planning to take over Earth and rule the universe.

Incidentally enough, series antagonist Professor Monster bears somewhat of a resemblance to another popular Marvel character – Doctor Doom. Though it was never explicitly stated by Toei that Professor Monster's appearance was based on Doom, there is a clear resemblance. Both have their faces obscured by a metal mask, sport a dark green cloak, and are skilled leaders.

Professor Monster is the head of the Iron Cross Army, the force attempting to take over the world. None of Spider-Man's classic villains show up – no Green Goblin, Electro, Doctor Octopus or Kraven the Hunter here. This falls more in line with a classic tokusatsu setup; while there is still a "monster of the week" format with a new creature to defeat, the minions all wear the same uniform and everyone is working for the same organization with a single leader at the helm. Other examples of this would be the Shocker organization in *Kamen Rider,* or Rita Repulsa and

Lord Zedd's Putty Patrol and Tenga Warriors in *Mighty Morphin' Power Rangers*.

The UFO that Takuya sees is actually an alien warship known as the "Marveller" that was sent from Planet Spider. After encountering the Iron Cross Army, Takuya falls down into a cave and is rescued by the ship's original owner, Garia. In order to save Takuya's life, Garia – who is at the end of his lifespan himself – injects Takuya with some of his own blood.

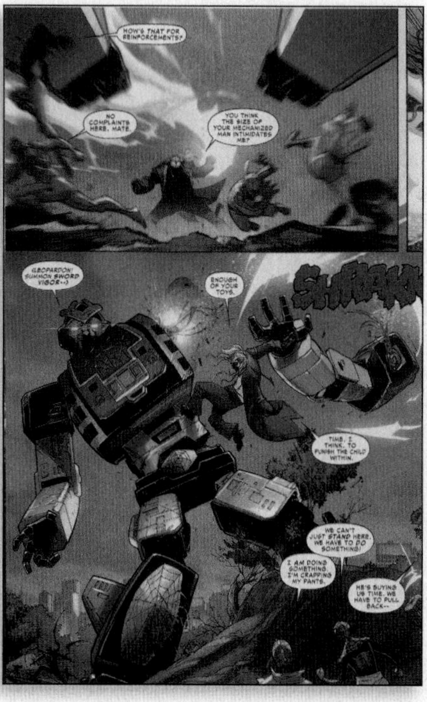
HOW'S THAT FOR REINFORCEMENTS?
NO COMPLAINTS HERE, MATE.
YOU THINK THE SIZE OF YOUR MECHANIZED MAN INTIMIDATES ME?
‹LEOPARDON! SUMMON SWORD VIGOR--›
ENOUGH OF YOUR TOYS.
TIME, I THINK, TO PUNISH THE CHILD WITHIN.
WE CAN'T JUST STAND HERE. WE HAVE TO DO SOMETHING!
I AM DOING SOMETHING. I'M CRAPPING MY PANTS.
HE'S BUYING US TIME. WE HAVE TO PULL BACK--

The blood of someone from Planet Spider gives Takuya his Spider-Sense ability as well as other spider-like traits, such as being able to climb on walls. Unfortunately, he also gains the weaknesses of spiders as well, becoming more sensitive to cold and certain sounds.

Takuya is also given a gadget known as the Spider Bracelet, which contains "Spider Fluid" which he can turn into nets and strings to trap and tie up enemies, as well as swing from. The Spider Bracelet also contains the superhero's suit – known in this version as the "Spider Protector" – allowing Takuya to instantly transform into Spider-Man when needed. There's also a homing device in the bracelet that allows Takuya to pick up distress signals as well as summon the Marveller.

The Marveller ship is usually accessed by Spider-Man by way of Spidey's flying car, the Spider Machine GP-7. Though the Spider Machine itself was equipped with a variety of weaponry in a similar fashion to the Batmobile, Takuya rarely spent much time in it for defensive purposes and most often used it as a means to access the Marveller. The Marveller itself is a massive ship at 45 meters tall, and because of this, it's usually stored underground. When Spider-Man summons the Marveller, it bursts through the Earth's surface before flying to Spidey's location.

The Marveller's best asset, though, was its ability to change into the giant fighting robot known as Leopardon. While Marveller is clearly a spaceship, Leopardon is more humanoid in appearance. It stands at 60 meters tall, making it an absolute force for the Iron Cross Army to reckon with. Leopardon is equipped with a number of weapons, including an arm rocket and the "Arc Turn." The latter would have Leopardon throwing its V-shaped head decoration like a boomerang at the enemy. The robot's best weapon, though, was the Sword Vigor, a sword attached to Leopardon's leg. Interestingly, Leopardon would never wield the Sword Vigor as if it were a traditional sword and instead opted to throw it at the enemy, resulting in destroying the enemy in a single hit in most cases. Leopardon also had a shield called the Spider Protector, which could be emitted from its legs and took the shape of a spider web – however, this was only ever shown in promotional materials for the show and was never actually seen in action. This might have been because Spider-Man's suit was already called the Spider Protector.

Those who grew up on *Power Rangers* in the 1990s are familiar with the Megazord, the team's powerful fighting robot. But the Megazord might not have ever come about if not for the success of Leopardon in *Spider-Man*. Leopardon was actually the first giant robot to be featured in any of Toei's tokusatsu television series, and the merchandising opportunities that the robot spawned made it a success. Toys and model kits of Leopardon continue to be made now, almost 40 years since the series ended.

Part of Leopardon's lasting popularity stems from the fact that he was nearly invincible. Toei's official website has called it "the mightiest instant killing giant robot in the history of tokusatsu programming." Battle scenes with Leopardon versus one of the Iron Cross Army's monsters were often short and always ended with a one-hit death via Leopardon's Sword Vigor.

The reason behind this, though, is somewhat ironic. The Leopardon suit, being one of the first of its kind, was somewhat primitive; the person inside the suit had a difficult time moving, and the suit became quickly damaged and later totally lost. So, by halfway through the 41-episode run, the Leopardon suit was no more. This led to the use of old stock footage being used of Leopardon to help create the fight scenes. Leopardon rarely ever appeared in the same shot as the giant monsters that it was fighting anyway, making it easy to stage fight scenes with different creatures. Numerous episodes featured Leopardon unsheathing the Sword Vigor and throwing it at the opponent as soon as it transformed, leading to unbelievably quick fight scenes – and leading to Leopardon not ever taking any damage itself even in the final battle against Professor Monster himself. So because of a damaged, lost and broken suit, Leopardon became known as the strongest fighting robot ever. Funny how these things work out.

Spider-Man ran from May 1978 to March 1979 for 41 episodes and also had a movie debut on July 22, 1978. The film takes place between episodes 10 and 11 and introduces the character Juzo Mamiya, an investigator in charge of Interpol's Secret Intelligence Division, who works alongside Spider-Man in an attempt to take down the Iron Cross Army. His story arc carried into the series through episode 13. Though it ran for less than a year, the series was received well and has maintained a cult following even in other parts of the world for the unusual premise and kitschy special effects.

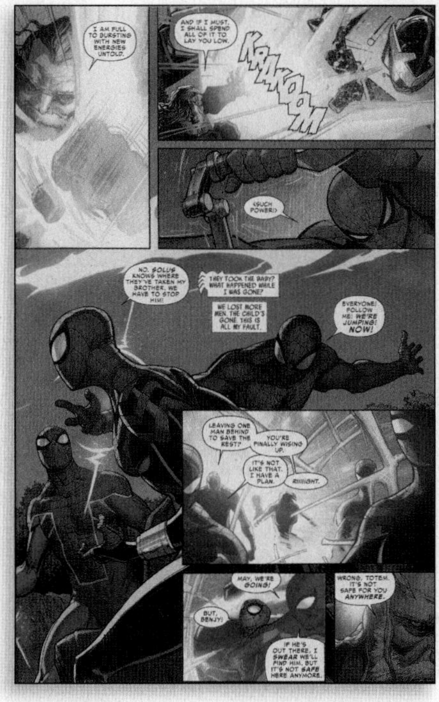
I AM FULL TO BURSTING WITH NEW ENERGIES UNTOLD.
AND IF I MUST, I SHALL SPEND ALL OF IT TO LAY YOU LOW.
KRAKOOM
‹SUCH POWER!›
NO. SOLUS KNOWS WHERE THEY'VE TAKEN MY BROTHER. WE HAVE TO STOP HIM!
THEY TOOK THE BABY? WHAT HAPPENED WHILE I WAS GONE?
WE LOST MORE MEN. THE CHILD'S GONE. THIS IS ALL MY FAULT.
EVERYONE! FOLLOW ME! WE'RE JUMPING! NOW!
LEAVING ONE MAN BEHIND TO SAVE THE REST?
YOU'RE FINALLY WISING UP.
IT'S NOT LIKE THAT. I HAVE A PLAN.
RIIIIIGHT.
MAY, WE'RE GOING!
BUT, BENJY!
IF HE'S OUT THERE, I SWEAR WE'LL FIND HIM, BUT IT'S NOT SAFE HERE ANYMORE.
WRONG, TOTEM. IT'S NOT SAFE FOR YOU ANYWHERE.

However, because of the licensing deal between Toei and Marvel, finding the series today can prove somewhat of a challenge. A DVD box set was released in 2005, and no plans for any sort of Blu-Ray release have been announced. Toei retains the rights to use the original characters they had created for the series, such as Professor Monster and Leopardon, for merchandising purposes, and replicas of both Leopardon and the Spider Machine GP-7 car have been made quite recently.

Though Takuya's appearance in the "Spider-Verse" event was certainly memorable on its own – given he arrived on the scene in the Marveller itself – it marked the first time that the character appeared in an American comic book. However, it wasn't the first attempt to introduce Takuya to the western market. In 1979, Marvel planned a Fumetti magazine version of Toei's *Spider-Man*, but only a cover was ever made for this, painted by Joe Jusko. The painting shows Takuya in action against one of the Iron Cross Army's many monsters, as well as the Spider Machine GP-7 and Professor Monster.

"Marvel was trying to do unique things with their black and white magazines in the late '70s," Jusko said. "When the idea of doing a book based on the then-current Japanese *Spider-Man* TV show, editors Rick Marshall and Ralph Maccio thought using a Fumetti approach – using sequential still photographs in lieu of art to tell the story – would not only be different, but give a true representation of the show."

Fumetti was a fairly popular approach in Europe at the time, but only had limited success in the United States; other series that used the medium were *National Lampoon* and *Star Trek*. Jusko at the time was new to the industry with only a couple of covers under his belt when given the assignment.

"As I remember, John Romita Jr. did the initial cover layout using Marvel's version of Spider-Man instead of Toei's, probably for newsstand recognition," he said, "I was given the layout and several stills for reference to complete the cover. It was a fun job, and looking back on it, I think it came out well for the time it was done and the limited experience I had at that point. I actually had never seen an episode of the show until it appeared on YouTube many years later. It was a unique interpretation, to stay the least, which is probably why it has gained such cult status over the years."

The magazine ultimately ended up scrapped, due to the low quality of the stills that Marvel finally received from Japan – "They were pretty much unusable," according to Jusko. But. fortunately for Marvel and Toei, Takuya's *Amazing Spider-Man* appearance was well-received by fans and critics alike. Though Toei's *Spider-Man* show had a distinct Japanese twist to it, the impact it had has already been felt in other parts of the world via the popularity of *Power Rangers*' Megazord – and perhaps this legacy will allow Takuya and Leopardon to make future Marvel Comics appearances.

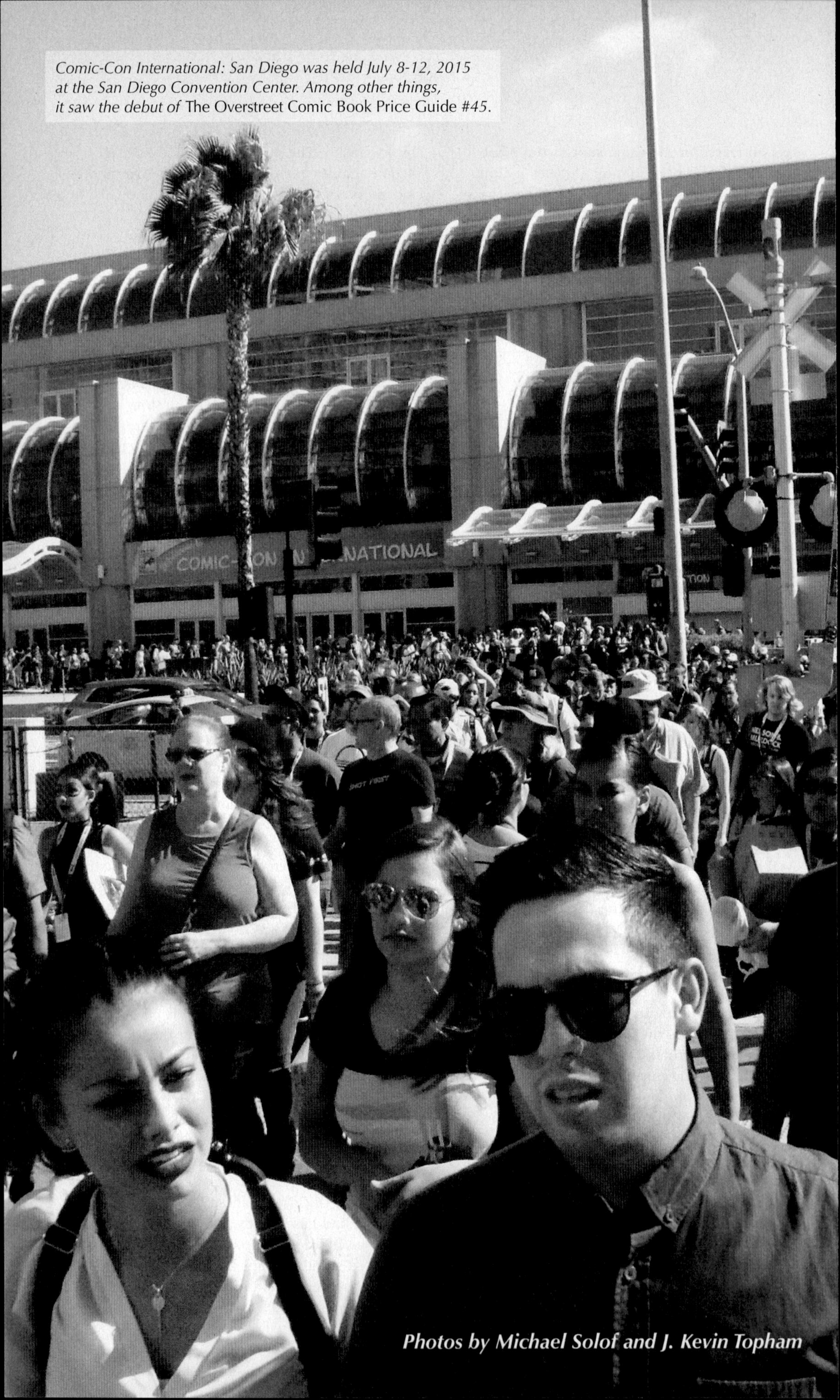

Comic-Con International: San Diego was held July 8-12, 2015 at the San Diego Convention Center. Among other things, it saw the debut of The Overstreet Comic Book Price Guide *#45.*

Photos by Michael Solof and J. Kevin Topham

Market Reports

Robert M. Overstreet
Author and Publisher
The Overstreet Comic Book Price Guide

The San Diego Comic-Con is such an important event for the comic book market. It was a pleasure for Carol and me to attend the 2015 July event, especially since we were there to hand out *The Overstreet Comic Book Price Guide* #45 to advisors and advertisers set up at the convention on the day of its release. I enjoyed visiting with everyone and also being able to meet some of the new advisors such as Torpedo Comics' Stephen Houston.

I enjoyed being able to visit with Gary Carter, Larry Bigman (early Overstreet Advisor), Ron Pussell, Chuck Rozanski, Richard Evans, Matt Nelson, John Verzyl, Jamie Graham, Bill Cole, Billy Tucci, Josh Nathanson, Vincent Zurzolo, Rob Reynolds and Frank Cwiklik, Barry Sandoval, Bill Ponsetti, Harley Yee, Michael Carbonaro, and so many others.

It is always fun being able to meet with my longtime friend Steve Geppi. I thoroughly enjoyed sitting in on our discussion with Paul Levitz about the beginnings of direct distribution, and most of all being able to visit with two of my colleagues, J.C. Vaughn and Mark Huesman, my top creative assistants at Gemstone who always get each new price guide to the printer on time.

It was a pleasure meeting and visiting with Dave Johnson at the Hero Initiative booth where we signed his Spirit cover on the Hero exclusive edition of the *Guide* as they were being sold.

But most of all I really enjoyed my special Hero Initiative luncheon with Steve Borock and the five top bidders at Roy's Hawaiian Fusion, where we were able to exchange collecting knowledge and better get to know each other. This luncheon was arranged by Jim McLauchlin, president of Hero Initiative, and it was a fun way to help such a great charity.

As we saw in the build-up to *CBPG* #45 and at Comic-Con, the market continues to be vibrant and exciting. Original comic art continues to be very interesting, but that hasn't stopped records from being set in comic books, too.

As you'll see in the following market reports, there are plenty of things worth noting going on.

Bob Overstreet and Diamond Comic Distributors President and CEO Steve Geppi caught up at the con.

Terry O'Neill
Terry's Comics/Nationwide Comics/CalComicCon
Orange, CA

This report focuses on Convention and mail order aspects of comic collecting. Sales from 2014 to 2015 have been strong. My advice to a young collector, who was frustrated about prices going up on many of the 1st appearances and other minor keys, was to "buy it all." This collector asked how he should know what title, character, or theme he should look for; he wanted to be ahead of the game before the next comic-related TV series or movie was announced. As we have seen these past few years, a comic character or storyline used in the media almost always increases demand, which almost always increases prices. How much and how long depends on the popularity of the character(s) and scarcity of the issue(s).

Now that Disney owns the Marvel and *Star Wars* franchises, we should see almost every first, second, and third (or more) obscure character promoted (exploited?). My younger sister once told me that girls are loyal Disney customers with the princesses: (Snow White, Cinderella, Aurora, Ariel, Belle, Jasmine, Pocahontas, Mulan, Rapunzel, Merida, and Anna and Elsa from *Frozen*). Now it's the boys' turn with super heroes and super villains, for example, Captain America, Avengers, Iron Man, Agents of

S.H.I.E.L.D, Agent Carter and Daredevil. Also, don't forget, Warner Brothers owns DC comics. We have all seen what kind of money well-done superhero movies (Batman, Superman, Green Lantern) and TV series (Green Arrow, Flash, Gotham) can produce, turning lesser characters into licensable merchandise.

That said, awareness of true scarcity is elevated for comics like *Tales to Astonish* #13 (1st Groot), when suddenly everyone wants a copy, pushing prices up. Had I only known the 4th-rate group Guardians of the Galaxy would one day be the new "*Star Wars*, Marvel-style" for this generation. I would have been able to retire. Snap.

I sold a *TTA* #13 in Very Good for $900, *Marvel Preview* #4 (1st Star-Lord) in Near Mint/Mint for $2400, (1st appearance Rocket Raccoon), #7 in Very Fine-plus for $1200, *Incredible Hulk* #271 (2nd Rocket) in Near Mint for $250, and *Marvel Super Heroes* #18 (1st appearance of Guardians) in Very Fine/Near Mint for $350. Sounds good, right? A year earlier I sold a *TTA* #13 in Very Good/Fine for $45, would have sold those Marvel Preview magazines for $20 or less, and put the Hulk #271 in a "$2 each" box. Last year I sold a *Marvel Super Heroes* #18 in Fine/Very Fine for $15. In one year, the value had increased fifty times. While most comics cool in value after the release of the movie/TV series, the values of these are forever appreciated. Did we really think *Teenage Mutant Ninja Turtles* had peaked?

The point is, back in 1976 I sold my first comic with the intent to use the money to buy other comics to read. I could not have dreamt that these lines on paper would be great investments. So, what should a new collector buy? If not one of each, or one of every 1st appearance, then my advice is to buy what you like. Maybe someday someone will like it enough to make a show of it. If not, at least you will have something you like to read.

Josh Nathanson
Douglas Gillock
ComicLink.com

Editor's note: *This market report from ComicLink's Josh Nathanson and Douglas Gillock just missed the deadline for* The Overstreet Comic Book Price Guide *#45 so some of the transactions they mention will seem a little dated, but given their stature in the hobby and the issues they discuss, it was an easy decision to include it in this edition of* Overstreet's Comic Book Marketplace Yearbook.

This past year was another exciting year in the hobby with ComicLink buyers and sellers utilizing ComicLink Auctions as well as the Comic Book Exchange and Comic Art Exchange in order to buy

SAN DIEGO
COMIC CON
INTERNATIONAL

Gemstone Publishing Vice-President of Publishing J.C. Vaughn, CCS President Matt Nelson, CBCS President Steve Borock, author Mark Waid, former CBG Editor Maggie Thompson, and Gemstone Publishing Creative Director Mark Huesman (left to right) at the "Overstreet at 45" panel at Comic-Con.

and sell valuable comic books and comic art to add to their collections and maximize their net sale prices.

2014 was a year of strength across virtually every collecting era. From Golden Age rarities of the 1930s and '40s, through the Silver Age keys of the late 1950s and early '60s, and right up to Bronze Age and Modern high grades, the bar was raised on record sales this year. Historically, it has seemed that as one era has a rise in collector interest, another gets a little quieter. This has not been the case recently, however, with collectors eager to compete for quality examples from virtually the entire time span of the hobby.

Demand is ever-present for comic books from the Silver Age genre. Major Marvel keys led the way in 2014 with exceptional results for several premiere and "1st app" issues achieved. There are way too many to list here but just a few examples include the record $275,000 sale of Thor's premiere in *Journey into Mystery* #83 CGC 9.4, the first Justice League appearance *Brave and the Bold* #28 CGC 9.2 for $120,000, *Tales to Astonish* #35 CGC 9.6 Western Penn, the first Ant-Man in costume, for $66,000, Spider-Man's first appearance in *Amazing Fantasy* #15 CGC 7.5 for $63,100, *Fantastic Four* #3 CGC 9.4 for $33,000, *Amazing Spider-Man* #1 CGC 8.5 for $29,750, *Incredible Hulk* #1 CGC 6.0 CVA for $23,100, *Amazing Spider-Man* #20 CGC 9.8 CVA for

$19,750, *Tales to Astonish* #44 CGC 9.6 Pacific Coast (first Wasp) for $17,000, *Fantastic Four* #49 CGC 9.6 for $11,939, *Amazing Spider-Man Annual* #3 CGC 9.8 for $8,601, *Tales to Astonish* #13 CGC 8.5 (first Groot) for $5750, *Detective Comics* #298 CGC 9.6 (first Silver Age Clayface) for $5500, *Batman* #121 CGC 9.0 for $5200, and *Batman* #210 CGC 9.8 for $3,300.

Major Golden Age runs and scarcities were also a focus for many of these buyers in 2014. Just a small sampling of record 2014 sales in this segment includes *Action Comics* #1 CGC 6.5 Extensive Restoration for $130,000, *Sub-Mariner Comics* #1 CGC 9.2 $105,000, *Batman* #1 CGC 4.0 for $52,000, *Detective Comics* #27 CGC NR (coverless, missing centerfold) for $27,500, a rare "Canadian White" *Nelvana* #1 CGC 6.5 for $13,750, *Detective Comics* #36 CGC 4.5 for $13,750, *Human Torch* #12 CGC 8.0 for $10,807, *Detective Comics* #73 CGC 9.0 for $10,000, *Marvel Mystery Comics* #30 CGC 8.5 for $7,900, *Captain America Comics* #62 CGC 9.0 CVA for $6,200, *More Fun Comics* #9 CGC 1.8 for $3,898, *Weird Science* #9 CGC 9.4 Gaines File for $3,378, *Haunt of Fear* #10 CGC 9.6 Gaines File for $2,920, *Strange Tales* #1 CBCS 6.5 for $2,900, *Teenage Romances* #9 CGC 5.5 (classic Matt Baker cover) for $2,350, *Hit Comics* #5 CGC 5.0 for $2,200, *Black Cat Comics* #50 CGC 6.5 for $1,901, and *Real Life Comics* #3 CGC 2.5 for $1,477. Scarcity and

Bob Overstreet (left) greets Josh Nathanson at the ComicLink booth.

particularly scarcity in grade are key factors here with buyers extremely educated on the availability of these items and stepping up aggressively when they did come to market. The Golden Age market is also extremely cover driven right now and even at the lower end of the pricing spectrum a book with a stand-out cover can blow the doors off *Guide* prices when properly promoted.

Highlights of the Bronze and Modern eras were also found with the very top of the grading spectrum leading the way. Issues connected to up-coming Marvel and DC films projects drew serious attention with some issues leaping from the "dollar bins" into three and four figure territory in just a matter of months and established keys continuing to rise. Some standout sales included *Teenage Mutant Ninja Turtles* #1 CGC 9.8 for $16,250, *Iron Fist* #14 CGC 9.4 Price Variant (first Iron Fist) for $15,000, *New Mutants* #98 CGC 9.9 (first Deadpool) for $6,203, *Tales of the Teen Titans* #44 CGC 9.9 (first Nightwing) for $4010, *Star Wars* #1 CGC 8.5 price variant for $3988, *Ms. Marvel* #1 CGC 9.8 for $1890, *Nova* #1 CGC 9.8 for $1500, *Howard the Duck* #1 CGC 9.8 for $1,399, *Tomb of Dracula* #3 CGC 9.8 for $1,100, and *Incredible Hulk* #271 CGC 9.8 (first Rocket Raccoon in comics) for $702.

Original comic art continues to draw the attention of more and more collectors and this segment of ComicLink's business has been incredibly dynamic in the past few years. Just a few standout 2014 art sales include an early 1960s Frank Frazetta "Bathing Girl" pin-up painting for $61,200, Dave Cockrum's *Iron Fist* #15 cover art for $55,178, Bill Sienkiewicz's *Elektra: Assassin* #4 cover painting for $50,000, John Romita's *Amazing Spider-Man* #141 cover art on vellum for $49,000, a Jack Kirby *Fantastic Four* #40 page for $42,000, a Steve Ditko *Amazing Spider-Man* #30 panel page for $39,000, a Jack Kirby Baxter Building pin-up from *Fantastic Four Annual* #1 for $36,100, Herb Trimpe's *Incredible Hulk* #119 cover art for $36,000, a John Byrne *X-Men* #113 panel page for $31,000 and a #114 panel page for $26,250, a Jack Kirby *X-Men* #9 Marvel Girl pin-up for $25,250, a Frank Miller *Wolverine* #2 panel page for $23,258, Greg Land's *X-Men* #500 cover art for $21,793, John Buscema's *Conan the Barbarian* #89 cover art for $20,583, a Jack Kirby *Mister Miracle* #12 title splash for $19,250, Tim Sale's *Batman: The Long Halloween* TPB cover for $16,100, a Jack Kirby *Silver Surfer* graphic novel page for $18,500, a Rick Leonardi *Uncanny X-Men* #212 half splash for $10,304, and an unpublished Joe Kubert Golden Age Hawkman page from *Flash Comics* for $6,600.

The first months of 2015 have already shown exceptional results across all eras with auction and exchange sales such as *Detective Comics* #27 CGC 2.5 (first Batman) for $275,000, *Avengers* #1 CGC 9.4 for $125,000, *Fantastic Four* #5 CGC 9.6 (first Doctor Doom) for $96,267, *Superman* #1 CGC 2.0 for $81,222, John Romita, Jr.'s *Amazing Spider-Man* #238 cover with the first Hobgoblin appearance for $100,000, and page 2 of *Avengers* #2 for $48,000.

With results like these leading off the year, 2015 seems poised to be another record-breaker not just for ComicLink, but for the industry as a whole. With nearly two decades online serving buyers and sellers in the collecting community, ComicLink is the longest running and most established consignment service in the hobby. We are excited to see what the next 20 years brings! It does not seem like we can get enough material of quality to satiate our collector-investors! If you've got some, give us a call!

Benjamin Labonog
Collector
Burlingame, CA

It is a great privilege to finally be an Overstreet comic advisor! Now, before I give my first market report, I'd like to give a warm "thank you" to fellow collectors/advisors Bill Ponseti, Todd Warren, and Greg Reece for their kind recommendations on my behalf. Also, a special "handshake" to Lance Washington, Frank Rohr, Isaac Flores, and Noel Jumaoas for all their longtime friendships in this hobby and for many lasting and impactful conversations during the early "pioneering" stages of my collecting days.

My roots in comics began with accumulating Original-owner Marvels in the early '80s at my local 7-11 store. From there, I found my LCS (Al's Comic Shop in Stockton, CA) where I'd purchase numerous Marvel titles off the rack (thanks Mom for waiting patiently on your corner seat!). I soon ventured into wall books, and I still have my high grade *Defenders* #10 that I purchased for a then-whopping $4.00 from Al's in 1985. In junior high, I can remember trading a stack of 1965 Marvels at a local Holiday Inn show for a low grade *FF* #8. It was the first time I ever saw a 12-cent circle Marvel and I had to have it. I took a break from comics in 1988, but would return in 1993 after I purchased a *Hulk* #3 at a local mall show and that hooked me into the vintage market. My focus is on pre-1964 Marvels, GA Schomburg covers, Timelys, and pre-Robin *Detective*s. There have been several key events that have impacted the buying and selling of comic books: the *Overstreet Comic Book Price Guide* (1970), the *Gerber Photo Journals* (1989), eBay (1995), online comic book auction houses, CGC grading (2000), pressing comics, and Hollywood movies based on comic books.

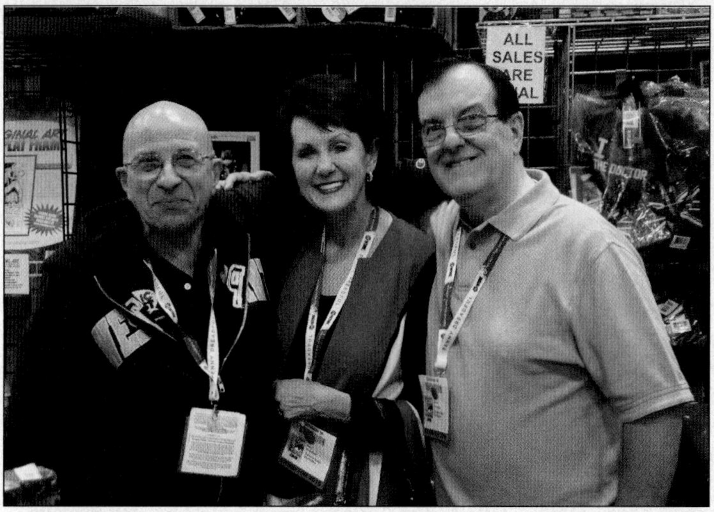
ALL
SALES

Longtime Overstreet Advisor Bill Cole caught up with Carol and Bob Overstreet for the first time in five years.

Golden Age

I get asked all the time if Superman, Batman, and Captain America-related titles are the best Golden Age books to invest in. Those sure have proven to be solid buys (and should continue to be), but comics should still be remembered to be bought and enjoyed for the creative, visual documents that they are. On the financial side, I have seen many collectors downgrade their more expensive keys as they approach and eclipse the five and six figure marks. I personally did that this past summer by downgrading my *Detective Comics* #31 from a CGC universal 5.0 to a CGC universal 2.5. I had owned the book for several years and it was good timing to cash out, pick up more books, and still keep a respectable copy in my wheelhouse. Supply and demand are strong factors in any purchase, but timing is equally important -- who's looking for what, how much they have to spend, and what books are actually available for purchase at that particular time -- all these factors affect private and auction prices. This is especially more important with GA books because of the very thin supply and relentless demand of classic covers and key books. Speaking of *Detective* #31, it has clearly passed *Detective* #29, #33, and #35 as far as price point goes. We can debate #29 vs. #31 forever, but I like them both with a slight edge going to the #31. Something some pre-Robin collectors may not have paid much attention to are Batman's "grey vs. blue" cowl/shoulders on the #31 cover. Look carefully, because they are two types. I have owned both and prefer the blue color as it blends better.

On the Timely front, *USA* #8 has proven to be the toughest in the *USA* run. Try to find one. The *USA* #7 gets all the attention (and rightfully so), but it is not nearly as tough to find as the #8. Both are strong sellers as are most Cap Schomburg covers. I will put a plug in here for *Marvel Mystery* #9: The mighty have fallen, but I sense a small upswing around the corner! A complete low grade copy will still run you $3000+. No copies have sold publicly since Spring 2014. Perhaps the next one will garner some attention. It's one of the best Subby covers of all time, and a battle issue to boot. The only *Marvel Mystery* books that seem to sell strong and fast are #40, #44, #46, which are all Schomburg covers. Speaking of Schomburg covers, the 9.0 CBCS *Suspense Comics* #3 is whispered to bring $100K+ in the August Heritage auction. By the time this goes to print, we shall see if that happened. *Suspense* #3 might be the best "cover only" book of the GA. I get a fair amount of requests for it, but some collectors won't spend 4-5 figures on a "cover only" book. For the rest of us, Schomburg's most powerful imagery of hooded Nazis, bondage, bonfire, guns, knives, swords, a full moon, bats, a steamy jungle, and of course the spear of freedom is too much to resist!

Silver Age

It's still quite amazing to see books like *Avengers* #55, *FF* #52, and *Strange Tales* #110 get mad respect and set record prices due to the Hollywood speculation hype. I think it is good and healthy for the comic market. It has reeled in new collectors (and old) and exposed them to characters and stories that they may not have been attracted to otherwise. We will see if those characters and first appearances will remain popular and in demand over time, or if the movie hype is just for a season. The Marvel and DC keys are strong and in non-stop demand. I've never seen *Brave and the Bold* #28, *Showcase* #4, and *Action* #252 in higher demand than now. There seems to be no stopping the *Amazing Fantasy* #15 train. Entry level prices for best copies are now at the $5K range, which is taking some collectors out of the race if they haven't purchased a copy yet. I remember thinking in 2012 when low grade copies were pushing $3K/point that it should slow down now...wrong! We have experienced the same with *Hulk* #1 the past 12 months... just red hot at commanding $3K-$4K/point. Non chipped books are most desired and sell strong. Especially on dark cover keys like *AF* #15, *Hulk* #1, and *TTA* #27 in which chipping degrades eye appeal. The earlier "12 cent circle price" Marvels are still my favorite such as *FF* #1-13 and *Hulk* #1-6. I got to meet Stan Lee two summers ago at a rare LCS appearance he made. I was trying to decide which book to have him sign, and it made sense that *FF* #1 was the right choice since it was the first title that started the Marvel

Silver Age. I hope *FF* #1 rebounds in the market. It deserves to be the #1 sought after Marvel key (with all respect to *AF* #15).

Bronze Age

Incredible Hulk #181 is the *AF* #15 of the Bronze Age. It has relentless demand and oodles of supply but still sells at about $200/point. Missing Marvel value stamps don't stop strong sales, especially if the eye appeal is VF or better. This is now a 40+ year old book and we will continue to see collectors in their 20s start buying these up as they begin to work and have money to invest with. *ASM* #121 has passed #122 as the stronger demand book. *ASM* #129 is snapped up in an instant as well. *Giant-Size X-Men* #1 is still a popular book as well as *X-Men* #94-143. *Sub-Mariner* #59 is a book that flies under the radar and is still cheap...a superb Everett black cover showing a Subby vs. Thor battle!

In closing, the comic book industry is very strong, profitable, and enjoyable. If you are a new collector, you may need to experience buying and selling different genres of comics before you find your niche and know what you truly enjoy. It is common to buy books and get bored with them and move on before you find out what makes you happy. The "hunt" is half the fun. Be patient and network with other dealers and collectors. The CGC comic boards are a great avenue to do so. Thanks for reading and happy collecting!

Doug Mabry
The Great Escape
Madison, TN

This spring and summer have seen quite a bit of volatility in the comic book marketplace! Every week we have someone looking for some first appearance of an obscure character on the off chance that they might make an appearance in a movie or TV show. Prices on many of these first appear-

ances seem to go up weekly. Even second and third appearances of characters like Deadpool are now receiving lots of attention.

I've also seen lots of movement in the regular runs of the mainstream Marvel titles, such as *Incredible Hulk*, *Iron Man*, and *Captain America*. Books that I used to have several runs of, I suddenly find myself out of. It's especially exciting to see the 1980's *Captain America* and *Avengers* runs finally move out of the boxes.

On the other hand, the DC back issue movement seems to be almost exclusively in the New 52 books. I do still have a strong demand for *Batman* and *Detective* and of course any key issues, but most of the other titles like *Justice League of America*, *Green Lantern*, etc., just haven't been moving unless it's a key issue. And lots of the classic Silver Age books just don't have any demand here. Titles like *Metal Men*, *Metamorpho*, *Hawkman*, *Atom*, *Doom Patrol*, and the Superman family of titles just seem to sit here.

Independent comics are hit or miss with us. *Walking Dead* is a perennial, and *Saga* sells great, but for most of the independent titles, anything over a month or two old will never sell unless deeply discounted. We tend to see most of our demand for Image comics in the trade paperback area. Folks seem to try an issue or two, and then wait for the trade.

Some sales of note:

Amazing Fantasy #15, Good-, $3000, *Amazing Spider-Man* #1, Fair, $1200, *Avengers* #57, FN/VF $400, *Dr. Strange* v2 #1, VF/NM $100, *Incredible Hulk* #181, Fair, $405, *Iron Man* #55, Good $210, *New Mutants* #98, FN/VF $163, *Star Wars* #1 (35¢ Variant) $1,000, *Uncanny X-Men* #1, Good-, $1,000, and *Showcase* #22, Good, $1,400.

That's it from Tennessee and Kentucky. Good luck hunting down those treasures!

Sure, the San Diego Convention Center was crowded, but the effort to farm some of the activities out to the nearby hotels actually seems to be succeeding in making the show floor more navigable.

Jamie Newbold
Southern California Comics
San Diego, California

2014 ended successfully for our store. Back issues, new comics, trades were selling at a high level. I'd say all three genres floated the store in roughly equal percentages. Those daily and weekly numbers can and were easily rocked by the sales of high-dollar back issues like *Amazing Spider-Man* #1 CGC 5.0 $5.5K and *Incredible Hulk* #181 CGC 9.6 $5,300.

2015 started with fervor equaling the end of 2014 indicating that the comic book world was still thriving on numerous levels. For instance, back issue sales for us extend backwards to the 1930s. Like many Golden Age–to-present dealers, we are rarely disappointed by the annual output of our older comics. They sell steadily with additional sales anointed by our presence at a couple of conventions.

No steadfast rules were broken in 2014 or early 2015 regarding old book sales, no surprises occurred. Marvels trumped DCs in back issue sales. Dells sold like Dells do. Westerns, funny animals, teen comics and Disneys appealed to small numbers of buyers. Archies published after 1960 fly out the store for only a buck apiece. Pre-Code Horror and Crime comics are hard to come by and relatively easy to sell if priced more conservatively than the recent past. DC ten cent-ers from the early to late 1950s are in great demand in high grade and so on.

Collections of Golden Age comics seldom showed up at our shop. This past year saw the least amount of Golden Age brought in to sell to us from the public. Oh, occasionally we would see small groups of books that we really wanted such as superheroes, Sci-Fi and Horror. We've seen infrequent quantities of War comics from Dell, Atlas and DC walk into our store with a few seen on road picks. Mostly, the old comics were represented by kid comics and *Classics Illustrated*. Our problem is selling that stuff.

It's still the same ol' story. Wait for the right buyer, often from an older age group, to come along at the store or at a convention. The older non-superhero comics are still a tough haul to sell at *Overstreet* prices. They probably will never generate awesome sale prices on those books ever again. War comics sales were an exception to the descent in popularity of the other genres. Right through the early 2000s the War comics market was still viable, worth hunting down collections for resale.

I read War comics produced these days. I also read much of the output from Atlas/Marvel and DC growing up. Unfortunately, passing time and new generations have left War comics sales in a downward slump. Low grade copies used to sell well for us at a dollar if we segregated them for easy perusal. Haunted Tank and Sgt. Rock titles flourished but even those comics languish in modern times.

We all know where the market is:

Stop me if you've heard this one before:

KEYS ARE HOT! In that regard absolutely nothing has changed in the market so I'm not gonna work that meaning over. What is damning is the increase in the number of customers, newbies in particular with "must-own at all costs" attitudes. We receive lots of customers looking to submit to CGC or CBCS through our more conservative submission prices (comparative to other stores in town). So we see a lot of other people's key books enroute to grading and a lot of that stuff is low grade. We used to see equal numbers of lower and higher grade stuff from original owner collections. Collectors that bought through contemporary markets seemed aware of the need to buy at particular grades. Those grades needed to be high enough to offset purchase and submission costs and still be worth more than the effort to encapsulate them. Through a variety of sources we've gained information that more submissions originate from a new gathering of speculators. Unfortunately, these guys are working without a net (to coin a circus phrase). Collectors buying from sellers with neither party dialed into proper grading with the results ending in poor choices.

We've tried to modestly educate customers, successfully gaining the attention and trust of some. Others operate with their belief "does grading really matter?" Yes. Yes it does and always has.

In their world it appears they've not bothered to be challenged by comic grading education. Instead, they are willing to trust dealers based upon price tags alone and then let the grading companies make sense of it all.

We shared a Facebook post with others regarding a poll taken by a comic book fan. The story involved fact-gathering from some 20 comic book stores worldwide. The conclusions drawn by many dwelled upon the state of new comic book sales versus back issues versus trade paperbacks. New comics were seen as holding their own against trades while back issues were not priorities for many stores. Strangely, new comic sales are thriving while digital comics exist. We expected new comics to reach a point where stores could not survive competing with digital but that seems not to be the case.

Trades sales at the store level at our store do quite well. We know we are small potatoes in a market overwhelmed by Amazon sales. I think

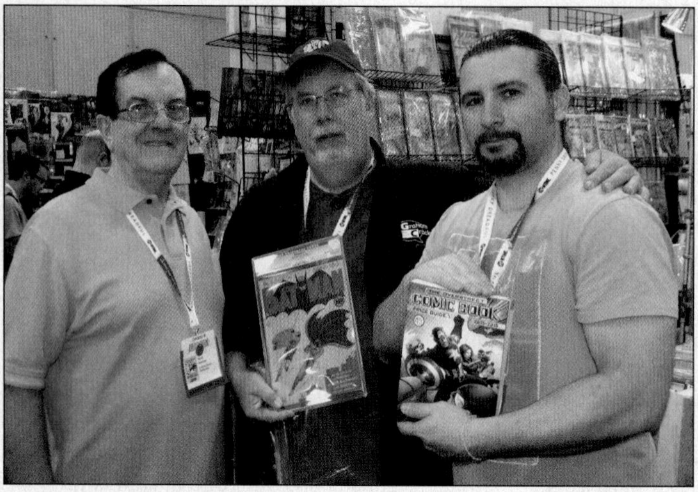
BATMAN
COMIC BOOK

Bob Overstreet with Graham Crackers Comics' Jamie Graham and Torpedo Comics' John Dolmayan (left to right).

Amazon misses the boat on gearing up customers on which trades to buy. That's something we excel at by talking customers through the various mythos of each company, sort of an initiation process. It's this "boots on the ground" scenario that keeps trades sales active at our store. Our store has just completed its third expansion just to provide adequate shelf space for the graphic novels we sell. We wouldn't do it if it were not profitable.

We have to say this about new comic book/trades sales in regards to DC and Marvel. The poll addressed this with statements from other store owners that match ours. DC's Convergence change-up did no one any good. The New 52 imprint sold comics. Numbers seemed to be similar to pre-New 52 in 2011. But the titles were steady sellers. AND they sold to a younger crowd. I ran an after school program at a near-by high school in the winter and spring of 2015. The 20 or so kids in that class had access to any current comics they wanted to read. They almost all chose New 52 titles. They liked a mix of many of the character titles. So what went wrong? Why did DC produce another upheaval event?

DC's new direction literally killed sales for DC titles for us. We ended up sitting on dozens of unsold copies of many of the Convergence titles. Nobody wanted the stuff. They were still adapting to the New 52 upgrades and felt another change was a change too much. By the time this article sees print hopefully DC's titles will have exceeded the Convergence interruption and the new versions of older characters will excite readers. It was the same with Marvel's simultaneous crashing of realities into each other to make huge alterations to the Marvel Universe. Jamie read many of the titles from both companies and found he shared apathy with other readers tired of having to hit the ground running one more time with their favorite comics. The poll we read recounted the same opinions from other stores.

The industry editors/writers seem to be struggling with character changes to keep them fresh and relevant. Marvel's alterations - having white male characters replaced by their black doppelgangers, and women of all hues is indicative of the new comic book market from 2014 to the present. *Howard The Duck* makes light of that in one of the recent issues. Every company is attempting to up-sell each issue with multiple covers, limiteds, variants of dubious future value and revelations that have but a momentary grip on their audience. Look at *Sex Criminals*' attempts to make each issue as sales-important as all previous issues by playing within the system. They had a moment of whimsy and produced a second printing of a fourth printing. That's genius, because the industry is filled with customers that don't even understand how that could be! They won't go near a second printing if they sense no profit in it so imagine their consternation over a popular fourth printing to the second power!

We remember when *Captain America* #25 featured his death. That shocker held value a lot longer than most surprise issues. Nowadays "death" issues are so common that comic book death has lost its shock value. Now it's any issue that could be the first appearance of some character that might possibly be in a movie or TV show. The buyers are literally jumping from one lily pad to the next trying to stay afloat financially while buying comics we all know have little gain in their future.

All of us are trying to establish the whys and wherefores of the directions comic books seem to be heading. Our store sells back issues. We started out as a back issue business formed along the templates we set for exhibiting at comic conventions. Our Diamond account came a year later after we resisted the necessity of selling new product for as long as we could. Since that time we've evolved with a philosophy that new comics pay the bills while old comics purchase the fun. Other stores, some that were polled as well, have shied away from back issues. Some have reduced while others have bowed out completely. This will never be the

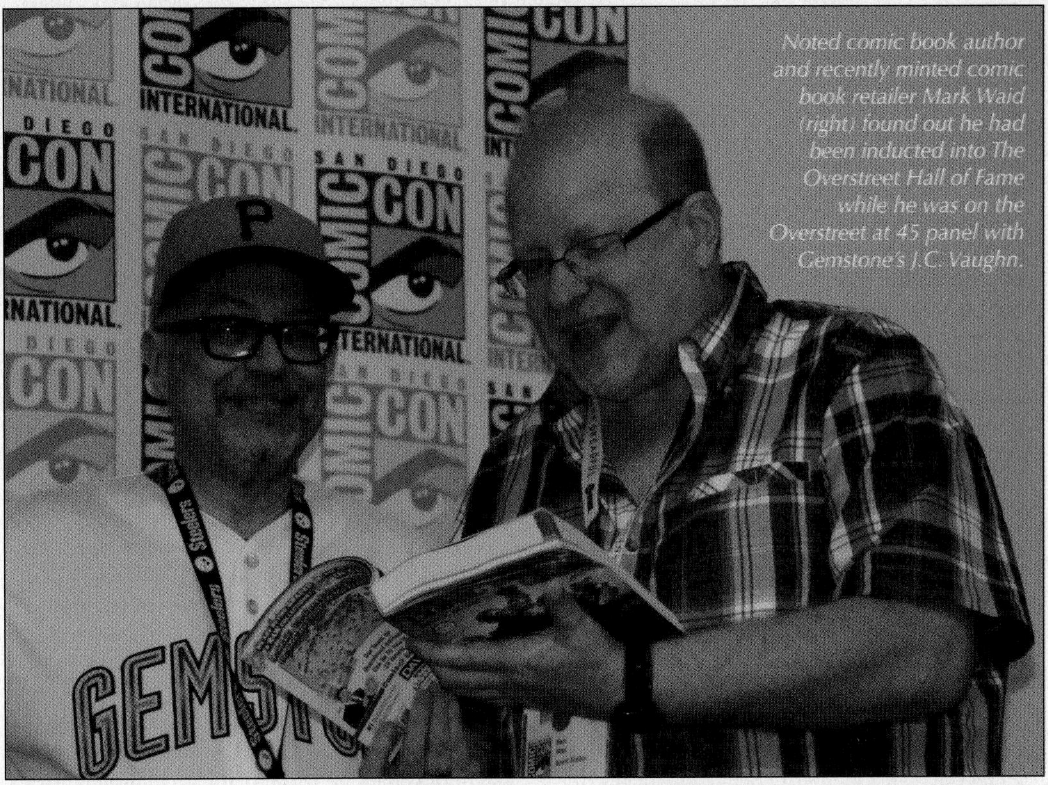
INTERNATIONAL
SAN DIEGO
CON
GEMS
Noted comic book author and recently minted comic book retailer Mark Waid (right) found out he had been inducted into The Overstreet Hall of Fame while he was on the Overstreet at 45 panel with Gemstone's J.C. Vaughn.

case for us. We practice what many others have do not; a four-pronged approach to the market. We sell on four fronts - the store, our web site, eBay and conventions. We've either enjoyed or suffered sales totals through these four methods over the years. The strength of the back issue market has proven worthwhile far more often than not. We've stayed with the reliability of constant, daily acquisition of comic collections and subsequent sales of those same collections. Without a doubt store sales of back issues have reigned in our neck of the woods for many years. Each year seems to be better than the previous.

This success in is direct correlation to the trades we sell that reprint some of the exact same stuff occupying our back issue bins. It seems people want choices and when those choices are present they spread the wealth over several styles of reads.

We know that we are successful when we see the explosion of comic collection want ads on Craigslist. Few are generated from actual stores with most of them guys working from home. The competitors work from Craigslist to buy and then to Facebook to sell. Some of the more energetic do shows within driving distance. Others still show up to sell at swap meets while a select few will sell from home by invitation only, usually to others within select Facebook groups, or some such entity.

Comic book stores can be fragile things. We've seen four local stores close in the past year and more than that open in the same period. The market must be good when new stores open in quantity.

The immense attention (frenzy) over comic-related movies has had other ramifications. It induced us to attach values to the 1980s comic book market where we used to just toss them in the bargain bins. We now mine them for additional profit from just the sale of single issues. Still most of it is valuable by content not quality. High grade '80s commons rarely see a profit after third-party grading involvement. Challenge yourself to find a 9.8 common '80s comic that is not a first appearance and would still be worth more than the cost of submission for grading.

My employees spend as much time as I do ordering and selling comics. They share all my experiences with the customers and store logistics. They are impacted by whatever weekly plusses and minuses the current comic book publishers and Diamond Comics throw at us. All have marketplace experience so I will take this space to share insights from three of them:

Dennis Schamp starts the comments with:

One disturbing trend (at least to me) is that modern comics seem to be returning to the frenzy of the late '80s/early '90s, as evidenced by the increased number of variant cover editions being produced, especially by DC and Marvel. Although many are being offered to retailers without conditions, there are increasing numbers of editions which require an order threshold to be met. When one must order 15, 25, or 100 copies (or more) of an issue, it has the effect of artificially skewing the print numbers for numerous titles, giving the impression that the modern comic book is enjoying an upswing in popularity. In addition, many retailers feel pressured into ordering one, two, or all variants in order to please their customer base. This can lead to retailers who may get stuck with unsold copies of threshold quantities, and customers who come in looking for something from which they can make a quick buck, rather than becoming a steady source of revenue. Do we retailers really need 68 different cover versions of a single book (*Star Wars* #1)? No. But as we see from the various eBay listings, clearly the public does. Perhaps it's time the publishers began looking at ways to keep their readers and retailers happy, rather than greedy...or broke.

Robert Mediavilla delivers:

Issue. Number. One. These three words have come to represent something massive, something unwieldy in the world of comic collection and distribution. Once upon a time the hot item in the comic collecting world was the landmark issue.

"Don't miss the exciting the 50th or the 100th or the 500th issue of your favorite funny book!"

Sure, the trend still exists today - Gold and Silver Age landmarks remain popular books. *Spawn* recently celebrated its 250th issue, and whenever Marvel wants to flaunt its publishing chops it reverts to old school numbering—but it has largely been supplanted in the mind of the modern collector by the craze for the almost mythic Issue #1. Ask any funny book pusher, number 1s sell like hotcakes, but sales of subsequent issues are often lukewarm. A number of factors have certainly contributed to the meteoric rise of the #1. For the wet behind the ears speculator, #1s smell like easy money.

"He paid how much for the first issue of *Spider-Man?*"

Without the discerning eyes or a seasoned comic veteran they snatch up every #1 with unwarranted voracity. Equally responsible for this trend is the new zeitgeist permeating the modern comic sphere, which is the ever growing desire for inclusivity in the medium. Many younger fans have argued that the modern numbering system, which resembles the "seasons" model utilized by television shows, is a more welcome system for new readers. The modern reader, they argue, can often feel put out or intimidated when faced with comics numbered in the hundreds, which insinuates that the reader must have pages upon pages of back story to enjoy one single issue. In my humble opinion, this is an entirely valid argument, but it seems as if the publishers are taking this to a new extreme, peppering the market with myriad new titles and re-launching already ongoing titles seemingly on a whim. While this provides the reader with ample reading material, it provides shop owners with a "special retailer's incentive" headache when it comes to managing these unmovable titles.

Case and point: one of our regular customers visited us recently hoping to sell several boxes worth of comics he had proudly accumulated. An eBay search had led him to, what he believed to be, a valuable collection comprised of 30 copies each of issues #1, #2 and #3 of Marvel's newest event redux Secret Wars. Tagging along were multiple copies of variants from DC Comics' recent Convergence story arc. At that point in time he was sitting on three month old books which held the honorable distinction of mirroring our overstuffed modern back stock and dollar bins. Thanks to poor market awareness on DC's part and infrequent release schedules on Marvel's, neither series picked up any traction. Here we have two diametrically opposed situations which aptly highlight the pitfalls of the #1 craze. On the one hand we have retailers cradling an excess of these titles, looking to unload them however possible. On the other we have the unaware speculator who has snapped up a large quantity of #1s with the intention of turning them over for a profit without taking into consideration elements such as timing and importance. The end result isn't so much a vicious cycle as it is a lackluster... anti...cycle, where someone must suffer a financial miscue.

Mark Huesman, Creative Director of Gemstone Publishing (left) checks in with SoCal Comics' Jamie Newbold (right) at his booth.

Despite everything I've just noticed there are certain benefits to this craze. The savvy retailer can capitalize on a wave of issue #1s without sinking in a sea of back issues. The emergence of so many titles can be interpreted as a sign of a thriving market, one where publishers have the money to back new and often experimental titles. The hype generated by titles featuring popular creative teams or that tie into the growing number of popular comic-inspired films often leads to an influx of customers, new and old, into stores. But if the publishers don't learn to slow down the #1 train, or at the very least make the train more appealing, speculators and retailers alike are going to be more than happy to get off and wait for the next one.

Charlie Ough says:

We are halfway through 2015 and we still see DC and Marvel continue their respective "Big Event" storylines to little success. Social media shows customers aren't interested. Neither the tired death or rebirth of a famed character(s) has made so much as a ripple in the community waters. Instead, the dialog consists of something more haunting...the Variant Cover. History lessons weren't learned as a new generation has reattached itself to the "collect every variant" that once plagued the 1990s. The same acclaimed variant books that exist in dollar bins today.

Image and other smaller companies continue to generate new monthly titles that remind me of movie pitches hoping to get one to stick. They are not even necessarily well-done stories!

Is this the problem? Is Generation Squirrel more concerned with 1:100 variant covers or being able to flip the next "*Walking Dead* #1" than actual story? It makes one wonder if the big events that DC and Marvel continue to push out are turning readers off. Please just give me a good storyline without events of cosmic proportions. What will it take to bring the reader back into the light and away from the path of the "speculator syndrome?" That seems to be a question that I can't answer because there are many titles out there that aren't getting their due. All I can do is introduce a customer to titles I enjoy and hope the seed is planted. I want comics to be enjoyed on their creative merit...by reading them.

Brock Dickinson
Collector
St. Catherines, Ontario

As in my previous market reports, I'll be covering a specific piece of the larger marketplace, focusing on the late Bronze Age through to the present. While this is not where the hobby's most valuable books are found, it is where the largest number of collectors can be found, so there's always a lot to reflect on. There are perhaps two key forces driving this portion of the market at the moment: movie and television production on the one hand, and the continued rise of Copper Age books on the other. To some extent the two trends are related, but to help tease out some more specific trends, I'll tackle them separately.

First, I'm sure that anyone reading through these marketing reports will get tired of hearing about movies and TV shows. The move from page to screen has been a key driver of the market for a couple of years, given the influence of Marvel's first wave of *Avengers*-related movies, and the popularity of the *Walking Dead* television series. More recently, though, the intensity has ratcheted up a notch. *Guardians of the Galaxy,* Marvel's big movie release for 2014, lit a match to the back issue market, and films like *Avengers: Age of Ultron* and *Ant-Man* have kept the fires burning. Marvel has, in fact, accelerated this process by identifying its slate of upcoming movies through to 2020. DC has been in lockstep, also releasing details on a slate of upcoming movies, and both companies have been simultaneously pushing out successful television ventures including series featuring *S.H.I.E.L.D.*, *Arrow, The Flash, Gotham* and *Daredevil.* Much more is in the works, and collectors have been racing to acquire anything and everything linked to these properties.

Over the past year, TV and movie-related first appearances and key issues have skyrocketed, often on the basis of minimal information. Marvel books have been particularly hot, with a focus on those linked directly to the current crop of movies (such as the first appearance of Scott Lang as Ant-Man in *Marvel Premiere* #47 and #48, and his first team up in *Avengers* #181) or to recent developments on the *Agents of S.H.I.E.L.D* television series (such as Mockingbird's first appearance in *Marvel Team-Up* #95). At DC, we've seen the explosive emergence of *Shazam!* #28 with the first modern appearance of Black Adam (to be played in an upcoming movie by fan-favourite Dwayne Johnson), which routinely fetches $300 or more in NM, and has topped $1,000 repeatedly in CGC 9.8 (one sold for $1,325 on eBay in November of 2014). DC's TV shows have also driven prices up, with increased attention on characters such as Green Arrow, the Flash, and more recently Supergirl. Some of the greatest TV-related movement, however, seems to be coming on secondary characters, with early issues of *Firestorm*, for example, rising on his appearances in episodes of the *Flash.* The announcement of a 2016 *Suicide Squad* movie featuring some of Hollywood's biggest stars has also begun to shake up the market, though it is likely that we are seeing just the front end of this trend. *Suicide Squad* #1 (1987 series) has become an easy $40 sale, while the group's first appearance in *Legends* #3 has also spiked. The movie announcement has pushed up the already stratospheric price of *Batman Adventures* #12 (1st Harley Quinn), and is beginning to drive books like *Detective Comics* #474 (1st Deadshot).

Steampunk Joker, Harley Quinn and Riddler

One niche that seems to have had a kick start from movie and TV sources this past year is DC's Vertigo imprint. Movie and TV production (or rumours of production) around *Sandman, I Zombie, Preacher* and others propelled these books to new heights. While these titles have long been admired within the hobby for their sophisticated writing, they were not generally seen as collectable in the same way as more mainstream titles. As movie and TV news drove collectors to this space, many quickly realized that overall supply is quite limited, causing prices to jump rapidly. The first to jump were books like *Sandman* #1, *I Zombie* #1 and *Preacher* #1, but the announcement of the *Constantine* TV series sparked further jumps from books like *Swamp Thing* #37 (1st Constantine) and *Hellblazer* #1. Studio options for other books drove the process further, lifting books like *Sandman* #4 (1st Lucifer) and *Lucifer* #1, at which point the floodgates broke. Speculators began to realize that many Vertigo books were perfectly-suited for the movie or TV market, and price spiked on books including *Scalped* #1, *Y – The Last Man* #1 and *100 Bullets* #1. Previews and early appearances of these titles and characters were also hot.

Over at Marvel, speculation began to swirl around Marvel's "cosmic" characters. The success of *Guardians of the Galaxy* prompted many to believe that more space-faring and sci-fi oriented characters would soon be joining their superhero counterparts on the big screen. Books like *Captain Marvel, Nova, Ms. Marvel, Warlock* and the various *Infinity Gauntlet* miniseries all rose rapidly in demand and price, a trend that has been cemented by the announcement of a *Captain Marvel* movie and the increasing importance of the infinity gauntlet itself in Marvel's movies. This trend has catapulted many late Bronze Age books through the roof. Once considered all but uncollectable, *Nova* #1 and *Ms. Marvel* #1 now routinely surpass $100 in NM, and have commanded multiples of that in CGC 9.8. Even obscure books like *Micronauts* #8 (1st Captain Universe) are climbing - $20 in NM, and $300 in CGC 9.8. This trend has spilled out of the Bronze Age, rolling right on into current releases. *Guardians of the Galaxy* #1 (2008 series) sells easily for $150 in NM, while issues of the massively printed Copper Age *Infinity Gauntlet* fetch $20-$30 each. Even *Captain Marvel* #1 (2012 series) has been selling for $15-$20, as has the first appearance of the new Ms. Marvel in *Captain Marvel* (2012 series) #17.

Ironically, the movie speculation frenzy may have touched off wider effects. With books like *Nova* (1976 series) #1 and *Ms. Marvel* (1977 series) #1 sailing past $100, there has been an explosion of interest in late Bronze books, and a continued rise of the Copper Age. I have written about the rise of the Copper Age in previous market reports, but the trend has begun to move far faster and further than many of us anticipated. Certainly late Bronze has been heating up, particularly first appearances, key issues, and anything that might connect to a movie. Who would have imagined that *ROM* #1 would be a hot book, with sales between $30-$50 in NM and CGC 9.8s approaching $300 or more? Collectors are recognizing that these books are now almost 40 years old, and that many have not been well-preserved. Further, the excitement around Bronze is causing "knock on" effects with Copper books.

Copper is a huge and largely under-researched mass of first appearances, new origins, revamps, and experimentation, much of which is providing grist for the current generation of both comic writers and filmmakers. This past year, almost everything was hot – obscure first appearances (like Suicide Squad's Vixen in *Action Comics* #521 for $30, or Cloak and Dagger in *Spectacular Spider-Man* #64 for $60), popular artists (with McFarlane issues of *Amazing Spider-Man* starting to rise again), or revamps (like *Power Man and Iron Fist* #50 for $60 or more).

In past market reports, I have provided a list of what I saw as the top 40 key books for collectors of the Copper Age. However, I've always been a fan of "crowd sourcing" – the idea that online technologies allow us to bring large groups together to work on common issues. So this year, I went to the CGC Boards, where one of the most active communities of Copper Age collectors gathers, and asked for their input. Now, anytime you ask 10 collectors for their opinion, you'll get 11 responses, so the final list is a result of my "editorial control" – but I think it represents a pretty good overview of what the Top 50 Copper Age keys are. To get this list, the discussion limited itself to the 1982-1992 timeframe:

- *Albedo* #2
- *Amazing Spider-Man* #238, #252, #298, #300, #361
- *Archie's Girls Betty and Veronica* #320
- *Batman* #357, #404, #428
- *Batman: The Dark Knight Returns* #1
- *Batman: The Killing Joke*
- *Bone* #1
- *Caliber Presents* #1
- *Comico Primer* #2
- *Crisis in Infinite Earths* #1
- *The Crow* #1
- *Daredevil* #181
- *DC Comics Presents* #47
- *Evil Ernie* #1
- *G.I. Joe: A Real American Hero* #1
- *Harbinger* #1
- *Incredible Hulk* #271, #340
- *Iron Man* #282
- *Marvel Graphic Novel* #4
- *Marvel Super Heroes Secret Wars* #8
- *Miracleman* #15
- *New Mutants* #87, #98
- *Sandman* #1, #8
- *Spectacular Spider-Man* #64
- *Superman* #75
- *Swamp Thing* #21, #37
- *Starslayer* #2
- *Tales of the New Teen Titans* #44
- *Thor* #337
- *Transformers* #1
- *Teenage Mutant Ninja Turtles* #1
- *Uncanny X-men* #221, #248, #266
- *Vampirella* #113
- *Warrior* (UK Magazine) #1
- *Watchmen* #1
- *Wolverine* (limited series) #1
- *X-Factor* #6, #24

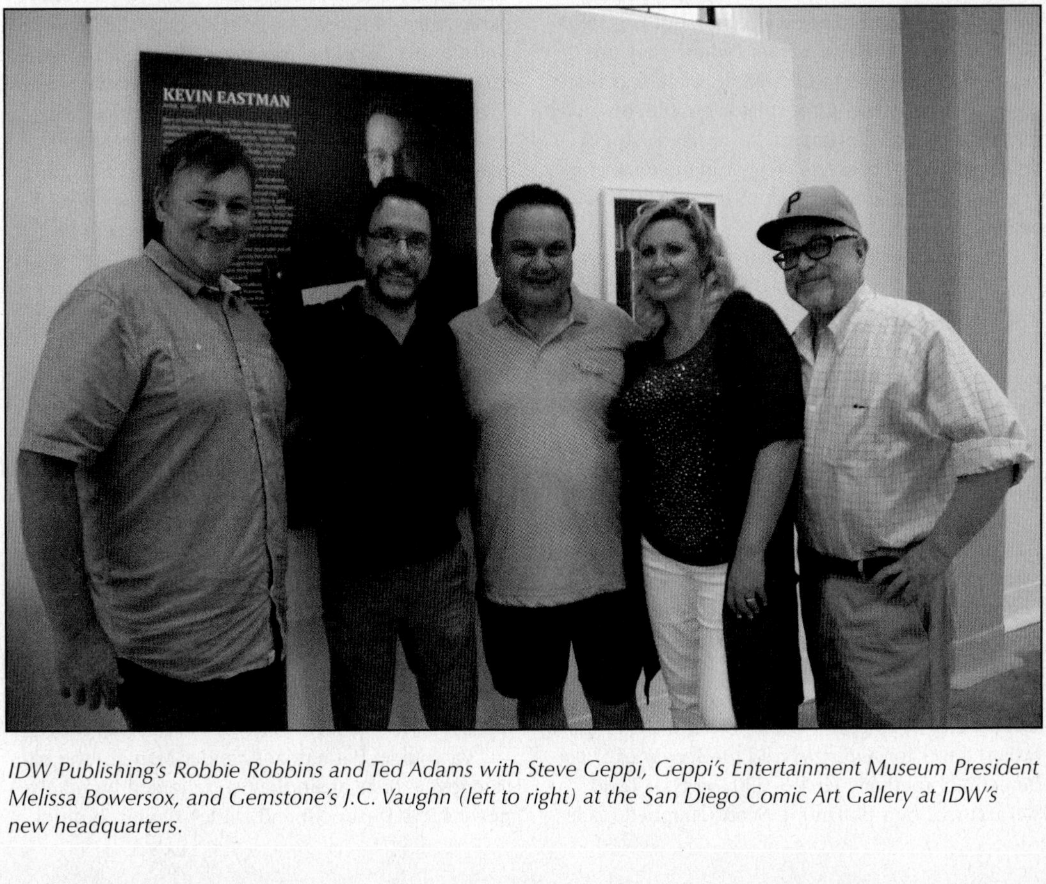
KEVIN EASTMAN

IDW Publishing's Robbie Robbins and Ted Adams with Steve Geppi, Geppi's Entertainment Museum President Melissa Bowersox, and Gemstone's J.C. Vaughn (left to right) at the San Diego Comic Art Gallery at IDW's new headquarters.

Virtually all of these books took substantial price jumps over the past year. If this list is of interest – and it should be, given that so much of the current market is driven by the search for "keys" – I'll try to do this crowd sourcing bit again in future reports. Special thanks this year to all the CGC boardies who took part in the discussion, and a special shout out to Ryan Leskiw (aka "kimik") who not only helped out with the discussion, but shared some great sales data as well.

While movie/TV hype and the continued rise of Copper are big stories, there are lots of other trends to be seen. Image Comics continues to launch a range of remarkable new series, continuously innovating to bring collectors some of the finest comics on the market today. Titles like *Walking Dead* and *Saga* continue to be strong sellers in the back issue market, but they were joined by a range of new titles this year. The relatively low print runs of many Image titles – and those of other smaller publishers – often combine with the spottiness of Diamond's direct-order distribution system to cause frequent and rapid sell-outs of many issues. An entire army of "flippers," operating like speculative day traders in the stock market, has emerged to take advantage of these distribution disparities and gaps. This phenomenon causes many, many books to escalate in price quite rapidly upon release, though prices tend to settle after a month or two as books make their way from "where they are" to "where they need to be." While some fear that this activity may fuel a speculator bubble, my own sense is that this flippers are more like scalpers selling tickets to concerts or sporting events, commanding a premium because of unmet short-term demand.

The continued rise of encapsulation, though CGC, CBCS and others, also continues to re-orient the market. As I've argued previously, I do see cover artists playing a larger role in determining future values. Neal Adams covers from the Bronze Age continue to be strong; this trend began with his *Batman, Detective* and *Green Lantern* books, and spread to *Action, Superman* and the DC horror titles like *House of Mystery*. I suspect that *his* covers for *Justice League of America* and *World's Finest* will also start to heat up, and – over time – this will creep forward to more and more modern books. The same trend can be seen with other classic Bronze Age artists like Michael Kaluta and Bernie Wrightson. In the modern period, Adam Hughes books continue to grow in popularity. *Catwoman* (2002 series) #51 is now a $60 book, while Hughes' variant cover for *Supergirl and the Legion of Super-Heroes* #23 routinely fetches $300 in NM. Todd McFarlane, Brian Bolland, J. Scott Campbell (espe-

cially his Mary Jane Watson and Black Cat covers) and Dave Stevens are also popular in this vein. Many of Hughes' *Catwoman, Tomb Raider* and *Wonder Woman* covers routinely sell for $10-$20, as do several of the covers from Bolland's *Wonder Woman* run. Popular Campbell covers often command $20-$40 each.

While artists have seemed to generate more heat than writers recently, there are exceptions. Writer Brian K. Vaughan in particular seems to be enjoying the favour of the marketplace at the moment. His Vertigo-published series *Y – The Last Man* (#1 at $200 in NM) has been selling well for a couple of years, and *Saga* (#1 at $125 in NM) has been one of Image's best-selling titles. But this year, his past work on titles including *Runaways* from Marvel, *Ex Machina* from Wildstorm, and *Swamp Thing* from DC has also been heating up. *Runaways* (2003 series) #1, for example, frequently sells for $60 or more.

Although artists and writers are attracting attention, there are still plenty of character-based collectors. Flash, Firestorm, Green Arrow, John Constantine, Deathlok, Mockingbird and others all benefited from increased television exposure, for example – but the big characters this year remained those perennial favourites Batman and Spider-Man. Early issues of the latest "New 52" *Batman* series were hot, with #1-10 selling quickly. Bronze and Copper *Batman* keys were also hot, including #357 ($80 for the 1st Tim Drake appearance), #404 (Year One), #417 (1st KGBeast appearance rising on movie rumours), #428 (Death of Robin) and many more. Certain spin-off titles were also doing well, led by the red-hot *Batman: the Dark Knight Returns* #1-4, *Batman: Harley Quinn, Batman: Mad Love* and *Batman: The Killing Joke*. As hot as *Batman* was, though, issues of *Amazing Spider-Man* were even stronger… #194 (1st Black cat at $200 in NM), #238 (1st Hobgoblin at $140), and #300 (1st Venom at $300 and CGC 9.8s routinely passing $1,200) led the way, but many, many issues are commanding an increasing premium. The renumbered issues #1-58 (from 1999 to 2003) were also hot, especially #19-29, #30 (1st Morlun at $15-$20), and #36. Any J. Scott Campbell covers were hot, but especially those like #51 ($12), #52 ($10), #601 ($30), #606 ($25), and #607 ($40) that have covers featuring Mary Jane Watson or the Black Cat. Even some annuals were heating up, with *Amazing Spider-Man Annual* #21 (wedding of Spider-Man and Mary Jane) showing particular strength with frequent sales in the $20-$25 range.

Of course, Batman and Spider-Man are the old standbys – once again they were joined by relative newcomers Deadpool and Harley Quinn. Both of

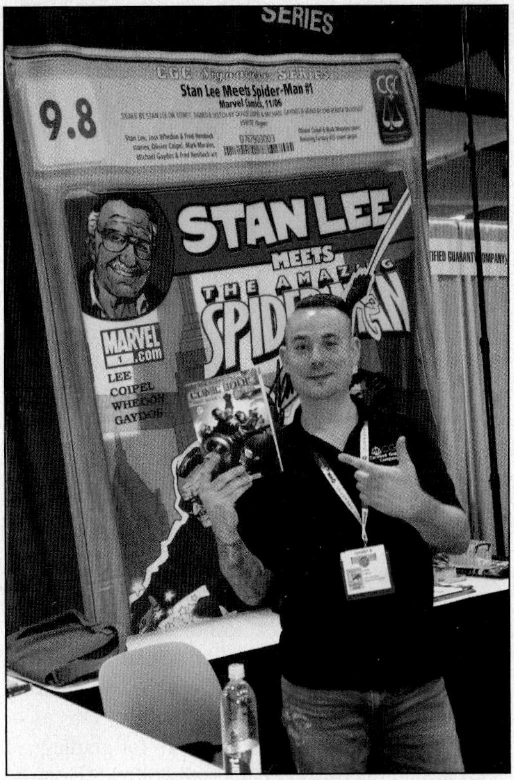
SERIES
9.8
Stan Lee Meets Spider-Man #1
STAN LEE
MEETS

CGC's Shawn Caffrey with the newly released 45th edition of The Overstreet Comic Book Price Guide.

these characters were created around the tail end of the Copper Age. Deadpool's first appearance in *New Mutants* #98 appears to be plentiful, but much like *Incredible Hulk* #181, a plentiful supply seems to have little effect on price. The book routinely reaches $350 in NM, and $800 or more in CGC 9.8. For the past few years, prices on some of his early appearances (early *X-Force* issues, his 1993 *Circle Chase* miniseries, and his 1997 regular series) have been holding steady in the $5-$10 range. These prices are now starting to rise, and while sales vary, it's not unusual to see many sales in the $15-$20 range, and higher for issues perceived as scarce. Harley Quinn is DC's closest counterpart to Deadpool, and her books are also rising rapidly. Her first appearance in *Batman Adventures* #12 now commands $450, while CGC 9.8s are in the $1,800 range. Unlike *New Mutants* #98, this book is genuinely hard to find in high grade. With Hollywood bombshell Margot Robbie playing Harley in the upcoming *Suicide Squad* movie, it's hard not to believe that this book will continue to go through the roof. All Harley Quinn appearances have been hot, commanding multiples of *Guide*. Early appearances in various titles related to the Batman animated television shows command $20-$50 apiece, while appearances in titles like *Harley Quinn* (2000 series) and *Gotham City Sirens* are $15-$25 each.

Still on the character front, the New Teen Titans appear to be gaining strength. Their first appearance in *DC Comics Presents* #26 is now a $200 book in NM, while many issues of *New Teen Titans* (1980 series) are also hot, including #2 (1st Deathstroke at $120), #16 (1st Captain Carrot at $20), #21 (1st Brother Blood at $10) and *Tales of the Teen Titans* #44 (1st Nightwing at $120-$150). The rise of this title leads me to suspect that other popular 1980s titles, like John Byrne's run on *X-Men*, Frank Miller's run on *Daredevil* and Walt Simonson's run on *Thor*, might also be poised to heat up again.

Another area that seems to be gathering steam is the early issues of long-running independent titles. Some have been strong for awhile, but as collectors begin to recognize how rare it is for a series to last for 100, 200 or even 250 issues, longevity itself seems to generate interest in early issues. Books benefiting from this effect include titles like *Femforce, Furrlough, Gold Digger, Knights of the Dinner Table, The Simpsons, Strangers in Paradise, Tarot: Witch of the Black Rose, Teenage Mutant Ninja Turtles* and many more. And at a time when Marvel and DC titles rarely make it past their 20th issue, long-running Image titles are also getting attention. As *Spawn* cruises past its 250th issue, interest in early issues is rising, though plentiful supply makes prices vary pretty widely. Early issues of *Witchblade* are also strong, though *Savage Dragon* – now well past its 200th issue – has yet to show any movement.

Looking ahead, I see a number of areas starting to heat up that could be very big moving forward. While the Dark Horse-published *Star Wars* series has its fans, there seems to be genuine excitement about the return of the *Star Wars* property to Marvel. I suspect that the release of *Star Wars: The Force Awakens* movie in December of 2015 will lift all *Star Wars* prices, but I think the original Marvel series will show particularly strong growth. Issues #1, #42 (1st Boba Fett), #68 (Boba Fett solo story) and #107 (low distribution) of the original are already heating up, but the entire series still has lots of room for growth. The new Marvel *Star Wars* launches have been sales juggernauts, but watch out if a future movie character is first introduced in a Marvel comic – prices for first appearances of that kind will likely go through the roof.

I also think the impact of crowd-funded comic books – emerging from sites like Kickstarter – will become more widespread. Artists can now use these sites to bypass traditional publishing and distribution structures, taking their books directly to consumers. This system will produce a wide range of material, and while much of it may be of little interest to collectors, it is likely that we will see select books "break out" from this model. Their lack of availability through traditional distributors or retail outlets suggests that – in a few instances at least – there could be some massive hits and price spikes. Books like *Cerebus* #1 or *Teenage Mutant Ninja Turtles* #1 or *Bone* #1 showcase the potential for creators outside the mainstream to produce highly sought after and valuable books. Now imagine that those books were never sold through retail outlets, but were only available to collectors who supported the creator's vision *before* a single page was ever published. I suspect that this new system will produce some extremely valuable books in the future, but predicting what book or which creator will kick this off will be something akin to predicting winning lottery numbers.

Finally, my thanks to all those who work so diligently to produce the *Yearbook* each year, and to my fellow advisors – I am constantly in awe of the knowledge and passion that this group brings to the industry. It's been a pleasure getting to meet some of you in the field, like the afternoon I spent with Michael Pavlic at the great Purple Gorilla Comics in Calgary. I hope that my modest contributions add to the mix, and, as always, I welcome feedback and suggestions for future reports!

Grant Adey
Halo Certification Pty Ltd.
Australia

Certification numbers continue a strong growth, and the last six months have seen an upward spike in grading all comics with Silver and Modern variants slightly out-running Bronze age. Establishing an Australian grading company has certainly increased the collector interest in comic collecting, and people who would not normally collect comics are showing good interest in learning about the hobby, reflected in strong sales growth for associated shops. Norm Bardell, proprietor of Fats Comics, has certainly shot to instant success riding a wave of what appears to be an insatiable appetite for graded Silver Age here in Oz. Displaying a multiple range of graded keys and #1s, Norm's approach to full disclosure and *Overstreet* priced books has resulted in Australia's premiere comic shop for specialty comics. Not since Nigel Johnson's comic shops in the '70s thru to the '90s has such an array of cherries been available for sale. His shop stocks *Incredible Hulk* #181, *Giant-Size X-Men* #1, *X-Men* #1, *Amazing Spider-Man* #129, *Amazing Fantasy* #15, *Amazing Spider-Man* #1, *Green Lantern* #1, *Fantastic Four* #1, *Amazing Spider-Man* #121 & 122, *Strange Tales* #110, and so on.

Ace Comics & Games run a huge smash of new releases, selling from their two stores and suppling smaller retail comic shops from their warehouse, working closely with the staff on new issue Wednesday, producing a good amount of 9.8s & 9.9s. Diamond factory case lots of 250 per box yield more than enough 9.8s to satisfy regular customers. Variants arriving boarded and bagged assure that the quality is superb.

The amount of restored books in for grading is up in number, mainly higher end Silver Age. A few particularly nasty examples of pro restoration have been submitted, so part of the job is delivering disappointing news sometimes. A number of books I see have the tell tale sign of interleafing or micro chamber paper left inside. Closer inspection reveals colour touch, page missing or coupon clipped. A frequent question I'm asked is why there is apparent visual discrepancies in grading, certain defects such as spine split have a impact on the limitation a comic can grade. A comic may also have writting in the margins, child colouring in, panels clipped - these are hidden defects. For cover visual defects, I would also draw attention to the notation that says "certain defects are allowed if other defects are not present." This is in effect to 8.5 and gives the grader some latitude.

When teaching new graders, I start with pre-digit grades, for them to master Poor, Fair, Good, Very Good, Fine, Very Fine, Near Mint and Mint, and then the finer points of plus and minus. Some prefer just to go to digits but my observation is though the first takes a bit longer to learn, speed comes later once a VG is obvious then its a matter of considering a plus or minus. Fourteen years of counter service

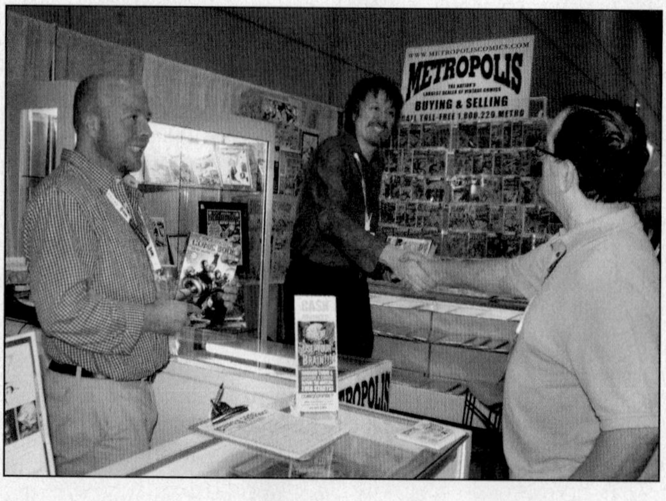
METROPOLIS
BUYING & SELLING

ComicConnect's Rob Reynolds, Bob Overstreet, and Metropolis Collectibles' Frank Cwiklik talk about the new Guide.

in the industry taught me not to offer up over-graded books.

Let's get to Gem Mint 10. Manufacturing in the printing industry is of the highest standard today. I have partly finished a study of modern manufacturing and distribution methods, and so far it looks like more 9.9s and Gem Mint 10s should be achievable. Some of the independents are going to extraordinary lengths to be sure books arrive with the highest level of care.

I spoke with Norm Bardell at length about the benefits of buying an established shop, his first year in the industry at Fats Comics. Here are his observations:

There are some very significant trends that I have noticed since taking the reins at Fats Comics. As usual the fastest trends are the ones most closely bonded to the Internet.

We have all seen a significant trend in speculation buying. Obviously the significant investment made by Hollywood into the Marvel Universe and the DC Universe have turned the gamut of popular superheroes into cultural icons. Many new collectors are entering the market and with the easy availability of information, these collectors are able to identify potential investment comics in a way that their older predecessors were never able to do. This causes a speculation bubble surrounding various books that fluctuates in volume at a rate hitherto unknown. These turbulent price fluctuations have affected many of the key issues and have made even some dollar bin books into rising stars. *New Mutants* #98 comes from obscurity less than 12 months ago to peak at around $1200 US for Graded 9.8 and settle at a little more than half that at about $700 US. In Australia, this book never had "Collector Pressure" affecting the price. As such it remains to be seen if this book which exists in vast quantities will sustain the prices it has risen to. Collector Pressure for the more traditional major and minor keys has been coupled with "Speculator Pressure" and we can see the supply and demand curve increasing at a staggering rate.

The purchasing pressure from both speculators and collectors have caused many comics to rise in price to where even low grade books are highly sought after and as such are barely affordable to the average working person. Mid-grade keys sell most easily and Marvel Keys far outsell DC keys. Silver Age books are in such high demand that it is hard for a shop in Australia to keep up. Bronze Age is becoming increasingly active and is more and more collected and stocks are hard to keep.

The desire to supply the expanding market in Australia for these books has caused me to investigate new arenas and methods for purchase and sale which brings me to the next trend I wish to talk about.

Steampunk Princess Leia and Darth Maul

The world is familiar with eBay and the "joys, trials and tribulations" we endure with it. Other online auctions are also available like Heritage Auctions and many of the large online stores. Listing your books can be costly, and purchasing from these sites can involve paying buyers premiums, and carry other risks as well. Many of the disenfranchised are taking to internet forums and social media networks like Facebook as a new medium for the Buy and Sell of specialist items like our beloved comics. These are fast becoming a virtual treasure trove for those people hardy enough to brave the quagmire of scammers, shill bidders, and other pitfalls. It was here that I immersed myself for months on end, to explore, learn, adapt and incorporate this as best as I could into my comic store.

Facebook users can find any number of specialist groups including groups dedicated to comic enthusiasts. These groups are often public, however the most active are "closed" or "invite only" groups which connect buyers and sellers in an amazingly hive-like fashion.

Specialized comic related Facebook groups exist in many countries. U.S. based groups like "Comic Book Collecting Buy Sell Trade" (15,000+ members) or "Nick's Comic Auctions, Buy and Sell" (3,000+) are as easy to find as Aussie groups like "Comics Australia Buy/Sell/Trade" and "Australian Comic book Auction House." These haunts are awesome places to buy or sell Keys and comics of all values. Fees are non-existent. PayPal is the bank of choice and offers the only protection you can get for a deal gone wrong. While honesty is the catch cry in an arena where the individual is almost autonomous, it is also Buyer Beware, for, like everything, there are a high number of scams and scammers. Group Administrators do what they can, but it is always after the fact. The same scams that exist on eBay thrive here too. Trusts are built over time and are treasured within this community. Sellers list comics for sale or auction in such a way that the pictures show quality and grade which helps the buyer choice. Hundreds, maybe thousands of comics are listed in various groups and it is common for a buyer to be involved with multiple auctions at once. If a buyer wins, they are expected to pay, usually via PayPal and the seller ships the books as soon as they can. These groups keep online lists of Star sellers, Star buyers and scam artists to keep the new members informed.

I have met, and over time, made friends with a number of individuals in these groups and would indeed trust thousands of dollars to them in advance for the books that they end up sending me. While this trust is quite common, it is not the same experience for everyone.

These groups are not for the faint of heart or the uneducated buyer. Read your *Overstreet Grading Guide*, keep track of your Key comic prices, research your trends, be informed. Take your time building relationships, keep notes. There is little room for error and errors can be costly.

This quintessential schoolyard is always evolving, for in the virtual world, nothing remains the same for long. My exploration into this world has been, I think, very successful. I learned from my mistakes. I made some great friends and I bought some great books which culminated in purchasing an *Amazing Fantasy* #15.

There is always a 'but.'

The truth for me is that the online social phenomena, while awesome and adventurous won't ever replace the comfort of hanging out at your local comic store (LCS). My view is, the local comic store lets enthusiasts indulge their passion in a more personal way. They get to have an in-depth conversation with other devotees who actually know what they are talking about. There is an excitement in holding a "grail" while bargaining over the price. There's safety in buying a book you can see and touch, and the feeling you get when searching for and sometimes finding that missing issue. Big kids and little kids down the local comic store excited about their heroes.

There seems to me to be a satisfaction gained from this that isn't easily found in the information corridors and the impersonal virtual meeting rooms. Facebook groups and even eBay are a useful tool. I like the Facebook groups, but I love hanging out at the comic store.

Frank Simmons
Coast to Coast Comics
Sunny California

Hello comic book enthusiasts out there everywhere in the Comic Book Marketplace Galaxy!

What better way to start this year's market report than with "COMING SOON TO A MOVIE THEATER NEAR YOU!" Yes, without a doubt the year 2015 and its comic-related, comic-themed, comic book hero movies dominated the big screen. They dominated our imagination and in many ways our hobby and wallets as well. Brick and mortar comic book stores were buzzing with phone calls asking for the 1st appearance of Deadpool in *New Mutants* #98, the same phone lines buzzed with calls for *Avengers* #181, 1st Scott Lang as Ant-Man, and *Marvel Super-Heroes* #12, 1st appearance of Captain Marvel, and also *Marvel Super-Heroes* #13, 1st appearance of Carol Danvers who later becomes the Marvel superstar and heroine known as Ms. Marvel. This year's epic movies introduced us to many existing superheroes in brand new ways on the big screen, in addition it brought about newfound fame for characters like Rocket from Marvel's monster hit movie *Guardians of the Galaxy*. The sudden popularity explosion of seemingly dormant characters such as this not only had comic stores busy to meet a seemingly endless demand for key 1st appearances, it also had the buzzing and to meet the demand from the blitz of enormous demand for all these new key and 1st appearances.

Super Nova e-commerce sites like along with direct sales sites like ComicLink were up to their elbows in requests as well for this explosion of movie related key issues! Coast To Coast Comics sold at a very minimum a dozen raw copies of *New Mutants* #98 in NM/MT 9.8 between $350 and $600, it was almost the exact same amount of *Avengers* #181 that sold for between $275 and $425 with one of our awesome customers buying 4 copies himself. He later wrote me an email saying, "Frank, I don't think I can buy any more #181s from you right now, I have 18 copies on hand at the moment." I had another client write us, "Thank you for the incredible NM/MT 9.8 copy of *New Mutants* #98, I now have nine copies and would like to eventually put three more in my collection for a total of twelve."

That's right folks, newly found fame and new movie character popularity ruled the market place and in many ways as I write this update. One of our many favorite customers that simply goes by the name MO has been on a mission to drain the comic vaults of Coast To Coast Comics of every new movie related key and to do so as fast as humanly possible as to not miss a single one.

It has been a real pleasure to serve and help

Ron Pussell of Redbeard's Book Den with Bob Overstreet.

many awesome collectors out there in our hobby achieve their collecting goals. I would like to send out a special thank you to the Gemstone staff for the incredible job not for just this year's amazing comic guides and related publications but for the hard work and effort they put into this hobby each and every year. This is no easy, no simple task. We are blessed to have such amazing material to support a hobby I have loved and enjoyed personally for the last 42 years. Bravo gentleman and ladies, and thank you allowing me to play a small part in this wonderful publication as an advisor.

Stephen Barrington and Jon Chambers
Flea Market Comics
Chickasaw, AL

DC and Marvel are at it again with their annual big events. DC just completed its multi-crossovers with *Convergence* which morphed into Divergence and is faced with an uncertain future with our customers. Marvel is having a good year so far, in the movies and on the comic racks.

Secret Wars is proving to sell better than expected but Marvel's *Star Wars* titles are leading the way. The demand for these recent back issues has been incredible. Marvel's super-hero titles are strictly second banana when it comes to all to the *Star Wars* titles. The major developments for Marvel seem to be more promising than DC's. Marvel in the coming months seems to be drawing a lot more interest than

DC.

The independent market is faring well for BOOM!, Image, and IDW. The *Strange Fruit* mini-series was a big hit with Mark Waid writing J.G. Jones' instant classic. It's a cross between the 1951 original sci-fi classic movie, *The Day The Earth Stood Still* and *Mississippi Burning*. Set in the late 1920s in rural Mississippi following a disaster flood, this giant black man doesn't seem to be happy with race relations at that time. We ordered extras on this title and we still sold out (we did a lot of promoting, though, when we saw the initial solicitation in *Previews*).

Other best sellers include *Southern Bastards*, Turtles titles and the *Archie Vs. Predator* series. *Sabrina*, *Afterlife With Archie* and the *Sonic* titles all do well. Our well-placed kids comics section always pulls the parents and grandparents in. These reader-friendly comics, many based on cartoons, are creating a whole generation of fans. The girls go for *My Little Pony* titles and the boys, *Turtles* and *Sonic*-related books.

Back issue sales have sky-rocketed this year with the 25¢ and $1.00 comics flying out the door. These can sometimes be hard to keep in stock. We have quite a few regulars who come in each week to scavenge through these boxes. Comic supply sales are hot. Almost all DC and Marvel Silver Age titles move quickly when priced right. We sell all of our higher priced issues at a nice discount and we get a lot of repeat customers.

DC's *Harley Quinn* and Marvel's *Deadpool* comics are red-hot and are impossible to keep in stock. The first 110 issues of *The Walking Dead* never stick a around for long. The TPBs of this series sell very well and we keep them prominently displayed. Very few slabbed comics come through the door but there is still a special market for graded comics.

Overall, sales for new comics are good but the $3.50 to $4.99 price tags are making a lot of our readers think twice about what they buy.

John Chruscinski
Tropic Comics Inc.
Lyndora, PA

Over the last year our hobby has seen an even stronger than normal increase in first appearances, origin issues and variant covers. As the TV and movie industry has come to embrace comic related shows, we see a constant man-hunt for any new TV/movie appearance creating a fast influx of buyers for the related comics especially in high grade. It seems like every week there is a new hot book to be pulled out of a dealers $1 box and sold for $20 and up. Titles that you never would have thought of in a million years like *Crash Ryan* because of a TV or movie related tie-in, or even just the rumor of one, a book can skyrocket over night.

With Golden Age we constantly see high grade or first appearances being strong sellers with no sign of slowing down. Most of stock issues, unless rare or hard to find, seem to stay in stock in lower grade a bit longer but do sell well. This even holds true with main stream superhero comics especially.

The exception to this rule is as always Timely comics. Timely superhero comics have always been hard to track as the demand far exceeds the supply in any grade at over *Guide* prices.

Silver Age comics continue to show strong growth in most all grades for the mainstream titles and with movie/TV shows like *Agents of S.H.I.E.L.D.*, *Avengers*, *Flash*, *Arrow*, and *Gotham*, we see a serious increase in demand and price for related first appearances. *Incredible Hulk* #1 in any grade still seems to lead the pack in most sought-after Silver Age and in many cases is still undervalued due to high demand, even in restored grade.

Silver Age comics have become the new Golden Age for most newer collectors. For them this is where it all began. Since most of the movie/TV show characters first appeared in the Silver Age, this makes it the most in-demand of all the time periods to collect.

Bronze Age is also hot with a lot of our new collectors starting their runs in the 1970s because they are much more affordable than their Silver Age counterparts, and high grades can be bought for much more reasonable prices.

The new comics market is growing strong especially with the introduction of variant and sketch covers. With the growth of conventions, TV/movie exposure, news and media exposure, interest continues to grow in what normally would be an uninterested audience.

With more people collecting comics and comic related items than anytime before in our collecting hobby, look for more common books to become hard to find as they get bought and put in many collections that will not be sold for many years. As collectors continue to look for undervalued comics, new things are discovered, such as *True Comics* #48 with no copies to be found on any of the major dealers websites or on eBay. This book is on a lot of wantlists selling for up to 10X *Guide* in low grade. Why, you ask? Because even the religious affiliation of comic book characters has become a highly collected niche in comics. *True Comics* #48 being the 1st comic appearance of Desmond T. Doss, who was a real-life Seventh-Day Adventist. His 2nd apperance was some 48 years later in Dark Horse's *Medal of Honor Special* #1, and he is the only comic character today that is a Seventh Day Adventist, and as such, has increased in demand for people of that faith and others who collect comic book characters due to their religious affiliation.

Look for many more undiscovered treasures to become valuable for different reasons than was the norm 15 years ago with many more entering our hobby on a daily

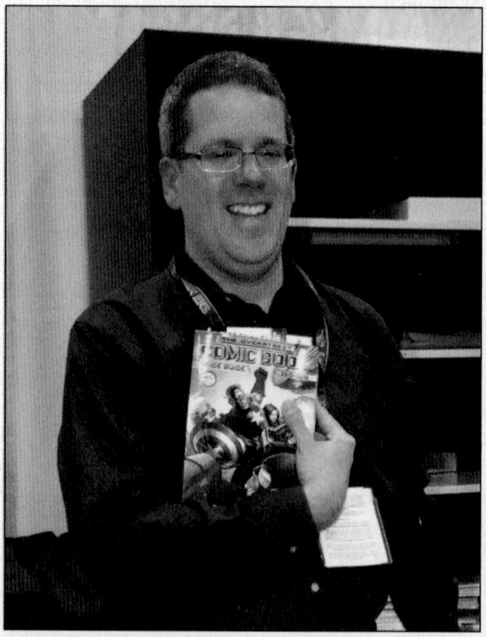
COMIC BOO

Heritage Auction's Barry Sandoval got his new Guide.

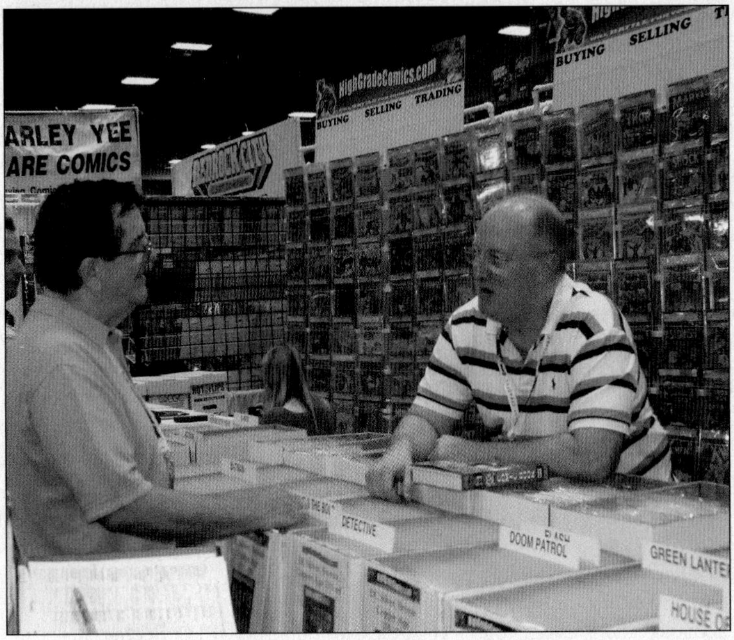
HighGradeComics.com
BUYING SELLING TRADING
BUYING SELLING
DETECTIVE
DOOM PATROL

Bob Overstreet chats with Bob Storms (left to right) about the market and the new Guide.

basis. More books that make you go "Huh" are going to be more sought after by the masses.

Remember to collect what you like and not what someone or website tells you that you should collect.

Michael Pavlic
Purple Gorilla Comics
Calgary Alberta Canada

As of this writing, the *Overstreet Guide* #45 has been out only a few weeks. After I and my good pal Sgt. Erock (OK, mostly Sgt. Erock) went through the *Guide* to compare year over year price differences on certain books, we noticed a few things that made us scratch our heads.

New Mutants #98 did not change in price. Not a dime. The day before I wrote this, I sold a 9.2 for $300. Deadpool is the most in demand character in my store. By far.

Deadpool: Circle Chase Mini-Series #1 easily sells for $60. *Guide* price is much less.

Amazing Spider-Man #361 (1st print) with Carnage's first full appearance is a steady seller at $150 which is 3x *Guide*. Carnage is by far the most popular comic book character not associated with an upcoming movie. Any Carnage appearance is a minimum $10 book.

Uncanny X-Men #94 in 6.0 or less went DOWN in price! I never thought I'd live to see the day that would happen. Truly the era when X-Men ruled the comic roost, which started in the late 1970s, is now over. That said, I've never had a problem selling lower grade key books for well over *Guide*. Even X-Men.

So what's with the discrepancies? Part of it must be due to the lag time between getting market reports and publishing the *Guide*, usually several months. But is there more at play? Is the Deadpool "phenomenon" a localized, regional thing? Can you dealers in say, Florida, only get $150 for *New Mutants* #98? Do they only get $50 for *Amazing Spidey* #361 in Denver? Is there more disposable income in Calgary than in other North American cities? More people buying comics here than elsewhere? My brain isn't big enough to answer these questions, only big enough to ask them. If your brain IS big enough, feel free to email me at purplegorillacomics@gmail.com and tell me what's what.

Art Cloos
Collector
Flushing, NY

As I type this it is mid summer and the weather is hot and humid. But for me that's far better and easier to deal with than the cold and ice of last winter. I find the vintage comic market to be hot as well and certainly not cold and many of the predictions I made in my *Overstreet* #45 report last December seem to be holding up quite well.

The influence of the hobby-based movies and TV shows continues. *Ant-Man* has been a success and there has been movement in the prices of his early comic appearances. *The Brave And The Bold* JLA issues continue to move up in value as does *Showcase* #4. It will be interesting to see how the reception to the *Fantastic Four* movie (which comes out a few days after I finish this) will affect the prices of early *FF* issues.

With Supergirl set to begin on CBS in October, there has been an increased demand for her first *Action Comics* appearance (issue #252 for those who are new to the hobby). Golden Age keys continue to sell well, especially DC and Marvel, but really at least at the shows I go to, the focus continues to be on Silver and Bronze books. With that in mind I suggest for those looking for potential investment opportunities to look for under-valued first edition late Silver and Bronze books, and for those just looking for good reads, I suggest the same. In addition there continues to be undervalued and under-appreciated books in many other areas of the hobby. Of course it goes without saying that speculation can bring rewards in terms of both financial value and reading enjoyment and financial losses if they do not appreciate in value. Thus ultimately the goal should always be to buy to enjoy first and foremost. See you in *Overstreet* #46 next July.

Jon McClure
Comics Historian
Portland, OR

Greetings from Portland Oregon! My general sales this year were of low grade Marvel keys, movie tie-ins and plain old Marvels of any kind starting at $4 in any grade selling best in antique malls at solid retail prices, often at multiple *Guide* due to the current shifting market. Zombie comics of all kinds sell well for me in the antique malls, while DC and others were so-so and Marvels sold extremely well as usual. I almost sold out of low grade Dells because they are

Worldwide Comics' Stephen Ritter

so cheap and so charming, going all the way back to the 1950s. Charlton was slower moving this year, and Romance and Western comics regardless of publisher were slower than last year. My most recent sales of interest in the first week of August 2015 are: *X-Men* #3 GD/VG for $216, the fanzine *Spa-Fon* #2 in Fine Plus for $199, a run of *Toxic!* magazine in VF/NM for $75, and a *Tales to Astonish* #60 in Fair/Good for $24.

Notable variant sales that happened in 2014 include *DC Comics Presents* #22 (6/80) Whitman Type 7a cover variant that sold in January on eBay in CGC 8.5 for a stunning $1,525, one of only six copies currently confirmed to exist. Notable high end sales of Type 1 test market Marvel cover price variants include a *Conan* #63 (6/76) 30¢ cover in CGC 9.8 for $1,827, a *Fantastic Four* #171 (6/76) 30¢ cover in CGC 9.6 for $777, a *Fantastic Four* #184 (7/77) 35¢ cover in CGC 9.8 for $2,000, an *Iron Fist* #13 (6/77) 35¢ cover in CGC 9.4 for $1,700, an *Iron Man* #100 (7/77) 35¢ cover in CGC 9.2 for $1,100, a *Marvel Team-Up* #45 (5/76) 30¢ cover in CGC 9.4 for $580, a *Star Wars* #1 (7/77) in CGC 8.5 for $3,100, CGC 8.0 for $2,500, and CGC 6.5 for $1,850, and an *X-Men* #106 (8/77) 35¢ cover in CGC 9.4 for $3,802. Many non-key issues of Marvel Type 1 test market cover price variants continue to break the listed values of easy-to-find, so-called "Top 10" Bronze Age keys, and as of *OCBPG* #45 in 2015, Star Wars #1(7/77) in raw 9.2 is in first place at $6,000, and *Iron Fist* #14 (8/77) in raw 9.2 is in second place at $3,000, a 36% increase; such books have sky-rocketed in value since I discovered and published on their existence in *Comic Book Marketplace* #51 in the summer of 1997! An *Iron Man* #55 (2/73) Type 1a U.S. published U.K. pence cover price variant in CGC 9.4 for $2,000 sold on eBay in 2013 is another encouraging example of collector recognition of what had previously been considered a foreign edition of lesser value; CGC 9.4 cents editions of *Iron Man* #55 in the same grade were bringing $1,600 on average on eBay during the same time, and since then demand for pence Marvel Type 1a price variants

has increased dramatically across the board.

Pricing spreads remain numb to actual marketability and have decreased the stated values of low grade issues, and especially low grade keys, to a sub-wholesale point that makes it impossible for dealers to keep in them stock at 200-400% of *Guide*. In a world where most older comics exist in Good, Very Good, and Fine condition, the slowly lessening interest in low to mid-grade books, which are in my view the backbone of the hobby, is of concern and dis-heartening, as such comics have taken a back seat to film and television related hot books, and ultra-high grade investment books.

Matt Schiffman
Collector
Bend, OR

As the grading services allowed many collectors to take their foot off the brake pedal, there are still the majority of comics that are not graded out there and we want to buy them, collect them and hold them dear for decades to come. Many buyers are putting complete faith in the grading services to insure that books are not restored, and therefore the rudimentary skills required to spot restoration by collectors has fallen to the wayside. There was that brief window before grading services when a hand-held blacklight was in the back pocket of every high end collector and one saw countless buyer tilting a book back and forth under back fluorescent convention hall lighting trying to spot a color discrepancy, or a dot of black that was out of place on the spine This was a part of the hobby and spotting restoration continues to play a huge role in prices and future prices of books, and it is a skill we all need to prefect and re-learn.

Platinum, Victorian and early Unique Books

I'm starting to see more traction with these books in the broader market, but not from our traditional retailers or dealers. They are popping up in rare book auctions in London and NY auction houses with either a physical or online presence. Prices are strong when they do sell, and those dealers such as, Bloomsbury, Swann and Bonhams and Heritage etc. are making it their domain.

Golden Age

Prices remained strong for high grade books through the start of 2015 and Timely, DC keys, Fox, Nedor and Fiction House are finding new buyers at record prices. The caveat remains that most Golden Age non-keys are selling for a lower fraction of their *Guide* price. Buyers should do their homework and

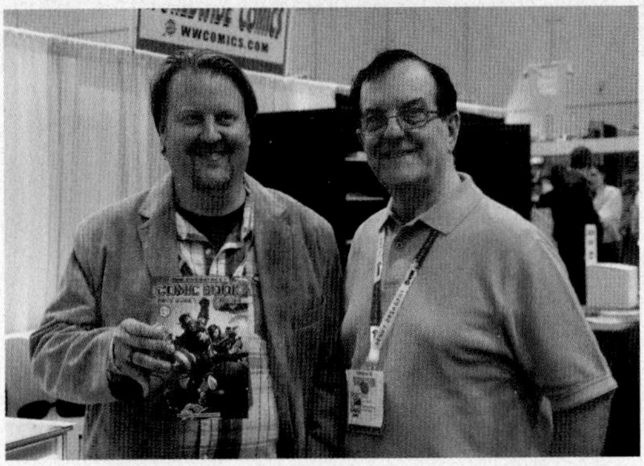
WWCOMICS.COM

Heritage Auctions' Lon Allen with Bob Overstreet.

study the market nuances when making these still relatively expensive purchases. Another focus to study is that restoration continues to take place at record breaking speed, so look carefully at each purchase. Early *Detectives* and *Actions* are in very high demand, as well as the Timely trifecta of *Marvel Mystery*, *Captain America* and *Sub-Mariner*, with *Human Torch* trailing.

Atomic Age

Outside of Fox Good Girl, high grade Fiction House, and Schomburg airbrush keys, prices have backed off slightly for the rest of the section. As with the rest of our hobby, the price spreads have continued to correct themselves and move outward. Collectors are finding that high grade Romance is very difficult to find and the census numbers prove that out and prices are starting to climb again. Oddball War titles are also on the increase in high grade and something to keep an eye on the pre-Code issues as they are not for the timid PC crowd.

Silver Age

Making the mistake and thinking that this run up of prices is overreaching and finished, think again. Collectors and investors have been reporting the over-inflated prices for high grade Marvel Silver and a few select DC issues since 2006 and it has continued in only one direction. This is not news, and not really even worth mentioning. Again. But, the new twist is that prices for key issues are finding higher and higher prices in that 6.5 to 9.0 range, which is not found in other Age categories. And for the top ten keys, this has dipped into the 2.0 and up grades. This might be seen in these other Age categories in the future, but besides *Detective* #27 and *Action* #1, nothing even comes close.

Bronze Age

Collecting Bronze has never been more fun, and trickier than right now. IF…IF you are very, very happy and satisfied by purchasing the very first Key 9.8 or 9.6 that comes to market and suffering the consequences that have been documented, then please continue onward and….downward. *Marvel Premiere* #7, *Green Lantern* #76, *Incredible Hulk* #181, *Giant-Size X-Men* #1, *All Star Western* #10. Advice? Learn the market, learn that some of these issues are, and will be out there. Others will not. Collect them all, but just be careful – if money matters to you. Others are having fun playing the movie appearance chase game and speculating pretty far afield with speculation of who is the next pop up villain to appear in any given movie trailer, or cameo/spin-off potential. *Marvel Feature* #4… you could not give that book away a few years ago. Spreads are probably the hardest to figure out of any given category here, with 9.4 the dropping-in value point and anything outside of a top 50 key finding itself the same price in any grade from GD to VF, and that is tough to digest.

Copper Age

Smaller print runs, heavy retail wear from long box slump and pawing through without the benefit of a backing board if what defines this era. Countless *TMNT* issues from #1 to #6 were battered due to oversizing and lower paper quality and inadequate back board protection. Have fun finding those other small, rare, and odd publishing houses that thought they should redefine comics by printing oversized books that are difficult to store in a conventional box. These are fun to collect and discover and good luck finding them in high grade.

Modern Age

There are warehouses, backrooms, attics and basements filled with long boxes of the most wonderful Modern Age books. Retailers were encouraged to over-order, collectors were urged to order and commit to multiples and the variant and multiple cover was shamelessly exploited for the first time. These are the increasingly frequent phone calls I receive from sellers. Now, there are starting to be some really, really great books buried in the tonnage. But, many retailers still cannot commit to buying such vast quantities and these collections still end up at thrift stores, storage auctions, and garage sales. Long time retailers are starting to haul their backstock out and digging through it all. This is where the fun for collectors starts and this is where the hunt flashes back to collecting of the olden days of yore.

Current

Small, tiny print runs. Not too much more needs to be said. These small numbers are staggering and would have been cancelled a decade ago, but that is the new reality. So, if you are looking way down the road, you'll kick yourself for not collecting some of these great runs that will be in demand down the road. And when your grandkid is going to see a movie costing $200 million to make and starring some character's first appearance in 2015 with a 12,000 print run, you'll wish you had that to slab up for him. Maybe….

Hake's Soars With Franco Toscanini Superman Collection

BY **MIKE BOLLINGER**

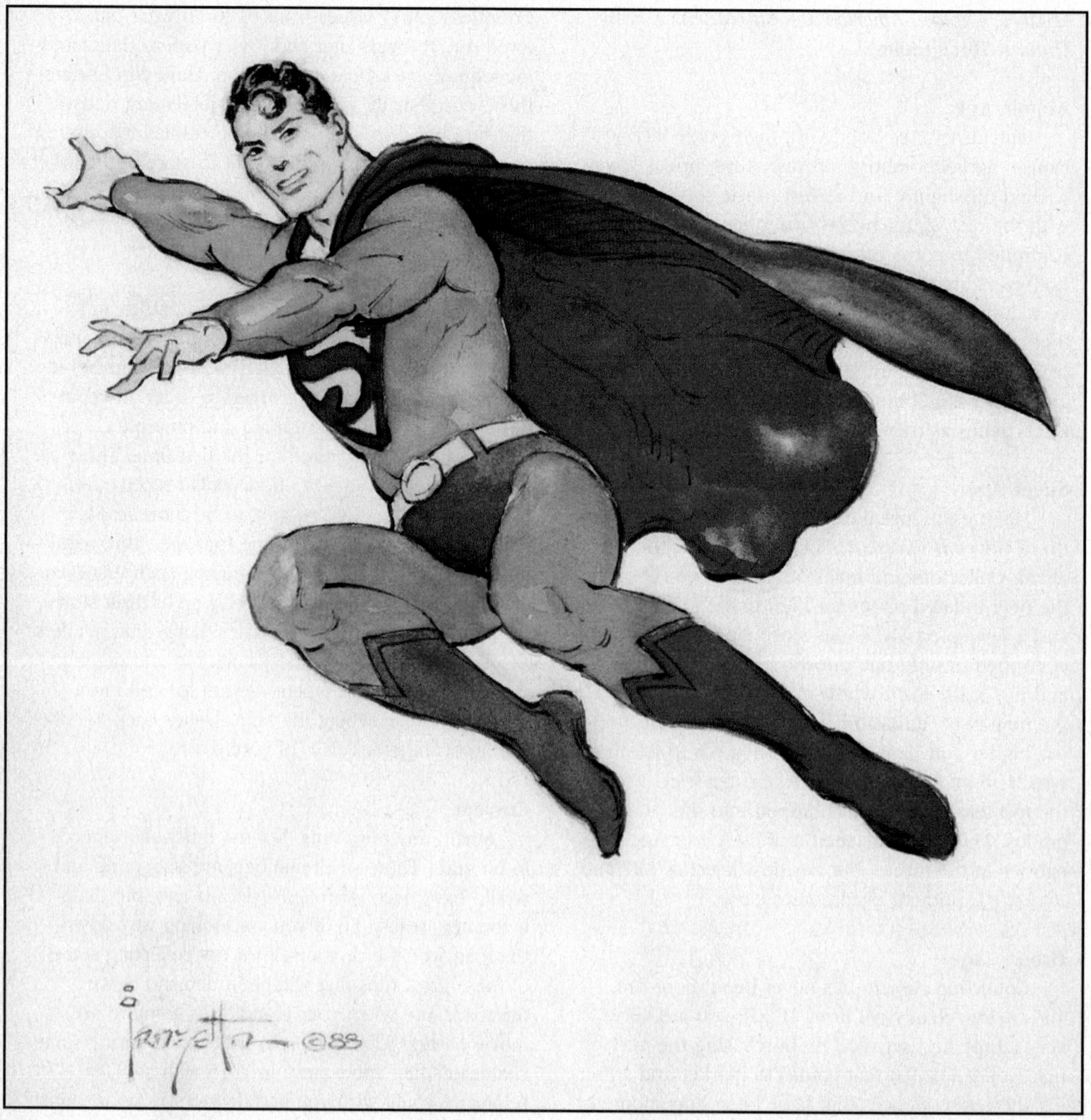

Easily one of the most merchandised characters ever created, Toscanini scoured comic book stores, comic conventions and collector shows, bid in auctions and searched everywhere in between, procuring countless Superman items, spanning from the early days of the character's history to modern day products that lined shelves of retail stores everywhere.

He enjoyed meeting with artists, writers, actors and anyone associated with the character he had grown to love. The sky was the limit regarding his collection and he was soon surrounded by comic books and all types of merchandise, premiums, promotional movie material, original art and anything else bearing Superman's trademark "S."

Since Toscanini's passing in 2011, his collection has remained in his "Fortress of Solitude." His widow Teresa recently decided it was time for other collectors to partake of the many great items he had compiled. To do this, she contacted Hake's Americana & Collectibles in York, PA.

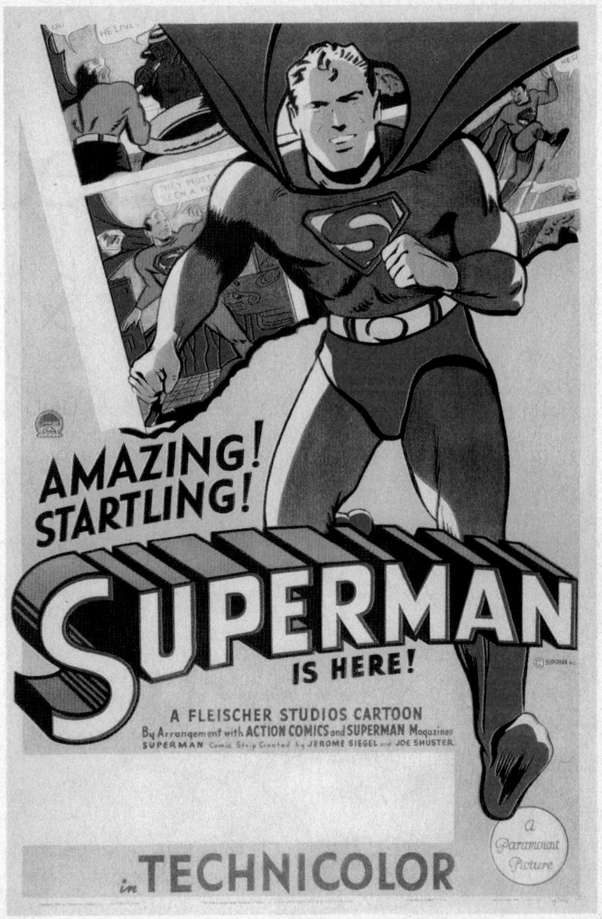
AMAZING!
STARTLING!
SUPERMAN
IS HERE!
A FLEISCHER STUDIOS CARTOON
By Arrangement with ACTION COMICS and SUPERMAN Magazines
SUPERMAN Comic Strip Created by JEROME SIEGEL and JOE SHUSTER
in TECHNICOLOR
a Paramount Picture

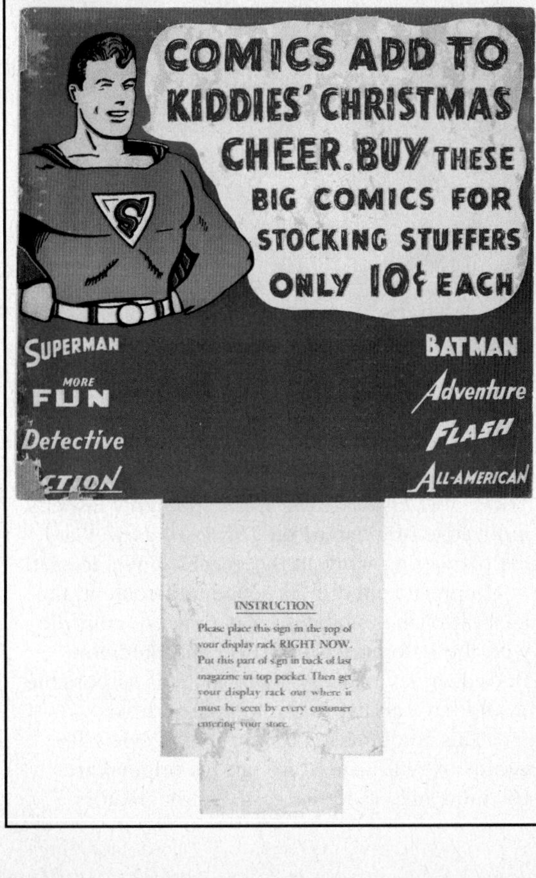
COMICS ADD TO KIDDIES' CHRISTMAS CHEER. BUY THESE BIG COMICS FOR STOCKING STUFFERS ONLY 10¢ EACH
SUPERMAN
MORE FUN
Detective
BATMAN
Adventure
FLASH
ALL-AMERICAN
INSTRUCTION
Please place this sign in the top of your display rack RIGHT NOW. Put this part of sign in back of last magazine in top pocket. Then get your display rack out where it must be seen by every customer entering your store.

The premier pop culture collectibles auction house offered the first wave of items from the Franco Toscanini Superman Collection in their July 2015 auction.

Needless to say, bidders were excited to have the opportunity to bid on the many high-quality Superman items being offered. A Christmas 1940 comic book rack topper sold for $24,035, while a rare one-sheet poster for the Fleischer Studios Superman cartoons brought $17,393. Other highlights included a standee for the 1948 Columbia serial that realized $15,028, a Fleischer pressbook that sold for $11,500; a one-of-a-kind Fleischer Superman model sheet soared to $10,436 while a newspaper syndicate promotional folder brought $9,867 in bids.

With 120 lots offered, Hake's pulled in a total of $257,000 in bids from the Toscanini Collection alone. Work has already begun on Hake's newest auction, with another super selection being prepared for the auction block. Just one of the highlights includes a piece of original Superman specialty art by legendary comic artist and illustrator Frank Frazetta. This and more will be featured in Hake's November 2015 auction. It'll be here faster than a speeding bullet.

75 Spirited Years:
Will Eisner & The Spirit

BY **CATHERINE SAUNDERS-WATSON**

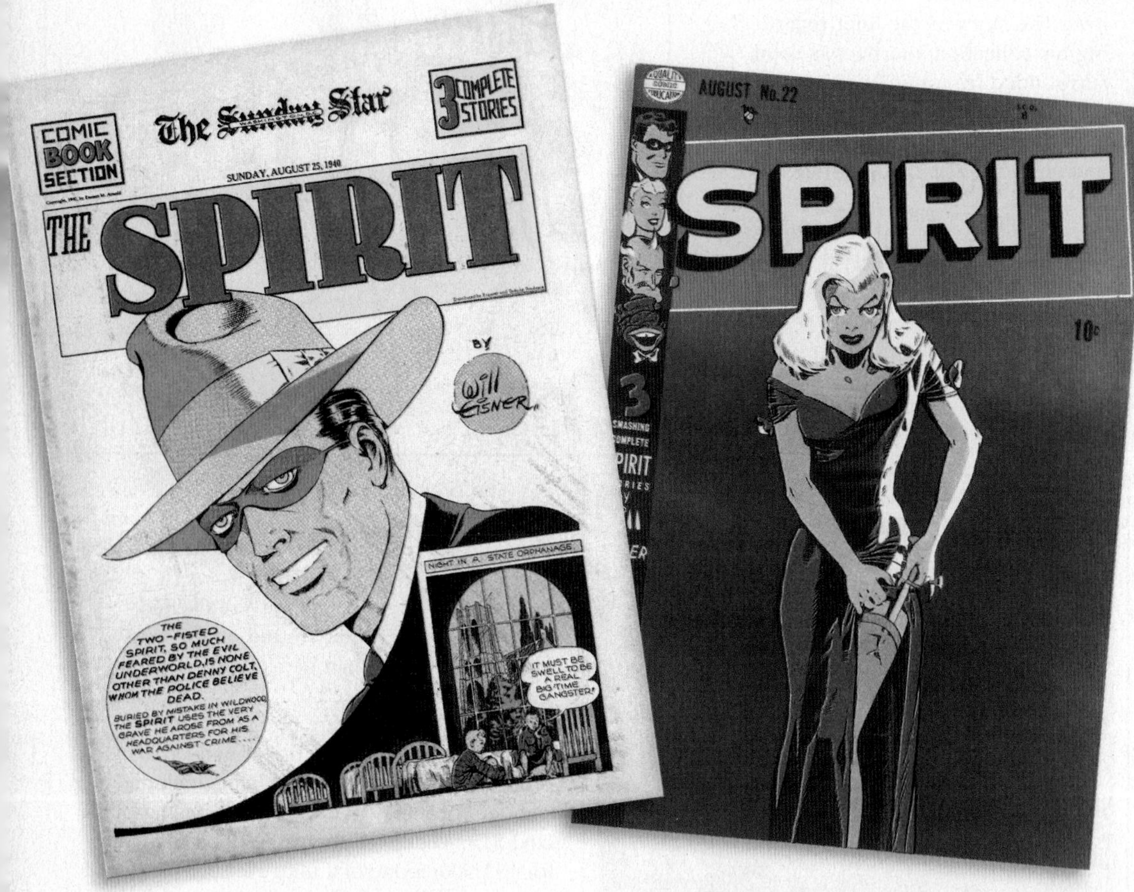
COMIC BOOK SECTION
3 COMPLETE STORIES
SUNDAY, AUGUST 25, 1940
THE SPIRIT
BY Will Eisner
THE TWO-FISTED SPIRIT, SO MUCH FEARED BY THE EVIL UNDERWORLD, IS NONE OTHER THAN DENNY COLT, WHOM THE POLICE BELIEVE DEAD.
BURIED BY MISTAKE IN WILDWOOD, THE SPIRIT USES THE VERY GRAVE HE AROSE FROM AS A HEADQUARTERS FOR HIS WAR AGAINST CRIME....
NIGHT IN A STATE ORPHANAGE
IT MUST BE SWELL TO BE A REAL BIG TIME GANGSTER!
AUGUST No. 22
SPIRIT
10¢

On September 26, 2015, *75 Spirited Years: Will Eisner & The Spirit*, the largest and most important anniversary retrospective exhibition of original comic art from Will Eisner's *The Spirit,* went on display at Geppi's Entertainment Museum (GEM) in Baltimore. Located in the historic Camden Yards sports complex directly across the street from the Baltimore Convention Center and immediately next door to Oriole Park, GEM will present more than 50 pieces of Eisner's rare original art in the exhibit, which runs through March 7, 2016.

Curated by Denis Kitchen, Eisner's longtime publisher, agent and friend, with the full cooperation of the Eisner family, *75 Spirited Years: Will Eisner & The Spirit* spotlights Eisner's innovative original art on *The Spirit* as well as his pioneering work in the graphic-novel format.

Unprecedented in its scope and content, the kick-off of the exhibition was timed to coincide with the Baltimore Comic-Con and Baltimore Book Fair, so as many comic art fans as possible would have access to the unique archive.

"This is a fantastic opportunity to view the genius of Will Eisner through his original art. His influence on future comic book creators

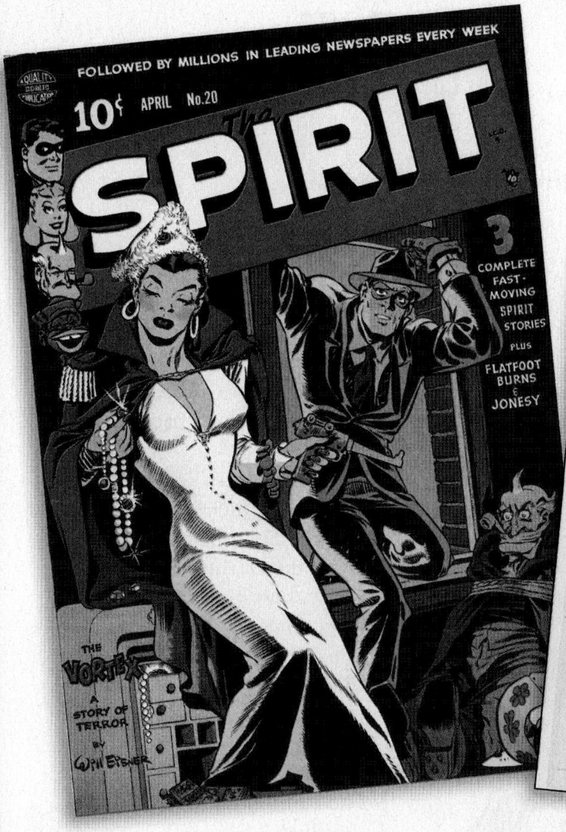
FOLLOWED BY MILLIONS IN LEADING NEWSPAPERS EVERY WEEK
10¢ APRIL No.20
The SPIRIT
3 COMPLETE FAST-MOVING SPIRIT STORIES
PLUS
FLATFOOT BURNS & JONESY
THE VORTEX A STORY OF TERROR BY Will Eisner

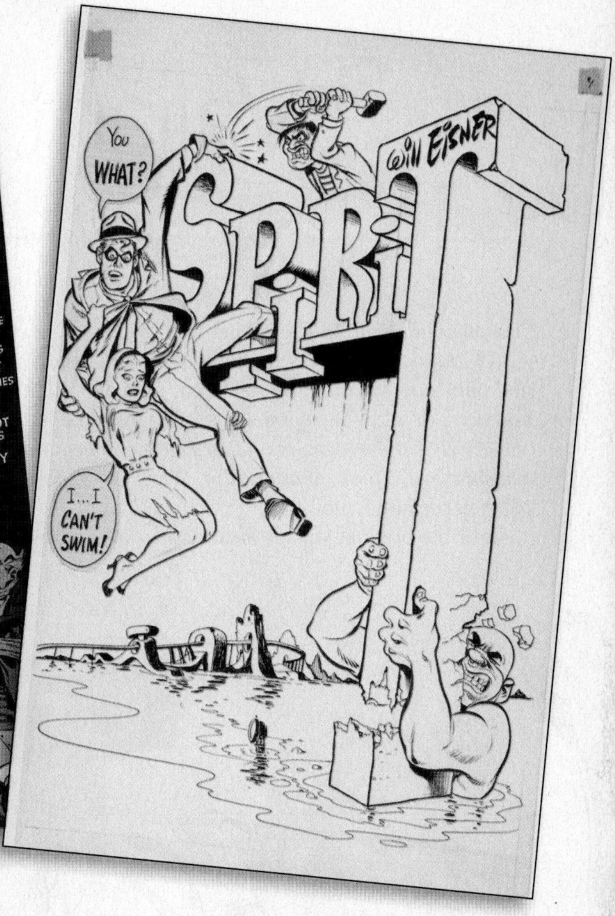
YOU WHAT?
Will Eisner
SPIRIT
I...I CAN'T SWIM!

and cartoonists was profound, and it also went far beyond his obvious artistic talent. When Mr. Eisner started in the business, comic book artists were not held in the same regard as comic strip artists," said Melissa Bowersox, President of Geppi's Entertainment Museum.

"During the Depression, there were 12 comic strip millionaires, but that wasn't the case for comic book creators. Eisner not only lived long enough to see important changes made, he helped make them. He became a leading advocate for creator rights and graphic novels, and his impact is still being felt today," she said.

From June 2, 1940 to October 5, 1952, Will Eisner's *The Spirit* appeared in a comic-book-size insert in local newspapers around the country, including in Baltimore. Noted for its inventiveness, wry send-ups of the superhero milieu, and its succinct, seven-page lead stories, *The Spirit* featured a never-give-up title character, strong females ranging from childhood friends to femme fatales, and creatively-designed title pages that worked the title into the art.

Escaping from the perceived second-class world of comic-book art and into the lucrative world of comic strips, Eisner built *The Spirit* sections into a calling card and never looked back.

Eisner introduced comics to the U.S. Army as an instructional tool for vehicle maintenance (in *P.S. Magazine*), presciently adapted his work to a graphic-novel format with *A Contract With God* (and many others), and taught at New York's School of Visual Arts. He remained vibrant and fully engaged with the creative community until his death in 2005, at age 87. In a single night, he won separate Harvey Awards for work created five decades apart, validating his foresight and enduring influence on those who followed in his footsteps.

Once the exhibit opens to the public, there will be no additional charge for museum visitors to view *75 Spirited Years: Will Eisner & The Spirit*; it will be included in the regular admission charge of $10 for adults, $9 for seniors (55+), and $7 for students 5-18. Children 4 and under are admitted free.

Geppi's Entertainment Museum is located at Camden Yards, 301 W. Camden St., Baltimore, MD 21201. It is open Tuesday through Sunday from 10 a.m. to 6 p.m. and is closed on Mondays. For additional information, call 410-625-7060 or visit www.geppismuseum.com.

Valiant at 25

BY **J.C. VAUGHN**

By September 1996, the dream was over.

X-O Manowar #68 was the final issue of all the Valiant titles and of their original universe. Video game publisher Acclaim Entertainment paid $65 million for Valiant and proceeded to mismanage the company – or allow the company's mismanagement – in a very challenging marketplace.

Eternal Warrior. Magnus Robot Fighter. Solar, Man of the Atom. Harbinger. Archer & Armstrong. Bloodshot. Rai. Turok. Shadowman. What Jim Shooter and his band of rebels and upstarts had begun in 1990 was seemingly no more.

All of the original Valiant incarnations of the characters had ended.

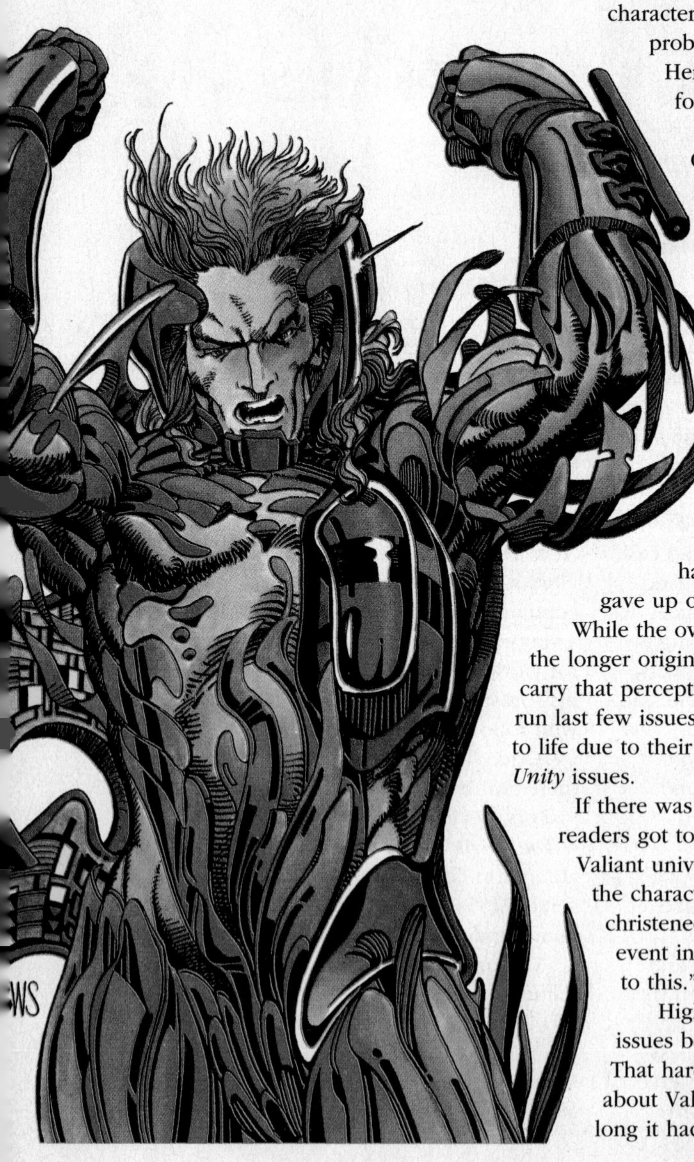

Acclaim relaunched some of them along with new characters, but the market had grown even more problematic at the time. Of the VH2 (Valiant Heroes 2) universe, only *Quantum & Woody* found any lasting impact with fans.

A third, smaller incarnation of Acclaim Comics brought a new incarnation of *Shadowman* and even brought back Shooter for *Unity 2000*, but Acclaim's own financial problems were manifest by that time and things finally ended. Unfinished.

Aftermath

Like many comics from the 1990s, the good were lumped in with the bad and the prices plummeted. Destination: 25-cent bins. Great characters and great stories make for unforgettable comics, though, and a hardcore contingent of Valiant fans never gave up on the issues they loved.

While the overwhelmingly plentiful middle issues of the longer original Valiant runs even now seem fated to carry that perception for the next few decades, the low print run last few issues of each series have long since sparked to life due to their rarity. And then there's the pre-*Unity* and *Unity* issues.

If there was ever a comic book universe that readers got to see coming together, it was the original Valiant universe. As Shooter and company wove the characters and story elements together and christened with that rarity of rarity, a comic book event in which it really has "...all been leading up to this."

High grade copies of the earliest Valiant issues began to slowly increase in value again. That hardcore group of diehard fans kept talking about Valiant, and it didn't seem to matter how long it had been gone.

Rebirth

Without the seeds planted by those early strong stories, the April 21, 2015 announcement from Valiant Entertainment and Sony Pictures of a five-picture deal for two superhero franchises – *Bloodshot* and *Harbinger* – never would have happened. Inspired by childhood love of the characters, Dinesh Shamdasani and Jason Kothari acquired the Valiant properties in Acclaim's bankruptcy sale.

They began the slow process of putting together a new universe based on the original, kicking off new interpretations of such characters as X-O Manowar, Harbinger, Shadowman and Ninjak.

At press time, *X-O Manowar*, their flagship title, is nearing its 40th issue, and between it and their other titles they've brought back a significant number of the original Valiant's top and secondary characters.

But they haven't been content with that. They turned the title *Unity* into an ongoing team book with no real ties to the original.

They launched a four-issue event title, *The Valiant*, which provided them with their best updated take on Eternal Warrior to date and gave them a trade paperback collection that promises to just keep selling.

They took the *Harbinger* concept and instead of just aping Jim Shooter and David Lapham's brilliant original run or offering twists on it, they carried it to a logical and potentially frightening next stage in *Imperium*.

They successfully introduced *Divinity*, their first title based on a new character with no ties to the original Valiant, and produced a hit with multiple printings in the process.

The Sony announcement followed news in March that DMG Entertainment, the Beijing-based entertainment firm, had made an eight-figure equity investment into Valiant, which the company will use in publishing, film, television, licensing and other areas. DMG also said that they had dedicated another nine-figure sum specifically for film production as well.

The result of all this to this point has been some very interesting comics. Going forward, though, fans have every reason to expect more.

Bloodshot, which is scheduled to arrive in theaters in 2017, will kick off the five-picture plan. It will be directed by David Leitch & Chad Stahelski (*John Wick*) from a script by Jeff Wadlow (*Kick Ass 2*) and Eric Heisserer (*Story of Your Life*). It will be followed shortly by *Harbinger*. The studio has already planned one sequel for each film, followed by the crossover *Harbinger Wars*.

And Valiant has other projects in the hopper as well.

My Pre-Unity Four

BY **SCOTT BRADEN**

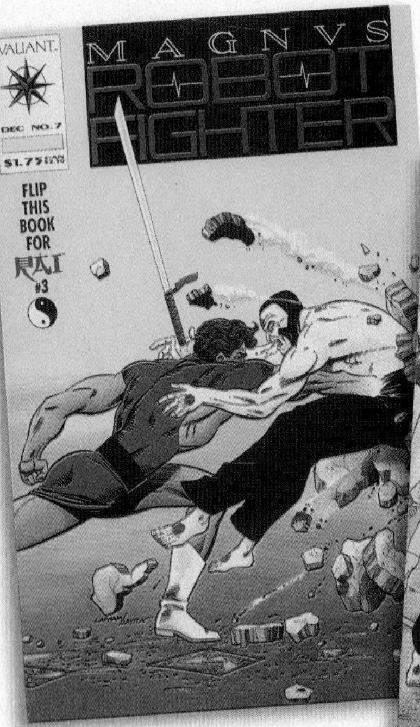
VALIANT
MAGNVS
ROBOT FIGHTER
DEC NO. 7
$1.75
FLIP THIS BOOK FOR RAI #3

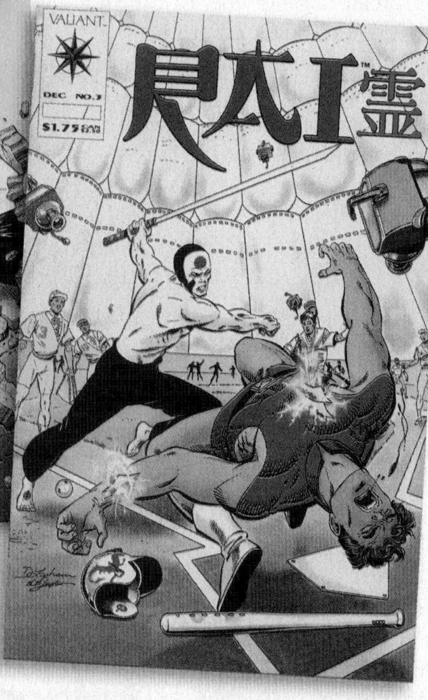
VALIANT
DEC NO. 3
$1.75
RAI

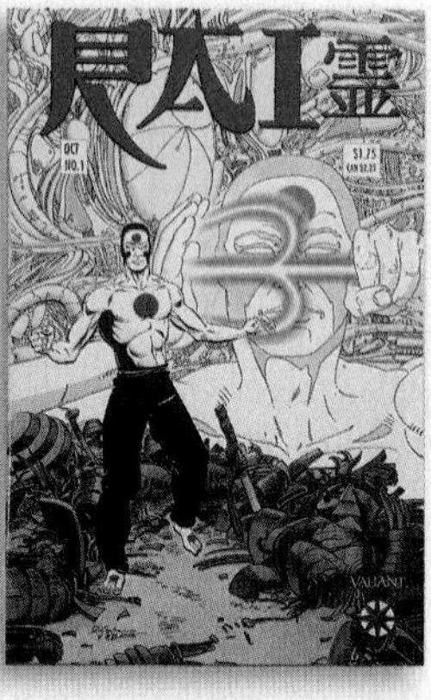
RAI
$1.75
VALIANT

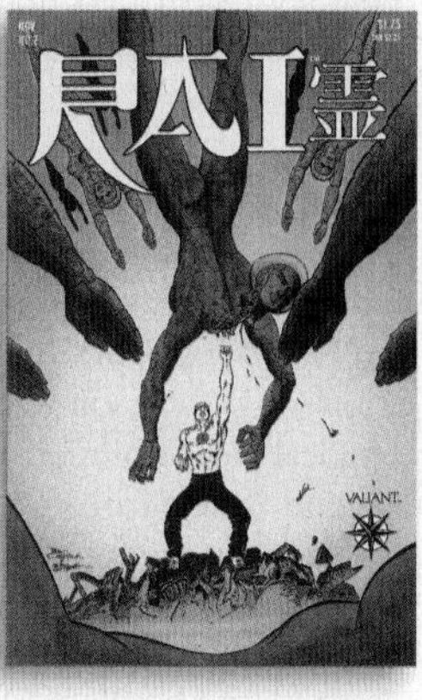
RAI
VALIANT

In the early 1990s, few comic book publishers matched the fan excitement stirred up by the Valiant universe. The company's new characters and those older ones that they revived captured the hearts of readers and spurred many to become long term Valiant enthusiasts, particularly of the material produced in advance of and during the event known simply as *Unity*.

Those early Valiant stories crafted by or under the direction of Valiant founder and former editor-in-chief Jim Shooter not only carved out Valiant's identity, two and a half decades later we can now safely say that many of them have stood the test of time.

Saying that, what were the specific elements that made Valiant books stand out on the comic rack? Was it they published comics with great storytelling and popular art? Was it the development of then-up-and-coming superstars like Joe Quesada and David Lapham, among others?

Could it have been all of that and more? I certainly think so.

In his introduction in the *Valiant Era Collection* trade paperback, writer-artist Kevin VanHook, a former Vice-President and Executive Editor for the company, wrote "…there was an excitement that's hard to describe…" while colorist and production guru Janet "JayJay" Jackson and others have publically commented on this as well.

There was something magic going on there, and it shows in the pages of those stories.

Here are my top four pre-*Unity* Valiant stories…

Magnus, Robot Fighter #5-#8

The first appearance of Rai, the futuristic Japanese guardian who has been carried over to

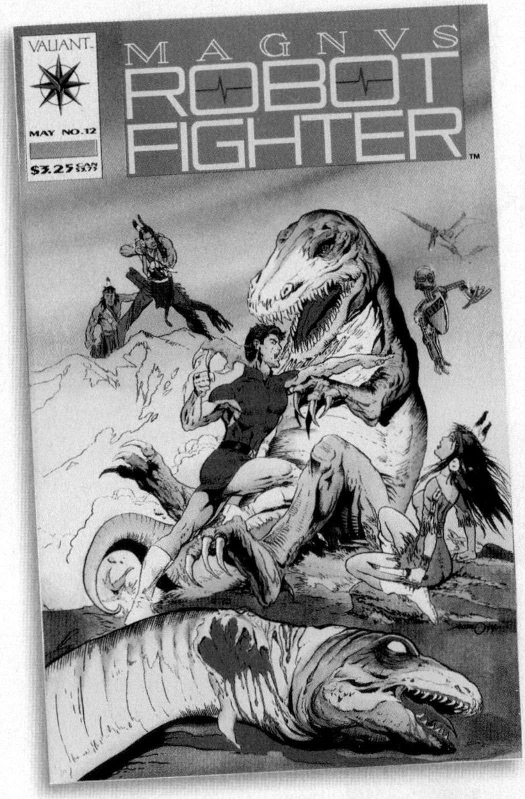
VALIANT
MAGNVS
ROBOT FIGHTER
MAY NO.12
$3.25

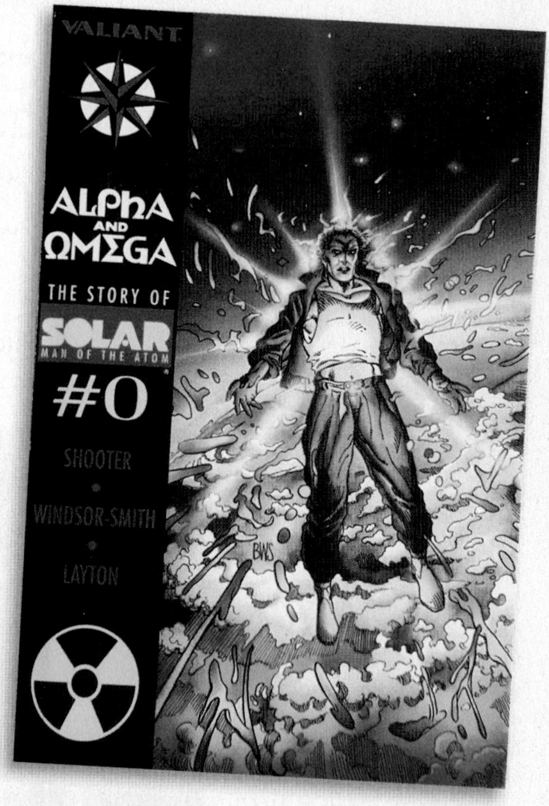
VALIANT
ALPHA AND OMEGA
THE STORY OF
SOLAR
MAN OF THE ATOM
#0
SHOOTER
WINDSOR-SMITH
LAYTON

an acclaimed series by today's Valiant universe, was first chronicled in *Magnus, Robot Fighter* #5-#8 with the story "Invasion," which was told in chapter form with flip books (*Magnus, Robot Fighter* on one side, *Rai* on the other). Besides unveiling Rai's character, courage and dedication, it was also the first story that readers experienced future Japan's massive – and strongly anime-tinged – Dragon form. Manga kids, look it up. You will find that the storyline is epic indeed!

Magnus, Robot Fighter #12

The classic Issue introduced the rest of the Valiant universe to Turok, a Native American warrior who would later be known to his millions of fans as the Dinosaur Hunter. It also gave readers a sneak peek at the Lost Land – the battleground and/or backdrop for the fierce war to come. With that said, both Turok and the mythical Lost Land would play pivotal roles in the *Unity* event.

Solar, Man of the Atom: Alpha and Omega

Known by many as one of Valiant's best-loved stories from its early days of publishing, "Alpha and Omega" was a stellar origin story featuring the publisher's godlike superhero, Solar. The story was told in multi-page inserts inside *Solar* #1-10, and then eventually in a trade collection and a hard-to-find slip-case edition. "Alpha and Omega" reintroduced comic readers to the early adventures of the Man of the Atom. It also examined the woman who would become the maniacal Mothergod in Valiant"s best-selling crossover event, *Unity*. To that end, the "Alpha and Omega" storyline gave fans a taste of the powerful storytelling they would later experience in the comics line, both in *Unity* and many more Valiant comics to come.

Solar, Man of the Atom #10

While part of the "Alpha and Omega" story appears as an insert in this one, this issue itself is also a stand-out. This key comic book featured a black embossed cover and dynamic content inside. Within the pages of this issue were the first appearances of the Eternal Warrior, and a young man who was the latest in a long line of Geomancers.– two characters and concepts that would continue under the auspices of the new Valiant Entertainment years later. Besides introducing two powerful characters to the Valiant universe, *Solar, Man of the Atom* #10 also planted the seeds for the *Unity* event, which was then just on the horizon.

What are your favorite pre-Unity Valiant stories or issues? You can drop us a line at feedback@gemstonepub.com and let us know!

Looking Under The Black Hood

BY **CARRIE WOOD**

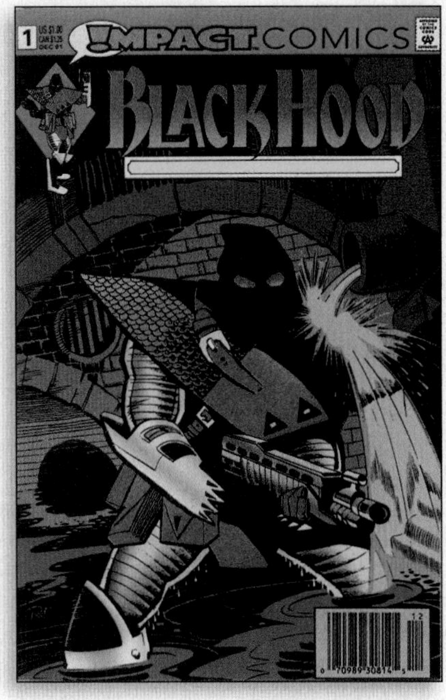
1
IMPACT COMICS
BLACK HOOD

Of all the characters in Archie's new Dark Circle line-up, the Black Hood has easily gone through the most changes over the years. The original Hood was a man by the name of Matthew "Kip" Burland who made his debut in MLJ Comics' Top-Notch Comics *#9 in October of 1940. Burland had been trained by a hermit to battle evil; an ex-cop, he was framed for larceny and left for dead, and while he eventually cleared his name, he continued to fight crime throughout the Golden Age.*

Burland's nephew, Thomas, became the Hood in the 1970s revival under Archie's Red Circle Comics line. This Hood could be seen riding a fancy motorcycle and was armed with custom Pepper-box pistols. He was featured in three issues of his own title in 1983 but most often was featured in The Mighty Crusaders *and* Archie's Super Hero Comic Digest.

The Black Hood *jumped to DC Comics in 1991 when the company began its Impact Comics imprint. Impact was only around from '91 to '93 and primarily featured old heroes licensed from Archie Comics, including the Comet and the Shield in addition to the Black Hood. Impact ended up ending due to poor sales, but of the comics in that line,* The Black Hood *was definitely a standout. This version of the Hood actually featured three different characters as the vigilante, and the titular hood itself was an executioner's hood that would grant its wearer heightened strength and agility – but would force them to only use these abilities for good.*

As The Black Hood celebrates its 75th anniversary and with a highly touted new version of the character launched in Spring 2015, Gemstone's Carrie Wood spoke with artist Rick Burchett and writer Mark Wheatley about their involvement with Impact's Black Hood series.

CBM: Did you have any specific story objectives going in?

Rick Burchett (RB): We were to create stories that would be good jumping on points for new comic readers of all ages. Stories that weren't bogged down by decades of continuity and would be complete in a single issue.

Mark Wheatley (MW): I was under orders from Mike Gold to shake things up and ignore everything that had ever been done with *The Black Hood.* The Impact line of comics was guaranteed three years to establish the stories, characters and commercial viability. So my objective was to create a set of fascinating characters and a setting that had a deep back story. The plan was to lay the foundation of a major new line of comics. I was weaving a tapestry that would be able to still be paying off stories a decade after our launch.

CBM: Do you think you were able to achieve these?

MW: With the help of Rick Burchett and the other

artists, I think we managed a near 100 percent of our goals for the first year. I was very pleased and gratified that fan response was so strong, as well. *The Black Hood* was a hit, with sales growing constantly. I was very excited, anticipating the next two years of the series. The future looked bright for *The Black Hood*.
RB: I think so, at least in *The Black Hood*. Some of the rest of the books in the Impact line started that way, but then began to feature continued stories.

CBM: The Black Hood you wrote for Impact different pretty significantly from the previous iterations of the character in Mighty Comics and Red Circle Comics. Why was that the case?
MW: Mike Gold was the mastermind behind Impact. He felt that the character names of the Mighty Crusaders were our major asset. He felt that the actual characters and their back stories were so messy, muddled and largely forgotten, we should concentrate on creating something essentially new. No one was lobbying for a return of these characters. We would have created entirely new characters, but Mike felt that we needed the name recognition factor. And since it also took the Archie company out of the superhero market, that played into the DC strategy.

2
US $1.00
CAN $1.25
JAN 92
IMPACT COMICS
THE BLACK HOOD IS DEAD!
--LONG LIVE THE BLACK HOOD

CBM: There were three different Hoods in this series. Did you have a favorite?
MW: Nate was absolutely my favorite. And my long term plan was to have Nate becoming The Black Hood and then abandoning the hood, over and over again. As other people would wear the hood for a while and have their lives shaken up or ended, Nate would be drawn back into the world of crime and super heroes. We would follow Nate as he grew into a man, seeing him struggle to keep his own identity, to have a normal life, to connect with people and family – and then to be dragged back into the fray. That said, the opportunity to cast other people as The Black Hood allowed for the potential of some delightful and extreme characters to be super heroes, people you would not usually expect to see in that role. You know – I think your count is off. There were at least three Hoods in the regular *Black Hood* comics. But I think there were two, maybe three more in the annuals. We had short back-up stories of historical Black Hood characters. This was part of the deep back story I was developing for the series.
RB: Yeah, I liked Nate the best. I'm a sucker for traditional heroes – ordinary people who find themselves in extraordinary situations and rise to the occasion. The first Hood in our series used the hood to serve an agenda, and Hit Coffee was an opportunist, using the hood to further personal gain.

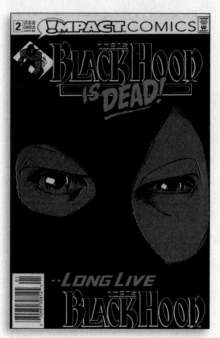

CBM: There were a lot of very colorful characters in the book besides the Hood himself. How did you go about designing the look of the book?
RB: I'm a big fan of the early Marvel books and one of the things I loved about them was the way Kirby and Ditko designed the characters. Not everyone looked like they had a lifetime membership to 24 Hour Fitness. Some of the bad guys were stout, some were lanky, many different body types. If you wield a power like Doctor Octopus, you don't need defined musculature. The mechanical arms do all the work. The same with the Vulture. It's probably better if the wings don't have to lift a lot of muscle mass. Different types of figures give the strip visual variety.

CBM: The Black Hood series seemed really reflective of societal fears at the time – The G-NE drugs, the ozone-afflicted villain, and so on. How were you able to integrate these issues into the book without seeming as though you were pandering to your audience?
MW: Pandering is exactly what I always avoid in my work. An audience is a moving target. If you aim at where they are, by the time your comic is in their hands six months later, they will have moved on. Pandering is usually wasted effort. I was writing *The Black Hood* based on my own interactions with the world. I was pulling from my own reactions and concerns with society. That's what I always do.

RB: That was Mark's doing, and I think he was just following in the footsteps of those writers who came before. When DC started the Silver Age, science was the underpinning for the characters and the stories. When Stan created the Marvel Universe, the touchstones were Radioactivity and the spread of Communism.

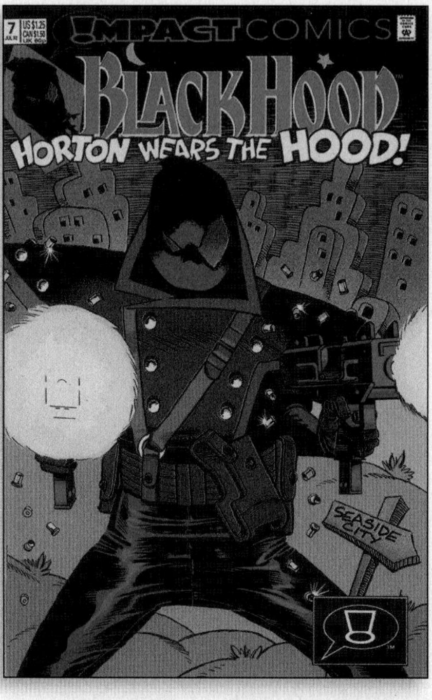
!MPACT COMICS
BLACK HOOD
HORTON WEARS THE HOOD!
SEASIDE CITY

All of these things reflected the times in which the stories were written. Comics have always reflected their times. You could put together a pretty good look at America in the 20th century just by reading the comics.

CBM: Was there any single stand-out moment or issue in the series for you?
MW: Most of the issues have moments I loved. Rick Burchett is an amazing storyteller. His ability to get the maximum visual impact from what I had written was a real joy for me. There is a three page sequence in one of the issues where the Hood is trying to climb out of a sewer that just blows me away. Issue #7 is probably my favorite, entire book. "Horton Wears The Hood" was inspired by two sources. First, it was my whimsical effort at telling a crime story in the style of a Doctor Seuss children's book – and I think we managed that very well. Second, the founding of the city was based on my own family history. Weaving details of my first ancestors to arrive in the new world and how they settled on Virginia's Eastern Shore was a sly nod to my roots.
RB: Actually, there are a couple. When Nate is in the tunnels under the city and they begin to flood. That turned out pretty good visually. The other was a quiet moment. Nate is in his room, feeling unsure of himself and he puts the Hood on and it gives him confidence. I started the sequence with the action in the panel tilted and, as he put on the Hood, the panels rotate to a visually more stable composition. I was trying to reach the reader's subconscious by indicating that without the Hood, Nate's emotions were uneasy. With the Hood, he was on firmer ground. I think that worked.

CBM: When you started on this project, what was your initial thought on the character and on the Impact line as a whole?
MW: It was a fun experience. I got to work with some of the most talented people working in comics at that time. We had several group retreats and spent a good deal of time cross-pollenating ideas and plans. I remember thinking that it would be an opportunity to do some world building in the same collaborative way that the early Marvel Comics under Lee, Kirby, Ditko, Heck, etc. had done – to be a part of a group of talented creators all working for a common goal.
RB: I thought the Impact line was a great idea, something that was desperately needed in the industry. It was intended to be an entry point for new readers, a way to expand the audience. I was familiar with the MLJ heroes before this, and I always felt there was a charm to them and unlimited potential. It's funny, but the one I gravitated to was the Black Hood. There were great possibilities to the character. When editor Mike Gold called to offer me the job and told me it would be *The Black Hood*, I was thrilled. Given a choice, it was the one I would've picked. What Mark did with the character was brilliant, not unlike the early Spider-Man. It was great fun. To this day Mark Wheatley is still the most creative person I've ever worked with. His influence helped me get better at what I did.

CBM: Did those thoughts change once the Black Hood finished?
MW: Well, I did get that creative experience that I was looking for. But the market was in turmoil at the time. And in spite of Mike Gold's best efforts to keep Impact on the rails, we were still hit with last minute changes and some astoundingly bad production problems. One of the issues was published without ANY of the caption boxes included – so the story made only partial sense and had little relation to the story I was actually telling, since the captions were explaining characters' hidden motivations for their actions that were on view in the art. Also, with so many other comics being released at the time from all the publishers, the creative teams were being tempted

away by big money and more assured opportunities. I was so fortunate that Rick Burchett stayed with the book as long as he did. And the other artists on the book were turning in amazing work. Ultimately, we had the rug pulled out from under us at the end of the first year. While it was acknowledged that my *Black Hood* was the standout commercial success of the line, for some odd reason, it was decided to throw out the baby with the bath water. *The Black Hood* was cancelled while at a very high and growing circulation, so they could mount a re-boot of the entire line. So my three year plan to pay off the stories and characters had only reached the end of their first act. In many ways we had only scratched the surface of the potential for that title. And the fans loved what we were doing. So, in the end, it was a somewhat frustrating experience.

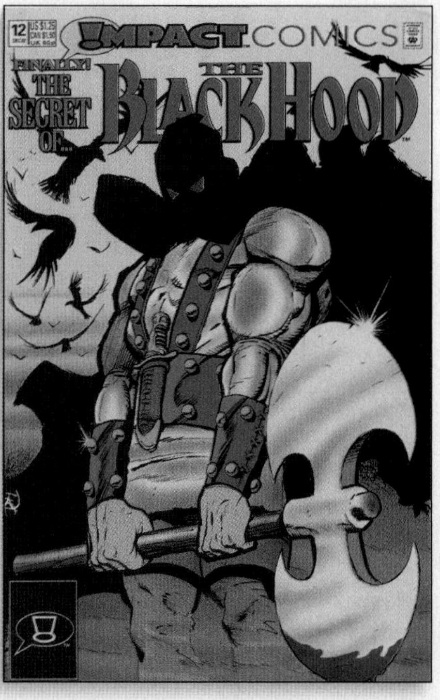
12
!MPACT COMICS
FINALLY! THE SECRET OF...
THE BLACK HOOD

RB: My thoughts on the Hood didn't change. The Impact line, as a whole, seemed to lose its way and DC stopped promoting it. I'm not sure the reasons behind those changes, but it was a shame. Impact was a noble experiment and I wish it would've been more successful. Its failure doesn't mirror the quality of the work that was done. There were some good comics produced in that short period of time.

CBM: Now that Archie is redeveloping their Red Circle line as Dark Circle, and now that your material will be available in digital format, what would you tell new readers about your stories?

MW: I think Rick and I managed to create some great characters in *The Black Hood*. They have interesting lives and unexpected things happened to them. In some ways, it was a subversive book. We were creating an anti-vigilante story that featured a prime vigilante. We enjoyed poking at some of the accepted super hero tropes. I think it started as a reaction to the silly elements in other comics. But it actually led us into some serious and fascinating areas of story. Things that usually get passed by while creators and readers all race to the usual super conflicts and complications. I wish I had had a chance to do at least 36 issues of *The Black Hood*. But the 12 issues, annual and short stories that we got done tell a cohesive story.

RB: Those stories were intended to engage the reader and entertain them. They were stories that were meant to be fun and filled with a sense of wonder. I'd just like readers to have a good time and for a few minutes forget that they're looking at pixels on a screen and believe they're watching the lives of real people unfold.

CBM: Is there anything you've got lined up for the future?

RB: There will be a mini-series coming out this summer that I did with writer Chris Mills called *Gravedigger*. It's a print collection of a crime comic we did on the internet. It's a three issue series that will be published by Action Lab. The first issue drops in July. Then there's the web comic I've been doing with Greg Rucka for the past four years, *Lady Sabre and the Pirates of the Ineffable Aether*. It can be found at ineffableaether.com. It's free on the web and we've done a print volume that collects the first five chapters of the story. That will be available through the website. Other than that, I don't have anything.

MW: Currently I'm working on a new television pilot for CBS. I'm working with Greg Garcia, creator of *My Name Is Earl* and *Raising Hope* and *The Millers*. We started working together in 2013 on this same show, called *Super Clyde*. It never really got turned down by CBS, but they took his other show, *The Millers* and were reluctant to give him two shows at once. I ended up doing work for two episodes of *The Millers* that were much like what we did on *Super Clyde*. And that was a lot of fun and well received. So now they are asking us to revamp the *Super Clyde* pilot for a second version, with a new cast. It is unique work for me. I'm creating something like motion comics for 6-9 minutes of an episode, to illustrate the comic book fantasies of the main character, Super Clyde, who will be played by Charlie McDermott from *The Middle*. I've always said that drawing comics was acting on paper. And now, in a strange way, with my art I'm almost acting in a TV show.

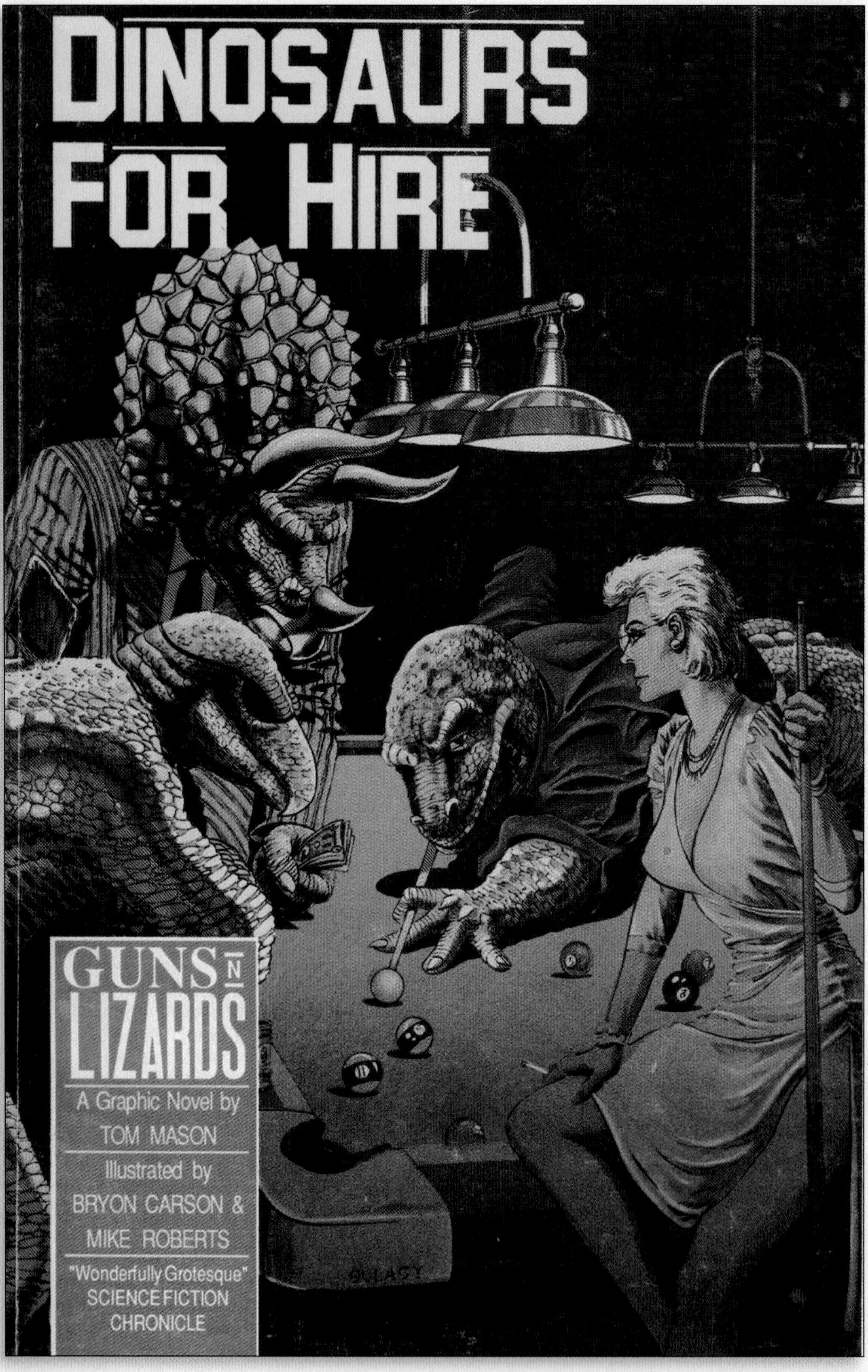
DINOSAURS FOR HIRE
GUNS N LIZARDS
A Graphic Novel by
TOM MASON
Illustrated by
BRYON CARSON &
MIKE ROBERTS
"Wonderfully Grotesque"
SCIENCE FICTION
CHRONICLE

Dinosaurs For Hire

TOM MASON INTERVIEWED BY J.C. VAUGHN

Tom Mason was one of the founders of Malibu Comics, the founding editor of its creator-owned imprint, Bravura, and an original founder of their Ultraverse line. Since leaving comics, he's worked extensively as a writer and story editor in television. Along with fellow Malibu veteran Dan Danko, he has written or chaperoned 500 episodes of animated television, and they took home an Emmy in the process. He also he co-writes the Captain Awesome *books for Simon & Schuster under the pseudonym Stan Kirby, and serves as a consultant for Space Goat Publishing.*

Tom Mason

Paralleling the early days of Malibu, Mason developed a creator-owned title called Dinosaurs For Hire, *which featured a trio of walking, talking, thinking dinosaurs who worked for the federal government and who packed what seemed like an inordinate amount of firepower in just about every situation. The original black and white series, later followed by one in full color, captured the imagination of our J.C. Vaughn well before he was ours, and actually helped set him on the path to Gemstone Publishing's door. Which is to say, you can blame Tom Mason and* Dinosaurs For Hire *for everything since.*

CBM: *Dinosaurs For Hire* is what put you on the map with me, Tom. What had you done up to that point?

Tom Mason (TM): I'd been around, but not where people would know me. I'd been a cartoonist and had my work published in *Playboy* and *Cosmopolitan*. I was an art director at Fantagraphics where I created the humor magazine *HONK!*, then I recreated it freelance for Jan Strnad's Mad Dog Graphics as *SPLAT!* When I left Fantagraphics, Dave Olbrich had called me to launch Malibu Comics with him, and that was being backed by Scott Rosenberg, who owned Sunrise Distribution.

And I was content for awhile to be just an office guy. My official title at Malibu back then was Creative Director, and I'm officially one of the four founders, and I was happy just making comics with Dave and Chris Ulm who was the Editor-In-Chief. Up until that time, I'd had no interest in writing comic books. Technically I was in the industry and had been for a few years, but I never saw my jobs as stepping stones to working for the Big Two, Marvel and DC. The two humor magazines I'd done I was just the editor. I wasn't writing for them or pushing my own stuff into the pages. I became a comic book writer by accident. When Scott Rosenberg made the decision to shut down his Eternity office in New York and move everything to the West Coast so that everything came out of Malibu, we picked up some Eternity titles that weren't finished yet. One of them was the last issue of a mini-series called *Battle To The Death*. It was written Marvel-style, so there was a plot and finished art, but no dialogue. And it was late and in danger of having its orders cancelled by the distributors. So Chris Ulm and I wrote the dialogue for it in a couple of days after the original writer declined. There are traces of the *Dinosaurs For Hire* sensibility all over that issue. But I started writing comics because there was one that urgently needed to get done, and I happened to be sitting in front of a computer.

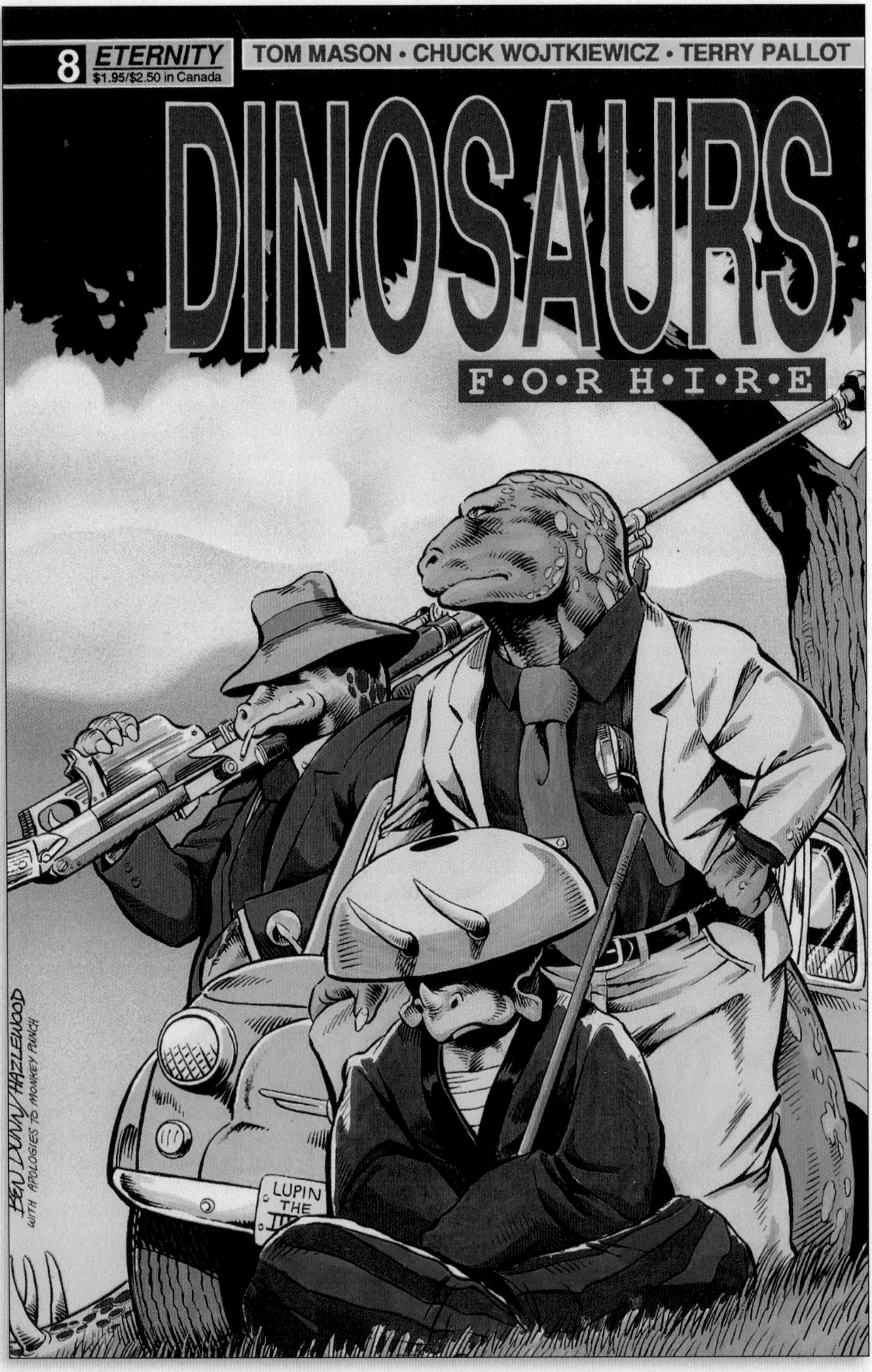
8
ETERNITY
$1.95/$2.50 in Canada
TOM MASON • CHUCK WOJTKIEWICZ • TERRY PALLOT
DINOSAURS
F•O•R H•I•R•E
BEN DUNN / HAZLEWOOD
WITH APOLOGIES TO MONKEY PUNCH
LUPIN
THE

After that, I wrote a couple of odd things – including two issues of *Solo Ex-Mutants*, an *Ex-Mutants* spin-off. Those issues have some humor, but are mostly played straight. And I discovered that I really liked this whole writing thing. Plus the company was bootstrapped and we weren't making big bucks by being on staff, so writing some stuff freelance became a way to pick up extra money.

CBM: I remember Eternity had published the *Ex-Mutants* comics by that point and also a trade paperback collection of Dave Cockrum's *The Futurians*. How did that all fit into Malibu? What was the plan?

TM: That's the craziest part of the whole story! Pre-Malibu Comics, Scott Rosenberg owned Sunrise, the southern California comic book distributor. He secretly financed four (yes, that's right) comic book companies with the idea that they would publish comics, he'd push them through his existing distribution channel at Sunrise, then sell individual copies by mail order through yet another company of his called Direct Comics. Having a distribution company that distributes books from multiple publishers, then expands to publishing its own books while also running a mail order division isn't a bad way to create a vertically-integrated company without many assets. Unfortunately, he did it in secret, and had been trying to manipulate the market to create "hot" comics that could be sold at higher prices post-publication, and it all went bad when the bubble of inflated high-priced "hot" comics burst. Sunrise was bankrupt and shut down leaving behind a trail of bad debt that hurt a lot of small publishers at the same time Malibu was launching.

Of his four original secret companies, Amazing and Wonder were run out of West Virginia by David Campiti, and Imperial and Eternity were run from Brooklyn by Brian Marshall. Imperial, Amazing and Wonder were closed down, and Campiti went on to his own company, Pied Piper (and later Innovation). *Ex-Mutants* had been created by David Lawrence and Ron Lim, and was published by Campiti through the Amazing imprint. But they lost control of the title in a bizarre dispute with Scott that I could never figure out – this had all happened just before I signed on to Malibu. The end result was that Scott ended up with *Ex-Mutants* being published through Eternity on the East Coast. Eternity still had some books that were selling well, but Scott wanted to move its operations to the West Coast

so we inherited the Eternity books that were in the pipeline. That included *Ex-Mutants* and *The Futurians* hardcover and books like *Ninja* and *Yakuza*. Then because the Eternity name had a much, much higher brand recognition among retailers than Malibu Comics, we dropped the Malibu name as an imprint and carried on under the Eternity Comics name with Malibu as the parent company. Had enough yet? A lot of this is archived via *The Comics Journal's* website.

Getting back to the other part of your question, the original Malibu plan was created by Dave Olbrich who would be the publisher. He was working at Sunrise and he pitched Scott on creating a comic book company – at this time not knowing that Scott was already secretly backing his four other companies. The concept for Malibu at the time was not exactly revolutionary, but the stuff that Dave wanted to publish would be creator-owned black and white titles with the idea that while we wouldn't pay a lot of money upfront, we would pay, and pay on time, we'd publish them and the creators would retain all the media exploitation rights. And they'd get publishing rights back after their project had run its course. And except for the occasional glitches that were quickly resolved, we managed to pay on time or early for the bulk of the company's run – right up until the year leading up to Marvel buying the company. That last year was when we were running out of operating capital and started deferring payments.

CBM: What was the original spark for you when you came up with *Dinosaurs For Hire*?

TM: Jan Strnad (DC's *Sword Of The Atom*, *Dalgoda*) and I used to live in the same neighborhood in Hollywood. I was having lunch with him and a mutual friend of ours, Mike Valerio. This was before I joined Dave to launch Malibu. Jan was trying to find interesting books to put out through his own comic book company, Mad Dog Graphics. One of the ideas that was kicked around at lunch was the idea of Elvis Presley as a crimefighter (he had been famously "deputized" by President Nixon back in the 1970s and used to drive around at night pulling people over).

It was a ragged idea, and Mike agreed to write it, and it was going to be called *Elvis: Undercover*. But as fate would have it, Mike couldn't get a handle on it and passed. I picked it up, and though I'd never written a comic book before, Jan sat with me and gave me a master class in comic book writing. I owe him everything for that! I finished the script, Jan lined up artist Don Lomax, pages were done, *The Los Angeles Times* got wind of it and wrote a story about it. Then Jan got worried about getting sued by the Elvis estate and pulled the book. So I had a finished script laying around.

And that's what it did for awhile. Just sat in a drawer. But I subscribe to the old saying of "Never throw anything away." Shortly thereafter, Dave Olbrich got the backing for Malibu Comics and brought me onboard. We'd been up and running for several months and working on the schedule. We started kicking ideas around for new projects. I mentioned the script I'd done for *Elvis: Undercover* and Jan's concerns about publishing it. Dave suggested that I change Elvis to something else - how about a dinosaur, he said. It was his basic idea and he just threw it out there. I loved it,

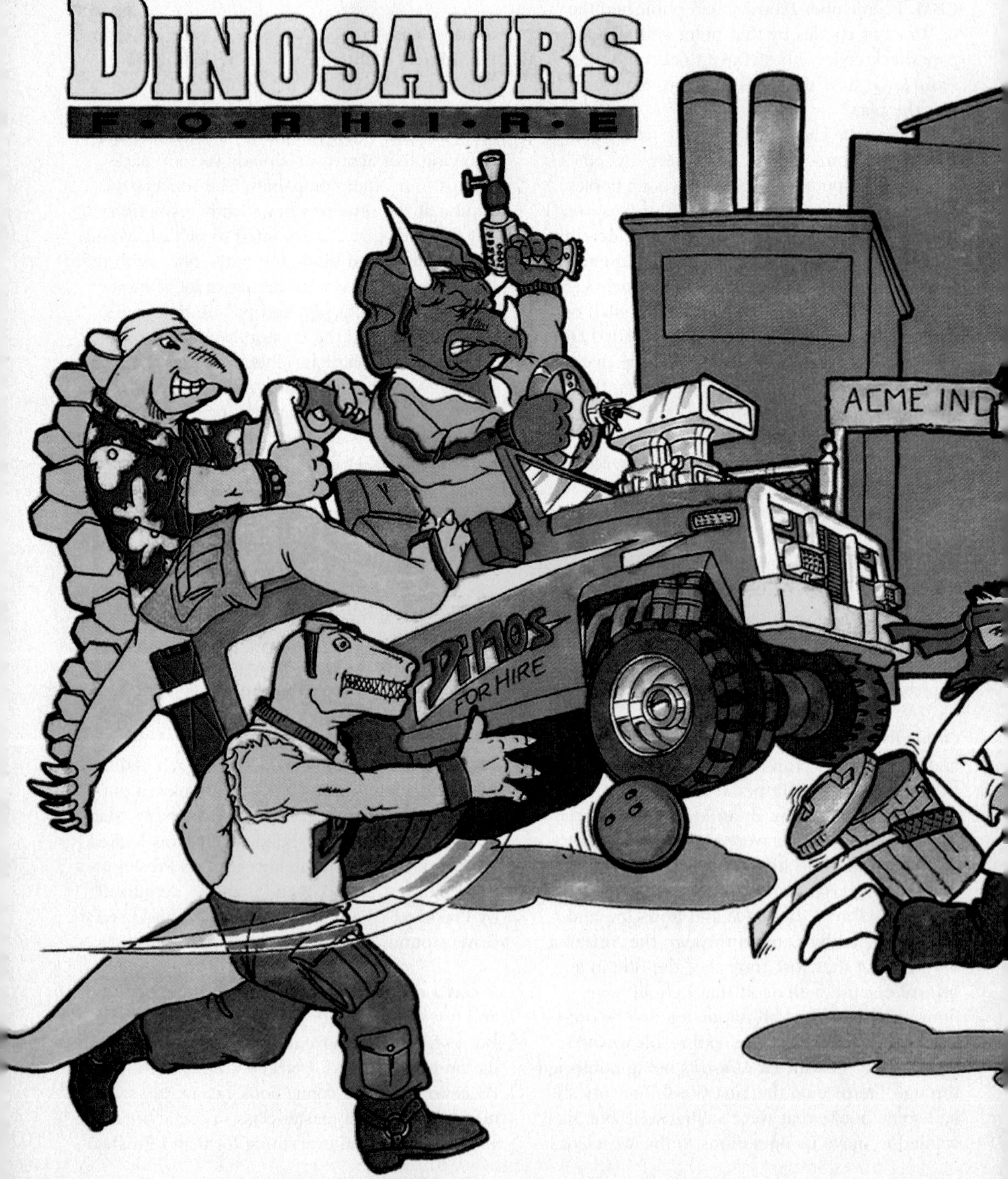
DINOSAURS
F•O•R H•I•R•E
ACME IND
DINOS
FOR HIRE

and went one better. I split the Elvis character into three distinct personalities and made them a trio of dinosaurs. And that became *Dinosaurs For Hire*. I went through the old script, chopped it up and added new stuff, and then we were off and running.

CBM: After you got the basic idea, what were your next few steps?
TM: I had to find an artist. I knew Bryon Carson because he'd done some other stuff for us earlier. He was a good artist and fun to work with, and he said he liked to draw dinosaurs. I sent him the script and he was on board. Then it was the usual publishing stuff – get a cover, press release, solicitation copy for the distributors, all that. More importantly, I also had to figure out the second issue. I'd never written a second script for *Elvis: Undercover*, so I didn't have a script I could crib from. I had to write a *Dinosaurs For Hire* script entirely from scratch.

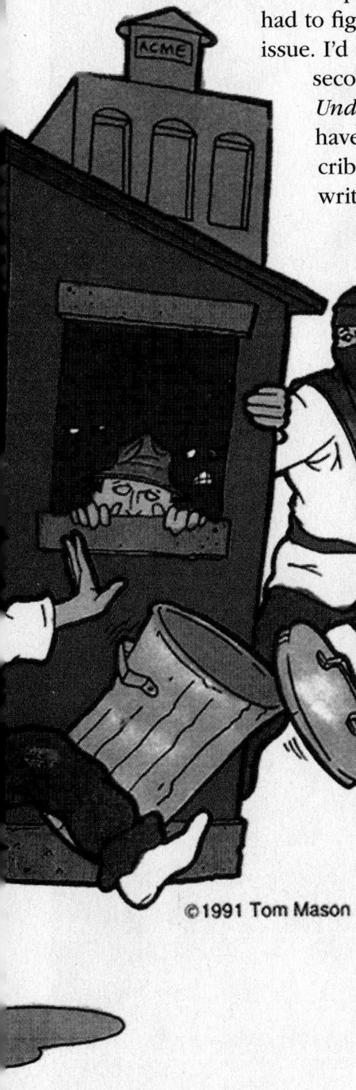
ACME
©1991 Tom Mason

CBM: How long did that second script take you to write? What hurdles did you face with it?
TM: It took the full month and then some. I think Bryon was waiting on me to get it done. *Elvis: Undercover* was basically a one-shot joke. It was never intended to be more than that. Rewriting that first script into *Dinosaurs For Hire* #1 was just that – rewriting. I hadn't done any preparatory work – no world-building, no character bios, no deep background, no origin. So there was nothing to base a second story on – I was winging it, trying to think it through, and write a script that wouldn't close off future story opportunities.

CBM: When did you think things were really beginning to come together for the property?
TM: I think the third issue of the original black and white series is when I started to figure things out. The first issue was a rewrite of the Elvis story. The second one was written in a hurry and picked up on a vampire tease from the first issue. The third one I had some time to think things through a bit and the cover by Scott Bieser really clarified it in my head. It was a good companion to Bryon's cover to the first issue. Put the two covers side-by-side and that's the series.

CBM: I think when you say "Scott Bieser really clarified it in my head" other writers will know what you mean, but could you explain that a bit?
TM: Scott did the guest cover for issue 3, and it was a pin-up style illustration of Professor Tyrell (the "Boss" of the dinosaurs), standing in front of the dinos, and everybody has a gun. It was a real "attitude" pose and it captured my vision perfectly. That's what the team was – confident, can-do, skilled, and the fact that it was dinosaurs led by a woman made it fun to me.

CBM: Since you guys had just started Malibu at the time, what was an average day like for you at that point, if there was such a thing?
TM: An average day? It would sort of go like this – Dave would get to the office first. I'd try to get there around 8:30. There wasn't any email in those days to worry about, so I'd spend the morning going over the upcoming business with Dave, figuring out what had to be done by the end of the day. And then FedEx and UPS would show up around 10, and that would take priority – it was going to be either scripts, pencils, inks or letters or cover coloring, and it would have to be logged in and shipped back out that day by 4:30 when they dropped by again to pick everything

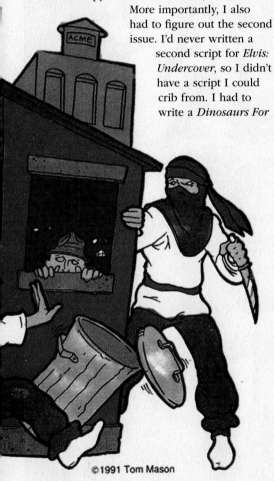

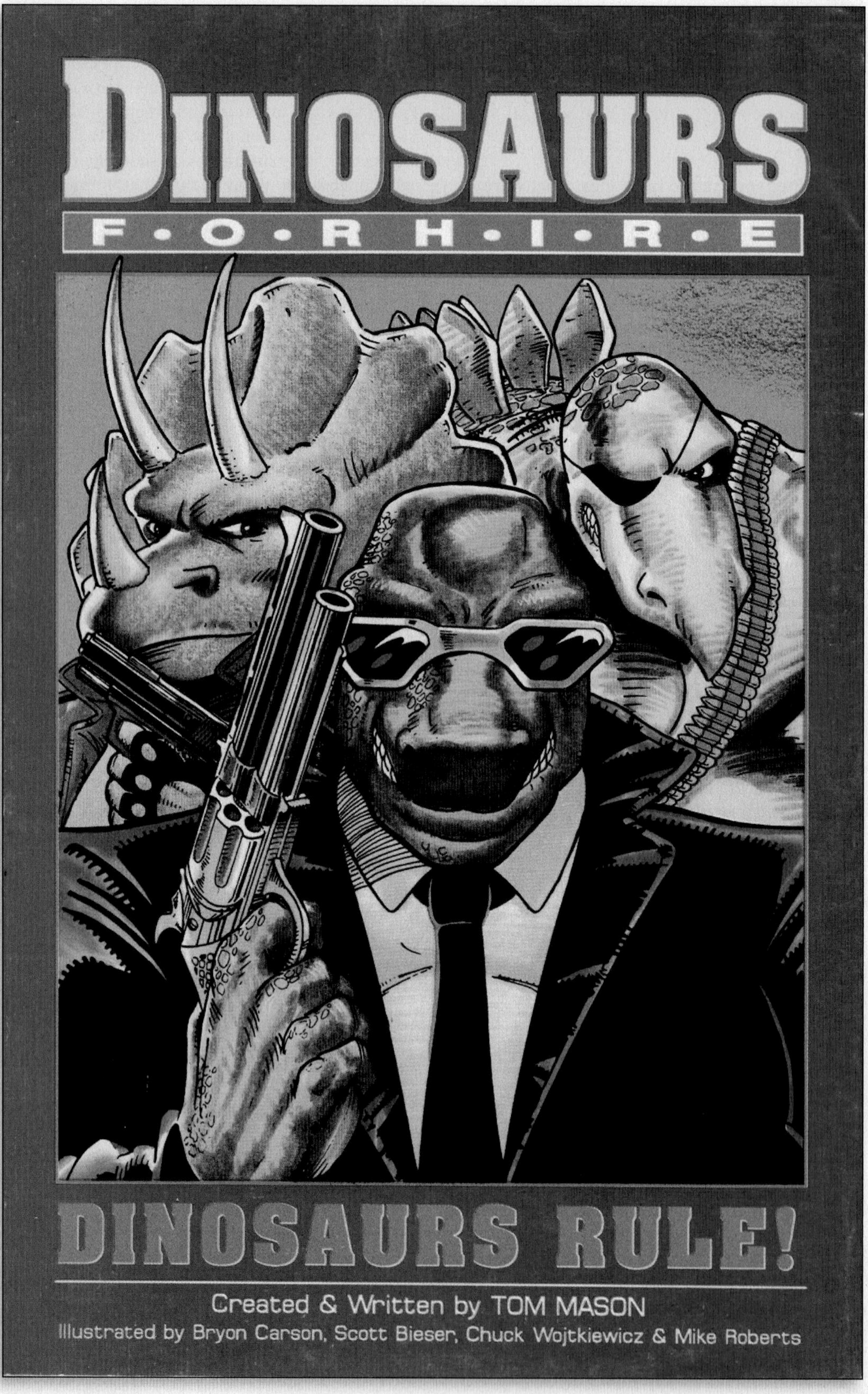
DINOSAURS
F•O•R H•I•R•E
DINOSAURS RULE!
Created & Written by TOM MASON
Illustrated by Bryon Carson, Scott Bieser, Chuck Wojtkiewicz & Mike Roberts

up. The afternoon would be spent trying to get ahead, find new projects, handle any problems that cropped up during the day, deal with any creator issues, the usual publishing stuff. During the course of each month, I'd still write the solicitation copy, write and design the print ads, and write and send out the press releases. And every Tuesday, we'd send completed books to the printer, so that meant designing all the text features, and paginating each issue, and dropping in the ads and stuff. We'd probably knock off around 7 PM. Chris and I would occasionally go out for dinner or a beer after work, and still be kicking around ideas. On evenings and weekends, I'd try to have a non-work life, but still do some writing.

CBM: Those kinds of periods are inherently hard to sustain over protracted periods, but they also tend to be fertile for the imagination. What were the best and worst parts of those days for you?
TM: The best part of it is that you're really in the middle of things. It's game on, and all of us, the four of us (Chris, Dave, Scott and me), were putting in crazy hours. But we were learning as we went, trying to build up a company and keep it going from month-to-month. We got to try a bunch of things, really experiment with marketing and promotional ideas, and the types of books we could publish. It was tiring, but very exciting, and very creative to have people to bounce loopy ideas off of and try to turn them into something practical. The worst part is you eventually just get tired and your brain shuts down. The last thing you want to see when that happens is a printed comic where the word balloon fell off somewhere between your desk and the printing press and nobody caught it. So you have to take a couple of days and detox.

CBM: If *DFH* #1 was largely a rewrite of *Elvis: Undercover,* was the humor in the first issue mostly intact from the earlier version?
TM: Very much so. Some of the jokes no longer worked, because they were Elvis-specific, but lot of the jokes did stay the same. Archie was basically the reworked Elvis, and Reese and Lorenzo were added as his buddies. Red was Elvis' main pal, Sonny, but he was called Red in both versions of the script and was always a little person. The love of guns, girls and snark was in both, and the overall attitude was similar. I still had the two government "handlers," Smith and Jones. I kept them from the original script, too.

I still have the original draft of the *Elvis: Undercover* #1 script. I've gone back to it and

reworked it a little to update it and tighten up the jokes. I think it's still funny and different enough from *Dinosaurs For Hire* #1 and I'm trying to line up a publisher for it.

CBM: From the first page, it was clear that you were willing to make fun of just about anything or anyone, left, right or center, and that even though you weren't particularly vicious about it, you didn't seem to have too many sacred cows. Is that accurate? And how much of that is still reflected in your approach to humor?
TM: I love poking fun at pop culture, and celebrities and politicians and any sort of big powerful thing. And I'm unapologetic about it, too. I've pissed off a bunch of people who did think I was too vicious, but I won't walk back a joke because of that. They're just jokes. I do have a couple of sacred cows. There are subjects that I don't think are funny or are too serious and "messagey" or that I can't make funny so I avoid them. Everything else is fair game. I might have a character represent a certain point of view for the sake of the story, but my goal isn't to make a political point or to be seen as either liberal or conservative or anything else – I want to make fun, knockabout comics about dinosaurs with guns. My background is humor, but humor on its own doesn't sell, so being able to mix it with action made it appealing to me and gave me a broader audience. It also gave me a wider range of subjects to pick on. I can do funny stuff and wrap it around big dinosaurs shooting things repeatedly.

CBM: From the original series, I always remember the line "The three bullets I was saving for a Beatles reunion" seemed a bit harsh, but then you had a cover blurb, something like "Outraged Beatles Fan letter included" a few issues later, it actually made the original thing funnier. What sorts of other angry letters did you get?
TM: That was my early brush with angry fans. That was a lot of fun, and I actually had more fans in support of the joke – it was just the one Beatles fan who was incensed. But there were other incidents as well. When the first issue of the color series came out, I was asked to participate on a radio call-in show at the last minute, but they deliberately sandbagged me. There was a woman on the show (an outraged mother, not one of the hosts) and she was thoroughly pissed at me because it was her belief Dinosaurs were strictly for children and shouldn't be co-opted for "this kind of awful attempt at humor." She wanted me to walk back the comic, apologize for it and

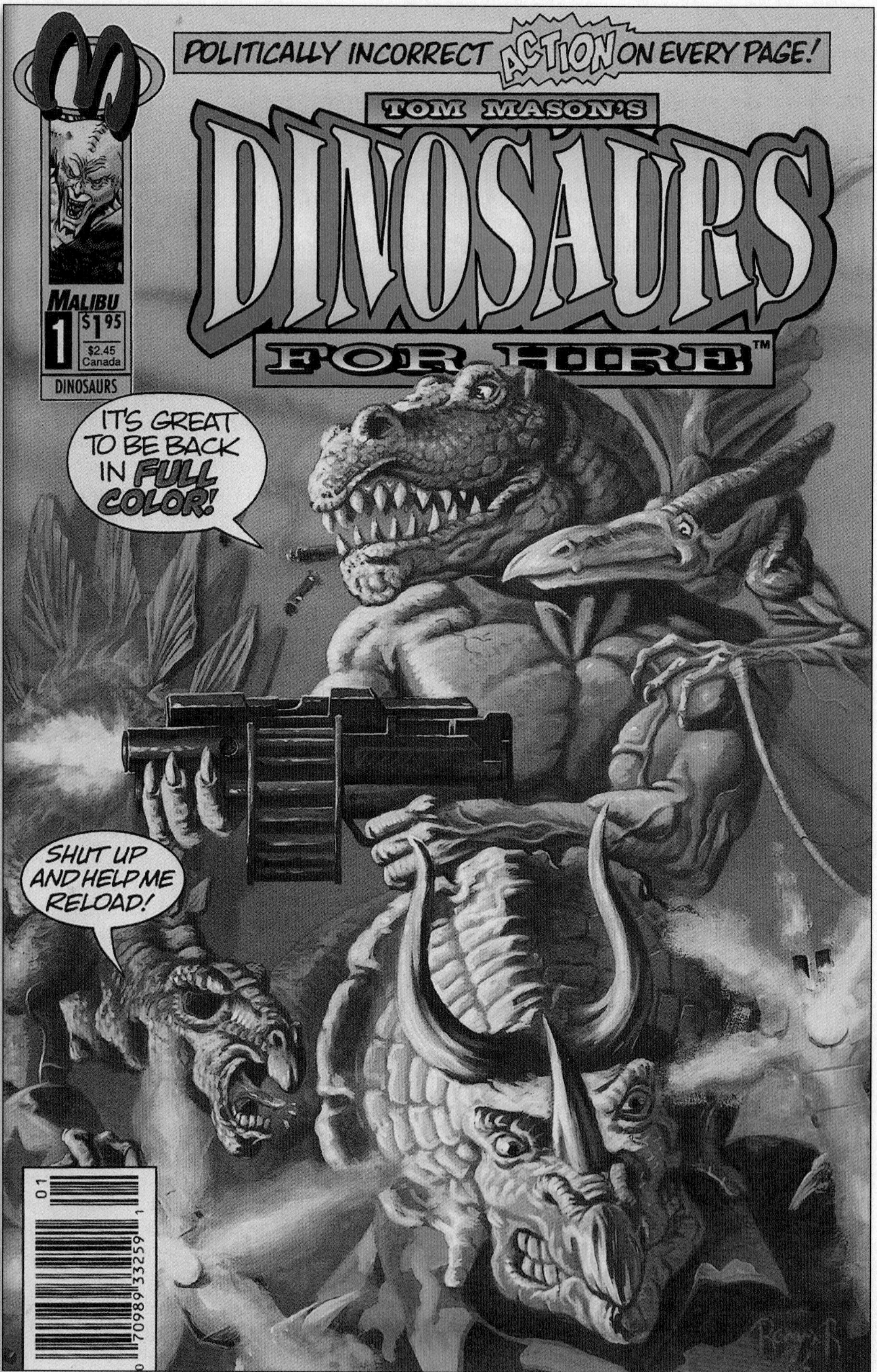
POLITICALLY INCORRECT ACTION ON EVERY PAGE!
TOM MASON'S
DINOSAURS
FOR HIRE™
MALIBU
1 $1.95 $2.45 Canada
DINOSAURS
IT'S GREAT TO BE BACK IN FULL COLOR!
SHUT UP AND HELP ME RELOAD!

promise to keep dinosaurs as a child's plaything. When the hosts gave me my chance to respond, I said that she should be a better mother and more carefully scrutinize her child's reading material. The interview ended shortly after that.

The biggest criticism I got, oddly enough, was from inside Malibu Comics. Malibu's co-president Bob Jacob was furious with me over the first issue of the color comic. He had earlier merged his videogame company with Malibu and liked to throw his weight around, calling himself "the new sheriff in town." He drove over from his office after the first issue shipped and took me outside to scold me about the content – he hated it, didn't think it was funny, didn't like the art, didn't like the tone. What he wanted was a comic book that he could license into toys and stuff and what he got was an embarrassment to him. "I can't show this book to people!" he yelled at me. That was great. I enjoyed every second of that.

What got me was that he then accused me of pushing the issue through Malibu in secret – that somehow in front of everyone I had gone behind his back, behind everyone's back, to create the issue he hated without anyone overseeing it. I told him that was total bullshit – all of the material, including the press and promotion for the series, had gone through the proper channels, the script had been vetted by both Dave Olbrich and Chris Ulm before a panel was drawn, and that Chris, in his role as Editor-In-Chief at the company personally trafficked the book at each stage. Further to that, I reminded him that *Dinosaurs For Hire* was not a Malibu title, it was a creator-owned title that was published by Malibu. He snorted and stomped around like an angry leprechaun for a bit then finally said, "That's what's wrong with creator-owned comics!" Our relations were quite strained after that, and he was eventually forced out of the company - not by me, though but by the investors Worldwide Sports & Entertainment who came aboard after the launch of the Ultraverse.

CBM: How were the sales on the early issues?
TM: Pretty darn good actually. Each issue of the black and white series hovered around the 9,000 copy level which doesn't sound great, but was profitable for the company and the talent. Then when the color series launched it was doing around 90,000 for that first issue.

CBM: Other than the Eternity collection of *The Futurians*, I seem to remember that everything Eternity did was black and white. Is that correct?

Was there any thought given to doing color material?
TM: Eternity had big plans to launch a color series back when the company was still operating out of New York in the pre-Malibu era. It was *Pirate Corp$* by Evan Dorkin. The first issue was done and colored and it went to the printer during the shift of Eternity from New York to California. It was scheduled to debut at the San Diego Comic Con that year. When it came out, though, the color printing was awful. The cover was muddy and dark and it just ruined Dorkin's terrific art. There would be no second issue, and even though the coloring for that issue wasn't done by the Malibu half of the equation and we hadn't supervised the printing, we'd have to take the blame for it. And it would be a long time before we'd try color again. The expense and the risk were too great until we could find a way to do it right.

CBM: After you got up and running, and after you got a handle on the series with #3, what sort of challenges did you face with *Dinosaurs For Hire*?
TM: Keeping me on schedule was one, and finding the time to write an issue was two. I had to write them in my off time, when I was home. I would write for about a half hour every morning after I got up, and put in an hour or two in the evenings after work. I developed a trick to always stop in the middle of a scene and leave it unfinished so it was easier to get back into the next time I sat down. It was a bi-monthly book because of that schedule. I just couldn't write it any faster. A perk to being in the office was that I was also rewriting and forever tweaking the script – when I'd go over the pencils before sending it to the letterer, I'd punch up the dialogue and the jokes, and then do it again just before an issue went to the printer. I was never really done writing until the original art was in the envelope and off to the printer. Another difficulty was finding an artist who could stay on the book. Sales were okay on the black and white series, but the money still wasn't big enough to have someone stay on the book as a full-time gig, so I was doing stand-alone issues just in case.

CBM: Bryon Carson, who you've mentioned, penciled the first three issues and the fifth issue. Who else was involved with the original black and white series?
TM: Scott Bieser did an issue, Chuck Wojtkiewicz did several issues, Scott Benefiel did one, and Nigel Tully did the *Fall Classic*.

CBM: Which issue of the first run is your favorite and why?

TM: I have to play the weasel card. I love them all – not because of my writing because what writer loves their own writing unconditionally? Certainly not me. I just love seeing what each artist did to my scripts – how they took my words and then elevated them by bringing the script to life. It's a magical process to see it happen, and after I'd send out a script, I'd be like a kid at Christmas waiting to see what the artist did with it, waiting for that package with the art to arrive. That's everything to me.

CBM: Why did the first series come to an end after nine issues?

TM: I was approaching some serious creative burnout and I just couldn't maintain the hours that I was putting in. Writing in the morning, going to work, then writing more in the evenings. It was just a lot. Issue #9 was a stand-alone issue that was essentially a fill-in by Scott Benefiel. Chuck had left for another gig, so if the series was to continue I had to find yet another artist to do #10 as I was writing it, and I was just too tired.

CBM: You mentioned that you started out as more of an editor-producer at first, and that you were pulled in multiple directions with your job as Creative Director. What sort of growth did you go through as a writer during that period?

TM: It was an incredibly fertile time because I was writing almost everything and writing constantly. During the day I was editing books, and in the evening I was writing my own scripts, and in between I was writing promotional copy, ad copy, letters pages, press releases, writing introductions for books, proofreading, conducting promotional interviews. It was everything. What I learned first was speed – writing very, very fast – and a great appreciation for computers. Without a computer to cut, paste, edit, repurpose I don't think I could've done any of it.

By actually working in comics and putting together comics, I was seeing how others wrote – reading a couple dozen scripts every month rubs off on you. I would pick up tips and tricks

from other writers – structure, dialogue, staging, characterization – just by osmosis. But mostly, it's speed – get the first draft down completely and as quickly as possible and spend the rest of your time fixing it.

Writing is a very solitary craft – it's just you and the computer. But during the day I was surrounded by people and activity and I could bounce ideas off the room. We had an open office for a long time and Chris's and Dave's desks were within feet of my own. We were always hollering out "What about this?" or "How about that?"

CBM: What happened with the property in the interim between the end first series and its revival as the full color second series?

TM: It sat. I assumed that after the black and white series was over, that the property was too, at least for awhile. I didn't really think about it again for a long time. There had been some movement to try to turn the comic book into a movie during its black-and-white days, and if I'd been smarter and known then what I know now, I would've stopped it all. The movie technology of the time didn't exist to make a real movie of the comic that anyone would want to see – so every conversation was about how to minimize the appearance of the dinosaurs to keep the budget down. I'd had a meeting with Jonathan Betuel, the guy who did *The Last Starfighter* and *My Science Project*. He was interested in optioning the comic, but I didn't think we were a good fit. It was eventually optioned by two goofballs who had no money and no track record, but they had optioned a couple of other comic books including *The Trouble With Girls*, and they were actually in the business, but in non-producing jobs.

I had one meeting with them after we signed a deal, and then they cut me loose. They had a script written that was just terrible and from a writer who hasn't done anything since. I had no input into it and they were shopping it around without me. The script thankfully went nowhere, but *Dinosaurs For Hire* ended up at Fox being developed as an animated series. And I had one meeting at Fox, and it was clear that they wanted a series that was much closer to *Teenage Mutant Ninja Turtles* with lots of slapstick hijinks and catchphrases that could take the world by storm. The meeting with me was basically a courtesy to see if I had any ideas for how they could dumb down the concept and make it kid-friendly for TV. Well, I didn't have any ideas for that direction. And fortunately the series never made it out of development, and the option lapsed. I was very lucky that nothing happened because I could've lost my comic during that time and in exchange gotten either a terrible movie or a worse cartoon show. That's the way Hollywood works and I knew that even at the time, and it still happened to me. I wasn't mad at anyone or even the generic "Hollywood," but I was very disappointed in myself. I got smarter after that, but only incrementally, of course.

The upshot is that after all of that, I was content to just keep the *Dinosaurs* on the shelf for awhile and do nothing with them. Nothing. During this downtime, however, Malibu Comics found a financial partner - the company merged with a local video game company called Acme Interactive. The new combined company had two distinct divisions – Malibu Comics which would make comics, and Malibu Interactive that would continue to make video games. Acme (now Malibu Interactive) was run by Bob Jacob who was now co-president with Scott. Bob immediately announced how stupid he thought we – Chris Ulm, Dave Olbrich and me – were. From his POV, we had once been publishing Image Comics, then we "let" Image get away and go off and publish on their own. He thought we somehow, magically, should've made a deal that kept the Image titles with us once the creators left – we should've owned those titles. Well, that's not the deal we made with Image, and it's not a deal they

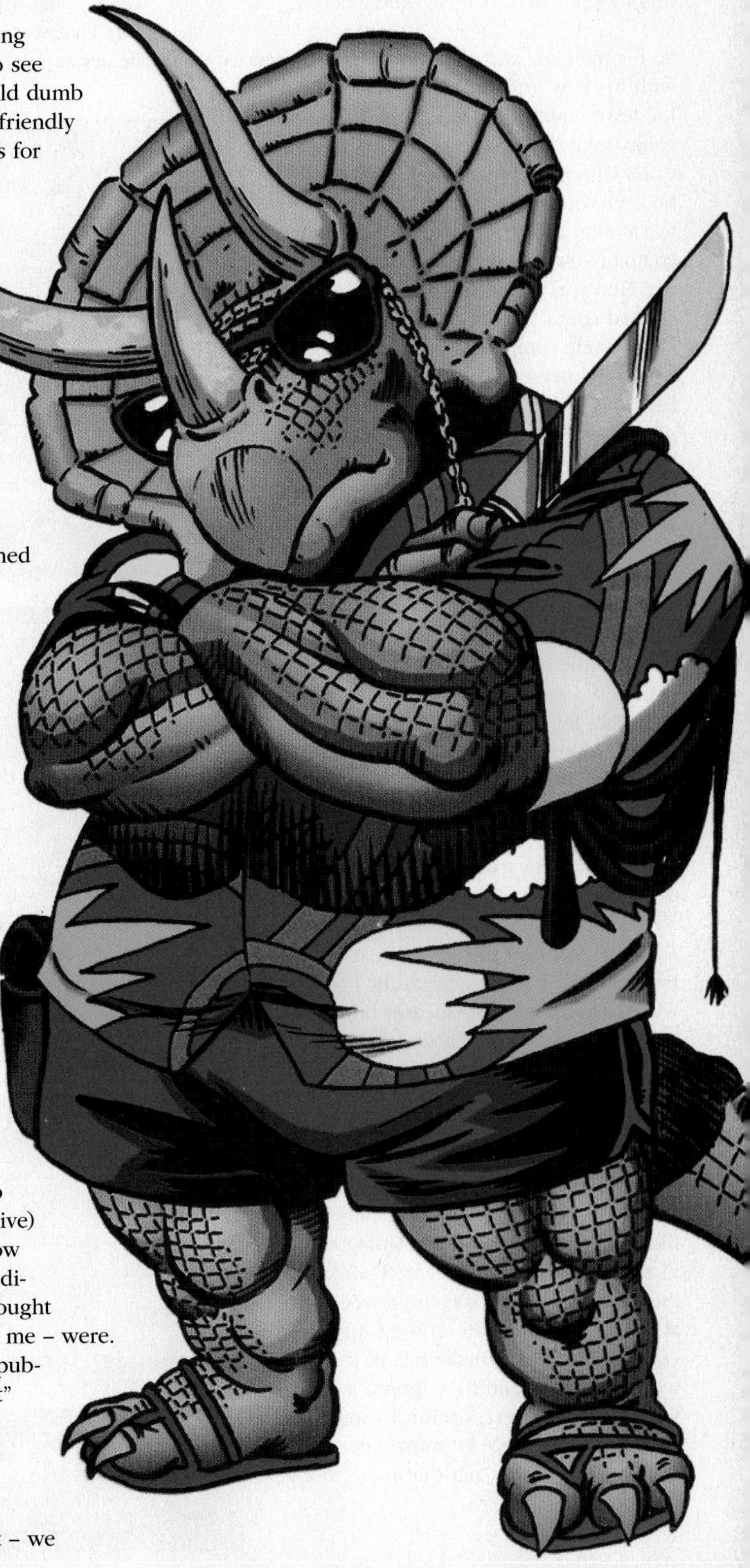

would've signed. It's a complete misreading of the business and the deal. Bob would have none of that though. He obviously knew better.

So his mandate was that Malibu going-forward with his new guidance would be publishing fewer creator-owned titles and more company-owned projects. This was when Chris Ulm pitched the idea that would become the Ultraverse. But in the interim, Malibu didn't really have that many company-owned properties in its arsenal, and Bob was antsy to start licensing out. He had contacts at Sega, and all the other video game companies because of the work he'd been doing at Acme, and he got Sega to pick up *Ex-Mutants* for a video game, and sure enough they also wanted *Dinosaurs For Hire* as well. And one of the stipulations was that to support the game, everybody wanted the comic book back on the racks. And so, I dusted it off and was back in the prehistory business.

CBM: So, was that the origin of the Genesis line or imprint, or did that follow later?
TM: That followed later, after the second series, the color one, was up and running. Malibu was breaking off into sub-imprints at the time. We had the Ultraverse books, the Bravura books, and all the licensed books. Suddenly, there were three books that didn't fit into any of those categories – *Ex-Mutants*, *Protectors* and *Dinosaurs For Hire*. Sales on them were just okay, less than the UV titles certainly. I forgot who came up with the idea of bunching them together, but it was mostly to increase sales and give them an identity of their own so they felt less like orphans. Roland Mann was the editor on all three, and he may have proposed it. I'm pretty sure he came up with the Genesis name. I agreed to go along with it because it felt like a way to keep my book going, even though it was a creator-owned book and the other two were company-owned. I also said I'd participate in the unifying crossover if I could make fun of it as it was happening, and then ignore it afterwards. In retrospect, I think I should've insisted that the title be moved over to the licensing group, but that might not've worked either.

CBM: For the second series, you added a fourth dinosaur. Was that driven by the video game or was it something you just wanted to do?
TM: That was something I wanted to do. When the series was greenlit for the new color run,

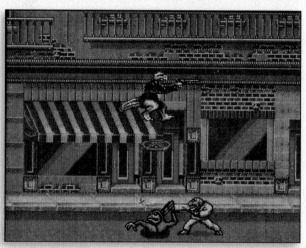

Chris and I talked about what I could do with the concept to add something to it. I thought bringing in a flying dinosaur could add another dimension to the book – basically air support for whatever they got involved in.

CBM: Given that you'd had a lot of new experiences between the two series, did you change your approach to the property in any way for the second one or did it feel like you were just picking up where you left off?
TM: I talked it over with Chris and Dave, and we all felt that as a relaunch, I should do something a bit different, find a way to bring something new to the book. I put more thought into the writing, into the background of the characters, and their

role in their universe. I tried to be a bit more "cerebral" about a book that's essentially about dinosaurs shooting stuff.

CBM: On the logo of the second series, it said *"Tom Mason's Dinosaurs For Hire"* rather than just *"Dinosaurs For Hire."* Given what you said a bit earlier, was that a message to Bob Jacobs or was that just coincidence?
TM: It's so funny – I was happy making comics, and happy in the day job helping to launch the Ultraverse and later Bravura, but now there was my comic book, and a video game. I had a courtesy meeting with the video game people in Diamond Bar, California and they were really nice and open about what they were doing. We talked

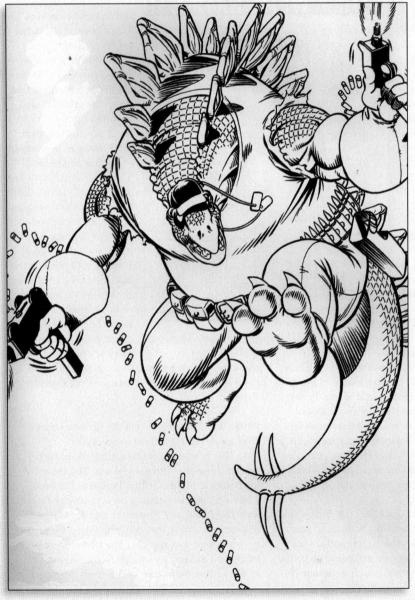

about the concept and the characters and the limitations of game technology at the time. The game was going to be a side-scrolling shooter and I was content to just let them run with it and check in periodically. But at the Malibu end, I was having trouble wading through the deal with Sega, the company that would actually publish the game. I kept thinking that because I was one of the founders of the company and one of the operational heads of it, that I should get some kind of favored-nations status, but every time something happened with *Dinosaurs For Hire*, I felt like I was getting Bill Fingered. I had been trying to figure out what my rights were and what was going on with the licensing. There's this terrible clause in most contracts that uses the phrase "best efforts" which means that no one will really do anything they're not required to do. I couldn't get a straight answer from Bob about how I'd be credited in the game, and my worry was that either I'd get no credit or that all credit would go to Malibu, like "based on a Malibu Comics title" or that I'd get a really tiny credit tucked away in the instruction manual. So since *DFH* was a creator-owned comic, I had the logo redesigned to incorporate my name in such a way that if someone wanted to strip it out they'd have to pay to redesign it. But the comic would be several issues into print by the time the game was out and it would mess up the branding if anyone did that. So I changed to logo to guarantee my own credit. A totally ego-driven FU.

CBM: What were the differences and similarities the second time around?
TM: Mainly the difference is that the writing process was a bit crazier. I would write full script, but with instructions to the artist – Mitch Byrd for the early relaunch issues – that he could mess around with it to help with the pacing. I always try to cram too many things into a page, and that makes the layouts unwieldy at times. When the pencils came back, I'd go through and do balloon placement for the letterer, and punch up the dialogue a bit, especially if Mitch added some fun stuff which he always did. Then when the lettering came back, I'd go through it again before sending it to the inker, and when it came back inked, I'd do a final pass on the dialogue. It's one of the benefits of having an inhouse lettering department and coloring department. They were all very patient with my selfish system, and I tried not to take advantage and just get changes made when they had gaps in their day.

CBM: Just a bit ago you described the "magical process" of comic book writing, waiting to see what the artist does with the script, and so on. For you is that something you still enjoy or is that something that fades naturally with experience?

AND YOU THOUGHT THEY WERE EXTINCT!
THEY'RE BIG
THEY'RE BAD,
THEY PACK SERIOUS HEAT,
AND THEY WORK FOR THE
U.S. GOVERNMENT.
CREATED BY TOM MASON
DINOSAURS FOR HIRE™ trademark & copyright © 1992 Tom Mason
DINOSAURS
F•O•R H•I•R•E

TM: I still enjoy it. It's all good – you send something off to someone else, you hope it connects with them, and when the art comes back it's always amazing to me. Artists make the work so much better, and I don't like to try to "control" them – here's my script, have at it. Everytime an issue came in, it was like Christmas for me.

CBM: You've written for a lot of different fields. How does that process compare to any of the others?
TM: It's still the same for me. Television and books actually take longer to get to the final result than comics do, but the process is the same. On TV shows that I've worked, I'm still writing and tweaking the script even as it's being recorded in the booth – if an actor has trouble with a line or something on the page sounds bad when it's said out loud, then I'm there to try to fix it. It's all that team stuff that you hear about – making comics and TV shows and books are all team efforts. It's just the size of the team that varies, and how you can manage the process to make something good. The big difference is the audience – I hardly ever hear from TV watchers or book readers, but I know how to find the comic book audience. They're online, and they show up at conventions, so I can interact with them and get that real "I love you!/You suck!" dynamic going.

CBM: What happened that the second series of *Dinosaurs For Hire* came to an end?
TM: This is where I made a strategic mistake, one of those live and learn deals. The cut-off for books at Malibu at that time was between 20,000-25,000, depending on a variety of factors. *DFH* (and *The Protectors* and *Ex-Mutants*) had been heading that way and based on projections the end was coming. The books were going away, and Roland was going to transition over to the Ultraverse where he'd already been edit-

ing a couple of books. So sales did it in. It seems outrageous now that a comic would be cancelled at sales of 20,000 copies, but it was a different industry then.

What I should've done was taken over the book as a packager and tried to take it somewhere else (or package it for Malibu) as an outside vendor, and looked at other options like going back to black and white and/or relaunching it. But the industry was collapsing at just around the same time, so any of those moves might not have succeeded. But I would've like to have tried.

CBM: With a given that you'll probably play the weasel card, again, can you pick out any particularly favorite issues from the second series?
TM: I won't weasel this time – the first issue of the second series. It had been quite a while since I written the guys, and I had a lot of stuff swirling around inside just dying to get out. That first issue is just an explosion of a billion thoughts, ideas, jokes and characters.

CBM: Was there anything with the series that you wanted to do but didn't get around to?
TM: Not really. I was always writing close to the wire just to get the current issue completed, so I wasn't thinking long-term and hadn't plotted out any spin-offs or side projects. There was one idea that always lurked around in the back of my head, but it was just an idea: a 4-issue series of solo issues, all #1s, starring each Dinosaur.

Tom Mason back in Malibu days

CBM: What is the property's status at this point?
TM: It's funny. It was in limbo for awhile. Malibu Comics had certain publishing rights, but I held all the media exploitation rights. As the second series ended, Malibu was up for sale. The company was partially owned then by the Malaysian billionaire businessman Ananda Krishnan, through an organization called Worldwide Sports & Entertainment (WSE) which was made up of some ex-Goldman Sachs suits. As the comic book market was crashing, they were anxious to get their money out before they lost it, so they were trying to force a sale or find investors to take their place. Dinosaurs For Hire's publishing contract was list-

ing as one of the assets and I couldn't get it back. Then Malibu was sold to Marvel and my publishing contract went with it.

I tried to negotiate those rights back because Marvel had no other rights beyond publishing and they weren't interested in it. But I couldn't make it happen – they held firm. But there's also a clause in the contract that Malibu Publisher Dave Olbrich had added in years earlier – I don't remember the exact wording, but it basically said that there couldn't be a *Dinosaurs For Hire* comic book without my direct participation and approval. So the property was just at a standstill until those rights lapsed. And I forgot all about it, until a friend of mine named J.C. Vaughn emailed me and said "I think that contract has expired now." And he was right. So I contacted Marvel and got the rights back. It was lucky too, because it was about a year before Disney bought them. If I'd waited, I'd have to deal with Disney legal instead of Marvel legal, and who knows how that would've gone?

That's where *Dinosaurs For Hire* is now – fully in my hands. And I've been working on some scripts for a possible relaunch.

CBM: Is there any time table for that or is it just as the opportunity presents itself?
TM: The opportunity has definitely presented itself. I'm just negotiating the deal points to see if we can make it happen. I'm hopeful! But making comics is a funny business, and there are lots of twists and turns getting something published.

CBM: What else are you working on at present?
TM: Dan and I wrapped up production on 52 episodes of an animated series called *Bat Pat* that should be out in late 2015 or early 2016. Dan and I are working on our 16th Captain Awesome book for Simon & Schuster. I'm doing some development work on an animated series that's going to Cannes in the fall, and I have a couple of pitches in at Space Goat for possible mini-series in 2016. And I've just started writing for a new show for Netflix – the series got a 20-episode commitment. Beyond that? It's anybody's guess.

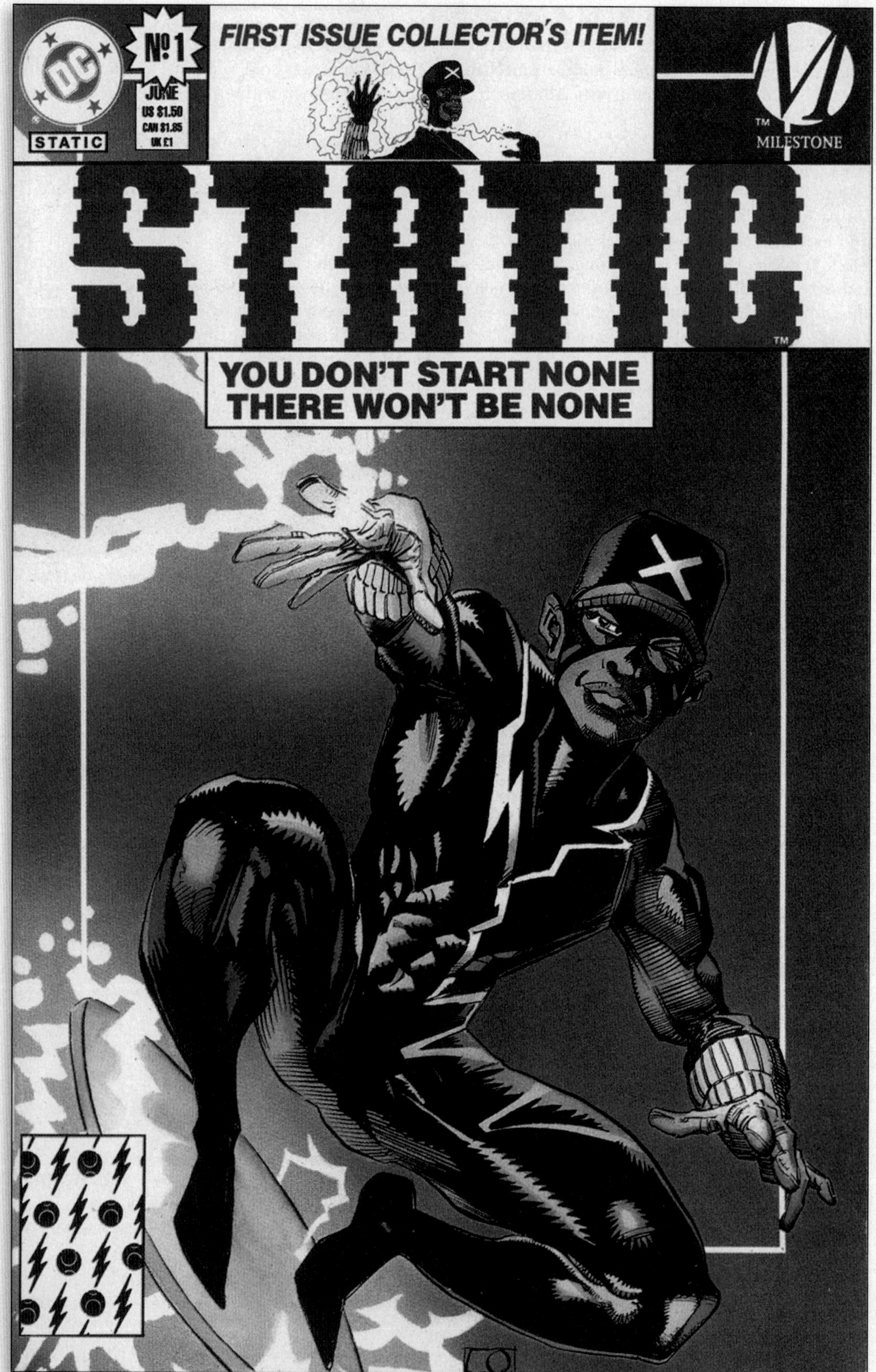

DC
STATIC
№1
JUNE
US $1.50
CAN $1.85
UK £1
FIRST ISSUE COLLECTOR'S ITEM!
MILESTONE
STATIC
YOU DON'T START NONE
THERE WON'T BE NONE

Electrifying!

An Issue-by-Issue Tour through the Incredible First Year of Static

BY **SCOTT BRADEN**

In the early 1990s, the comic book market was flooded with new titles, new characters, new publishers and new superhero universes. Many of them are gone and perhaps best forgotten, but among the standouts was high school student Virgil Hawkins, who became much more than a electrifying young hero anew to the comics scene. In the eyes of many critics and large number of fans, the hero Static became Milestone Media's thematic analog to the energy, relationship angst, feelings and trepidations of the earliest days of Stan Lee and Steve Ditko's Amazing Spider-Man *at Marvel.*

With a quick-witted big mouth and originally not much to back it up, the intelligent, opinionated Hawkins was caught up in the Big Bang, the event that transformed a number of citizens of the fictional city of Dakota into super-powered beings and Hawkins into the electromagnetic-powered Static.

Produced by writers Dwayne McDuffie & Robert L. Washington III and artists John Paul Leon, Steve Mitchell & Shawn C. Martinbrough, the young superhero helped make his city safe from the likes of Hotstreak and Holocaust, but the comic book Static *was more than just about super-powers. It focused on kids growing up and the issues that were important for the time – and for all times. It went deeper than many other super-hero titles in that era, and gave the reader his or her money's worth with every issue.*

The first year of the title, some have asserted, was the best monthly superhero comic book on the market at that time. Join us for this tour of Static *#1-12 and we'll show you why.*

Static #1
DC Comics; Milestone Media; June 1993
Trial by Fire Part One – Burning Sensation

"You don't start none there won't be none" is scrawled on the forefront of the premiere issue's front cover, and that's just about the high level of bravado that Virgil Hawkins gets up to when he's the hero Static.

Inside the comic, in his identity as Static, he's trying to protect an arcade that Frieda Goren, a young schoolmate who he's got a crush on, frequents. Suddenly, a group of gangbangers who work for a heavy named Hotstreak go after Frieda, and that's when Static enters the scene.

Taking out the "trash" like an electrically charged Spider-Man, he saves the day while reminding himself that as Static, he's not supposed to know his potential "girlfriend" while bidding her adieu.

The scene then changes to Static returning home as Virgil, where the reader meets his strong-willed mother and his overbearing sister, Sharon. After brief banter, he heads up to his bedroom to talk to Frieda on the phone, who has called to tell him how the hero Static saved her life.

The next day, Hawkins meets up with his friends at school – the ultra-cool Larry Wade and the overly sensitive ballet dancer Rick Stone – as well as Hotstreak's boys. Given the task to round up Frieda for Hotstreak, the toughs intimidate the students, with one of Hotstreak's thugs pulling out a gun.

Leaving the scene, Virgil transforms into Static, and he finds Frieda coming face-to-face with her pursuer, the mysterious Hotstreak. Super powers collide as Static and Hotstreak go head to head, with our hero getting the upper hand by binding a metal chain around the villain.

Then, as Hotstreak melts his bindings, Static recognizes his opponent as Biz Money B, a thug who bullied him at school. Falling to the ground after multiple punches, Static is defeated by Hotstreak, unintentionally shedding his mask and revealing his secret identity to his beloved Frieda while saying, "You don't understand. I can't fight him. I can't beat him. I can't... I can't..."

Not bad for a first issue, huh?

STATIC
2
JULY
MILESTONE
STATIC
THE SHOCKING ORIGIN!

STATIC
NO. 3
AUG
MILESTONE
STATIC
ROAD KILL!

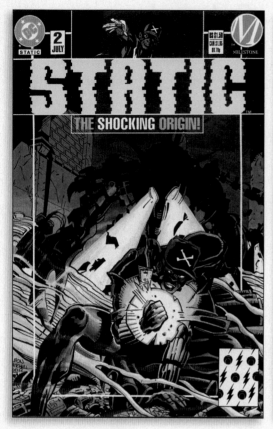

Static #2
DC Comics; Milestone Media; July 1993
Trial by Fire Part Two – Everything But the Girl

Static's origin issue opens up a little time after the end of the exciting series premiere, with Hawkins and Frieda discussing the climactic events of the first issue. This melds into a flashback of Hawkins' first meeting with Biz Money B, where he gets beaten up by the thug for attempting to defend Frieda's honor in school.

Flash forward to the present where Hawkins, crying and revealing his insecure side to Frieda, continues his story by describing the events that transpired on Paris Island on the night of the Big Bang – the genesis event that caused a number of Dakota's citizens to become super-powered.

With a gun that he acquired from his friend Larry firmly in hand, Hawkins was preparing himself to have his revenge on Biz Money B. While telling himself that he is not "a walking bullseye" and "a loser," he also comes to the sober conclusion that more importantly, he's not a killer either. This epiphany serves to reinforce Hawkins' character and shows the reader just what kind of hero he really is, and he makes no bones about it.

Just as he's dumping the gun into the river, though, Hawkins gets caught up in the gas of the Big Bang. Laid unconscious for some time, Hawkins awakens to see Biz Money B down on the ground and mistakenly considered dead, and then looks up to find super-powered people flying toward the city. Then, Hawkins finds himself the target of the mysterious "Indigo Base" authorities, which prompts him to first use his electromagnetic powers to defend himself.

His first show of force works, and he flies out of Paris Island no longer Hawkins – but now the super-hero Static. Coming back to the present, Hawkins tells Frieda that "so a legend was born," and chronicles the time it took to practice his skills, so he could bust up crack houses, street thugs, and fight other crime – victories that stopped when he met Biz Money B again. Realizing what he had to do, he sets out to face Hotstreak once more – and this time, to the reader's surprise, there's little or no resistance from the super-powered bully.

Triumphantly returning to Frieda's house where he stands floating just outside her upstairs window, Static learns to his displeasure that she only thinks of him as a friend. Meanwhile, he's caught the eye of another, Holocaust, who wants Static to either work for him . . . or die.

Static #3
DC Comics; Milestone Media; August 1993
Trial by Fire Part Three – Pounding the Pavement

"Pounding the Pavement" starts off with lots of action – and lots of sparks! Static spends the first several pages of the issue saving armies of victims from near disaster using a combination of his superhuman abilities and the lessons he learned from his Chemistry One class.

Then, after all the excitement, we see him at his part-time job, performing mundane tasks like washing dishes. It's through this plot point that we see another of Hawkins' impressive traits: modesty. It's also at this time that he receives a phone call at work from Frieda, who informs him that some "terminator guy" is after Static.

Hawkins immediately tells his boss, Ms. Ervin, that he's got to go and that it's an emergency – whether she decides to fire him or not. Fast forward to Static in downtown Dakota, where he learns that his pursuer is named Tarmack. After acquiring this knowledge, Static returns home and prepares for school the next day.

It's at school that he learns that Tarmack is nearby, and a battle between the two soon takes place. The fight turns out to be a draw, when suddenly, Tarmack throws a car on an innocent bystander and demands that he and Static settle their differences once and for all in Bradshaw's Parking Lot at midnight.

DC
4
SEPT
STATIC
US $1.50
CAN $1.95
UK 70p
MILESTON
STATIC
PLAYING WITH FIRE.
J.P.L.+
S.M.

After the fight – and after school – Hawkins and his friends are taking the subway home and talking about the big fight between Static and Tarmack. It's during this exchange that Frieda tells Hawkins and the others that Tarmack is older and bigger, and that Static should leave him to the more powerful Milestone character, Icon.

Before leaving the train, Hawkins whispers to Frieda that he has two things for the upcoming fight that Tarmack doesn't – a brain and a plan. Later, outside of Bradshaw's, Static meets up with Tarmack for a fight to the finish.

But after a relatively one-sided battle where Static is winning, the hero finally takes Holocaust's soldier down for the count…but not without Holocaust bringing the fight to Static.

Static #4
DC Comics; Milestone Media; September 1993
Trial by Fire Part Four – Playing with Fire

Picking up where the last issue left off, Static

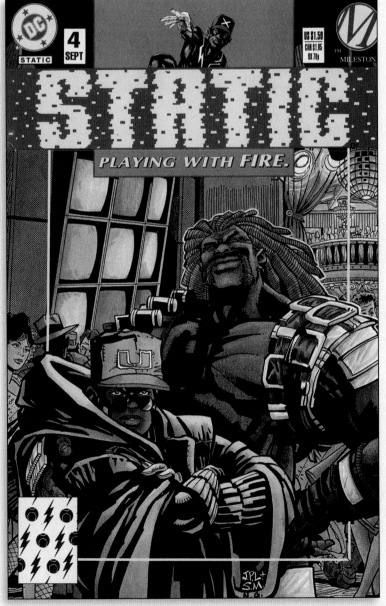

talks with Holocaust. On the surface, it seems that Holocaust wants Static to understand that he either takes or "he'll be took," that the rich are only rich because of their "birthright" and luck, not because of brains or talent.

It comes down to one thing: Holocaust wants Static to watch his back. To that end, Holocaust shows Static his gratitude by introducing him to his women, and presenting a life that the young hero could have.

The next panel finds Static (flying) and Holocaust (relaxing in his limo) entering Don Giacomo Cornelius' mansion at 1:15 in the morning. Holocaust starts using his fire powers on the thugs, before Static interrupts and says he'll take care of them (in a more humane way). Holocaust then screams that Cornelius family got most of their wealth "off the backs of my people."

After leaving the compound in flames, Static makes his way to Frieda's home, where he finds her in the arms of his friend, Larry. After blowing up at his discovery, he leaves while remarking that he can't "trust anyone else around here."

The next day, Hawkins is woken up and confronted by his mom and his sister about losing his job. To his surprise, his mom has Sharon take over his job and informs him that if he finds "something to do with himself, to let her know."

Hawkins then hangs out with his friends and finds out that Larry and Frieda have been an item even before they met – and that everybody knew but him. The scene then changes to Hawkins' bedroom, where he gets a call from Frieda trying to explain herself, which pushes him over the edge.

On the way out of the house, he tells his mom that he's going to see a man about "a real job." Next, we find Static next to Holocaust's SUV, where he is taking care of business and laying waste to mobsters everywhere. Once they get inside Don Cornelius' mansion, Holocaust decides to hurt the mobster's young son – at least that's the intent until Static steps in, saves the day, and says his piece.

After a less-than-friendly send off by Holocaust, he then talks to Larry in his bedroom, who tells him that he doesn't have to lose his friendship with Frieda because of the couple.

Meanwhile, as he picks up the phone – it's Frieda – his mom asks him whether the job he talked about earlier was "no hoodlum kind of job." He says no, and she replies: "Good, we raised you better than that."

DC
STATIC
NO. 5
OCT
US $1.50
CAN $1.95
UK 70p
APPROVED BY THE COMICS CODE AUTHORITY
MILESTONE
STATIC
THERE'S A RIOT GOIN' ON

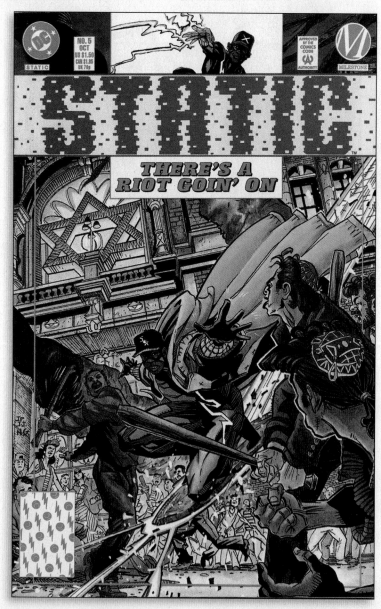

Static #5
DC Comics; Milestone Media; October 1993
Louder Than a Bomb Chapter One – Megablast

Page one finds Hawkins right smack dab in the middle of a race riot between blacks and Jews. While trying to separate the warring parties, he creates a repulsion field to keep everybody away from each other until they calm down.

Flashback to Hawkins at his favorite comic book store playing a role-playing game with friends when one of them remembers that he has a date with Daisy Watkins. After saying that he didn't remember any date, Daisy walks in, confronts Hawkins, and leaves in tears. Processing that she really wanted a date with him, Hawkins then hears about the riot at Temple Beth Ad and, next thing he knows, he's running crowd control – super-powers style.

Fast-forward to a Jewish rabbi and a black pastor holding hands, jointly lecturing and pointing out the uselessness of continued violence. Afterward, the rabbi and the pastor meet with Static and ask him to speak at an assembly against Commando X and his recent bombings – the reason for the riot. Static at first doesn't know what to say – then accepts.

Segue way to Hawkins in school, where after some small talk between Larry and Frieda, our hero uses his electromagnetic powers to activate the sprinkler system after Commando X attacked his school. Later, at a restaurant, Hawkins and his friends debate Commando X and his tactics, when he tells Frieda and everybody else that Static will be at the peace rally on Saturday.

Finally, the big day comes, and Static gets ready for his big speech, when all of a sudden Commando X makes himself heard at the assembly – putting Static on the defensive. Then, Commando X unleashes a plethora of bombs on the peace rally – leaving Static seemingly helpless!

Static #6
DC Comics; Milestone Media; November 1993
Louder Than a Bomb Chapter Two – War at 30 Frames Per Second

As Static fights to save the people assembled at the peace rally from Commando X, he remarks: "Listen X, we came here to get a little peace – not wind up in little pieces." He then uses his electromagnetism to have the stadium chairs scoop up the bombs and move them safely away. Static then chases after Commando X – until he loses his magnetic field after Commando X touched something that just blew up (that's his power).

NO. 6
NOV
STATIC
MILESTONE
STATIC
BLOW UP
DIRECT SALES

7
DEC
STATIC
MILESTONE
STATIC
CASUALTIES OF WAR
DIRECT SALES

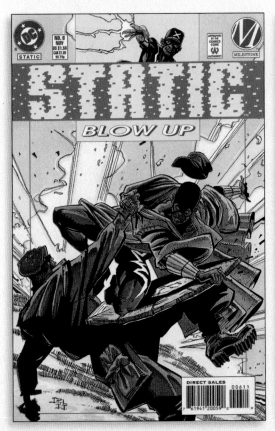

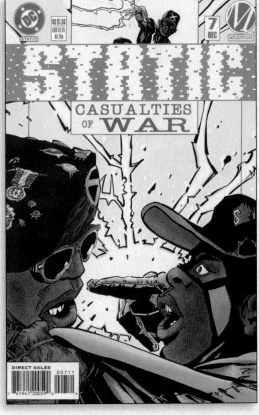

Static then flies atop the loud speaker and says: "Commando X! I don't care if you can hear me or not -- we are at war! Armageddon is in effect! There will be no late pass! Whatever it takes, you're going down!"

Then, at the Dakota Library, Hawkins and Frieda talk about the peace rally and the fact that a lot of people would have been hurt if not for Static. Hawkins also finds out that Commando X is a black militant zealot named Howell X, and that he's been sending op-ed letters to both of Dakota's newspapers, *The Chronicle* and *The North Star*. Hawkins also learns that Howell X had a public access TV show, and calls the cable company to get a tape.

At home, he watches the tape to get leads on Commando X's next target. On the tape, he finds one show referencing "pigs" – so he knows he's after the S.H.R.E.D. and anti-gang unit, G.R.I.N.D., at the old downtown precinct. Getting into costume, Hawkins becomes Static and heads towards trouble. Near the precinct, he finds some cop effigies that are set to explode. He then sends them flying and the bombs safely explode several stories higher in the air above the cops.

The next day at school, Hawkins, Frieda and Rick talk about the success found in both the Jewish and black communities. Hawkins and Rick also talk about what happened to Daisy, and how our hero should apologize – and he does, while also inviting her to a matinee. And as luck would have it, she agrees to the date.

Later, at home, Hawkins discovers that the tapes were made at the Rockdale Housing Apartments – or better known as the Rock. At the complex, he comes across Howell X, and pretends to be a fan. Hawkins learns that Commando X has planted some more bombs, and is offered the chance to get out all the statements to the media. The last image is Howell X offering Hawkins the phone.

Static #7
DC Comics; Milestone Media; December 1993
Louder Than a Bomb Chapter Three – You're Gonna Get Yours

The first page picks up right where we left off on *Static* #6, with Howell X (a.k.a. Commando X) offering Hawkins the chance to call the media. Through coming up with distractions (excuses for going to the bathroom, getting change for phone calls, getting gas), he heads to City Hall, where he finds the hidden bomb in a van parked in the garage. Drawing enough power to shoot the van into the air, it explodes harmlessly over City Hall.

SHADOW WAR
THE BIG BANG WAS JUST THE BEGINNING...

9 FEB
STATIC
COMING DOWN WITH A LITTLE SOMETHING

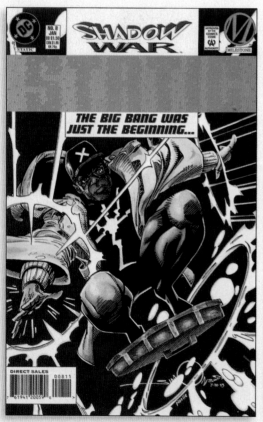

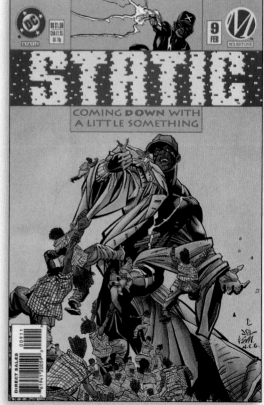

Hawkins then returns home to find his mom and dad (first appearance) waiting up to talk to him about the militant "Malcolm 10" program he was using for his investigation of Howell X.

Meanwhile at Frieda's house, her father and mother are talking to Frieda about the Jews easier integration into American society because they are white, and how racism, sadly, works both ways for them. Right afterward, Hawkins and Frieda call each other on the phone, and decide that they both have a lot to talk about. At the same time, they try to figure out Commando X's next target – and they come up with WDKA Studios.

Much later, Static finds his quarry on the studio's grounds. Commando X tries to take Static out of the way by exploding gasoline, but he gets away and wraps Commando X – and his bombs – up in wire. And by wrapping Commando X's hands, prevents the militant from using his power.

Returning late at home with his mom and dad still awake, he's left to climb his wall and get to bed. In the morning, Frieda calls him up and tells Hawkins that Static is famous and running on Channel 11. Our hero – fighting the good fight no matter what!

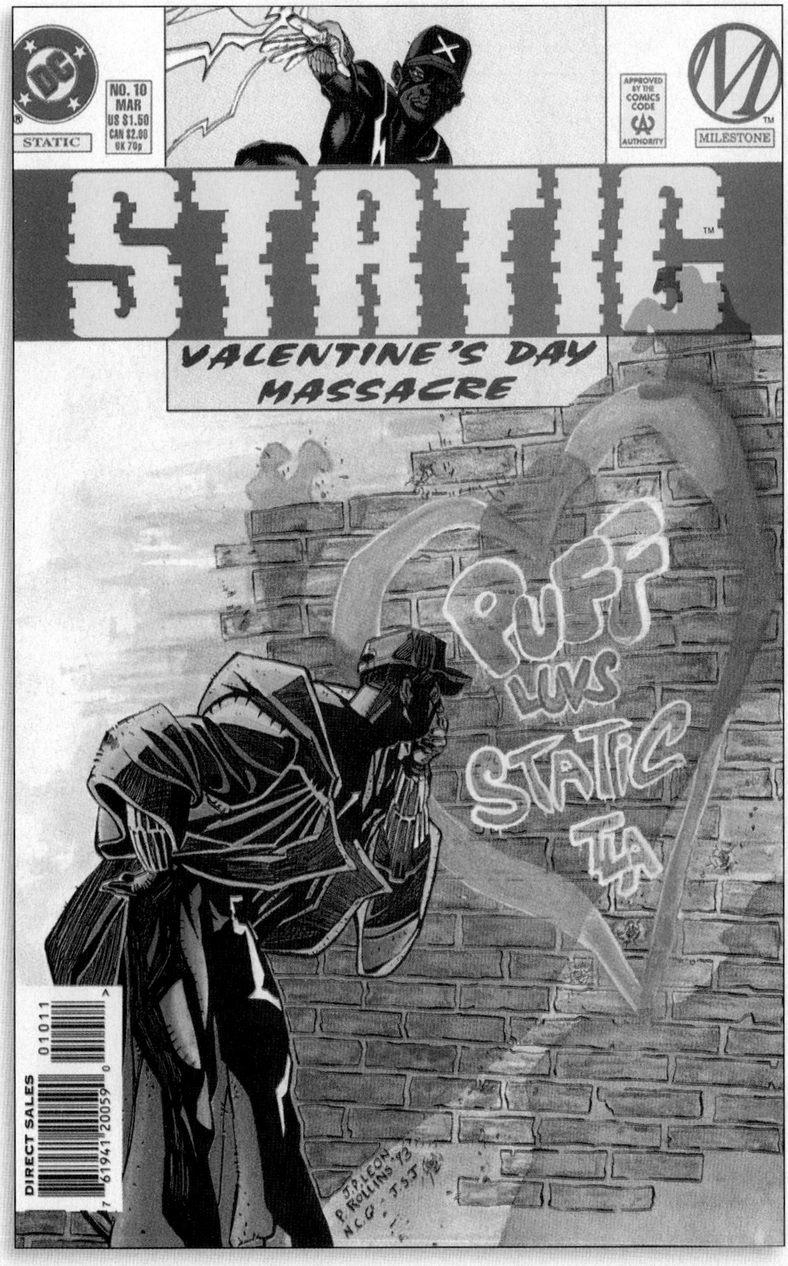
DC
NO. 10
MAR
US $1.50
CAN $2.00
UK 70p
STATIC
APPROVED BY THE COMICS CODE AUTHORITY
MILESTONE
STATIC
VALENTINE'S DAY MASSACRE
PUFF LUVS STATIC
DIRECT SALES

Static #8
DC Comics; Milestone Media; January 1994
Shadow War Crossover – Needless to Say, The Party Broke Up

Featuring a cover by comics legend Walter Simonson, this issue starts with Static versus a villain by the name of the Botanist, who has the unlikely power of making plants grow. After defeating him, the comic segues to members of the Shadow Cabinet – Dharma and Plus – discussing Static, with Plus calling him "talky but huggable." She is reminded that Static is important to both the Shadow Cabinet . . . and the world.

Meanwhile, Frieda is buying snacks for Hawkins and his friends, and talking about the role-playing games she *won't* be playing with them, as well as the house party that they all have to attend (her parents are gone for three weeks, after all).

Then, when he's off on his own and going to his secret garage headquarters,

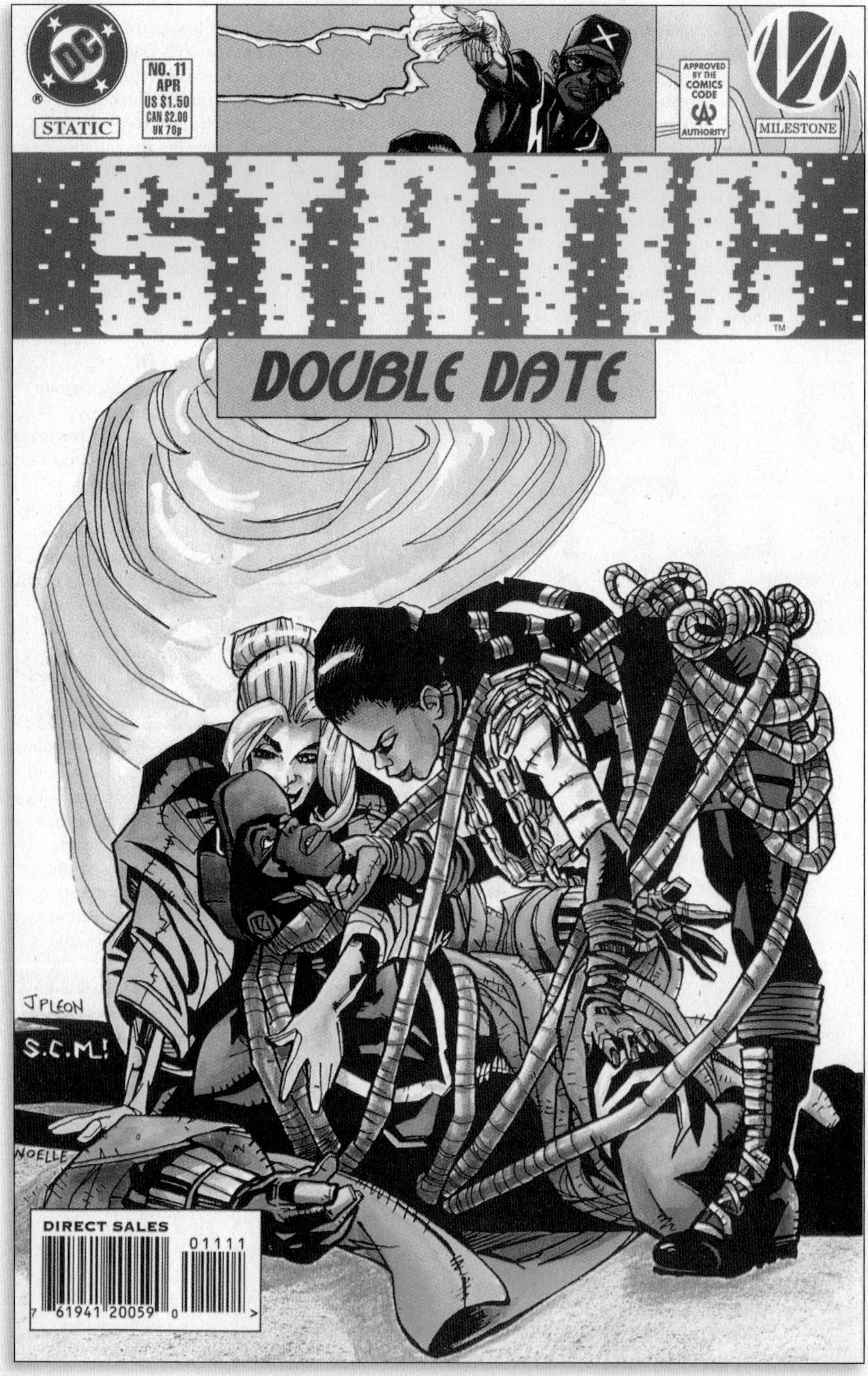
NO. 11
APR
US $1.50
CAN $2.00
UK 70p
STATIC
APPROVED BY THE COMICS CODE AUTHORITY
MILESTONE
STATIC
DOUBLE DATE
JPLEON
S.C.M!
NOELLE
DIRECT SALES

Static runs into Funyl, a member of the Shadow Cabinet who "funnels" him to the top of the Eiffel Tower in Paris, France. After they agree to talk, Funyl transports them both back to the garage, where Hawkins learns about the Shadow Cabinet – and their place for him.

After saying that he'd join the Shadow Cabinet, he heads out to Frieda's house for the party. There, he meets Plus, who comes at an inconvenient time. (Daisy comes up to see Hawkins when he's "alone" . . . and then subsequently turns around and leaves.) Then, Funyl comes out of nowhere and, with Plus, tells Hawkins that some gangbangers are moving against him. Hawkins – who wants nothing to happen to Frieda's house or his friends – turns into Static, and with Plus' help, take down the bad guys.

Funyl comes back to get Static and Plus – only to let slip that they had a homing device in Static's badge, and that's how they were able to keep tabs on him. With Funyl leaving, Plus takes Static to a dark closet – and they both disappear to the amazement of the partygoers.

The action then continues in *Shadow Cabinet* #0.

Static #9
DC Comics; Milestone Media; February 1994
Static Needs a New Pair of Shoes (In which our fab phenom finds fashionable form-fitting footwear fit for foe-fighting)

Static starts things off by leaping into action in the mall, chasing down a shoplifting operation. He unarms the would-be felons and reverses their polarity so they are stuck to the ground, ready for mall security.

Flashback to Hawkins riding the train downtown with Frieda, who is surprised to learn that he wants to spend his last dollar buying "fighting" shoes for his Static costume. As he says, he hasn't had a decent pair of shoes since he fought Tarmack in issue #3. When he gets to the store, though, he realizes a theft is taking place – by little "hardened criminals." Transforming back into Static, he confronts one of the thieves, who says, "Mamma's sick, she's been in the basement too long. I gotta get stuff. Lemme go!"

In the middle of that, the little guy drops some gold rings and runs off with his twin. Hawkins, changed back to his normal self, finds Frieda and they head off the jewelry store to return the rings. They do just that, but the store manager thinks they were part of the operation and calls security. Suddenly, the manager sees micro-versions of the thieves running around

the jewelry display case and picking up pricey trinkets for themselves. Hawkins scoops them up with his hat, and finds himself chased by the rest of the thieves, all identical except for their varying sizes.

Trying to find a place to change (again), Hawkins climbs down an elevator shaft and becomes Static. Then the little thieves fall down around him, transforming into a single enemy named Virus, who's out to protect a mannequin he calls Mamma. After a fierce battle, where the mannequin catches on fire, Static learns Virus' "origin" and wants to help out the teenager. He makes him a bike, makes the big juvenile promise not to steal again, and then flies him over to St. Peter's Mission.

When all is said and done, Hawkins catches up with Frieda and misses out on his shoes – or does he..? The store manager of the shoe store recognizes Hawkins as the kid who stopped the earlier robbery, opens up the store, and says there's a "special discount for junior crime stoppers." Frieda, on the other hand sees the hero's reward as another reason for Hawkins to play super-hero – and she thinks that's one thing that should be stopped now.

Static #10
DC Comics; Milestone Media; March 1994
Escort Etiquette for Guyz Chapter One – Mystery Date

The comic starts out with a bang, as Static and Frieda fly out of the page and into the story. Static is giving Frieda the thrill ride of her life, when suddenly he remembers – via flashback – that he, Rick, Felix, and Frieda were playing a role-playing game (Frieda beats Hawkins, for shame, and gave her the right to wear a t-shirt that would say "I Beat Virgil O. Hawkins on His Best Day"), when suddenly the boys show her their self-made comic book, *Captain Lightning*.

Afterward, and with some polite words concerning the comic book, Frieda is confronted by Hawkins, who says he'd do anything if not for the t-shirt. And thus, the joyride begins. Then, Frieda jumps off Static's back and points out a car theft in progress. Static comes in and saves the day, and tracks the stolen car and gets it to the cops. He then picks up Frieda – who's impressed – and finishes up the joyride.

At his secret garage headquarters, he changes while talking to Frieda about Daisy. The next day at school, Hawkins tells Daisy that the Indian super-hero girl who appeared and disappeared at Frieda's party was looking for Static,

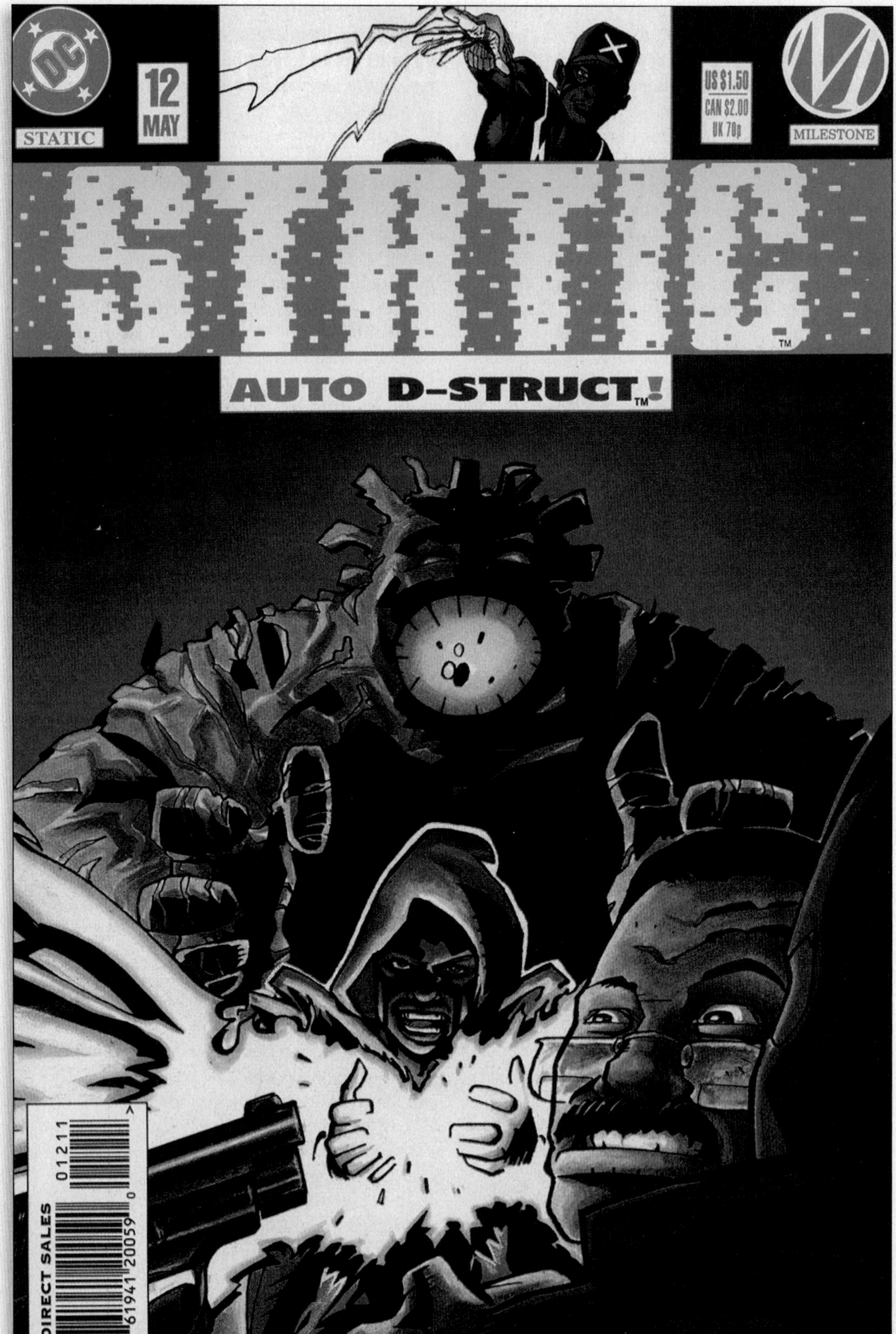
STATIC
12
MAY
US $1.50
CAN $2.00
UK 70p
MILESTONE
STATIC
AUTO D-STRUCT!
DIRECT SALES

and there was nothing to it. Daisy ponders it and says with a giggle that maybe she'll call Hawkins later.

Happy, Hawkins then comes across his old friend, Larry, who is dating Frieda. Making up, the two friends wander down the school hallway when another friend comes up to Hawkins and talks about how his cousin is in love with Static.

After stopping by the Fish Shack to harass his sister, he heads to the Tab to meet Puff, a girl who seems to have a serious crush on him. After passing her flowers in mid-air, she wants to get physical. When Static tries to slow things down, she turns violent – revealing that like Static, she too is a Bang Baby.

In response to this, he realizes that "gas girl" just ate through a concrete piling. A battle ensues and it looks like Static is going to get away, except he gets wrapped in chain by Coil – and things don't even begin to look good!

Static #11
DC Comics; Milestone Media; April 1994
Escort Etiquette for Guyz Chapter Two – Double Date

Picking up where the last issue left off, Coil tells Static that he's been set up and the flowers that he brought will be put on his grave. Puff poses with a strung up Static for a picture. Then, Static swings his chain into the Puff's lingering acid cloud and breaks loose from his femmes fatale. Static asks if they are trying to use this attack on him as a way to get in good with a gang. They reply that they want all the gangs, and that the girls are going to run Dakota. Finally, he gets away – but they say they've still got the photo of Static tied up.

After the super-powered battle, he heads by the Fish Shack to see if he can get his old job back. And after an impassioned appeal for the job, he succeeds. The next day at school, the usual bickering is going on (Rick takes serious offense when his friend calls his shirt "fruit-flavored"), and Daisy and Hawkins have a chat (Hawkins forgets the date that he promised last issue). So, he either fights the supervillains or has a date with Daisy. Following his gut reaction to treat life like an *Archie* comic, he chooses both.

After choosing his proper attire – both civilian and super-hero – he meets up with Larry's car, and goes to the concert with his friends . . . and Daisy. At 6:45, Hawkins makes his move, telling everybody he's going to the concession stand, when actually he turns into Static and searches for Coil and Puff. Finding Puff's acid cloud, the brawl begins.

Static splashes her with water, diluting her acid and, paraphrasing our hero, bringing her "acid reign" to an end. And with all the water she absorbed, Hawkins made Puff fat. He then goes back to the concert and brings the food back to his friends, He gives the food to Frieda, and says he's going to go into the t-shirt line – when he's off to fight Coil. He challenges her inside Bradshaw's, where she can't control anything outside. He uses his force field, breaks out of his chains, and gives her a kiss – as well as takes a picture of her defeat.

Back at the concert, he gets Daisy a t-shirt and learns that Frieda covered for him – he supposedly had digestive-trouble from eating Indian food.

Static #12
DC Comics; Milestone Media; May 1994
Getting Out

The end of the series' first year begins with Static on patrol, when all of a sudden, a Buick flies out from nowhere and almost hits him. The culprit was D-Struct Briggs, another Bang Baby, who is jealous of Static. And when some thugs take D-Struct's father and say they'll kill him if he doesn't kill Static, then he knows what he has to do.

But that also leaves Static to think of a way to save his own butt. So, when D-Struct comes into school, Hawkins transforms into Static and confronts his new nemesis. He tells him that by working together, they'll save his dad – and that he has a plan.

While D-Struct takes pot shots at him, Hawkins gives him a grand tour of Sadler and the other neighborhoods of Dakota. The last location is where D-Struct's dad is being held, and they literally crash the party. As D-Struct goes after Static, he's taking out one gangster after another – to the point that the thugs think they're working together. As Static joins in and kicks major booty, D-Struct finds his father . . . safe and sound.

Segue to D-Struct meeting Static and telling him he and his father are leaving Dakota. In D-Struct's words, he doesn't want to be a super-hero or a super-villain, he just wants to go to college.

And at the end, he tells Static that he hopes he and the Superman-esque hero Icon and the others keep fighting, because some day he wants to come home.

Comics historian and journalist Scott Braden is an Overstreet Advisor.

THE
ONLINE MAGAZINE
OF

www.fandomnetwork.com

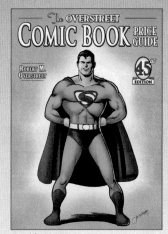

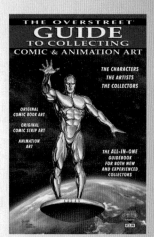

LIGHTS! CAMERA! ACTION!

The Overstreet® Guide To Collecting Movie Posters

takes our "How To" series to the cinema to explore the history and artistry
of movie posters, old and new, American and foreign, across the genres of
horror, Disney, adventure, comedy and many more...

Full color, filled with plenty of visual examples
and all the basics of grading, preservation and storage.

Directory Listings

Dr. David J. Anderson, D.D.S.
5192 Dawes Avenue
Seminary Professional Village
Alexandria, VA 22311
PH/FAX: 703-578-1222
DJA2@cox.net

Comic Book Certification Service (CBCS)
P.O. Box 33048
St. Petersburg, FL 33733-8048
PH: 727-803-6822
PH: 844-870-CBCS (2227)
www.CBCScomics.com

ComicLink Auctions & Exchange
PH: 617-517-0062
buysell@ComicLink.com
www.ComicLink.com

ComicWow!
www.ComicWow.com

Diamond Comic Distributors
10150 York Rd.
Suite 300
Hunt Valley, MD 21030
PH: 443-318-8001

Diamond International Galleries
1940 Greenspring Drive
Suite I
Timonium, MD 21093
GalleryQuestions@DiamondGalleries.com
www.DiamondGalleries.com

Stephen A. Geppi
10150 York Rd., Suite 300
Hunt Valley, MD 21030
PH: 443-318-8203
gsteve@diamondcomics.com

Geppi's Entertainment Museum
301 West Camden Street
Baltimore, MD 21201
PH: 410-625-7089
FAX: 410-625-7090
www.geppismuseum.com

E. Gerber Products
1720 Belmont Ave., Suite C
Baltimore, MD 21244
PH: 888-79-MYLAR

Hake's Americana
P.O. Box 12001
York, PA 17402
PH: 866-404-9800
www.hakes.com

Heritage Auctions
3500 Maple Avenue
17th Floor
Dallas, TX 75219-3941
PH: 800-872-6467
www.HA.com

Nick Katradis
PH: 917-815-0777
ndde@aol.com
www.NickKatradis.com

BACK ISSUES OF COMIC BOOK MARKETPLACE

Looking for back issues of the original CBM?
Check out the "Gemstone Magazines" section of our website,
www.gemstonepub.com.
Also, CBM's founding editor, Gary M. Carter,
still has a few uncirculated copies for sale.
He can be contacted at **garymcarter@gmail.com**.